Conjectures and Evidences:

Methods of Inquiry in the Political and Social Sciences with Elementary Statistics

Rakhahari Chatterji
Partha Pratim Basu
Jyotiprasad Chatterjee
Suprio Basu

Routledge
Taylor & Francis Group

LONDON AND NEW YORK

Levant Books

India

First published 2023
by Routledge
4 Park Square, Milton Park, Abingdon, Oxon OX14 4RN

and by Routledge
605 Third Avenue, New York, NY 10158

Routledge is an imprint of the Taylor & Francis Group, an informa business

Print edition not for sale in South Asia (India, Sri Lanka, Nepal, Bangladesh, Pakistan or Bhutan)

British Library Cataloguing-in-Publication Data
A catalogue record for this book is available from the British Library

ISBN: 9781032526836 (hbk)
ISBN: 9781032526843 (pbk)
ISBN: 9781003407843 (ebk)

DOI: 10.4324/9781003407843

Typeset in Knuth Computer Modern
by Levant Books

LEVANT

Preface

The title of the present volume is undoubtedly reminiscent of Karl Popper's famous work, *Conjectures and Refutations*, although in no way it aspires to present an alternative view of scientific knowledge. Neither does it propose a new methodology or pretend to be original in its discussion of the various methods. It is not one of those 'complete' methodological textbooks in which one finds some discussion, however brief, of almost every problem having relationship to research methods. Neither is it exclusively a discussion of statistical techniques of analysis.

On the positive side, it is enough to state that this book discusses some methods of inquiry and statistical techniques which are most commonly practiced by political and social scientists these days. While discussing them, attempt has been made to summarize and synthesize and to put simply what is already known. In this, the authors have been guided by their knowledge of the needs and problems of post-graduate students and young researchers acquired through their experience as teachers giving courses and seminars in research methods in several universities and colleges in India.

More specifically, this book in its first part focuses on the uses, problems and limitations of alternative strategies of empirical social and political research. The strategies discussed include analysis of aggregate data such as census and event statistics, survey research, experimental and quasi-experimental research designs, content analysis, focus group study and participant observation. In the discussion, emphasis has been placed both on the procedures of data collection and on the techniques of data analysis. Secondly, an attempt has been made to bring to surface the prospects and problems of each of the alternative strategies, and also, to suggest, as far as possible, some practical solutions to the problems. The discussion is introductory rather than exhaustive. Further, it does not assume that the alternative strategies discussed exhaust the methods of empirical political inquiry, not to speak of political science research. To buttress this point a chapter has been added on the relationship between quantitative and qualitative methods. In a word, the book makes an attempt to constructively introduce its readers to an important fragment of the vast literature on social science methodology.

In the second part, the book introduces some essential and commonly used statistical techniques like measurement, measures of central tendency and dispersion, correlation and regression, non-parametric measures of correlation with examples and exercises for students. Important formulas have been separately listed, the whole idea being to make it easy for beginners to learn and practice on their own.

The point of view that runs throughout and threads the book is that methodological knowledge is purely instrumental to substantive and theoretical knowledge. The value of a particular research method and techniques depends on what one is able to learn by its use. A student of political science, sociology and other social sciences must first direct her attention to substantive issues and theoretically significant problems and then choose the most useful method and statistical tools for dealing with them rather than allow a method to determine her substantive concerns. The book deprecates 'barefoot empiricism' however much methodologically informed. It may be mentioned here that the first part of the book has been written by Rakhahari Chatterji and Partha Pratim Basu and the second part by Jyotiprasad Chatterjee and Suprio Basu.

It gives us great pleasure to be able to acknowledge our intellectual debts to our teachers, colleagues and friends. Most importantly, we have learnt a lot from our students who have helped us understand the best way to teach a subject to which they are being exposed for the first time.

Most importantly, we are indebted to our family members who stood by us for more than a year with patience, understanding and in good humour.

26 January 2023

R. C.

PPB

JPC

SB

List of Tables

List of Figures

Contents

PART I

1

Research Strategies: Quantitative and Qualitative

... (T)he description of the research strategy as 'quantitative research' should not be taken to mean that quantification of aspects of social life is all that distinguishes it from a qualitative research strategy.

Alan Bryman

Social research is understood as academic research into questions relating to issues relevant for different social sciences such as politics, sociology, economics, human geography or criminology. Social research is often inspired by diverse socio-political concerns such as intensification of caste conflicts, rise in crimes against women or surge in farmer suicides. Inquiry into these issues, however, draw on various ideas and traditions of social sciences in formulating research topics, collecting evidence for answering research questions and deploying a range of techniques for analysing data for this purpose. Again, while dealing with these methodological issues, it is customary to draw a distinction between quantitative and qualitative methods. For some scholars, this distinction is of fundamental importance, but others hold that the barriers between the two are progressively collapsing. On balance, however, the qualitative-quantitative split continues to provide a useful means of classification of social science research methods as well as addressing a host of attendant considerations. At the same time, we should be careful not to convert these distinction into watertight compartmentalization and remain open to the possibility that a certain piece of research exhibiting the broad characteristics of one research approach could very well incorporate elements of the other.

On the face of it, the contrast between these two strands of research would seem to boil down to those who prioritise counting the numbers – of people or other social units such as groups, households or communities – the quantitative researchers – and those who do not, i.e. the practitioners of qualitative methods. For example, Durkheim at the outset of his famous study on 'suicide' began with a count of the number of people per thousand who committed suicide. Qualitative researchers, on the other hand, analyze words, conversations, texts or images which are not amenable to ready quantification. However, a broader understanding looks upon the quantitative-qualitative divide in terms of two distinct research strategies reflecting divergent orientations to conduct of social research. Going beyond their respective inclinations towards counting and measuring – without diluting its significance though – these two research traditions are perceived to be influenced by a number of factors: perception of the relation between theory and research, epistemological foundations and ontological considerations which in turn shape how each negotiate the steps involved in the research exercise. This chapter would begin by identifying the differences between the two approaches to research in terms of theoretical, epistemological and ontological commitments; consider how these differences in turn impact the planning and execution of research activities, summarize the major criticisms of the two strategies, and conclude with a brief reference to the areas of overlap between the two.

Bryman's schematic presentation[1]gives us a convenient entry point into our discussion before we elaborate: quantitative strategy which emphasizes quantification in collection and analysis of data is marked by three characteristics: (a) it adopts a 'deductive' view of theory-research continuum and is interested in testing theories; (b) it imbibes the 'explanation-oriented' norms and practices of scientific analysis inspired by positivism; and (c) it operates with an 'objectivist' view of social reality. In contrast, qualitative research which relies on words and narratives in gathering and scanning data carries the following features: (a) it follows an 'inductive' account of the connection between theory and research which underscores generation of theories through research; (b) it abandons the positivistic and scientific research practices and harps instead on how individuals 'understand and interpret' the social world; (c) it looks at social reality not as given but a constantly shifting 'creation' of individuals.

Theory and research: The linkage between social theories and the research process as well as reading of research findings could be perceived from two ends[2]: theories inform and underlie social research but they get enriched in turn once research outputs replenish theoretical repertoire of knowledge. This brings us to the contrast between deductive and inductive theories associated with quantitative and qualitative research strategies respectively. In the **deductive** model, the researcher undertakes theoretical reflections in the initial stage of research which generates hypotheses – a tentative answer to a research questions – which are then subjected to empirical test through collection of data and evidence. These hypotheses contain variables – or concepts which can take on two or more values, e.g. annual income of a household or number of children in a household. The objective of hypothesis testing is to look for contingent relationships among variables, e.g. whether the sum of income influences the number of children in a household. Thus theory, and hypotheses deduced from it drive the process of data collection which in turn leads not only to confirmation/ rejection of the hypotheses but also lends support to or calls for revision of the theory itself.

This last step, however, introduces us to the alternative – **inductive** – research mode which views theory as an outcome of the research process, i.e. something that is precipitated at the end of the journey. In other words, the researcher following the inductive path seeks to draw inferences which are generalizable and applicable to situations which go beyond the data sets she has worked with. The inductive method thus represents a more flexible and open-ended research strategy in which theoretical ideas emerge out of the data. However, if the deductive method, as suggested, contains an element of induction, presence of deductive concerns could also be traced in the inductive research exercise. Once during the course of the inquiry the investigator carries out theoretical reflections on a preliminary set of data gathered by her, she would be interested to delve into more data to find out the conditions under which these theoretical insights would (or would not) be sustainable. This moving back and forth between theory and data is known as 'iterative' strategy which is especially evident in grounded theory and further affirms our earlier statement that inductive and deductive alternatives could be better viewed as broad tendencies rather than hard and fast distinctions.

Table 1.1: Deductive and Inductive approaches to research

Deductive model	Inductive model
Theoretical insights	General research questions
Hypothesis testing	Data collection
Confirmation/refutation of theory	Theoretical reflections

Epistemological concerns[3]: A second set of differences between quantitative and qualitative methods stem from views and assumptions regarding how research should be conducted which are known as epistemological issues in social science parlance. One dominant view has been that social research should follow the scientific canon – which involves hypothesis testing as described above – though this view is far from being universally shared. Its critics contend that the subject matter of social science – human beings and social institutions – is fundamentally different from the scientist's objects of study which calls for devising methods that are more sensitive to and accommodative of these differences. The key epistemological position which asserts that social scientists should follow the same principles and procedures in studying the social reality as do the natural scientists is **positivism**. Its major components have been identified thus:

- Knowledge generated through sensory experience alone should be considered acceptable knowledge.

- Knowledge comes from collection of facts which form the basis of laws about social developments.

- Social scientists would refrain from making normative or evaluative statements which cannot stand the test of experience and are therefore unfit to be considered a form of knowledge.

- Theories which seek to explain these social laws are supposed to spawn hypotheses which through further testing help in assessing the veracity of these explanations.

Sociologist Maurice Duverger offered one such law/law-like generalization – popularly known as Duverger's Law – which states that simple majority electoral systems where the party that secures the highest number of votes is declared the winner (such as the first-past-the-post system that prevails in India), tend to become two-party systems. One of the explanations offered for this proposition has been in terms of a psychological factor – that voters are reluctant to waste their votes on losers.

The school of **interpretivism** poses a counter-point to the positivists and furnishes the bedrock for qualitative research. Its practitioners plead that since social researchers focus on studying 'thinking' individuals and their institutions rather than the material world which preoccupies natural scientists, they need to develop research norms and procedures that build on these differences. The interpretivists draw on the hermeneutic tradition, a term which was originally associated with theology and deciphering the meaning of religious texts. In the study of society, it has been deployed as an alternative to the efforts of the positivists to *explain* social behaviour and events with reference to facts and evidences. The interpretivists instead seek to *interpret* human action through empathic understanding, i.e. exploring the meanings and motives underlying such action rather than the external forces that allegedly shape this behaviour. For example, two persons who take part in voting can hold different understandings about the act: for one, it might amount to political activism; for the other, it might simply mean carrying out a citizenship duty.

In this connection, we can refer to Max Weber's concept of **Verstehen** (roughly translated, *understanding*) which has been one of the major intellectual influences on the interpretivist tradition and elucidated elsewhere in this volume. Interestingly, Weber described Sociology (a description that could be extended to social sciences in general) as a 'science which attempts the interpretive understanding of social action in order to arrive at a causal explanation of its course and effects'. In a sense this could very well be considered as an attempt to bridge the positivistic and interpretivist traditions through a combination of explanation and understanding. Yet the point to note is that he proposed 'causal explanation' to be undertaken in terms of 'interpretive understanding of social action' rather than giving priority to the external determinants of human behaviour as the positivists would be inclined to do.

Table 1.2: Varieties of epistemological positions

Positivism	Interpretivism/ hermeneutics	Verstehen
Knowledge comes through experience and facts	Knowledge comes through empathic understanding	Explanation of action in terms of
Explanation through theory and hypothesis testing	Interpretation through accessing meanings and motives of action	Interpretive understanding

Ontological questions[4]: Thirdly, the assumptions about the nature of social phenomena – which, we have noted above, partially accounted for the differences between positivism and interpretivism – take us into the domain of ontological propositions. Here the two major orientations, i.e. objectivism and constructionism (also known as constructivism), part ways as to whether social entities can and should be looked at as objective entities that exist external to and independent of social actors, or they should be regarded as social constructions rooted in the perceptions and actions of social actors. **Objectivism**, which influenced scientifically inclined positivistic-quantitative research activity, implies that social phenomena confront us as external facts that remain beyond our control or influence. Thus a social organization can be viewed as a tangible object defined in terms of its rules and procedures, its hierarchy and division of labour which have a reality external to the individuals who inhabit it. These characteristics of an organization generate a set of values and behavioural expectations which exert a strong influence on the actions of its members. As against this, **constructionism**, to which the interpretivist-qualitative research tradition is heavily indebted, asserts that social phenomena and their meanings are far from pre-given – rather they are constructed, and continually reconstructed, through the behaviour and interaction of social actors. Thus from this perspective social organizations instead of having some pre-existing characteristics are more akin to being a negotiated order: they undergo a process of constant reassessment and reformulation as its members keep on modifying, if not subverting, its command and control mechanism through their everyday practices. Needless to say, the research questions put forward by those who uphold the scientific and quantitative research traditions focus on the formal properties of social organizations (such as law and constitutions) while the practitioners of interpretive and qualitative genre of research highlight the active involvement of the people (e.g. voting and agitations) in imparting flesh and blood to these objective structures.

Table 1.3: Ontological considerations

Objectivism	Constructionism
Social phenomena are objective facts	Social phenomena have no predetermined character
They exist independently of human actors	Their meanings are human constructions
They remain beyond the control of actors	These meanings are constantly reconstructed through social interaction and practices

Trajectories of quantitative and qualitative research[5]: Thesethree clusters of distinctions in terms of theoretical, epistemological and ontological concerns set the stage for exploring how they underlie the divergent courses of quantitative and qualitative research. All research, quantitative and qualitative, essentially aim at solving a puzzle or answering certain questions; yet the steps involved in the two kinds of exercises are distinct and different and hence call for a review. The starting point of quantitative research is selection of a topic for inquiry, a general area of study such as media and democracy. Since this represents a broad theme, it needs to be narrowed down to more specific research questions – to take one example: does concentration of media ownership pose a threat to democracy? Answering this question requires formulation of hypotheses with the help of theories derived from a survey of the existing literature. The next step – working out a suitable design for carrying out the research – involves a number of decisions which include first, devising appropriate measures for identifying the concepts that appear in the hypotheses (e.g. whether to include social media as an indicator of the concept of media); second, selecting relevant cases or samples for conducting the investigation; and third, choosing the right techniques to be employed for collecting data. The data collection stage has two aspects: recording of information, verified and expressed in numerical forms; and transcription of this data into computer readable format. This is followed by data analysis or condensation of the raw data through charts, graphs, tables and statistical measures. This leaves the researcher with the crucial task of interpretation of the data: use the findings in the light of theoretical insights to answer research questions raised at the outset. The researcher here is expected to consider alternative interpretations, and also contemplate what kind of contributions the research has made to the extant body of theories/literature.

This tight-knit approach involving a given sequence of steps is absent in the case of qualitative research which is marked by a high degree of flexibility and only a loose structure. Research questions, hypotheses or concepts are not elucidated in detail at the outset – if at all, they provide only a working framework that could get modified and concretised in the course of the research. The overall idea is to allow concepts and theories, analysis and findings to emerge over the entire period of study and therefore imposition of any premature closure is strictly discouraged. In other words, the researcher here begins with a loosely defined topic while a research question emerges only during the research process – once some data is gathered and the researcher carries out some preliminary analysis by examining this data. Thus J. Foster's study titled 'Informal Social Control and Community Crime Prevention' (1995) is launched by simply questioning the popularly held assumptions that (a) communities containing predominantly public housing societies in poorer areas of the city are marked by high levels of crime; and (b) communities with high levels of crime tend to have low levels of social control. She spent eighteen months in one such community and accumulated a huge volume of field data which led her to two findings: first, though the community in question had a high rate of crime, its residents did not really consider it problematic; and secondly, she also found evidence of functioning social control mechanisms, for example, in the form of shaming practices. Foster's work did not seem to indicate the emergence of any new theory or concept from these early interpretations of her data; nor was there any evidence as to whether she engaged in any further data collection exercise. However, in qualitative research, such preliminary interpretations often help in tighter specification of research questions which in turn initiates a new phase of data gathering. When this occurs, as for example within a grounded theory framework, there can be an interface between interpretation and theorizing on one hand, and data collection on the other.

Table 1.4: Steps in quantitative and qualitative research

Quantitative research (Structured)	Qualitative research (Flexible)
Research topic Specific research questions Hypotheses formulation Research design Data collection Data analysis	Loosely defined research topic and questions Data collection and preliminary analysis Firming up of research questions Emergence of theoretical insights Further data collection New theoretical reflections

Nature of data and techniques of data collection[6]: It would be useful here to elaborate on the nature of data handled by the quantitative and qualitative researchers as well as the data collection procedures followed under the two strategies respectively which, we have seen above, is often perceived to capture the core differences between the two. All research aims at collecting empirical data more or less systematically and examine emergent data patterns with a view to better understand and explain the social world. Yet a basic distinction could be drawn between quantitative and qualitative approaches to research in terms of the kind of data each deals with: quantitative researchers are interested in hard data collected in the form of numbers while qualitative studies involve collection of soft data e.g. words, sentences, photos, symbols and so on. These basic differences regarding the nature of data drive the differential data gathering techniques used by the two strategies as well. The most commonly used tool for quantitative researchers is the **survey** technique used to study personal experiences, perceptions, opinions and attitude of individuals to answer research questions. A large number of people are asked an identical set of questions contained in a questionnaire, and the respondents are often required to choose the answers from a given and limited range of options. The sample of respondents surveyed are considered representative of a wider population whose beliefs and opinions are important from the standpoint of the researcher's objectives of investigation. **Content analysis,** a second technique aims at systematically recording and analysing the contents of documents, reports, manuscripts, radio programmes, television news and other written, oral or visual material. Content analysis, like survey research, also enables researchers to explore the beliefs, values, attitudes and preferences of actors, for which a body of material is identified, and then a system for recording specific aspects of contents (known as 'coding') is created. But it allows researchers to access subjects difficult or impossible to get in personal touch with, for example because they are located abroad or no more in this world. Quantitative researchers also engage in analysis of existing statistics (also known as **aggregate data**) which involves re-examination and statistical manipulation of quantitative data gathered by government agencies or other organizations. Here the researcher locates previously collected sources of information produced by government or non-governmental agencies. This body of information is then reorganized for the purpose of answering research questions.

For qualitative researchers, **ethnography** or field study where the investigator directly observes and takes notes on a people in a natural setting for a length of time remains a popular technique. Here the researcher sets out with a loose set of queries, then selects an appropriate group or site for study, and follows it up with careful observation of the field setting for the period of a few months to several years. Data emerges in the form of detailed notes prepared on a daily basis which finally evolve into an insider account of the day to day lives of the people being studied. This method is considered especially useful for promoting better understanding of institutions (an army, a media house or the World Bank) or cultures (migrant communities, fundamentalist religious outfits or insurgent groups) or events (a protracted ethnic conflict) etc. **Interview,** yet another widely used tool for qualitative researchers has similarities with surveys in that it also seeks to amass information about the social world by asking questions to selected individuals. In its more structured version, the interviewer operates with a pre-formulated set of questions though it allows the scope for probing, and adding new questions for this purpose, with the answers recorded by the interviewer. An unstructured interview is more like a free-flowing conversation: no fixed list of questions is used, and interviewees have the liberty to answer in their own words which deepens the qualitative flavour of this activity. Unstructured interviews are often combined with survey or structured interview – which yield factual data

– in addition to its own focus on delving deep into people's experiences. Finally, **focus group discussion,** a more recent addition to the arsenal of qualitative research methods, is akin to an unstructured interview and yet produces different kind of data. A focus group represents an assemblage of people selected because they are believed to be related to some phenomenon which is of interest to the researcher (e.g. retired judges or army officers). The investigator meets them in an informal environment, initiates a loosely organized discussion regarding something the participants have experiences and beliefs about with herself playing the role of the anchor, and this interaction is expected to reveal more in terms of the suppressed emotions and unconscious motivations of the participants than they would in the formal survey/interview setting.

Table 1.5: Nature of data/ data collection and analysis

Quantitative research: Hard data	Qualitative research: Soft Data
Techniques:	Techniques:
Survey	Ethnography
Content analysis	Interview
Aggregate data analysis	Focus group discussion

Major preoccupations of quantitative and qualitative researchers[7]: After outlining the trajectories of quantitative and qualitative research and looking at the variety of the methods of data collection, we proceed to take note of the preoccupations of the two sets of exercises, i.e. what the researchers seek to achieve in the course of their research. As to quantitative research, four such objectives can be mentioned – measurement, explanation, generalization and replication which are elaborated hereunder. Quantitative research, we have noted, seeks to establish contingent relationship between concepts/variables, and **measurement** makes a significant contribution here. To study, for example, the relationship between social class and life expectancy, it is important to measure class for which an inventory of social classes needs to be developed and individuals under study assigned to these different clusters. This data has to be read together with the information regarding the age at which people die, to find out if there is any correspondence between social class differences and the mean age of death. In the absence of measurement, it is impossible to test the theoretical ideas and verify contingent relationships embodied in hypotheses. Thus, to take the example of car insurance, if it were possible for car insurance companies to make precise estimates of how well (or otherwise) people drive, it would have been possible for them to more accurately predict accident rates, and fix insurance premiums accordingly. But in the absence of hard data, they have to depend on poor substitutes such as the driver's age, number of driving convictions, and number of previous policy claims etc. which are often responsible for calculation going haywire. Use of formal academic qualifications as the measure of an individual's educational attainments and IQ score as the indicator of one's intelligence have also attracted similar criticisms.

At this point we can introduce the issues of reliability and validity which guard against threats to accuracy of measurements. **Reliability** is concerned with stability and consistency of measures, i.e. the extent to which any measuring procedure yields the same result on repeated trials. This is most popularly sought to be ensured through 'test-retest method' where a test or a measure is administered on one occasion and is again repeated with the same sample on a different occasion. A robust correlation between the two sets of observations made at different points of time would also indicate a strong relationship between the variables concerned (and vice versa). Similarly, when a substantial subjective judgement is involved – for example, when content analysts have to take decisions about how to categorize media items – and for this purpose more than one 'observer' is deployed, reliability is demonstrated if all of them reach similar conclusions regarding the content of the media items in question (known as 'inter-observer consistency'). Again, the **validity** of a measure refers to the correspondence between a measure and the concept it is supposed to measure, i.e. whether an indicator or set of indicators really measure the concept in question. A measure's validity is more difficult to demonstrate due to lack of adequate information as to the relationship between measurement of a concept and the actual presence of the concept itself. However, validity is sought to be established through a number of ways, of which assertion of face validity remains the simplest when the researcher asks others, presumably with acknowledged expertise and experience in the field, to judge whether a particular measure has effectively captured the concerned concept.

Measurement and establishment of contingent connections, however, are not enough because contingency might very well reflect specious or chance relationships; hence quantitative researchers look for **explanation in terms of causality**. Thus while studying a phenomenon like caste or racial prejudice, they of course begin by ascertaining how much prejudice prevails in a certain group of individuals or what proportion of its members is highly prejudiced and vice versa. But ultimately they are interested not just in how things are but why things are the way they are, or they are concerned with the causes – in this case, of the pattern of distribution of caste/racial prejudices in the said group. Thus a researcher might trace this prejudice to an individual's psychological make-up, e.g. one's authoritarian nature; or social characteristics such as level of education, location in the caste hierarchy or experiences of social mobility. In this connection, the researcher is inclined to think in terms of two sets of variables, dependent and independent, which help her to think in terms of cause and effects. In this example, racial prejudice constitutes the dependent variable whose explanation is being sought, and authoritarian streaks in an individual is to be regarded as having a causal influence in shaping a prejudiced mind-set.

It may be noted in this connection that affirmation of a causal connection between two variables has to satisfy two conditions: first, a change in the value of the 'independent' variable at the point of time t1 brings about a change in the 'dependent' variable at a subsequent point, t2 (and not the other way round). Thus, it is the authoritarian psyche in the above example, which is regarded as inherent in an individual's nature that would be taken to account for the caste or racial prejudices harboured by him or her. Secondly, we have to make sure that the contingent relationship between the two variables is not the product of a third – antecedent – variable. Thus, while seeking to confirm a contingent relationship between age and annual income, one should duly take note of and eliminate the role of education which could be related to both advanced age and enhanced income. All this prompts the practitioners of qualitative research to engage in sophisticated multivariate analyses to show that a projected causal connection between two variables is valid or specify the conditions under which they are likely to hold in future.

A third preoccupation of quantitative research is **generalization**, i.e. the claim that the research findings would remain valid even in situations which go beyond the immediate context within which the research has been carried out. Thus in the example cited, the researcher would expect that the findings of the study on caste/racial prejudices conducted with a questionnaire administered to a select body of respondents would be applicable to a wider cross-section of individuals as well. This concern with generalization of findings finds expression through the emphasis survey research puts on developing a representative sample for executing the survey. It is easy to appreciate that a survey can never cover the entire population it is directed at – of a city, a party or a factory – by despatching questionnaires to all the targeted individuals or interviewing all its members, which makes sampling a necessity. However, the sample has to be as representative as possible so that the results it yields would not remain confined to that particular group but are generalizable beyond the cases included in the sample. The quantitative researchers resort to probability sampling techniques based on random selection to make the samples representative and bias-free though the process has its obvious limitations (as discussed elsewhere in this volume). Moreover, when we talk of representative sample, the question naturally crops up: representative of what? The answer obviously would be that it is representative, for example, of the male members of a particular political party, or the elderly population of a certain community. However, researchers in their enthusiasm to discover positivism-inspired 'law-like generalizations' become oblivious to this built-in pitfalls of sampling and claim wider applicability of their findings and invite at times serious troubles for themselves.

Finally, quantitative researchers, following the footsteps of natural scientists, take great pains to eradicate all contaminating influences on their research findings introduced above all by their value orientations. Presence of biases and values are taken to mark a gross departure from the ideal of objectivity and undermine the claim to present a reliable picture of the social reality. One suggested remedy has been for the researchers to replicate or reproduce each other's research projects, the idea being that if a certain study failed the test of **replication**, the validity of its findings would become open to serious doubts. Again, replication demands that the steps and procedures adopted in executing a particular research exercise should be made as explicit as possible so that other researchers could traverse the same course to see if the same results were arrived at or not. True, replication of social science studies remain rare in practice; still with increase in the transparency of data collection processes and methods of analysis, the possibility of confirming or rejecting the findings of previous studies has certainly been expanded.

While the quantitative researchers begin their venture by looking at theories, formulating hypotheses and developing reliable and valid measures for the concepts involved, the starting point for their qualitative counterparts is **establishing rapport with their research subjects**[8]. This in fact reflects their basic commitment to develop an enhanced interpretive understanding of the social world which requires gaining access to the subjective meanings through which it is understood by the participants. Hence their emphasis on seeing the social world through the eyes of others – the people they study – and frequent references to empathic understanding of their points of view. Thus a study on teenage girls' views on and experience of violence has to begin by listening to their accounts of such encounters however personal and subjective these might appear to be. Indeed, qualitative research can also bring out aspects of the social reality that may not have been grasped the research subjects as well. Thus a study conducted by Zimmerman in the 1970s on a welfare agency disclosed a peculiar rule of thumb followed by its officials: whenever a client said something that seemed to point to her *ineligibility* for welfare benefits, it was taken at face value; but statements made by clients that bore on their *eligibility* for welfare benefits were not believed unless backed up by supportive documents.

Again, qualitative researchers place much greater stress on descriptive details while presenting the course and outcome their research as against the quantitative researchers' penchant for unearthing 'causal connections'. This fascination with 'thick' description comes largely from the qualitative researchers' interest in **context-based understanding** of social behaviour, of which the popular maxim 'one man's terrorist is another man's freedom fighter' remains a pertinent example. They assert, in other words, we cannot understand the behaviour of the members of a social group – police personnel, gender activists or drug peddlers – without taking into account the typical social environment in which they operate. Thus, behaviour that might appear awkward and irrational in one social milieu could make perfect sense once we look at it in terms of the context in which it took place.

Thirdly, quantitative researchers with their proclivity to arrive at generalizations prefer to work with a large number of cases, but qualitative researchers are comfortable with a **case study approach** which comprises concentrating on a single or a few cases. For them, the intensive, in-depth study of a limited number of cases replaces the extensive, surface-level study of numerous cases typical of the quantitative format. The study of cases is seen to deliver complex explanations or interpretations in the form of an unfolding plot or a narrative regarding a particular people or a specific events. This often makes the passage of time integral to the explanation/ understanding which in turn accounts for the qualitative researchers' insistence on viewing social life in terms of a process. This **focus on process**

– defined as a sequence of individual and collective events, actions and activities unfolding over time in context – helps uncover how a change of government has been precipitated, the phases through which a conflict evolves, or the way a social relationship unravels. Thus, two scholars through unstructured conversations with about fifty couples in which the man was unemployed sought to understand what kind of adjustments both the men and the wives had to go through over time in negotiating the phenomenon of male unemployment.

Finally, the quantitative scholars prefer a research approach which is **highly flexible**, loosely structured and minimally invasive vis-a-vis the research subjects. This open-endedness and conscious reluctance to impose any preconceived frame of reference upon the people being studied is considered necessary to encourage the participants to comfortably share their perspectives with the researchers. For the same reason, qualitative researchers do not strictly delimit their areas of inquiry but operate instead, as already mentioned above, with a few general rather than specific research questions. Associated with it is the preference for ethnography as a research method where the investigator as participant observer immerses herself in a social setting with a general research focus in mind. The wide array of observations that follow helps her to gradually narrow the emphasis and formulate more specific research questions out of the collected data. This again could be the first step towards data-driven theory building or ground theory in data which by facilitating interaction between theory and data adds to the flexibility of qualitative research. This grounded theory approach compared to other ways of theorizing tends to be less abstract and much closer to concrete observations or specific events.

At this point the question is likely to come up: does qualitative research concern itself with **reliability** and **validity** issues? Two views emerge in response, one favoured adoption of the criteria employed by the quantitative researchers with minimal changes in meaning; the other suggested alternative criteria for evaluating qualitative research. Scholars who subscribe to the first view play down the measurement issues – the focus of reliability and validity criteria in quantitative research – and call for replication of research or generalization of finding though the difficulties of attaining these objectives in the qualitative mode is duly acknowledged. The proponents of alternative criteria on the other hand emphasize assessing trustworthiness of research through, for example, triangulation or respondent validation. **Respondent validation**, also known as member validation, is a process where the researcher shares her findings with the people she has studied with a view to seek confirmation from them as to the authenticity of her understanding of their social world. **Triangulation**, yet another way of assessing credibility of research findings, pleads for using more than one method or sources of data in the study of social phenomena. Finally, since qualitative research is concerned with in-depth study of a few cases and heavily context-intensive, the **thick description** – the rich and detailed account they furnish about the context – is likely to provide others with a dense database for making judgments about wider applicability of the findings.

Table 1.6: Major preoccupations of quantitative and qualitative research

Quantitative	Qualitative
Measurement to test relationships among variables	Establishing close contact with research subject to access subjective meanings
Causal explanation in terms of independent and dependent variables	Interpretive understanding of social action
Sampling and generalization	A case and context oriented approach
Replication to confirm findings	Alternative criteria for validation of findings

Critique of quantitative and qualitative research[8]: Over the years, both quantitative and qualitative research strategies have been exposed to certain standard criticisms directed at each other by the exponents and practitioners of the two rival traditions which we briefly summarize in this section. To begin with **quantitative research**, its epistemological foundation – especially its insistence, following the positivist precepts – on adopting the natural science methods for exploring social phenomena has been seriously questioned. This position, it has been contended, rests on a flawed objectivist **ontology**, i.e. an insufficient appreciation of the basic differences between the inanimate objects the physical sciences deal with and human beings and institutions studied by the social sciences to the extent the behaviour of the latter, unlike that of the former, is suffused with meanings and call for interpretation. Secondly, **measurement** which constitutes the heart of quantitative research is viewed as artificial and its claim to precision and accuracy has attracted stiff contestation. It has been pointed out that the 'fit' between the measures developed by the 'scientists' and the concepts they are supposed represent is often assumed rather than real. Similarly, the claim that during survey research the respondents answer an identical set of questions, i.e. are exposed to the same experimental stimulus, is problematic because the meaning of the same question or the concepts used in its formulation could vary from respondent to respondent and impact their responses. An allied criticism is that creation of **artificially controlled experimental situations** far removed from everyday human experiences or use of 'instruments' such as self-administered questionnaires and structured interviews by quantitative researchers could very well appear to be intimidating for the research subjects. On the other hand, a respondent might take a 'politically correct' stance while answering a question on racial prejudice while her actual behaviour could be grossly at variance with this copybook response. Finally, it has been asserted that studying the social world through establishing relationships of variables is bound to produce a **static and partial understanding of the social reality** for it omits the process through which concrete individuals constantly engage in creating and recreating the meaning of this reality through their everyday interpretations and practices.

On the other hand, perhaps the foremost complaint made against **qualitative research**[9] is that it is highly **subjective** in the sense that its findings are primarily dependent on the researcher's impressionistic understanding of what was significant and what was not. This element of subjectivity is further compounded by the close rapport the researcher develops with the research subjects which introduces their values and biases as well into the study thereby further contaminating its conclusions. Again, this unstructured character of qualitative research and its heavy dependence on the ingenuity of the researcher has implications for possible **replication** of qualitative studies. Though replication admittedly has never been an easy target in social sciences, it has been argued that absence of any standard procedures to be followed, and the researcher acting as the chief instrument of data collection virtually rules out possibilities of reproducing qualitative studies by others. This **absence of transparency**, thirdly, regarding, for example, how people were chosen for observation or interview – in sharp contrast to the detailed accounts of sampling procedures contained in quantitative research reports – or what the researcher actually did or how did she arrive at her conclusions expose the findings of qualitative research to serious doubts. The final objection pertains to the **lack of generalizability** of the conclusions of qualitative research: after all conclusions following from participant observation conducted at one particular research site or qualitative interviews conducted with a few individuals could hardly be generalized to other settings or a wider body of individuals.

Table 1.7: Critique of quantitative and qualitative research

Quantitative	Qualitative
Adoption of 'scientific' method based on flawed conception of the nature of social world	Highly subjective approach
	Probability of infiltration of researcher bias
Viability and accuracy of measurement	Case and context based orientation
Artificiality of experimental research	impedes generalization
Search for relationship among variables	Unstructured course of research thwarts
ignore dynamic social processes	replication

By way of concluding, an overall comparison of the two research strategies can be attempted through a tabular representation below:

Table 1.8: Overall comparison of quantitative and qualitative research strategies

Quantitative research	Qualitative research
1. Theories and concepts tested through research	1. Theories generated at the end of the research process
2. Social behaviour sought to be explained with reference to objective factors external to the actors	2. Social action sought to be interpreted or understood with reference to its subjective meaning
3. Researcher maintains conscious distance from research subjects to meet the demands of objectivity	3. Researcher's concern with empathizing with the research subjects to grasp their perspectives engage the two into close interaction
4. Emphasis on hypothesis testing and establishing contingent or causal relationship among variables	4. Stress on studying social processes or unfolding of social events over time
5. Approach to research highly structured and involves a sequence of given steps	5. Approach to research flexible often involving backward and forward movements
6. Emphasis on 'hard' data collected in numerical form through use of sophisticated techniques	6. Concern with 'soft' data in the form of words or images gathered through relatively informal methods
7. Data collected in contrived and artificial context	7. Data collected in more natural setting
8. Aims at generalization based on observation of many cases	8. Interested in rich context-specific understanding based on one or a few cases

Nevertheless, we would like to conclude on a note of caution: the differences between quantitative and qualitative approaches to research should be seen as broad tendencies and not in dichotomous terms. Thus the association of quantitative research with positivistic theory of knowledge and of qualitative research with an interpretivist epistemology should not be seen in absolute terms. Quantitative researchers, for example, are often found to engage in study of meanings through use of attitude scales, while qualitative researchers may want to understand people's behaviour in terms of 'social facts' (to borrow Durkheim's expression) such as norms and values of a community or organization. Again, qualitative researchers at times resort to a quantification of their data even if in a limited way, while analysis of quantitative data yielded by survey research often has an exploratory character which facilitates generation of theories and concepts. Finally, quantitative data collection techniques are often perceived as more invasive and less natural; however, even a participant observer especially when functioning in an overt manner can become a source of 'interference' in the natural flow of the participants' lives. In sum, the qualitative-quantitative divide is far from insurmountable which indeed has encouraged a section of researchers to combine the two strategies through mixed method research since the 1980s.

Endnotes

1. Alan Bryman, *Social Research Methods*, (Oxford: Oxford University Press 2012), 35-36.
2. Ibid, 24-27; W. Lawrence Neuman, *Social Research Methods: Qualitative and Quantitative Approaches*, (Essex: Pearson 2014), 69-70.
3. Bryman, 27-32; A. P. Kelly, *Social Research Methods*, (London: London School of Economics and Political Science 2016), 21.
4. Bryman 32-34; Kelly 21-22.
5. Neuman, 17-22.
6. Ibid, 46-53.Bryman 168-178; Kelly 27-29.
7. Bryman 399-405; Kelly 27-29.
8. Bryman 178-179.
9. Ibid 405-407.

2

Research Methodology: Concept, Hypothesis and Variables

> Methodology is in essence prophylactic.
>
> *Stanislaw Andreski*

Since World War II social science research has gained a new respectability. One finds rapid expansion of social research not merely in the universities but in business and government as well. Those disciplines which have been directly affected by the post-war behavioural movement, namely, anthropology, psychology and sociology, are the main beneficiaries of this expansion in research. Political science, being rather deeply though not as directly affected by behaviouralism, has also experienced considerable expansion in research. While political science only partly committed itself to the first of the two major tenets of behaviouralism, namely, dealing with individual human behaviour (for political science never gave up its interest in aggregative and institutional behaviour and legal and constitutional documents), its commitment to the second major tenet of behaviouralism, that is, "scientific" study of its subject matter, was total and complete.[1] It is true that there is considerable scope for debate regarding the meaning and implications of "scientific" study of one's subject matter in any of the social sciences. For political science, however, "scientism" has meant primarily two things : first, it means a great concern for empirical theories capable of generating testable propositions, and secondly, it implies a search for useful methods, methods that facilitate data collection as well as permit an exhaustive examination of theory-data fit.

Interestingly, both theoretical developments and the methodological innovations have taken place under the rubric of comparative politics. There are a number of political scientists who believe that the resultant "revolution in comparative politics" would be sufficient to create a paradigm for research that would finally terminate the pre- paradigm state of our science. Hence, they talk in terms of such fundamental goals of social science as "achieving accurate explanations and predictions of human behaviour." There are others, however, who, while cherishing such goals as achieving law-like generalizations in the social sciences in general and in political science in particular, still recognize certain basic and hindering problems. In spite of the rapid proliferation of "frame works," "paradigms," and "theories", they still find the development of a cumulative science of society a far cry. For them, most research is still idiosyncratic in style, and unable to test hypotheses. As Sidney Verba says, "they do not easily add up". Hence, such writers cannot suggest anything braver than "a disciplined configurative approach".[2]

A thorough examination of these two viewpoints would invite a discussion of the philosophy of science (or at least of Social Science) which we do not propose to undertake here. While it is admitted that any serious methodological discussion would finally raise issues relating to philosophy of science, our purpose in this chapter (as indeed, in this book) is much more modest. We want to point out that one major contribution of this new concern with empirical theory and methodology in political science has been that its practitioners today look much more critically at the concepts they use or the problems they probe. A lot of effort is now consciously spent on refining the concepts, constructing testable hypotheses and defining the relevant variables more precisely. These are now considered to be the minimum requirements for any piece of research that hopes to be systematic. Hence, it is necessary that a student of research methodology knows what is meant by concepts, hypotheses and variables. But before we take these up for elucidation, let us make a few brief remarks regarding what methodology is or is not for.

WHY LEARN METHODOLOGY?

With the elevation in the status of social science research in the post World War II period, the teaching of research methods has also become popular. Since 1950's, the social science departments in American universities have been offering courses in research methods and over the years they have gained in popularity among the students. Universities in India, however, have introduced courses in research methods mostly in 1970s and by now, social science departments in a number of universities (most Indian universities do not yet have a separate social science faculty, and the social science departments are still huddled together under Arts or Humanities faculty) as well as a few other institutes (such as the Indian Institutes of Management or Indian Council for Social Science Research etc.) regularly offer courses in research methods.

Concern with methods of research is common for any science when it decides to come down from the level of vague generalities and attempts to concentrate on specific problems of a much narrower focus. This very point was clearly made by Emile Durkheim in his short introduction to the *Rules of Sociological Method*.[3] While lamenting the fact that the problem of methodology had been generally neglected by Spencer or Comte, Durkheim noted that such neglect should not surprise anyone, for the great sociologists prior to him "seldom advanced beyond vague generalities on the nature of societies, on the relations between social and biological realms and on the general march of progress". Hence, such issues as the "precautions to be taken in the observation of facts, the manner in which the principal problems should be formulated, the direction research should take, the specific methods of work which may enable it to reach its conclusions" were kept completely untouched. But as soon as the scientist would abandon the very "general questions" and decide "to attack a certain number of definite problems," he would be led "to construct a method".

By 'method' Durkheim in his *Rules* was not meaning certain techniques of practical research; rather, he was taking it to mean "an exercise in clarification of logical issues."[4] This wider meaning of method has indeed become, as Anthony Giddens points out, a part of European social science tradition. However, for purposes of the present volume, we define method somewhat narrowly. The chapters that follow will primarily discuss some of the more technical aspects of research methods, namely, the technique of data collection and analysis. But even in this narrower sense, the study of methods cannot altogether exclude discussion of the logical issues, for the techniques of data analysis essentially mean looking at one's data from the perspective of certain logic. Only by doing so is one able to find "meaning" in one's data and can explicate the theoretical significance of the data.

Thus, some formal training in research methodology is always helpful. It helps young social scientists to do better research by developing disciplined thinking. It gives an opportunity to young scholars to look critically at other people's research procedures: how they formulate their questions and problems; how they go about finding the data; once they have the data, how they utilize them in answering their most fundamental questions or in advancing their understanding of the stated problems. The students of methodology can carefully scrutinize if the procedures followed by others in data collection and analysis were the most appropriate ones under given conditions. Thus, training in methodology helps the young scholar to learn from the research experience of others.

Training in methodology particularly equips a young scholar for independent study and criticism. As Paul F. Lazarsfeld and Morris Rosenberg pointed out, such training would enhance "the social scientist's ability *to cope with new and unfamiliar problems in his field*."[5] By familiarizing him with some of the basic problems and issues of his science, methodological training equips the young scientist to confront new developments in his discipline and "to judge their merits, to relate them to past trends and to make a reasoned choice as to what he wants to integrate in his own thinking, thus furthering self-education which every responsible scholar continues most of his life."[6]

In an important sense, methodological training enhances awareness of what the researcher already knows. It alerts him to the theoretic and analytic potentialities in his data which he might sometimes overlook. At the same time, it makes the young scientist aware of some of the very common fallacies and pitfalls.

But to say that methodological training is useful is not to encourage what C. Wright Mills calls, "methodological inhibition," nor to suggest that methods should be used "to delimit the problems we take up."[7] Indeed, it does no harm to admit that no amount of methodological training can really generate the originality of approach, the ingenuity in locating and solving problems and above all, that rare quality which can be labelled, following Wright Mills himself, as "sociological imagination" which are essential characteristics of a truly innovating genius. Good analysis of data is an "art" which calls for "insight." No course in methodology can teach one how to acquire insight, or develop imagination or flair. A mature and creative scholar has, in fact, very little to gain from a formal training in methodology. The best thing in his case would be to leave him to his own devices. Yet, as Lazarsfeld and Rosenberg correctly point out, "during the period of his training, during the time when he tries to acquire knowledge and modes of thinking which he might use later, during this formative period, a thorough grounding in methodology will be valueable."[8]

CONTENTS AND HYPOTHESES

Concepts

Concepts are basic to any scientific thinking or research. Any science that is interested in exploring some part of the reality has to develop appropriate concepts. For, concepts are about the reality, though they are not themselves the reality. Concepts symbolically represent the phenomena that the scientists are studying. In fact, they are abstractions from the reality, abstractions which the scientists use as building blocks for the construction of hypotheses and theories.

Concepts are unitary; that is, they are not statements about relationships between phenomena. Further, a concept is neither true nor false; it may only be more or less useful. Concept has to be judged in terms of its contribution to the development of scientific knowledge.

Three different standards of judgement may be applied to evaluate concepts critically. They are: scope, clarity and systematic import.

SCOPE OF CONCEPT

By *scope* of a concept one refers to the "inclusiveness of the class of situations to which the concept applies". A concept to which lots of other concepts are logically related will have greater scope. Thus, in terms of scope, one can talk about general or "universal" concept and specific concept. The former belongs to the higher rungs of the ladder of abstraction while the latter belongs to the lower rungs. Take, for instance, the concept of "social stratification". It is a universal concept. In some sense, stratification is present in all societies; that is, all societies are stratified societies. But only some of them are "class societies", some are "estate societies", some are "caste societies". These latter represent more specific concepts than the concept of "stratified society". (Figure 1.1).

Figure 2.1: Classification of concepts in terms of scope.

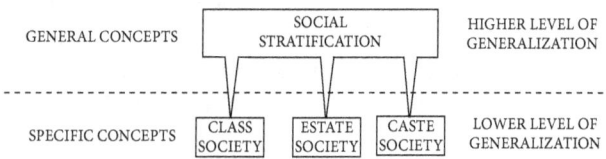

As the general or universal concepts are more abstract than specific concepts, they are often less useful analytically. This constitutes a special problem for the social sciences where the practitioners more often use universal concepts. To say, for instance, that a society is stratified will make much less empirical sense than to say that a society is a caste society or that a society shows certain characteristics of class society. Thus, to be of empirical significance, concepts need to be specified. As Reinhard Bendix suggests, "to be useful analytically, universal concepts require specifications which help us bridge the gap between concept and empirical evidence".[9] In the absence of necessary specification, much of the sosial sciences suffer from a situation where "concepts and theories are difficult to relate to empirical findings and much empirical research is devoid of theoretical significance"[10].

CLARITY OF CONCEPTS

The *clarity* of a concept refers to its capacity for empirical identification and measurements. Since science aims at objective knowledge, the concepts that a scientific discipline uses should have clearly specified meanings and should be uniformly used by all the practitioners of the discipline. That is to say, to be useful, concepts should have meaning specificity or "determinacy" and "uniformity of usage". Clarity of a concept depends on both meaning specificity and uniformity of usage. The more a concept refers to one specific empirical phenomenon and the more such a referent is "inter subjectively certifiable", the higher is clarity of the concept. These also enhance the reliability of a concept. As Carl Hempel writes,

"the reliability of concepts .... is usually understood as an indicator of two things : the consistency shown in its use by one observer and the agreement in the use made of it by different observers".[11]

Clarity of concepts is seriously affected by whether or not the terms used in connection with a concept are part of the vocabulary used by the laity. In the natural sciences it has become possible to gradually abandon common sense frameworks in favour of much more rigorous and specialised lexicon. As Thomas Kuhn points out, with the development of paradigm in a field of science, it becomes possible for the researcher to report his research in the form of "brief articles addressed only to professional colleagues who prove to be the only ones able to read the papers addressed to them"[12]. Practitioners of such sciences need not write whole books starting from first principles and justifying the use of each concept introduced, for whatever they write is meant not for anyone who might be interested in the subject-matter but for a special group of men, the ones who share a common framework of knowledge with the writer. Quite obviously, this raises barriers to the understanding of scientific concepts by the common man and in the case of highly specialised sciences, even by one's colleagues in the other fields of specialisation. But the justification of such a "widening gulf", separating the professional scientist from his colleagues in the other fields on the one hand and from the lay public on the other, lies in the fact that it enormously facilitates communication within the sciences. Kuhn identifies this as an important feature of "normal science" and he even considers that there is an "*essential relationship* between that gulf and the mechanisms intrinsic to scientific advance".[13]

While such a relationship may, in fact, be true in the natural sciences, at least in what Kuhn calls their "normal" states, the position in the social sciences is vastly different. Here the scientist is very often using terms which are frequently used by the laity in everyday speech and this often obscures the meaning that the scientist may want them to convey. But the danger may not come only from lay use of the terms. Social scientists themselves may use the same concept in different senses on different occasions. This creates the problem of multiple meanings of concepts in the social sciences;[14] that is to say, concepts, may assume different meanings in different frames of reference. Thus, the concept of bureaucracy may mean a particular type of organizational structure in sociology. But at the same time, the concept may be used (even by sociologists themselves) in the sense of "red tape" or administrative waste or official disregard of public interest. Again, a single concept may refer to different phenomena. The concept of "function", for instance, may refer to occupational phenomenon, or may imply dependence (in a mathematical sense, e.g., X is a function of Y), or may even denote (as in biology) the contribution of a given part of a whole to the maintenance of the whole (as contrasted with *dysfunction*). Conversely, different concepts may refer to the same phenomenon; that is, a number of concepts may have overlapping meanings.

Situations such as these greatly hinder the development of conceptual clarity, for they contribute neither to meaning specificity nor to inter-subjectivity. In order to remedy the situation, a tendency may increasingly be detected among numerous contemporary social scientists to develop a more rigorous and "professional" vocabulary which will protect their sciences from the unintended lexical interference by the laity. In other words, these social scientists insist that in order to gain scientific objectivity, the social sciences must develop a vocabulary which would make social science discourse inaccessible to the common man. To what extent the development of such a specialized lexicon will contribute to the attainment of scientific objectivity in the social sciences remains controversial.

Nevertheless, it may be pointed out that while the "widening gulf" between the scientist and the common man that we have referred to above might have benefited the natural sciences as Kuhn claims, its recurrence in the social science may be very unfortunate as well as self-defeating. For the objective of social science is to develop greater understanding of man in society not merely for the scientists alone, but for the general public as well. Even if one assumes that the social sciences should be policy oriented, it may safely be asserted that social evils can be eradicated only when the lay public--not merely the social science community, develops a good grasp of the problems and realizes the need for their solution.

Several ways other than developing a specialized lexicon have been suggested for enhancing clarity of scientific concepts in the social sciences. One of these, as suggested by Reinhard Bendix, is to develop "contrast conception".[15]Bendix argues that a concept becomes more clearly understandable and empirically usable when it is contrasted with a similar, yet different, concept. Through such contrast, the inner meaning of a concept may be properly explicated. As Bendix writes:

"Bureaucracy" is hardly a usable concept as long as it stands alone. It gains clarity when we contrast it with the "patrimonial" form of government because in this way we learn of a non-bureaucratic type of government administration that has a century-long development of its own ..... while such paired-concepts are never wholly satisfactory, they do enable us to delimit the space-and-time dimension of a given concept to some extent."[16]***

The more frequently advocated method of enhancing clarity of concepts is through developing "operational definitions" of concepts and scientific terms. The idea of "operational definition" was first systematically advanced by the physicist P.W. Bridgman in his *The Logic of Modern Physics*.[17] As Hempel writes, the operational definition of a term is supposed to provide "objective criteria by means of which any scientific investigator can decide, for any particular case, whether the term does or does not apply".[18] According to the advocates of operationalism, it is only through concepts and terms whose meanings are operationally specific that objectively testable statements can be made by a discipline, and if statements are not so objectively testable, they are scientifically meaningless. For the advocates of operationalism the meaning of intelligence, for instance, would simply be that which is measured by an intelligence test. The operationalists, thus, put emphasis on clear and precise public criteria of application for scientific terms. The nature of such public criteria of application is that they are inter-subjective in the sense that different observers are able to perform "the same operation" with reasonable agreement in their results.[19] The meaning of a concept, from the operationalist standpoint, would then simply consist of a description of the operations used to measure the concept.

Operationalism undoubtedly performs a salutary role by emphasizing clarity, precision and inter-subjectivity of concepts. But extreme operationalism has its limitations. After all, all concepts are abstractions in some form. To concretize a concept like intelligence simply by defining it as whatever is measured by an intelligence test is to lose many other significant dimensions of the concept. Take education, for instance. One may operationalize 'education' by interpreting it to mean the years of formal schooling that one has. But then, we know that such an interpretation is only partial, for education means a lot of other things than merely the number of years of formal schooling.

Operationalism also implies, in a sense, putting the cart before horse. For, unless one has an abstract notion of the concept of intelligence or of education, one cannot even construct, assess and improve tests and the measuring instruments concerned. That is to say, one must first have the concept as an abstraction; only then is it possible to think of ways of measuring it. When one has already constructed the measuring instrument and the test, one can talk about the "operational definition" of the concept. But then, the operational definition is sure to lose the full theoretically possible range of the concept. In this sense, an operational definition is always a "partial definition" or a "partial criterion of application."

Besides, an excessive emphasis on operational definition might lead to the abandonment of theoretically useful concepts for which measurement procedures may not immediately be available.

Finally, it is necessary to admit that every term used in a particular scientific discipline cannot be operationally defined. That is to say, even in operational definitions it is necessary to use abstractions, for it may not be possible to operationally define all the terms that a particular operational definition uses. As Hempel says, "in any definitional situation (quite independently of the issue of operationalism), some terms must be antecedently understood." [20]

Attaining clarity and objectivity is certainly desirable. But it has to be remembered that essentially it is a matter of degree. Even observations of object through microscope or telescope or through X-ray photographs are not totally immune from inter-subjective variations among experts. Hempel rightly remarks :

> "What matters is, I think, to be aware of the extent to which subjective factors enter into the application of a given set of concepts, and to aim at gradual deduction of their influence."[21]

SYSTEMATIC IMPORT OF CONCEPTS

The third important criterion for the evaluation of   concepts is their *systematic import*. Precisely, it refers to the extent to which a concept can be incorporated in a theoretical framework.   To be scientifically useful, a concept must contribute to the systematization of knowledge in a particular discipline in the form of law-like generalizations and theories. Hempel, in fact, considers systematic import as more important than clarity in the form of "operational definitions". He deplores the tendency in contemporary methodological literature in the social sciences to emphasize the need for "operational definitions" as the most promising way of furthering the growth of these fields of knowledge as scientific disciplines, "leaving it to subsequent research to discover whether these concepts lend themselves to the formulation of fruitful theoretical principles". He thinks that "concept formation in science cannot be separated from theoretical considerations."[22]

While in the long run, systematic import of concepts is surely the most important criterion for either retaining or abandoning a particular concept, too much emphasis on systematicimport, especially, at the early stages of development of a science, may do more harm than good. In its early stages, a science must spend lot of its energy in search of new concepts, although apparently they may have little systematic import. In such a state of a discipline, the importance of a concept would lie on less pragmatic criteria--for instance, on the authority of the person using the concept, or the status of the journal in which the publication appears, or the connections--in somewhat loose and ad-hoc manner--that may be established between this new concept and the ones already in use etc. In view of this, the emphasis put on clarity more than on systematic import in contemporary social science seems somewhat less unwarranted.

Hypotheses

Once we have a body of interrelated concepts or a conceptual framework, it becomes possible to formulate hypotheses. And if we have a theory which rigorously systematizes facts and establishes relationships among them through concepts, hypotheses can be deduced from it. A theory creates certain expectation about the reality. Hypotheses are systematic statements of these expectations in a verifiable form. Since hypotheses are statements about the reality, they will be either true or false. A verified hypothesis will strengthen the theory from which it is deduced while a falsified hypothesis will weaken the theory, though it need not necessarily lead to the rejection of the theory.[23]

The relationship between theory or conceptual framework and hypothesis is a very close one. Any worthwhile theory will certainly generate additional hypotheses, for a theory itself is a sort of an "elaborate hypothesis" which implies more than it incorporates. Verifiable hypotheses, through rigorous testing of these implications, will match facts with theory and thus will articulate the theory under varying and stringent conditions. Thus, hypotheses are indispensable tools for scientific knowledge (Figure 1.2).

Figure 2.2: Process of development of scientific knowledge.

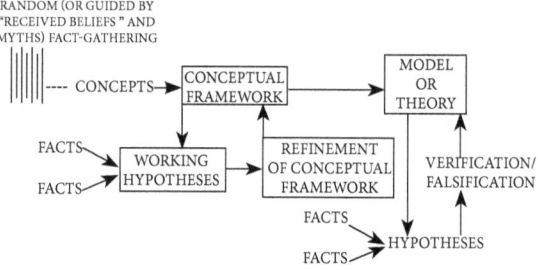

FUNCTION OF HYPOTHESES

The above figure (1.2) clearly indicates that hypotheses play a very crucial role: they mediate between facts on the one hand and theories on the other. That is why any reference to the critical function of hypotheses in the development of scientific knowledge automatically brings up the controversy regarding the relationship between fact and theory. For a long time it has been the subject matter of discussion in methodological literature as well as in the philosophy of science. Very simply, the crucial question here is: where does a scientist start? Should the scientist first build up a catalogue of facts and then, by following the logic of inductive method, arrive at generalization (theory), or must he first have the theory and then, look at facts to make sure that the theory is correct (or rather, that it is not incorrect)? The first procedure is known as "post-factum" analysis while the second one is called the "method of hypothesis". In the former, the researcher starts with the data and seeks an interpretation which is consistent with the data. The latter procedure, however, requires that the researcher must have a specific interpretation first and then determine whether the data are consistent with it.

The conventional empiricist position has been that one must look at facts first, for how can one offer an interpretation without first confronting facts? Emile Durkheim, for instance, in his *Rules of Sociological Method* takes the position that sociology must try to construct theories about externally visible human conduct by looking at such conduct. It is out of such prior observations, which are necessarily pre-theoretical, that theories are born. Empirical tradition in political science also took such a "facts would speak for themselves" position for a long time.[24]

In the early stages of the natural sciences also one could detect a tendency toward random fact- gathering. Pliny's encyclopaedic writings or Bacon's works are examples of such a "natural history" stage of modern science. But as Kuhn says, such random fact-gathering soon "produces a morass," and it becomes apparent that such natural history cannot be interpreted in the absence of "at least some implicit body of intertwined theoretical and methodological beliefs" that permits selection, evaluation and criticism.[25]

But before we come to the "method of hypothesis" which Kuhn's statement obviously implies, let us examine some of the problems of post-factum analysis. The first problem arises out of the fact that in the post-factum analysis one offers an interpretation in the light of the facts before him and hence, one can freely choose or change one's interpretation at will. If one finds, for instance, that the unemployed poor in urban areas are more likely to vote for rightist parties, one can offer several interpretations for this. If, on the other hand, one finds that the urban unemployed poor are more likely to vote for the left, one can similarly offer equally satisfactory interpretations. Thus, as Rosenberg points out, "excessive flexibility" is one of the weak points of post-factum analysis.[26]

Again, post-factum interpretations are not falsifiable. If, as in the above example, one finds that the unemployed poor are more likely to vote for rightist parties, one might interpret it to be due to their belief that under rightist regimes the industrialists are likely to invest more and thereby increase employment opportunities. Given the fact, there is no way to prove that this interpretation is incorrect.

Thirdly, which is corollary to the second argument above, if an interpretation is not falsifiable, it cannot be confirmed either. It is not possible for one confronting a post-factum interpretation to see whether the interpretation is correct by referring back to the data, for the interpretation itself is based on the data. Thus, the data cannot be taken as an external confirmation of the interpretation.

These problems severely weaken the empiricist argument that theories can really develop out of such pre-theoretical observational statements. Indeed, Hume had already conclusively refuted the logic of inductive inference or the fact that generalization can ever be made on the basis of inductive fact-finding. In the absence of falsifiability, post-factum interpretations fail to resolve what Popper calls the "problem of determination" between science and pseudoscience,[27] and hence, they are of very limited use for scientific knowledge.

Carl Hempel, while discussing A. B. Wolfe's view of the stages of scientific enquiry, has made similar criticisms of the empiricist position that un-hypothesized findings can really lead to general principles.[28] Wolfe suggested that there were four stages in an ideal scientific enquiry. Chronologically, these would be : (1) observation and recording of all facts; (2) analysis and classification of these facts; (3) inductive derivation of generalizations from them and (4) further testing of the generalizations.[29] That is, Wolfe believed that hypotheses were unnecessary in the beginning : the real starting point for scientific enquiry would be observation and collection of facts.

Hempel calls such a position as "the narrow intuitivist conception of scientific enquiry" and points out first, that collection of all the facts is impossible; only the relevant facts can be collected, and the relevance of facts can be established only with reference to a given hypothesis. Secondly, that fact can be analyzed and classified in numerous ways, and hence, the choice of a particular mode of analysis and classification has to depend on hypothesis. Thus, without hypothesis, "analysis and classification of facts are blind".[30] Hence, Hempel observes,

"tentative hypotheses are needed to give direction to a scientific investigation. Such hypotheses determine, among other things, what data should be collected at a given point of scientific investigation".[31]

The burden of above discussion has been to demonstrate the weakness of the empiricist position. In Figure 1.2 above, at the left-hand end we have fact-gathering as the starting point of the process of development of scientific knowledge. The discussion in the above paragraphs relates to a very simple question: can fact-gathering at all be random? We see facts all around us. But can one discover anything by simply looking at these facts at random? Is it ever possible for any observer to look at *all* the facts? The answer to these questions is a simple 'No'. We surely will have to be grounded on facts, but not on all facts. We need something like a sieve which will help us to filter out the irrelevant from the relevant facts. A conceptual framework or theory is such a sieve. Fact-gathering, unguided by any conceptual or theoretical frame-work, will lead to nowhere. As Karl Popper says,

"........ the instruction 'Observe!' is absurd...... observation is always selective. It needs a chosen object, a definite task, an interest, a point of view, a problem."[32]

Random fact-gathering is thus impossible. It has to be guided by some theory. It is, of course, neither possible nor necessary to have a well-developed theory from which pre-formulated hypotheses can be derived in a strictly deductive fashion. As a matter of fact, the initial approach to facts may simply be guided by certain myths and beliefs or common sense considerations, and the hypotheses based on them may even remain implicit and non- specific. What is absolutely essential is that before one looks at facts, one must have some idea as to why does he want to look at them. That is to say, one must have a 'frame of reference'.

It is true that a scientist has to remain sensitive to the possibility of unexpected or "serendipitous" findings.[33] It is very common for a scientist to face a situation when his research assistant comes after a hectic search and says 'I tried hard but could not get what you wanted; however, I have found this (piece of information); I do not know if it will be of any help', and the scientist finds that this chance finding is something which he was not, but should have been, looking for. But even such unanticipated findings come only to those who had been anticipating something. Thus, the route to discovery and theory starts not strictly from facts, but from hypotheses which have to be invented. It requires inventive ingenuity, imaginative and insightful guessing. Facts help to test hypotheses, not to invent them. They provide "inductive support" by either confirming or refuting the hypotheses. That is why Popper in his *Conjectures and Refutations* advises the scientist to be bold in proposing hypotheses (i.e. making "conjectures") and in trying their best to demonstrate, in the light of empirical evidence (i.e., facts), if these are erroneous (i.e., attempting "refutations").

TYPES OF HYPOTHESES

Hypotheses may generally be classified into two types: *descriptive* hypotheses and *relational* hypotheses. The former are concerned with the existence or distribution of empirical uniformities while the latter are concerned with the exploration of relationships among variables.

One may, for instance, be interested in investigating the distribution of the population in a community by age. Similarly, one may be interested in investigating the degrees of conformism/non-conformism in the behaviour pattern of the first year undergraduates. In instances such as these, one is dealing with descriptive hypotheses.

On the other hand, one may be interested in investigating whether the size of the family has any relationship with income levels, or whether the frequency of exercising the right to vote is related to educational attainments or whether it is likely that a person belonging to a minority group is more likely to feel alienated etc. In all such cases, one is exploring relationships between variables and hence, one is dealing with relational hypotheses.

In the social sciences, the scientist is normally interested in relational hypotheses; that is, in other words, the scientist is generally interested in exploring relationships among variables. But that should not mean that the social scientist can, therefore, be solely interested in relational hypotheses to the exclusion of the descriptive hypotheses. For, normally, concern with description of empirical uniformities is a prior step towards examining more complicated relational hypotheses. Emile Durkheim in his *Suicide* was interested in exploring the determinants of suicide and hence, he was considering the relationship of suicide rates with such variables as age, marital status, religious affiliation, political crises etc. In this sense, he was essentially dealing with relational hypotheses. But in order to explore these, he also had to be interested in the description of the different individual variables. For instance, he had to know the suicide rate per year for a certain number of years, and also the frequency of political crises during those years in order to test the relationship between suicide rates and political crises.

Descriptive hypotheses, thus, merely add up facts, and thereby facilitate the exploration of relationships among facts.

EVALUATION OF HYPOTHESES

We have already seen that there are certain criteria for evaluating concepts. Analogous to those, there are also certain criteria for the evaluation of hypotheses. Broadly, these are two: *testability* and *theoretic relevance*.

As we have already stated, a hypothesis is a statement about reality, and hence, it may be either true or false. This automatically implies that a hypothesis must be so formulated that its truth or falsity can be empirically tested. Obviously, a hypothesis which is so formulated is useful; and the one which is not so formulated is unusable.

To be testable, a hypothesis must use concepts and terms whose meanings are clear. It is necessary to define the concepts and terms involved very clearly and also to make them as operationalizable as possible.

Secondly, testability also requires that a hypothesis is a specific rather than a very broad and general statement about reality. Although it is tempting for one to attempt to substantiate or refute such broad statements as 'class conflict is endemic to all industrial societies', or 'political democracy requires social pluralism', or 'democracy is the best form of government', it will be very unwise to try to test these as they are. In order to lend them testable form, it is essential that more specific hypotheses dealing with a much narrower range of matters are derived from them. The more general the statement, the harder is it to either substantiate or refute it.

Moreover, if the hypothesis is specific it will automatically bring into focus the problems of operationalizing the concepts involved and constructing Indices for measuring them. Thus, a specific hypothesis, by making such issues explicit, will offer the researcher a chance for checking the feasibility of testing a hypothesis.

Thirdly, testability implies that a hypothesis must be a statement such that it can be refuted. Statements such as 'God exists everywhere' or 'Black (or Brown) is beautiful' cannot be taken as testable hypotheses for the simple reason that they can neither be verified nor refuted. They are non-testable propositions or statements of faith. Astrological forecasting is also of that type: they are stated in such a way that whatever happens will be consistent, in some way or other, with the forecast. Hence, Popper, arguing for a more rigorous procedure, suggests the *"criteria of refutation"* (rather than of verification) and insists that such criteria must be clearly stated in advance: "it must be agreed which observable situations, if actually observed, mean that the theory is refuted."[34]

It may, briefly and in passing, be pointed out that the application of Popper's "criteria of refutation", however desirable, may not altogether be feasible in the social sciences. The difficulty of arranging satisfactorily controlled and crucial experiments in the social sciences will always keep the door open to alternative hypotheses and competing theories. Kuhn, while elaborately describing the process through which revolutions in scientific theories take place, shows that the unequivocal acceptance of the theory by scientific community, while depending initially and in part on the "faith" in its "future promise", will ultimately depend on the new theory's "comparative ability to *solve problems.*"[35] But this not merely requires some sort of agreement on what constitutes the major problems and what are their acceptable solutions on the part of the practitioners of a scientific discipline; in addition, this also requires that the solutions must be demonstrable. The social sciences in their present state of development do not permit fulfilment of these requirements.

However, setting the "criteria of refutation" in advance has one great value. It tends to curb that unfortunate mental tendency common to the whole human race; that is, the tendency to notice only those facts which support one's beliefs and wishes and to ignore or pervert those which do not. This tendency towards gathering "selective evidence," or what Francis Bacon called the "Idols of Tribe," arises out of the practice of verifying one's hypothesis (rather than trying to falsify them) as Popper argues. If one insists on verification, one will surely find confirmations of his hypothesis all around. The only way of establishing one's hypothesis, though only tentatively, is by trying hard but failing to refute it.

Finally, testability also requires that there should be some correspondence between the hypothesis and the techniques available for testing them. That is to say, while formulating one's hypotheses, a scientist must know what techniques are available through which he can empirically test them.

This does not mean that a scientist, while formulating hypotheses, should always be limited by the techniques available. It is quite natural for a scientist to formulate theoretically relevant hypotheses or concepts for which no satisfactory measuring devices or indices exist.[36]That is indeed a sure way for advancing not merely theory but the spectrum of available techniques as well. However, the knowledge of available technique is important for a researcher, because he must be in a position to make the best use of them.

Apart from testability, the other criterion for evaluating hypotheses is their theoretic relevance. The discussion above on the function of hypotheses has already delineated the fact that a hypothesis is normally connected with a body of explicit or implicit theory. A good empirical research tries to test a number of hypotheses which are connected with a major hypothesis or theory. To a young researcher numerous hypotheses may strike as interesting; but unless they can be linked to a theory, research would remain merely episodic. In *Suicide*, for instance, Durkheim tests a number of hypotheses regarding the relationship between suicide on the one hand and such variables as gender, age, marital status, income, political crises, religious affiliation etc., on the other. But they are all connected with his general hypothesis (or theory) that suicide, which appears to be "a highly individual and personal phenomenon, is explicable through the social structure and its ramifying functions." Without theoretic relevance, hypothesis-testing cannot be scientifically interesting or useful, for it cannot contribute to the development of systematic knowledge.

VARIABLES

Crudely defined, a variable is something that varies. In fact, it is a concept stated in such a way that it can take on two or more values. Gender, for instance, is a concept which takes on two values: male and female (it can have a third value if the third gender is taken into account). Hence, it can be used as a variable. On the other hand, skin as a concept is not a variable; but if one considers *colour of skin*, then that becomes a variable for the colour of skin varies from individual to individual. Therefore, to be used as a variable a concept must imply two or multiple values so that observations or cases can be categorized according to these values.

There are numerous concepts which, unlike gender, do not by themselves imply two or more values. But most of the times they can be so converted. Thus, the concept of ego can be converted into "ego strength", urbanization into "degrees of urbanization", education into "levels of education" and so on.

RELATIONSHIP BETWEEN VARIABLES

In social science research, as we have already pointed out, one is interested in examining relationships between variables. But not all bivariate (two-variable) relationships are of equal significance to the scientist. There are generally three types of relationship between variables: *symmetrical, reciprocal* and *asymmetrical*.[37]

In symmetrical relationships, the two variables may be very highly correlated; yet it would not be possible to talk in terms of one variable affecting or influencing the other. For instance, one may find that the amount of rainfall in Bombay correlates very highly with the amount of rainfall in Calcutta over the past several years. But this would not mean that the amount of rainfall in Bombay affects the rainfall in Calcutta. They are, in fact, the effects of the same cause, i.e., spread of the monsoon.

Similar symmetrical relationships one may find between the alternative indicators of the same concept (for example, the close correlation between having a television set at home and owning a car is due to the fact that both are indicators of being wealthy rather than one affecting the other) or between two component parts of a functionally interdependent system (for example, the presence of heart in an organism may highly correlate with the presence of lungs not because either is due to the other or either causes the other, but simply because they are functionally interdependent parts of a whole). Further, symmetrical relationships may be simply fortuitous. For example, one may find that whenever she goes to the airport to take a flight to Delhi, the plane develops some trouble and the flight is delayed. But this should not lead one to reason that herdecision to take the Delhi flight causes the delay in flight, for the correlation is simply accidental and fortuitous. While such symmetrical relationships are interesting, and often very revealing for understanding a larger system, they are by themselves not adequate for understanding and explanation. To understand and explain individual and collective behaviour, one must be able to identify the underlying asymmetries in relationships of variables.

But before we come to asymmetrical relationships, let us briefly refer to reciprocal relationships. In social research, reciprocal relationships are very common to find. While in case of symmetrical relationships we found that neither of the two variables are "causally" linked with the other in spite of high degree of correlation, when relationships between two variables are reciprocal, both variables may be said to be "casually linked" to each other. It is a case of mutual causation or interacting relationship. The relationship between room temperature and thermostat is a case in point. The thermostat determines room temperature which in turn affects the thermostat. Similarly, an individual with leftist political leaning, for instance, would be exposed to the leftist media and such exposure, in turn, would further strengthen her leftist political leaning or affiliation. Or again, political underdevelopment may lead to military intervention in politics and such intervention may help maintain political underdevelopment. The price-wage spiral is an example of such reciprocal relationships between two economic variables.

In this type of relationship, the same variable is both a cause and an effect. If, in a specific time period (t_1), A affects B, at the next phase (t_2),A itself is affected by B (figure 2.3). Hence, as Rosenberg says, it is a case of "alternating asymmetry."

Figure 2.3: Reciprocal relationship

$$A_{t_1} \longrightarrow B_{t_1} \longrightarrow A_{t_2} \longrightarrow B_{t_2} \cdots$$

But it is with locating and exploring asymmetrical relationships between variables that social research is centrally concerned. Asymmetrical relationships differ from symmetrical and reciprocal relationships in that they permit the researcher to postulate that one variable affects or influences the other. That is to say, when relationships between variables are asymmetrical, one can talk about 'independent' and 'dependent' variables (or 'describing' and 'response' variables).

Social research, like any other research, starts with a problem to be solved or a question to be answered. For example: why some countries failed to develop stable political institutions while others succeeded? Why does the military tend to intervene in politics more in some countries than in others? Why some individuals vote more regularly than others in national elections? To answer such questions one has to think in terms of causes, however incomplete or tentative may be the explanation offered. Whenever we are thinking in terms of causes, or are trying to *explain* something, we are in the area of asymmetrical relationships. The phenomenon we are trying to explain is the dependent variable, and the phenomenon with which we are explaining is the independent (explanatory) variable. A two-variable asymmetrical relationship would imply that one has one dependent and one independent variable. However, usually a social phenomenon is produced by not one but a number of factors. Hence it becomes incumbent on the researcher to identify as many of the factors explaining the phenomenon as possible. That is, one has in such situations one dependent and multiple independent variables. The former is known as bivariate (two-variable) analysis, while the latter is called multivariate analysis. (Figure 2.4)

Figure 2.4: Types of relationship among variables.

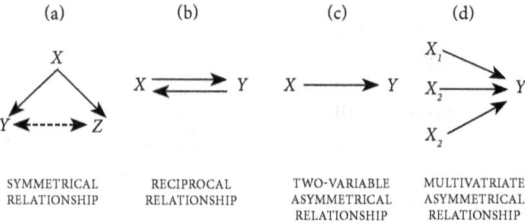

Thus, while answering the question, why some people vote more regularly than others, one may find that one is likely to vote more regularly than others if he/she is well educated, belongs to higher income group, has a respectable occupation and lives in an urban area. In this case, one can call the rate of voting as his dependent variable and education, income, occupation and place of residence as independent variables (Figure 2.5).

Figure 2.5: Independent-dependent relationship.

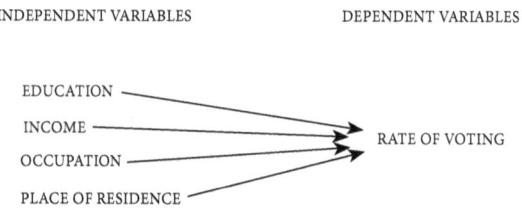

In asymmetrical relationships, then, we can talk about dependent and independent variables. But how does one know which one is the dependent and which one is the independent variable? Is there any concrete or statistical procedure for identifying the dependent and the independent variables? That is, in other words, even if we know that variables A and B are causally related, the problem would be far from solved. For, it would be absolutely necessary for us also to know which one influences the other, or in which way the causal arrow runs. The simple answer to this question is that there is no statistical procedure through which one can identify the direction of influence. This is entirely a logical problem, amenable only to logical solution. There are, however, two rules of thumb that one may remember while trying to determine the direction of influence: (i) the time sequence of the variables and (ii) their relative "fixity" or flexibility.[38]

Knowledge of time sequence is clearly important in determining causal relationships, for anything happening later cannot have influenced something that had happened earlier. That is, the causal factor (independent variable) must always be temporally prior to the effect factor (dependent variable). For instance, if one finds a close correlation between one's childhood political experiences within the family and his later political affiliation during adulthood, only the former could be a causal factor for the latter.

Similarly, in a causal relationship, it may be assumed that between two variables, the fixed one would be causal to the more flexible one. Thus, if one finds a relationship between gender and political affiliation, it is one's gender that might determine his/her political affiliation rather than the latter determining the former. Gender as an individual's attribute, is of a fixed nature than something like political affiliation which is flexible and variable.

While these are good rules of thumb and one should not violate them while identify the causal and the dependent variables, the point made earlier needs to be repeated that the determination of the causal factor is a logical operation. The statistical values of relationships (such as correlation coefficients) between variables never say which of the two variables is dependent and which one is independent. Edward Tufte remarks that,

> "Statistical techniques do not solve any of the common sense difficulties about making causal inferences. Such techniques may help organize or arrange the data....... All the logical, theoretical and empirical difficulties attendant to establishing a causal relationship persist no matter what type of statistical analysis is applied."[39]

TYPES OF VARIABLES

We have already talked about independent and dependent variables. We have seen that asymmetrical relationship between two variables implies the existence of a 'dependent' variable and an 'independent' variable. We have further pointed out that given the rules of time sequence and fixity, it is also possible to indicate the direction of the causal arrow between two variables. For instance, if it is found that the rural working class people in India usually vote for the Congress Party, it is quite obvious that their voting pattern does not determine their social class; rather it is their social class that influences their voting pattern. But even then, such a finding remains essentially in the realm of description. It does not indicate *why* this has to be so: is it that the rural working class people vote more frequently for the Congress Party because of their class affiliation, or because of something else? That is to say, is the observed asymmetry between these two variables genuine or only apparent?

It is possible that there is another variable somewhere which really determines this relationship, and once that variable is controlled, the relationship between social class and voting would disappear. For instance, it may be that the rural working class people vote for the Congress because of their low education. In that case, if one controls for education (that is, if one classifies the rural working class people according to the level of education attained and then correlates separately each of the different educational categories within the rural working class with "voting Congress") one may find that those among the rural working class who have received some education vote more frequently for the left parties than for the Congress. Such a finding would at once lead to the conclusion that it is education, rather than one's social class per se, that determines voting.

Therefore, it is not adequate for purposes of understanding and explanation merely to identify a dependent and an independent variable. One must further examine their relationship to explore the nature of asymmetry by introducing new variables. Such new variables are called 'test factors' or 'control variables', for they are used to test the genuineness of the asymmetry.

One may ask legitimately, how does one get the test factors or where to look for them. The answer to this is that individuals and groups have a number of characteristics and generally these are interrelated. Thus, when we talk about rural workers, we do not simply mean workers who live in rural areas. We also assume, that generally they are likely to be uneducated, more religion-minded, tradition-bound, less politically informed and less motivated about politics etc.

Therefore, 'rural worker' means a bundle of characteristics. When we talk about the voting pattern of these rural workers, what we really want to know is this: which one of these different characteristics of the rural workers accounts for its visible voting pattern. These associated characteristics then become significant variables that help one to explore the relationship between a dependent and an independent variable. Once the researcher is able to identify the most significant of these associated variables, he can draw his test factors from them.

Depending on their logical position vis-a-vis the dependent and independent variables and the function they perform, the test factors can be classified into four major types; extraneous variables, component variables, intervening variables and antecedent variables. Following Rosenberg, [40] we will briefly discuss these different types of variables below.

EXTRANEOUS VARIABLE

We have to remember that the whole idea of introducing test factors while examining the asymmetrical relationship between two variables is to see whether the observed asymmetry is real or only apparent. Sometimes, the observed relationship between two variables may in fact be due to an extraneous variable. For instance, one might see that older people read lesser number of books than younger people. Obviously, the question then would be: is there any relationship between age and the habit of reading books? Speculating on the basis of logical reasoning, one might feel that after all, the habit of reading books must also be associated with education. People with low education are likely to read lesser number of books than well-educated people. Is it possible then, that the older people read books less than the younger ones not so much because they are old as because these people belonging to older generations are generally less educated than people of the younger generation? On the basis of such reasoning, then, one may introduce the extraneous variable "education" as a test factor to examine whether the apparent relationship between age and the habit of reading books is correct or not, and in fact one may see that if education is controlled (that is, if one compares the book reading habits of old and young people belonging to the same educational levels), the relation between age and the habit of book reading disappears.

But how does one determine which extraneous variable can productively be used as a test factor in a specific two variable relationship? This decision essentially depends on two considerations: one *logical*, the other *statistical*. The logical consideration is that the extraneous variable must logically appear as relevant in the context of the relationship under study. Thus, to examine the relationship between age and book reading habit within a population one cannot look at its kinship structure or the size of the family. Logically, that does not make any sense.

The statistical consideration requires that the test factor must be statistically related both to the independent and the dependent variables. If, for instance, one knows that the test factor is not so related, it would not make any sense to introduce such a variable as a test factor. In the above example, education could be introduced as a test factor, for education is statistically related to age as well as to reading habit.

One may introduce extraneous variables not merely to test the validity of a given asymmetry in relationship, but also as a check on *suppressed* or *distorted* relationships. Sometimes, the true relationship between two variables may remain suppressed or hidden. When relationships between variables are suppressed, one may simply find them unrelated or negatively related. And yet, the variables may in fact be positively related. In this sense, negative findings may be as misleading as positive ones. Sometimes, through the introduction of the appropriate test factor one may expose the suppressed relationship.

Russell Middleton's study[41] of the relationship between race and alienation in the United States may be used as an example of dealing with suppressed relationships. Middleton wanted to know if people with subordinate social status (e.g., the Blacks in the U.S.) have a greater sense of alienation than others (e.g., the whites). Middleton developed six indicators to measure alienation and in five out of the six, he found the Blacks to be more alienated than the whites. But on one indicator, which he called "cultural estrangement," he found no difference between the Blacks and the whites. Suspecting that this absence of relation between race and "cultural estrangement" maybe false, he introduced "education" as a test factor. Interestingly, when he classified the Blacks and the whites by the level of education, he found that under each educational level, the whites demonstrated greater cultural estrangement than the Blacks.

The original non-correlation between race and "cultural estrangement" was due to the fact that "cultural estrangement" depended more on poor education than on race, and that the Blacks were generally poorly educated. Poor education of the Blacks in general had offset the greater sense of estrangement among the whites. The introduction of the extraneous variable "education" as a *suppressor variable* brought out the true implications of the relationship between race and "cultural estrangement". Extraneous variables, thus, can expose spurious non-correlations.

Similarly, extraneous variables also help to penetrate distorted relationship between two variables and bring out the true one. Relationship between two variables may be said to be "distorted" when the true relationship is just the reverse of the apparent relationship.

Sydney Verba and Norman H. Nie,[42]while examining the relationship between race and political participation in the United States, found that the Blacks, in general, participate much less politically than the whites. When the mean participation score of the whites was found to be + 1, for the Blacks it was - 12. To examine the relationship further, they introduced 'socio-economic status' (a composite of education, income and occupation variables) as an extraneous variable and found that the original relationship was completely reversed when the socio-economic status (SES) variable was controlled. That is to say, when one compares the rate of political participation of the Blacks and the whites belonging to identical socio-economic status groups, the Blacks appear to be greater participants than the whites. The original relationship was due to the fact that the Blacks generally belong to lower SES categories than the whites in the United States.

Thus, the original relationship between race and participation was distorted by the fact that an average Black in United States has lower education and income and worse occupation than the average white. As soon as one introduces those *distorter variables* in the relationship, one finds the distortion as well as the true relationship.

COMPONENT VARIABLES

Social research generally deals with variables which are 'global' and hence non-specific. A global variable is one which is a composite of several component or elementary variables. Therefore, when a social scientist shows the relationship between a global variable and a dependent variable, one does not know whether the variable is related in its global capacity or the relationship is due to the effects of any of the components of the global variable. The problem can be solved only if one is able to decompose the global variable in its component parts and then examine the relationship between each of the components on the one hand and the dependent variable on the other.

An example will clarify the problem. Durkheim, in his study of suicide, found that in given age groups, married people were less likely to commit suicide than single ones. While explaining such a relationship one would face the fact that marriage is a global concept with several component meanings. Clearly, marriage involves two types of relationships : (i) conjugal (husband and wife) and (ii) family (parents and children). Therefore, it becomes necessary to know which of these two aspects of marriage is important in reducing suicide rates. Durkheim examined this further and found that it is not marriage as such, but the presence of children that affects the rate of suicide for the married people.

Similarly, social class is a global variable and education, income, occupation, status of the family, caste, class consciousness etc., are its components. Social class may be related to variable X as well as variable Y; but, in fact, two different components or sets of components of "social class" may be related to X and Y respectively. (Figure 2.6)

Figure 2.6: Global variable and its components

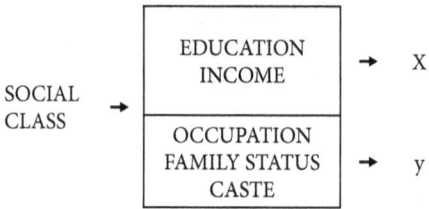

Thus while social class affects both X and Y, the meaning of social class differs on the two occasions. This will not be understood unless the global variable is split up into its components and relationships are examined by components. Thus, identification of the component variables and their use in analysing relationships are important for understanding what specific factors are responsible for a particular relationship.

INTERVENING VARIABLES

Intervening variables are those that intervene between the independent and the dependent variables, and hence, are casually related to both. They appear as *consequences* of the independent variable and as *causes* of the dependent variable.

As Rosenberg points out, the intervening variables have almost the same statistical properties as the extraneous variables. In both cases, the relationship between the independent and the dependent variables would appear to depend on the test factor (i.e., extraneous or intervening variable, as the case may be). That is to say, if the test factor is controlled, the relationship between the independent and the dependent variables would either disappear or would be seriously weakened. Also, in both cases, the test factor would be correlated with the dependent as well as independent variables. Yet, the intervening variables are logically quite different from the extraneous variables.

When a relationship between an independent and a dependent variable is due to an extraneous variable, there is, in fact, no direct relationship between the former two. The independent- dependent relationship, then, is wholly apparent, and it appears because both the variables are directly related to a third (extraneous) variable. When an extraneous variable is present the relationship would look like:

Extraneous Variable ⟶ ⎡ Independent Variable
⎣ Dependent Variable

In the example of the extraneous variable above, we found that education was associated with age, and education was also associated with book reading habit. These two associations led to an apparent association between age and book reading.

In the case of the intervening variable, however, the relationship between the independent and the dependent variables is mediated through the intervening variable :

Independent variable → Intervening variable → Dependent variable

For instance, Durkheim observed that Catholics had lower suicide rates than Protestants. He argued that this relationship became more meaningful when one discovered the intervening variable, namely, social integration. Thus, Catholicism, by enhancing a sense of integration, reduces suicide rates among its adherents.

Similarly, many students of voting behaviour have found that education is positively correlated with voting. But they have reasoned that this relationship becomes more meaningful when one considers the fact that education enhances voting frequency not so much directly as through the enhancement of interest in politics. That is to say,

Education	→	Political Interest	→	Voting
(independent)		(intervening)		(dependent)

The presence of an intervening variable would imply three separate asymmetrical relationships: first, the relationship between the independent (e.g., education) and the dependent (e.g., voting) variables; second, the relationship between in the independent variable (education) and the intervening variable (political interest, which is a dependent variable to education); third, the relationship between the intervening variable (political interest) and the dependent variable (voting, which is dependent to political interest as well as to education).

ANTECEDENT VARIABLE

Antecedent variable is the variable which logically precedes the independent variable in a two-variable relationship. That is, just as the independent variable is supposed to answer the question: why is the dependent variable, so the antecedent variable is supposed to answer, why is the independent variable. This means that the presence of an antecedent variable would transform the so-called "independent" variable into a dependent variable (to the antecedent variable). In other words, in that three-variable situation, the independent variable would take the place of an intervening variable. A concrete example will illustrate the point.

Verba and Nie[43] in their study of political participation in the United States found that greater participation by the upper status citizens leads to greater governmental responsiveness to their demands. Diagrammatically it would look like:

Greater Political participation   →   Greater Governmental response
  (by upper status people)   (for the upper status people's demands)

That is, governmental responsiveness to demands is positively correlated with the degree of political participation.

In view of this, they further asked, why is it that the upper status people participate more? They found that the very fact of their belonging to the upper status group makes them greater participants. (Figure 2.7)

Figure 2.7: Different ways of looking at the variables

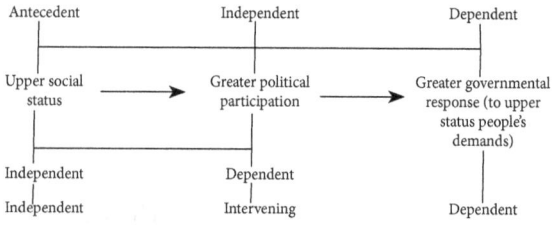

Thus, while greater participation can secure greater governmental response, upper social status remains an antecedent condition to greater participation. Another way of saying the same thing would be that upper social status is an independent variable to greater political participation which, in turn, becomes an intervening variable.

If one looks at the latter two variables as independent and dependent, upper social status is antecedent variable. But if one looks at the former two variables only, upper social status becomes an independent variable. On the other hand, taking all the three variables together, one may say that social status is the independent variable to governmental response (dependent variable), while greater participation is an intervening variable.

The presence of an antecedent variable in a two-variable situation would have the following statistical features: [44]

a. all the variables would be statistically related;

b. the relationship between the independent and the dependent variables would not depend on the antecedent variable;

c. in the absence of the independent variable, the antecedent variable would show no relationship to the dependent variable.

In the above example that was exactly the case. While all the variables were statistically related, and while there was a clear positive relationship between participation and responsiveness, when participation was controlled, the relationship between social status and responsiveness sharply declined.[45] That is to say, participation had a crucial role to play; social status did not directly lead to greater governmental responsiveness : it was mediated through greater political participation.

The major function of an antecedent variable is to elaborate the causal chain. The intervening variable also performs a similar function. While the intervening variable(s) tries to trace out what lies *between* an independent and a dependent variable, the antecedent variable explores the factor that lies *before* the independent variable. The purpose in exploring the antecedent variable(s) need not be a quest for the 'first cause'. Simply by bringing out the meaningful factors and by elaborating the relationship between two variables, both the antecedent and the intervening variables enhance our understanding of the relationship. While thinking about the possible intervening and antecedent variables and while bringing them into the analysis, one is, in essence, subjecting the basic two- variable relationship to further tests and trying to see whether in the so-called 'independent' variable one truly has a significant explanatory factor. The antecedent variable can be diagrammatically presented as,

Antecedent variable → Independent variable → Dependent variable

While the statistical features of the presence of an antecedent variable are important, simply the satisfaction of the statistical conditions would not mean that a particular variable is truly antecedent. The final criterion is obviously logical.

The variables discussed above, extraneous through antecedent, help one to subject a two-variable relationship to further elaboration and tests, and to deepen one's understanding of it. When one considers a two-variable relationship, one faces the obvious problem of knowing whether the relationship is genuine or not. The possibility that one might reject a true relationship as false (Type I error) or that one might accept a false relationship as true (Type II error) is always present. By introducing a third extraneous variable as a test factor, one imposes a check on that possibility. The component variables, on the other hand, help one to arrive at more specific findings. Intervening and antecedent variables permit one to further elaborate the causal chain. While it is admitted that no test factor can guarantee an absolutely genuine relationship, through the use of test factors one may avoid certain common fallacies and pitfalls and attain a sounder foundation both for the description of a relationship and its explanation.

Theory and Method

In the discussion above, especially in sections on concepts and hypotheses, we have attempted to draw attention to the importance of theory in a research which wants to be methodologically sound. Needless to mention that while scientific knowledge can be both inductively and deductively obtained, here our emphasis is on methods of inductive or empirical research.

The foundation of empirical research lies not on speculative or abstract thinking but on observable world of facts. It starts from observation of facts and ends in validation against facts. Using well-articulated methods is important for empirical research to achieve these objectives. But then these objectives are not ends in themselves; methodologically well founded observation and validation are meaningful exercises when they help empirical research to achieve its final objective, namely, making some contribution to theory.

Facts are gathered and their relations are examined not randomly, but with a certain idea in mind. The idea is to understand and to explain certain issues or problems. A good empirical research is organized around such an idea which informs the research with meaning. The task of research is to elaborate the idea with methodological discipline. Attempt to offer explanations through either description of certain facts or examination of relationships between facts is to act theoretically. A theory is often described as a 'proposed explanation for a set of coordinated occurrences, or relationships'.

It is of course necessary to remember that theory in the social sciences is soft compared to the hard theories in Physics. Social science theories may well be simply a network of certain logically interrelated ideas. A particular empirical research may borrow such ideas from an existing theory and by checking them against facts may further refine and enrich such ideas or prove them useless and false. Alternatively, a research may begin with some in-articulated or vague ideas or guesses and by systematically examining them against facts come to certain theoretical observations. In either case, this task (of critiquing a theory or creating a theory) can only be performed well when it is guided by an appropriate method.

Method has an important role in this research process. Method guides research from beginning to end, that is, from the stage of fact gathering and selection to proposing explanations. Unless the appropriate method is adopted for the particular task at hand research will lose direction and purpose.

Yet, no good empirical research can be based on methodological reductionism, that is, on the idea that the most important thing in research is the use of a good method. Whatever be the status of the method used, it does not guaranty success of research which depends on the theoretical contribution it makes. Method cannot dictate research agenda; it is the latter which must dictate the choice of the former.

Endnotes

1. Bernard Berelson, "Introduction to the Behavioural Sciences," and Robert K. Merton, "The Mosaic of the Behavioural Sciences," in *The Behavioural Sciences Today*, ed. BernardBerelson, (New York: Harper, 1968), 1-11 and 247-72. The other papers in this volume written from specific disciplinary standpoints are also very useful.

2. Sydney Verba, "Some Dimensions in Comparative Research," *World Politics* 20 (October 1967): 111-27; Alasdair C. MacIntyre, "Can There be a Science of Comparative Politics," University of Chicago, 1971 (Mimeo); On paradigm in science,Thomas Kuhn, *The Structure of Scientific Revolutions*

(Chicago: University of Chicago Press,1962; enlarged ed., 1970).

3. Emile Durkheim, *The Rules of Sociological Method*, ed., George E.G. Catlin and trans. Sarah A. Solovay and John H. Muellar (New York : The Free Press, 1964), "Authors' Introduction," lix-lx.

4. Anthony Giddens, *New Rules of Sociological Method* (London : Hutchinson, 1976), 8.

5. Paul F. Lazarsfeld and Morris Rosenberg (eds.), *The Language of Social Research* (New York: The Free Press, 1955), 9.

6. Ibid, p.10.

7. C. Wright Mills, *The Sociological Imagination*. (London : Oxford University Press, 1959), 50, 72.

8. Lazarsfeld and Rosenberg, *The Language*, 12.

9. Reinhard Bendix, "Concepts and Generalizations in Comparative Sociological Studies," *American Sociological Review 28, no. 4* (August 1963): 532-39; reprinted in Reinhard ix, *Embattled Reason : Essay on Social Knowledge* (New York : Oxford University Press, 1970), 175-86.

10. Ibid.

11. Carl G. Hempel, *Aspects of Scientific Explanation* (New York : The Free Press, 1965), 142.

12. Kuhn, *The Structure*, 20.

13. Ibid., 21 (italics mine).

14. William J Goode and Paul K. Hatt, *Methods in Social Research* (New York: McGraw-Hill, 1952), 44-48 for several examples of concepts with multiple meanings.

15. Bendix, "Concepts and Generalizations."

16. Ibid.

17. P.W. Bridgman, *The Logic of Modern Physics* (New York: McMillan, 1927).

18. Hempel, *Scientific Explanation*, 141.

19. Ibid. 124.

20. Ibid. 144.

21. Ibid. p. 146.

22. Carl G. Hempel, *Fundamentals of Concept Formation in Empirical Science* (Chicago: University of Chicago Press, 1952), 47; Also, *Scientific Explanation*, 146 ff.

23. Kuhn, *The Structure*, 146 ff.

24. David Easton, *The   Political System* (New York : Alfred A, Knopf, 1953), p. 77; also, 66-78.

25. Kuhn, *The Structure*, 16 ff.

26. Morris Rosenberg, *The Logic of Survey Analysis* (New York: Basic Books, 1968), 233ff.

27. Karl R. Popper, *Conjectures and Refutations* (London:Routledge and Kegan Paul, 1969),39-41 (3rd. Ed.)

28. Carl G. Hempel, *Philosophy of Natural Science* (N.J.: Prentice-Hall, 1966), chap. 2.

29. A.B. Wolfe, "Functional Economics," in *The Trend in Economics* ed. R.G. Tugwell (New York: Alfred A. Knopf, 1924); cited in Hempel, Ibid. 11.

30. Ibid. 13.

31. Ibid.

32. Popper, *Conjectures*, 48.

33. The term "serendipity" is applied to cases of unforeseen or unanticipated discovery. Merton describes it as "the discovery, by chance or sagacity, of valid results which were not sought for." R.K. Merton, *Social Theory and Social Structure* (1949, rev. ed. (New York: The Free Press, 1949, rev. Edn., 1968), 98; also, Rosenberg, *The Logic*, 217-22.

34. Popper, *Conjectures*, 38n.

35. Kuhn, *The Structure*, 155-58 (Italics mine); sec. XII entire. Also Karl R. Popper, *Poverty of Historicism* (London: Routledge and Kegan Paul, 1959), chap. 29 ("The Unity of Method"), esp. n.2, 131-32. It is necessary to mention here that there are some important differences between the positions taken by Kuhn and Popper on the notions of "verification" and "refutation." Kuhn, *The Structure*, 146-47; also, Giddens, 135-38.

36. David Easton, *A Framework for Political Analysis* (N.J.: Prentice Hall, 1965), 94-95.

37. Rosenberg, *The Logic*, chap. 1.

38. Ibid.11 ff.

39. Edward R. Tufte, *Data Analysis for Politics and Policy* (N.J.: Prentice Hall, 1974), 5.

40. Rosenberg, *The Logic*, Chaps.2-4.

41. Russel Middleton, "Alienation, Race and Education," *American Sociological Review* 28 (December 1963): 973-77; cited in Rosenberg, *The Logic*, 85-86.

42. Sidney Verba and Norman H. Nie, *Participation in America: Political Democracy and Social Equality* (New York : Harper and Row, 1972), 156-57.

43. Ibid. 336 ff.

44. Rosenberg, *The Logic*, 68-69.

45. Verba and Nie, *Participation*, 304-8.

3

Research Designs: Experimental and Quasi-Experimental

The hope of discovering a method that will "leave little to the sharpness and strength of men's wits" is one which finds no support from a careful study of the procedure of the sciences.

Cohen and Nagel

Ever since Francis Bacon, the experiment has come to be regarded as the foundation of scientific method. The natural and the biological sciences, during the course of their development, have frequently resorted to and profited by the experimental method. Lately, the experiment has also been productively applied to such other academic disciplines as psychology, education and sociology. In fact, since John Stuart Mill's formulation of Bacon's principles in *A System of Logic*, social scientists in general have become aware of the possibility of using the experiment as a method of data collection and analysis. It is possible for political scientists as well to make use of this method, particularly in its quasi-experimental forms.

This chapter will discuss some of the more common experimental and quasi-experimental designs for research. But we would first briefly discuss John Stuart Mill's considerations on the experimental method, for the logic of the experiment was well laid by him.

J.S. MILL AND THE EXPERIMENTAL METHOD

Mill conceived of the experimental method in terms of four major categories: the method of agreement, the method of difference, the method of concomitant variations and the method of residues.[1] He considered all of these as methods of both discovery and proof.

Mill's Methods

THE METHOD OF AGREEMENT

This method proceeds to establish the cause of an event or the effect of a cause by comparing apparently different instances to ascertain the factor on which they agree. In Mill's words,

"If two or more instances of the phenomenon under investigation have only one circumstance in common, the circumstance in which alone all the instances agree is the cause (or effect) of the given phenomenon."

Take, for instance, the case of two different groups of farmers showing equal eagerness to use chemical fertilizers to improve crop production. Suppose that the two groups are coming from two different villages with different systems of land holdings and irrigation facilities, widely different communication facilities with town centres etc. Suppose, further, members of the two groups also differ in their mean age, educational level, exposure to mass media of communications, rates of political participation etc. The identical attitude of the two groups to the use of chemical fertilizers, then, cannot be said to be due to any of these factors, as they are present only in one instance, and not in the other. But if we also find that both the groups were exposed to a film extolling the use of chemical fertilizers, the answer may be given. As this is the only common factor (i.e., a factor on which the two groups agree) between the two otherwise different groups, this must invariably be connected with their common attitude to the use of chemical fertilizer. The method may be diagrammatically presented as:

Figure 3 .1: Method of agreement

Groups of Farmers	Attitude to the use of Chemical fertilizers	Exposure to Film	Village of Residence	Village – Characteristics	Background characteristics of the group	
A	U	V	X	Y	Z	N
B	U	V	X^1	Y^1	Z^1	

A and B, while differing on X, Y and Z variables, share the U phenomenon. U (being the 'phenomenon under investigation' or the dependent variable), then, must be explained in terms of variable V which is the only circumstance in which the instances A and B agree. Thus, the method, according to Mill, helps both to "discover" and to "prove" the cause of the effect.

THE METHOD OF DIFFERENCE

This method permits one to investigate the occurrence of an event or the presence of a phenomenon by comparing two instances which have everything in common excepting the event or the phenomenon under investigation. In Mill's words:

> If an instance in which the phenomenon under investigation occurs and an instance in which it does not occur have every circumstance

in common save one, that one occurring in the former, the circumstance in which alone the two instances differ is the effect or the cause, or an indispensable part of the cause, of the phenomenon.

Suppose that the attitude of a group of farmers to the use of chemical fertilizers is the phenomenon under investigation (as in the above example). We may take a number of farmers coming from the same village and with exactly similar background characteristics. Yet, we may find that while some of them show an eagerness to use such fertilizers, others remain indifferent. Upon investigation, it may be found that even though all the farmers have a common background, there is one thing on which the 'eager' ones differ from the "indifferent" ones; that is, while the former were exposed to a film extolling the use of chemical fertilizers and demonstrating their effectiveness in increasing the output, the latter were not so exposed. In this case, under Mill's method of *difference*, it is possible to conclude that it is the exposure or non-exposure to the film that is responsible for the difference in the attitude of the farmers to the use of chemical fertilizers. The method may be diagrammatically presented as:

Figure 3.2: Method of Difference

Groups of Farmers	Attitude to the use of Chemical fertilizers	Exposure to Film	Village of Residence	Village – Characteri-stics	Background characteristics of the group	
A	U	V	X	Y	Z	N
B	U^1	V^1	X	Y	Z	

This is to say, while A and B are exactly alike of in terms of X, Y and Z variables, they differ in terms of variable 'V' (exposure / non-exposure to the film). The difference in 'V', then, must have caused the difference in 'U' (that is, attitude to the use of chemical fertilizers). According to Mill, the method of difference, just as the method of agreement, helps one both to "discover" the casual factor and to "prove" the interrelationship between cause and effect.

THE METHOD OF CONCOMITANT VARIATIONS

The logic behind the methods of agreement and difference is simple. If in a particular situation (A) I find that both U and V are present and from that I hypothesize that U and V are causally related, the best way to demonstrate the validity of that hypothesis would be for me to find out another situation (B) which is nearly *totally different* from situation A and yet characterized by the presence of both U and V (agreement). Alternatively or additionally, I may also find out a situation (B) which is almost totally similar to situation A and yet where both U and V are absent so that I can make the statement that 'U' is absent because 'V' is also absent, although everything else remains the same (difference).

Thus, both the methods of agreement and difference assume that it is possible to isolate 'U' and 'V' and to examine whether they are related to each other irrespective of the context.

However, it is not always possible to isolate the relevant variables from the irrelevant ones, or to isolate the hypothesized causal variable completely. For example, as Cohen and Nagel point out, if one hypothesizes that the sun and the moon cause tides, it won't be possible for the investigator to have a situation from where the sun and moon are absent so that he can check and see if, in consequence, tides are also absent.

Nor would it always be possible to have a situation (B) which is *completely different* from situation A (except for 'U' and 'V', as is required under the 'method of agreement') for, in addition to the 'cause' and 'effect' factors, some other common factors may also be unavoidably present in both situations (such as the position of the fixed stars in the case of locating the cause of tides).

In such cases, that is, in situations where it is not possible to eliminate the cause completely and see whether the effect is also eliminated thereby, one may introduce or look for variations in the degree or magnitude of U (or V) and examine if there is corresponding variation in V in (or U). Mill's *method of concomitant variations* can deal with such a situation.

Since this method allows one to observe the degree of variation and covariation in the hypothesized 'cause' and 'effect' factors, it is possible to focus on the quantitative aspects of the relationship with the help of this method. This method, thus, involves the use of measurement and statistical techniques. Mill describes the method in the following manner:

"Whatever phenomenon varies in any manner whenever another phenomenon varies in some particular manner is either a cause or an effect of that phenomenon, or is connected with it through some fact of causation."

THE METHOD OF RESIDUES

Suppose we have a set of causes and a set of effects. If a part of the former can explain a part of the latter, we may infer that the rest of the causes would be connected with the rest of the effects. For instance, if we have U_1, U_2, U_3 antecedents and V_1, V_2, V_3 consequences, and if we have established that V_1 is the effect of U_1 and V_2 of U_2 then the residue of the consequences (i.e., V_3) may be known to be the effect of U_3. In Mill's words,

> "Subduct from any phenomenon such part as is known by previous inductions to be the effect of certain antecedents, and the residue of phenomenon is the effect of remaining antecedents."

Evaluation of Mill's method

The methods of experimental inquiry formulated by John Stuart Mill have been very well evaluated by Cohen and Nagel.[2] The present discussion will generally follow their lines of argument.

We have already mentioned that Mill regarded all the four methods as methods of both "discovery" and "proof." As far as the element of "discovery" is concerned, a little reflection would suggest the inadequacy of the methods. In fact, the relationship between the dependant and the independent variables cannot be "discovered" by simply applying any of these methods. For instance, the idea that there may be some relationship between exposure to a film extolling the use of chemical fertilizers and the attitude of exposed group of farmers to its use is founded either on common sense or our prior knowledge about the phenomena. Otherwise, we might consider a number of variables and yet miss the real cause. There is nothing in these methods themselves that will inevitably lead us to "discover" the cause or the effect.

Similarly, there is also the problem about the number and types of variables which are to be taken into consideration. If you look again at Figure 4.1 and 4.2 (under the methods of agreement and difference), we find that the line dividing A and B has an 'N' at its right hand end. The 'N' refers to the fact that there are an unlimited number of variables on which A and B may differ or agree. It is impossible to examine all these variables. Hence, the problem arises, on which variables 'A' and 'B' are to be compared? The answer appears to be simple: we are to examine only the *relevant* variables. But what are they, or how do we establish that a particular variable is relevant while the others are irrelevant? Obviously, this has to be done with reference to a pre-formulated hypothesis. But the hypothesis does not follow from any of these methods. That has to be generated by the researcher himself on the basis of his prior knowledge and information.

Just as the methods fail to discover the causal relationship, they may also be fallacious in proving the relationship. For instance, a person might have severe headache on three successive nights. Thinking back, he remembers that on the first day on his way back home from office he had an hour's ride in an overcrowded bus and after taking his evening tea at home he had a walk. On the second, he waited for his friend in a street corner which had a pile of nauseating garbage nearby, and then, not meeting his friend, he had taken a walk himself. On the third day, he went to a movie which appeared to be particularly long and boring, and to overcome his boredom he took a walk. An application of the method of agreement would lead him to conclude that walking (apparently being the sole common factor) had caused his headache on those three successive nights. But, evidently, that would be an entirely false conclusion.

The method of difference might be equally misleading. For instance, as Cohen and Nagel point out, if someone drinks coffee and spends sleepless night and if, on the next night he does not drink any coffee and have sound sleep, this need not lead one to conclude (by applying the method of difference) that drinking coffee is invariably connected with his sleeplessness. For, in fact, his sleep might be allergic not to coffee as such, but to some particular element that the coffee contained. If it is difficult to make a causal statement even in a particular case, it is just impossible to make such a general statement as drinking coffee leads to sleeplessness.

Similarly, the correlations observed between two phenomena through the method of concomitant variations may be perfect, but entirely fortuitous. Thus, one may observe a perfect correlation between increasing shoe size and the clarity of speech among children; but this does not surely mean that one of these causes the other. In fact, as statisticians well know, correlation merely indicates association; it does not indicate cause and effect relationship. Even very high correlation coefficients do not signify an invariable connection. Thus, simple coincidence or correlation does not 'prove' anything. The methods do not guarantee that the necessary conditions for a phenomenon will be found.

Furthermore, as Cohen and Nagel point out, the cause of a phenomenon must be invariably connected with the phenomenon. Since we cannot examine more than a limited number of cases, it is not possible to claim that even a demonstrated causal relationship will invariably hold in all unexamined cases as well.

Yet, the methods suggested by Mill are not without value. Their value lies in their negative function. They help the researcher to eliminate one or more of the hypothesized causes which do not meet the essential requirement of a cause. They also help one to formulate hypotheses more precisely by suggesting possible lines of inquiry for detecting causal relations.

It may be further pointed out that Mill's methods of difference and of concomitant variations provide the logical foundation to the comparative method as it is commonly practised in the field of comparative politics. For comparative analysis focuses on 'comparable' cases, that is, cases which share a large number of common characteristics (so that these may be treated as "constants") but differ "as far as those variables are concerned which one wants to relate to each other."[3]

THE EXPERIMENT

To understand the nature of the experiment as a method, it is necessary to remember Mill's method of difference. In performing an experiment, one is interested in comparing two almost exactly similar situations which differ between themselves only in the fact that one of them is exposed to the experiment while the other is not. The idea is that under such conditions any observed difference between the two situations in the post-experimental stage can very appropriately be attributed to the experiment. Diagrammatically, it can be presented thus,

Figure 3.3: Model of the experiment

A	X
A^1	-

That is, the experiment (X) occurs to A alone, and not to A^1 which is similar to A in every respect other than the exposure to X. In terms of the experiment, A is called *experimental* group or situation and A^1 is called *control* group or situation.

The experiment as a method, therefore, assumes that the experimenter, through selection and manipulation, will be capable of achieving a situation when the two groups--experimental and control, will approximate each other in every respect excepting the experiment. Such approximation is not easy to achieve and total identity (at the pre-experimental stage) is almost unachievable. Thus, it raises the issue of relevant and irrelevant variables. That is to say, if complete equivalence or identity is not achievable, one must know the relevant variables (in relation to the proposed experiment) on which some degree of approximation must be achieved. The specific techniques that an experimenter uses in achieving such approximation between the two groups are generally two: randomization and matching.

Achieving Equivalence Between Experimental and Control Groups: Randomization and Matching

Randomization is the most commonly used and also, most efficacious technique for achieving equivalence between the experimental and the control groups. It is a procedure for placing the available respondents in an experiment in the experimental and control groups in such a way that the two groups become similar. It does so by selecting at random from the total initial pool of respondents a sample for the experimental group and another sample for the control group. That is to say, each respondent in the initial pool will have an equal chance of being placed either in the experimental group or in the control group.

Each of the two groups may thus be regarded as representative of the initial pool. Randomization procedure, therefore, achieves a matching of the experimental and control groups on *all* variables-- suspected or unsuspected -- that might possibly affect and confound the results of the experiment. Of course, matching or equivalence between the groups thus established is not absolute. However one may further enhance reliability by increasing the sample size.

The procedure known as *matching* tries to establish equivalence somewhat more precisely than randomization between the two groups on a *limited* number of variables about whose confounding effect the experimenter is highly suspicious. Matching can be achieved either through frequency distribution control or through precision control.

The procedure known as *frequency distribution control* permits the experimenter to establish equivalence between the experimental and the control groups on those variables on which control appears to be relevant. Thus, if the experimenter thinks that 'caste' variable should be controlled, she will have an equal number of respondents from the same caste in each group. Similarly, if she thinks that 'gender' variable should also be controlled, she will have an equal distribution of male and female respondents in each group. Under frequency distribution control the two groups may be equated on a number of variables, but the matching will be done separately for each variable.

The procedure which permits matching of several variables at the same time is known as *precision control*. Under this procedure the respondents will be paired on the basis of the number of variables deserving control and then, one of each pair will be assigned to the experimental group and the other to the control group.

Thus, if the experimenter wants to control 'caste' and 'gender' variables, she can do that *at the same time* under this procedure. The experimenter will have to find two males of the same caste, and having found them, she will have to place one of them to the experimental group and the other to the control group. Then, she will have to find two females of the same caste, and similarly place them in the two groups. Thus, precision control will not merely match the two groups in terms of the distribution of marginal frequencies on different variables (as in frequency distribution control), but also in terms of the distribution of their cell frequencies on each variable (Table 4.1).

Table 3.1: Precision control and frequency distribution control

		Experimental Group N= 100		Control Group N = 100	
		Male	Female	Male	Female
PRECISION CONTROL	Brahmin	20	20	20	20
	Non-Brahmin	30	30	30	30
FREQUENCY DISTRIBUTION CONTROL	Brahmin	10	30	30	10
	Non-Brahmin	40	20	20	40

Precision control is thus a better procedure than frequency distribution control, for it achieves more exact equivalence between the two groups. But both of these matching procedures have two serious drawbacks when compared with the randomization procedure. In both frequency distribution control and precision control the experimental and the control groups can be equated only on a limited number of variables whose confounding effects the experimenter can guess. But there may be other unsuspected factors equally contaminating; they will continue to bias the results of the experiment. On the other hand, randomization, however imprecise, will establish equivalence between the two groups on all variables through random selection (with an estimated degree of error).

Secondly, while randomization procedure will allow the experimenter to use all the respondents available for experiment, under frequency distribution control, and even more so under precision control, several cases will be lost in the process of matching and pairing. All those who cannot be properly matched or paired will have to be left out. The number of lost cases will increase as more and more variables are controlled. Hence, it may be difficult to apply these matching procedures particularly if one's initial sample is small.

The experiment is used as method of 'proof' if not so much as a method of 'discovery'. For, the researcher conducting an experiment is essentially interested in establishing the 'true effects' of the experiment. Thus, the experimenter will generally have two observations, one before the experiment ('Before test' or pre-test) and the other after experiment ('After test' for post-test), and she will expect herself to be in a position to say that the difference between the two observations is *due to* the experiment.

Such applications of the experimental method have yielded highly desirable results in the natural as well as biological sciences. But the success of the method in these sciences is primarily due to the fact that a researcher is capable of organizing the experiment under highly controlled conditions. In the social sciences, however, such control is just unachievable, regardless of the degree of perfection that one may reach either in selecting one's samples or in designing one's research. Thus, experiments, when they are conducted in the social sciences and the historical disciplines, are highly susceptible to several contaminating factors. We say 'contaminating', because it is in the nature of these factors that they tend to get mixed up with the 'true' effects of the experiment, and thereby, confound them. Also, some of these contaminating factors make it difficult for the scientist to generalize the results of the experiment beyond the specific experimental group. Randomization and matching procedures help the experimenter to exercise some control over a number of such contaminating factors, especially those that are associated with the process of selection of cases. However, we will very briefly refer to these factors now so that when we discuss the different experimental designs below we can evaluate them with reference to their independence from such contaminations.

Problem of Validity

If the results of an experiment are contaminated by unknown or uncontrolled factors, one's claims about those results as being *due exclusively* to the experiment cannot be regarded as valid. Hence, the intervention of these factors essentially raises the issue of validity. Donald Campbell has discussed this problem with emphasis.[4] Campbell draws a distinction between *internal* and *external* validity. The former refers to "the basic minimum without which any experiment is uninterpretable." Thus, with reference to internal validity, one asks questions such as: has the experimental treatment made any difference, or in other words, is the difference (if any) due to the experiment alone? *External validity*, on the other hand, raises the issue of generalizability. In Campbell's words, "To what populations, settings, treatment variables, and measurement variables can this effect be generalized?" While it is impossible to satisfy completely the demands of internal and external validity, the experimental research designs we select for application ought to be as strong with reference to both types of validity as possible.

Below we will define seven different classes of extraneous variables which, unless controlled for, might contaminate the experiment and confound its effects.[5] These will be further discussed and illustrated when we examine specific experimental designs.

a. *General march of external events* (other than the experiment): This refers to all those specific events (external to the members of the experimental and control groups but potentially affecting them) that may occur between the 'Before' and 'After' measurements (or pre-tests and post-tests) in addition to the experiment itself. Thus, unless an experimental design controls for such external events, it would not be possible for the researcher to say that the difference between the 'Before' and 'After' measurements is due to the experiment alone, and not to such other uncontrolled events against which the respondents were not 'sealed'.

b. *Internal development processes:* These refer to those physical and mental processes that may occur within the respondents as a function of the passage of time per se. For instance, during the course of the experiments the respondents may get more tired, or hungrier etc., and these developments within them may affect their responses to the experiment. Such internal developments (or processes of *maturation,* as Campbell and Stanley label them) happen *within* the respondents rather than in the world outside.

c. *Effects of the 'Before' test (or pre-test):*This refers to the effects that the 'Before' test may have on the scores of subsequent tests.

d. *Effect of measuring instruments:* This implies that changes in the measuring instruments--human or mechanical, may affect the measurement during the course of the experiment.

e. *Statistical Regression:*This refers to the fallacy of selecting groups or cases on the basis of their extreme scores. For it is a natural tendency that extreme scores gradually move toward their statistical mean. Unless one is careful, such statistical regression towards the mean may be taken as the effect of the experiment.

f. *Biased selection procedure:* If the selection procedure is biased, it might result in differential selection of the respondents for the experimental and control groups. In that case, the groups cannot be truly comparable.

g. *Respondent dropouts:* This refers to the differential loss of respondents due to refusals, change of residence, or death to the experimental and control groups. Such unsystematic loss of respondents also makes the groups uneven and potentially non-comparable.

All these seven factors are connected with the problem of establishing the effect of the experiment on the experimental group in the experimental situation. That is, unless these factors are controlled or otherwise taken care of, any change detected in the experimental group after the experiment cannot be ascribed to the experiment alone and not to any of these factors. While controlling these factors is absolutely essential in an experiment, the experimenter is equally interested in another aspect of the experiment as well. That concerns the question of generalizability.

Usually, one conducts an experiment on an experimental group not solely because one is vitally interested in the group per se, but because one is interested in knowing the effects of the experiment so that later on she can apply the experiment to the unexperimented universe and expect that the known effects would follow. Thus, one experimentally applies a newly discovered medicine to a selected small sample population because once the effects of the medicine are demonstrated convincingly in the experiment; she can go beyond the experimental situation and prescribe the medicine for the general population belonging to the unexperimented universe. Under certain situations, however, the results of the experiment become unique to the experimental group alone and hence, they cannot be generalized. The presence of such situations or factors in an experiment constitutes problems for generalizability or 'external validity'. Two most significant factors affecting generalizability are the following:

a. *Pretest-experiment interaction*: This refers to the fact that the pretest, by making the respondents conscious of the experiment, might enhance or reduce, as the case may be, the effects of experiment. This would make the results of the experiment unique to the pretested population alone, and inapplicable to the unpretested universe.

b. *Reaction of the experimental setting*: If the experimental setting or situation is such that it produces special reactions among the respondents and thereby enhances or reduces the effect of the experiment on them, the effect of such an experiment cannot be generalized to unexperimented populations.

EXPERIMENTAL DESIGNS

Classical Experimental Design

The purpose of the foregoing discussion was to make one alert about the need for a research design which would avoid as many of the threats to validity as possible. While the logic of the experiment can be applied through a number of designs, the most widely accepted design is the classical experimental design or the 'Pretest - Posttest design with one control group'. This design takes the following form:

Figure 3.4 : The Classical Design

Groups	Before Test/ pretest	Experiment	After test/Post Test	Before After Difference
Experimental Group	O_1	x	O_2	$d = O_2 - O_1$
Control Group	O_3		O_4	$d' = O_4 - O_3$

(0 is observation and X is the experiment in this and the following figures.)

Under this design, the experimental and the control groups must be recruited in the same manner, that is, either through randomization or through matching. Further, both groups must be at subjected to "Before" test (O_1 and 03) as well as to 'After' test (O_2 and O_4). Thus, the only difference between the two groups will be with regard to the experimental stimulus: while the first one will be exposed to the experiment (X), the second one will not be so exposed (Table 4.2).

Therefore, assuming that the two groups-- experimental and control, are broadly similar, d (in Figure 4.4) marks the effect of the experiment while d' functions as a control on regarding d as the true effect of the experiment. The strength of this design lies in the fact that it can successfully withstand the challenge of most of the rival hypotheses flowing from the various problems of validity discussed above. The following discussion illustrates the point.

Table 3.2: Experimental and Control Groups in the Classical Design

Experimental Group	Control Group
Selection of respondents through randomization / matching.	Selection of respondents through randomization / matching.
'Before' test	'Before' test
Exposure to experimental stimulus	---
'After' test	'After' test

PROBLEMS OF INTERNAL VALIDITY IN CLASSICAL EXPERIMENTAL DESIGN

While discussing the problems of internal validity above we have seen that the *general march of external events* may provide the first major rival hypothesis challenging the effect of the experiment. Suppose that we are interested in examining the effect of a film on the attitude of a group of farmers to the use of chemical fertilizers. After applying the pre-test to both the experimental group and the control group in order to assess their initial attitude, we expose only the experimental group to the film demonstrating the utility of the use of chemical fertilizers. Having exposed the experimental group to the experiment, we would expect that in the post-test, to be administered to both the groups, the experimental group's attitude to the use of chemical fertilizers would markedly differ from the control group's attitude and that the difference could be attributed to the experiment. But, suppose, before we took our post-test some reports on the good effects of the use of chemical fertilizers on the crops come out in the newspapers. Since, normally the members of the experimental group will not be sealed off from such things as newspaper reading, in the post-test it will be difficult for us to separate the effect of the experiment from the effects of such outside events as newspaper reports.

However, the classical experimental design presented above can take care of this problem. For, due to the presence of a control group, it is possible in this design to compare not merely O_2 with 0_1, but also 0_2 with 0_4. Since we can assume that the control group would be equally exposed to such newspaper reports (or other external events), the difference, if any, between d and d' could be taken as essentially due to the experiment.

The effect of *internal development processes* as well as the *effect of pre-test* would be similarly controlled in this design. For both the processes of internal development and the effect of the pre-test should equally affect the experimental and the control groups. They could be regarded as common factors present in both d and d', and therefore the difference, if any, between d and d' cannot be ascribed to such common factors.

The effect of *measuring instruments* can be controlled by relying on fixed instrument for both groups. For instance, one may use a printed questionnaire. But the use of interviewers may complicate the problem. If the number of interviewers is few, they will not be randomly assignable to either group. In that case each interviewer should be used for both experimental and control groups. This, or random assignment of interviewers--if their number permits such a strategy, would help reduce the effect of measuring instruments on the outcome of the experiment.

The effect of *statistical regression* will similarly be controlled as far as the mean difference between the pre-test and the post-test scores are concerned. For even if the pre-test scores had shown extremity, in so far as both the experimental and the control groups are assigned randomly from this 'extreme' sample, the control group would regress as much as the experimental group.

Similarly, the possibility of *biased selection procedure* affecting the outcome of the experiment need not jeopardize the experiment to the extent that both groups are randomly selected. Establishing group equivalence through randomization is the best possible statistical procedure. In this design, sometimes the pre-test scores of the experimental and the control groups may differ significantly. To bring down the difference in the mean pre-test scores of the groups, some form of matching may be applied as an adjunct to randomization rather than as a replacement for it. For matching by itself cannot guarantee initial equivalence between the two groups.[6]

There is also a good probability of controlling the effects of *respondent dropouts* in this design. The possibility of dropout becomes stronger if the time interval between the pre-test and the post-test is very long. In any case, if the dropout rate (i.e., the number of lost cases) affects both the experimental and the control groups equally and if the mean pre-test scores of the two groups remain the same even after such dropouts, the experiment can claim internal validity on this point.

PROBLEMS OF EXTERNAL VALIDITY IN CLASSICAL EXPERIMENTAL DESIGN

Pre-test-Experiment interaction: As far as the threats to internal validity are concerned, the classical design is a very strong design for, as we have seen just now, it can withstand most of these threats well. But the design shows some weaknesses with reference to the threats to external validity. This makes it difficult to generalize the findings of an experiment based on this design.

The possibility of an interaction between the pre-test and the experiment remains present as a threat to external validity in the classical design. It implies that since the experimental group is being pretested before being exposed to the experiment, the pre-test may particularly sensitize the group with regard to the experiment so that the experiment would be especially effective for the pretested group but not so effective or not effective at all for the un-pretested population. In other words, the pre-test and experiment might interact to produce an effect which neither the pre-test nor the experiment could alone produce.

This problem was very clearly detected in the study of an information campaign about the United Nations in the American city of Cincinnati conducted by the National Opinion Research Centre of the University of Chicago.[7] The idea behind this study was to see the degree of impact on the city's population of an intensive information campaign for the UN. For this purpose, two equivalent samples, of one thousand people each, were drawn from the city's population. One of these samples was pretested while the other one was left un-pretested. Following the pre-test an intensive publicity campaign through all the mass media of communication was launched in the city for two months. At the end of the campaign, the un-pretested group of one thousand people was interviewed. When the results of this interview (i.e., the post-test for the *un-pretested* group) were compared with the results of the first interview (i.e., the pre-test for the *pretested* group), no perceptible difference in attitude could be found. That is to say, in the post-test, the un-pretested group (which was as much exposed to the information campaign as the pretested group) did not show any impact of the campaign.

However, as the pretested group was also re-interviewed at the end of the campaign, the impact of the campaign could be checked for them as well. In re-interview the pretested group showed definite attitude change as well as a high degree of awareness of the campaign on their part. This clearly meant that the pretested group could *feel* the campaign simply because they were already sensitized about the issue involved in the campaign (i.e., the experiment) by the pre-test itself.

This interaction effect would be the greater the more the pre-test marks a break with normal activity. If the pre-test takes the shape of usual events, its sensitizing effect would be minimal. For instance, if in educational research the usual class-room examinations are used as pre-test and pos-test, the undesirable effects of interaction might be avoided.

Effects of reaction of the experimental setting: This refers to the effects of the experimental conditions on the results of the experiment. If the experimental procedure creates certain artificial conditions in such a manner that the participants in the experiment become too much aware of the fact of the experiment, it might generate a sort of 'I-am-a-guineapig' feeling among them. The results of the experiment in such a case might be inapplicable to the general un-experimented population. That is to say, the artificiality of the experimental conditions might react on the respondents in the experiment. The more an experiment has to depend on artificial conditions, the greater would be its impact on the experimental group.

This is particularly a problem in psychological and educational experiments (although, in the latter there are ways of avoiding it as Campbell and Stanley Show).[8] But, as the social sciences depend on quasi-experiments (to be discussed later in this chapter), this need not become a problem, for quasi-experiments are conducted in natural settings. On the other hand, all intrusive measures, whether of the experimental or of the survey type, will somehow or other be reactive.

Pre-Experimental Designs

The above discussion on the classical experimental design shows that such a design is very useful for it can stand against most of the possible alternative or rival hypotheses. But it is also apparent that the demands of such a design are very high and hence, there may be difficulties in applying this design to social science problems where often, due to the lack of laboratory conditions, such demands cannot be met. Consequently, the social scientist may have to settle for less satisfying designs. We propose to discuss some of these less perfect but more practicable designs below. But one thing needs to be mentioned here. While resorting to such "pre-experimental" (i.e., less than proper experimental designs) designs sometimes may be very practical and realistic, a thorough knowledge about the proper or classical experimental design is essential for, as Stouffer says, "we can at least keep the experimental model in front of our eyes and behave cautiously when we fill in missing cells with dotted lines."[9]

The classical experimental design, as we have already seen, permits a two way comparison ($O_2 > O_1$, $O_2 > O_4$) for establishing the validity of the experiment. But a lot of social science research is done through a design which does not permit any comparison at all. Such a design takes the following form:

Figure 3.5(a): Single Observation Design

$$X \qquad 0$$

In this case, the validity of our hypothesis is based on one single observation. In the context of the classical design it (Single Observation Design) would look like the following:

Figure 3.5(b)

O_1	O_2
O_3	O_4

That is, while we only observe O_2, we assume the condition of O_1 and O_4 without really investigating them. The total absence of control and no scope for comparison make this design significantly invalid. Since the crucial cells are missing from this design, however thorough our study and however careful our observation of O_2, any reference from this single observation regarding the effects of the experiment will be completely without scientific foundation. This, of course, is the weakest 'experimental' model.

A somewhat better design maybe the following one (Pre-test-Post-test Design without Control Group):

Figure 3.6: Pre-Test-Post-Test Design

$$O_1 \qquad\qquad X \qquad\qquad O_2$$

While this differs from the classical design, it permits at least one formal comparison ($O_2 > O_1$) between X and non-X. This is a widely used design where conditions for the true experiment (classical design) cannot be secured. Since under laboratory conditions experimental isolation can be attained, this design (Figure 4.6) has been rather successfully applied to physical and biological research. In the social sciences, however, due to the lack of laboratory isolation, the possibility of contamination of the experiment by other relevant variables remains present. Without the presence of a control group, it is not possible to validly claim that the $0_2 \sim 0_1$ differences are solely due to X rather than to some other relevant external event. In Collier's classroom experiment during World War II which is often referred to in this connection, while an experimental group of students was exposed to Nazi propaganda material, France fell to the Nazis. The changes in the attitude of the students (towards the Nazis) observed in the post-test appeared more likely to be the result of this external event (fall of France) than of the propaganda material itself.[10]

Similarly, it is quite conceivable that if in the course of an experimental testing of the attitude of a group of Indians towards Pakistan a war breaks out between the two countries, the outbreak of the war would have serious confounding effects on the experiment.

In a similar manner, other plausible rival hypotheses coming from sources like the process of internal development, effects of pre-test and measuring instruments, statistical regression, or reaction of experimental setting cannot adequately be checked in this design, and consequently, all or some of these may confound the effects of the experiment.

Finally, we may discuss yet another "pre-experimental" design which is also very commonly used in the social sciences. This may be called the 'Post-test Only with One Control Group Design'. In this design a group of respondents which has been exposed to the 'experiment' is compared with another group which has not been so exposed to it, and on the basis of such comparison the effect of the experiment is deduced. This design will have the following form :

Figure 3.7(a): Post-test only with one control group design

$$X \qquad\qquad\qquad\qquad 0_1$$

$$0_2$$

In this design we know little about the 'before' stages of either group. Comparing a group of people which has seen a particular TV programme with another group which has not seen it, or comparing a group of students which has taken a particular course of instruction with another group which has not taken it, or comparing two different societies one of which has experienced colonial rule and the other has not, will take the above form. Comparisons such as these are often very tempting, and sometimes, in the absence of any better and more feasible alternative, one may have to use such comparisons. Yet, such comparisons may very well be totally false, for in the absence of a formal investigation of the 'before' stages of the groups concerned, we have no way of establishing that the groups really had no other substantial difference save the experiment. In other words, there is no formal way of certifying that the groups would have been equivalent in the 'after' stage had there been no experiment. That is to say, such a design suffers from *biased selection* procedure. It may be that the two groups would have differed any way, even without the occurrence of the experiment. Only rough estimates can be made about the prior equivalence of the two groups.

An interesting example of the application of this design and its difficulties has been provided by Samuel Stouffer.[11] In *American Soldier*, Stouffer and his collaborators were interested in investigating the result of the innovation regarding putting 'Negro' soldiers in some white infantry companies so that they could fight beside white soldiers during World War II. As part of their inquiry, the investigators were interested to explore the reaction of the white soldiers to the idea of racially integrated companies. Hence, they asked the white soldiers of those companies in which the innovation had already been introduced whether they liked the innovation.

To have a comparative base, they also asked another group of white soldiers in companies *without* 'Negro' platoons about their attitude towards such an innovation. Interestingly, only 7% of the white soldiers in the companies with 'Negro' platoons (the experimental group) said they disliked the idea while 62% of the white soldiers in companies without 'Negro' platoons (control group) disliked the idea. It looked like the following :

Figure 3.7(b):

	PERCENT OPPOSING THE INNOVATION
	X
Experimental Group	7
Control Group	62

It thus appeared that those who were already in the racially integrated companies liked the idea of such integration while those who had only heard about the innovation, overwhelmingly rejected it. The question that obviously arose before the investigators was: why was this the case? Did the experimental group represent a unique (non-generalizable) sample? Or, was the difference between the experimental and the control groups solely due to the fact that while the former was in fact exposed to contact with 'Negroes' (X), the latter was not so exposed, and that such exposure itself reduced social hostility? To answer this question, one had to look at 'before' stages of the two groups; that is to say, one had to know whether the experimental group was as much opposed to the innovation as the control group *before* they were exposed to it. But such an inquiry into the 'before' stages was no longer possible. While some sort of initial equivalence between the two groups on the racial issue could be assumed as both groups had about the same proportion of southern Americans, it was not adequate as proof, for a host of other relevant variables might have been hidden. As second best, the investigators inquired if the members of the experimental group could recall what they felt about the innovation when it was first proposed (i.e., before it was actually implemented). They found that 67% of them said they were initially opposed to the idea.

Now the situation became like the following:

Figure 3.7 (c):

	PERCENT OPPOSING THE INNOVATION	
	X	
Experimental Group	67	7
Control Group		62

By thus reconstructing the upper left hand cell(0_1), the investigators could somehow establish the initial equivalence of the two groups (0_1, 0_4) more formally. This permitted them to conclude at least tentatively that under the conditions present, probably the innovation itself led to an attitude change among the white soldiers.

The above example very interestingly shows the fundamental weakness of this design. Stouffer and his collaborators solved their problem not strictly through this design (Figure 4.7a), but by transforming the design (Figure 4.7c). The main point about the 'Post-test Only with One Control

Group Design' is that it cannot solve the problem of selection as a source of internal validity at all. For unless we have some way of establishing the initial equivalence of the experimental and control groups (which this design does not permit), comparison at the post-test stage may be highly fallacious.

However, this design can be vastly improved and transformed into a true experimental design if the experimental and control groups are selected through proper randomization, as randomization is considered to be an all-purpose solution to the problem of equivalence. This design should then look like:

Figure 3.7 (d):

$$R \quad X \quad 0_1$$
$$R \qquad 0_2 \quad \text{(R=Randamization)}$$

This 'Randomised Post-test Only with One Control Group Design' may even be preferred to the classical experimental design in situations where the pre-test cannot be administered or where the pre-test is likely to be invariably reactive.[12] The major advantage of this design over the classical experiment is its simplicity.

Solomon's Four Group Design

Before we finish the discussion on experimental designs, reference should be made to 'Solomon's Four-Group Design' which is more sophisticated than even the classical experimental design and which controls the threats to external validity more specifically. The design looks like the following:

Figure 3.8: Solomon's Design

$$0_1 \quad X \quad 0_2$$
$$0_3 \qquad 0_4$$
$$\qquad X \quad 0_5$$
$$\qquad 0_6$$

In fact, this design represents a coupling of the classical experimental design (0_1 through 0_4) and the 'Post-test Only with One Control Group Design' (0_5 and 0_6). By doing so, this design permits determination of both the main effects of testing ($0_4 \sim 0_6$) and of interaction of testing and experiment ($0_2 \sim 0_5$). In addition, this design also permits repeated examination of the effect of the experiment in four different ways: $0_2 > 0_1$, $0_2 > 0_4$, $0_5 > 0_6$, $0_5 > 0_3$.

Thus, the net gain in this design over the classical design is an increase in generalizablity. The design assumes random sampling.

The weakness of the design lies in fact that the pre-test scores of the unpretested groups (0_5 and 0_6) will have to be assumed from the mean value of the pre-test of the first two groups. Besides, unless the initial sample is large, it may not be possible to have four sizeable randomized groups for experiment and control.

QUASI-EXPERIMENTAL DESIGNS

In a true experiment the researcher is able to determine the timing and the nature of the experimental stimulus as well as to assign respondents randomly to experimental and control groups. In natural social settings, however, there are situations which are worthy of rigorous inquiry but where such controls are lacking. Events may happen or public policies may be adopted whose necessary consequences the social scientist must verify. For instance, a community may decide to terminate capital punishment, and the advocates of such punishment predict an increase in the rates of murder; or television is introduced in a community and some predict that it would adversely affect the reading habits of the public; or a school appoints a disciplinarian headmaster and cases of indiscipline tend to increase etc. In such instances as these the researcher has no control either on the subjects of the "experiment" or on its nature and timing. Yet, for the social scientist, these may be really significant issues, issues whose exact consequences he must investigate.

Quasi-experimental designs assume significance in the context of such natural social settings.For these designs, as Campbell and Ross suggest, provide a mode of analysis that permits one "to deal with a common class of situations in which research must proceed without the benefit of experimental control."[13]

The logic of the experiment has three important components: first, it must establish the fact that variation has taken place in the independent variable 'X' (or just that the presence of 'X' has meant variation in an otherwise non-X situation); second, that covariation has been observed in the dependent variable 'Y'; and third, that all possible rival explanations to the hypothesized one(s) are ruled out. A proper experiment is founded on a thorough application of all these components of the logic of the experiment.

It is true that the ability to randomize and control is almost indispensable for the fulfilment of these three conditions. But it is also true that these conditions may be fulfilled, however approximately and tentatively, even in the absence of randomization and control--provided we assume that no experiment is absolutely perfect and also, that even a successful experiment does not 'prove' a theory; it merely saves theory from being rejected. Quasi-experimental designs, which may be applied to situations where true experimental conditions are absent, are accepted solely on the ground that better designs are not feasible.[14]While this constitutes a grave weakness of these designs, it also rather ironically becomes one of its strong points. Being less rigorous, these designs can be more freely practised; they can be applied to areas which are unsuited to proper experimentation. In political science, public policy analysis is an area where the application of the method of quasi-experimentation might prove to be highly productive. The most important thing, while applying any quasi-experimental design, is to be thoroughly aware of the specific variables which a particular design fails to control.

Several quasi-experimental designs can be constructed.[15] Here, however, we will discuss only two of these designs because of their simplicity and significance.

Interrupted Time-Series Design

Control groups are normally regarded as important and essential in an experiment. But sometimes they are somewhat over-emphasized so that their presence becomes synonymous with an experiment. This, then, would mean that we should not try to apply the experimental logic at all in the absence of a control group. Quasi-experimental designs, however, permit the application of the logic of the experiment even without a control group. Such designs, as the one under discussion show, can also be quite strong in the face of most of the sources of invalidity.

The 'Interrupted Time Series Design' is essentially an extension of the pre-experimental design called 'Pre-test-Post-test Design without Control Group' which we have discussed above. But the word 'extension' is important, for by extending the number of observations overtime, this design avoids, as we will see, some of the weaknesses of the pre-experimental design.

This design[16] would look like the following:

$$0_1, 0_2, 0_3, 0_4, 0_5, X\ 0_6, 0_7, 0_8, 0_9, 0_{10}$$

Figure 3.9 (a): Interrupted time-series design

Under this design the researcher observes a phenomenon at different points in time prior to the experiment (0_1 to 0_5) and then he introduces some change in it (the experiment X) and follows with several further observations (0_6 to 0_{10}) to ascertain if the change thus introduced has any effect on the phenomenon concerned. Such a design has wide applications in different fields of knowledge. For instance, one may apply it to test the impact of a nitric acid bath on the weight of iron bars, or the impact of Vitamin C intakes on man's susceptibility to cold, or the impact of a stricter law prohibiting drunken driving on road accidents.

The advantages of this design over the 'Pre-test- Post-test Design without Control Group' become very clear if we look at figure 3.9 (b).

Figure 3.9(b):

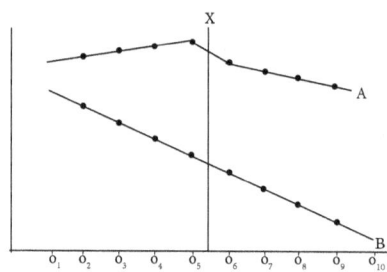

In figure 3.9(b) there are two cases (A and B) in which an exogenous event *(X)* has intervened and produced some change. Under the 'Pre-test-Post-test Design without Control Group' we would have only two observations (0_5 and 0_6). When we look at 0_5~0_6 difference, we find that the experiment has equally strongly affected both cases, for the degree of change (identified by the slope of the line between 0_5 and 0_6) is exactly identical for both A and B.

Under the present design, however, we would look not merely at 0_5 and 0_6, but all the observations ranging from 0_1 to 0_{10}. When we do that we find that while in the case of A the experiment has definitely and dramatically *changed* the pattern of events, in the case of B nothing of the sort has happened. In the latter case, the experiment has not affected the previous pattern at all. Thus, the nature and impact of the experiment (*X*) is much more revealed under the 'Interrupted Time-Series Design'.

This design by permitting a number of observations extended over time makes it possible, even in the absence of a control group, to demonstrate whether the experiment has produced any definite change in the dependent variable. Once it is seen that a definite change has taken place in the dependent variable following the experiment (i.e., fulfilment of the first two conditions of the experimental logic mentioned above), it would be necessary to show that the change is due to the experiment alone and not to something else. That is, is one must then examine the validity of rival hypotheses (i.e., the third condition of the experimental logic).

The most important threat to the validity of inference about the effect of the experiment in this design lies in external events. That is, it may be claimed that the change between 0_5 and 0_6 is not due to the experiment, but to some other thing that had happened more or less simultaneously with the experiment. Since, as we have already pointed out, in the social sciences it is not possible to isolate the subject of experiment from all known and unknown contaminating influences, external events will always remain a threat to validity. Along with and as part of this factor will also be factors such as the effects of varying weather conditions or seasonal changes, particularly because a time-series experiment will expectedly extend over long time periods. Take, for instance, the case of introduction of an incentive scheme for enhancing worker output in a factory. If such a scheme is introduced in the winter months and if it enhances worker output, it may plausibly be argued that the enhancement is not so much due to the scheme as to better weather conditions. If it is done in the summer and if it does not enhance the output, it may similarly be argued that the fault lies with the season rather than with the scheme. Extending the period of observation backward to cover the same season of the previous year when there was no experiment might be helpful but not decisive as seasons vary in their intensity from year to year.

The other threats to internal validity, namely, internal development processes, effects of pre-test or of measuring instruments, regression, biased selection procedure or respondent dropouts will not pose much of a threat in this design. For, we could assume if any of these factors was operative it should operate between *any two* observations (e.g., between 0_1 and 0_2 or 0_2 and 0_3 or 0_6 and 0_7 etc.). There is no inherent reason why any of these factors should operate only between two specific observations, namely, the one immediately preceding and the one immediately following the experiment (i.e., 0_5 and 0_6).

However, one potentially contaminating factor may still remain and may lead to a false confirmation of the hypothesis regarding the effect of the experiment: that is, the experimenter's own *expectation* about the result of the experiment. In cases where the experiment is a contrived one conducted by the human beings through survey methods this factor may create contaminating influence in the sense that the experimenter's subjective involvement with the experiment may lead her to find only the expected effects and to ignore the unexpected or undesired ones. But this factor, which may be classed under the 'effect of measuring instruments', will not create any problem if the data in use are aggregate data which are not collected to suit the purposes of a specific research.

Similarly, while the design cannot absolutely control threats to external validity coming from interaction of testing and experiment, reaction of experimental setting need not cause concern if one is dealing with aggregate data or if the design is applied to the area of public policy study. But in case of survey data or in case of a sample consisting of a select group of individuals these may create problems.

One important question may relate to the range of the time period over which the observation would spread. The exact period of time over which one should spread one's observations would obviously depend on the problem under study. However, the choice should be both logically defensible as well as sensible. One thing is important in this connection. It is absolutely essential that a relationship in terms of time between the experiment on the one hand, and the occurrence of its expected effects on the other must be clearly specified. That is to say, one must specify *beforehand* exactly *when* one is to expect the change to be produced by the experiment. Otherwise, any change taking place at any time after the experiment may be claimed to be the effect of the experiment.

The simplicity of the 'Interrupted Time-Series Design' diagrammed above need not lead one to think that in this design one can examine only a single experiment over time. In fact, this design can be used in studying the effects of two or more experiments (i.e., independent variables) on different data sets over different time periods. This is precisely what Caporaso and Pelowski have done in their methodologically informed paper on European integration.[17] The authors have developed nine dependent variables indicating the degree of integration among West European states and have examined the effects of three independent variables (or interrupting events, namely, the formation of the EEC in 1958, the adoption of the first agricultural 'package' decision in early 1962 and the Common Market agricultural crisis which began in June 1965 and ended in January 1966) on the dependent variables over three overlapping time periods. In fact, the largest number of variables and observations allowed them to make sophisticated statistical analysis as well as to make some inferences regarding the systemic nature of West European integration.

Multiple Time Series Design

The above discussion on the 'Interrupted Time Series Design' demonstrates that in quasi-experiments it is possible to apply the logic of the experiment even in the absence of a control group. For, in a time-series, the prior and the posterior observations themselves exercise some amount of control over possible inferences about the effects of the experiment.

Yet, in studies using time-series data and quasi-experimental models greater precision as well as confidence can be attained if a control group is added to the experimental group. Diagrammatically, the design then would be like the following:

Figure 3.10: Multiple time-series design

Experimental group	A	O_1	O_2	O_3	O_4	O_5	X	O_6	O_7	O_8	O_9	O_{10}
Control group	B	O_1	O_2	O_3	O_4	O_5		O_6	O_7	O_8	O_9	O_{10}

That is, in addition to the series of observations (*A*) with the interrupting event (or the experiment X), we have another comparable series of observations (*B*) *without* the interrupting event. Thus the effect of the experiment can be demonstrated not merely by holding the post-experimental observations against the observations prior to the experiment in series *A* (A - O_6, O_7, O_8, O_9, O_{10} > A - O_1, O_2, O_3, O_4, O_5), but it can also be demonstrated against the observations in series *B* (A- O_1, O_2,....O_{10} > B- O_1, O_2,.... O_{10}). This 'Multiple Time Series Design' does not achieve more than in the 'Interrupted Time-Series Design' in terms of external validity or generalizability. But, in terms of internal validity, it provides a further check because of the presence of the control group. Campbell and Stanley consider it as "perhaps the best of the more feasible (quasi-experimental) designs." Indeed, the design need not restrict itself to the comparison of nearly two groups. It can use any number of experimental and control groups depending on their availability and comparability.

An excellent example of both the interrupted and multiple time series designs has been provided by Campbell himself in collaboration with H. Laurence Ross.[18] In their paper on "Connecticut Crackdown on Speeding," the authors have examined the effects of a specific policy in one of the states in the U.S.A. In view of the higher rate of death due to automobile accidents in 1955, the state of Connecticut decided upon stringent law enforcement against highway speeding immediately before the Christmas rush. The result was that traffic accident deaths came down sharply in 1956 from the 1955 level. The question that arose was whether the Connecticut authorities were right in assuming that speeding was the most important factor in traffic deaths. Simple 'before-after' test (i.e., comparing 1955 with 1956 figures for the state of Connecticut alone) as well as interrupted time series test demonstrated that the assumption was not wrong. In order to be more thorough, they resorted further to multiple time-series experiment by collecting traffic fatality data for the same years (1951-1959) from four other neighbouring states (constituting the control group) which did not adopt any crackdown policy on speeding. The null hypothesis (i.e., that speeding was the most important factor contributing to high rate of traffic deaths) could not be rejected even after the multiple time series test. Thus, while not all the rival hypotheses could be ruled out (for example, statistical regression still remained a rival hypothesis), the interrupted time-series experiment combined with an examination of the multiple time-series data made possible a very interesting analysis.

The experimental, pre-experimental and quasi-experimental research designs presented and discussed above are only some of the possible designs. In this sense, the discussion is introductory rather than exhaustive. Experimental designs may be used in analyzing different type of data. For instance, one may use survey data or aggregate data, or data collected through intensive interviewing. In the social sciences, because of the lack of opportunity for experimental isolation, it is usually difficult for the scientist to apply the true (classical) experimental design. But that need not prevent her from making the best use of the pre-experimental or quasi-experimental designs. As some of the examples cited above show, an intelligent use of these latter designs may very well enrich data analysis in social science, especially in the area of public policy studies.

Endnotes

1.   Ernest Nagel, ed., *John Stuart Mill's Philosophy of Scientific Method* (New York: Hafner Publishing Co., 1950), 211-33.

2. Morris R. Cohen and Earnest Nagel, *An Introduction to Logic and Scientific Method* (New York: Harcourt, Brace & Co. 1937), 245-66.

3. ArendLijphart, "Comparative Politics and Comparative Method," *American Political Science Review* 65 (September 1971): 687

4. Donald T. Campbell, "Factors Relevant to the Validity of Experiments in Social Settings," in *Stages of Social Research: Contemporary Perspectives*, eds. Dennis P. Forcese and Stephen Richer, (New Jersey: Prentice-hall, 1970), 116-31, and Donald T Campbell and Julian C Stanley, *Experimental and Quasi-Experimental Designs for Research* (Chicago: Rand Mcnally& Co., 1970) 5.

5. The present discussion on contaminating factors generally follows the points raised and developed by Campbell and Stanley. See Ibid.

6. Campbell and Stanley, *Experimental*, 15.

7. S.A. Star and H.M. Hughes, "Report on and education campaign: The Cincinnati plan for the United Nations," *American Journal of Sociology* 55, no. 4 (January 1950): 389-400.

8. Campbell and Stanley,*Experimental*, 20-22.

9. Samuel Stouffer, "Some Observations on Study Design," *American Journal of Sociology* 55, no. 4 (January 1950) : 355-61.

10. R.M. Collier, "The Effect of Propaganda upon attitude following a critical examination of the Propaganda itself," *Journal of Social Psychology* 20 no. 3, (1944) 71, cited in Campbell and Stanley, *Experimental*, 7

11. Stouffer, "Some observations on Study Design."

12. Campbell and Stanley, *Experimental*, 25-26.

13. D.T. Campbell and H.L. Ross, "The Connecticut Crackdown on Speeding: Time –Series Data in Quasi-Experimental Analysis," in *The Quantitative Analysis of Social Problems*, ed. Edward R. Tufte (Reading, Massachusetts: Addison-Wesley Publishing Co., 1970),110.

14. It may be mentioned here that the three components of the logic of experiment mentioned in the above paragraph follow from Mill's methods of difference and concomitant variations. Mill himself thought that these methods were inapplicable in the social sciences because sufficiently similar cases could not be found. Thus, he ruled out the idea of their application to political science and said that any attempt to do so would be a "gross misconception of the mode of investigation proper to political phenomena." But from contemporary social science point of view, such a position may be regarded as too inflexible. Thus, Lijphart feels that such objections are "founded on a too exacting scientific standard," or the result of what Sartori calls "over-conscious thinking." Lijphart maintains that

"in looking for comparable cases, this standard should be approximated as closely as possible."

It is in the context of such feelings that the pre-experimental and quasi-experimental designs assume relevance for comparative research. Lijphart, "Comparative Politics," 688; Giovanni Sartori, "Concept Misformation in Comparative Politics," *American Political Science Review* 64, no 4 (December 1970): 1033-53.

15. See Campbell and Stanley, *Experimental,* 34-64.

16. This design is different from the Time-series design common in economics. In the latter, the exogenous independent variable (i.e., 'X') is present continuously along with the dependent variable(s). In the Interrupted Time-Series Design the independent variable is an event that interrupts the movement of the dependent variable over time. See Campbell and Ross, "The Connecticut," 115-16.

17. James A. Caporaso and Alan L. Pelowski, "Economic and Political Integration in Europe : A Time-Series Quasi-Experimental Analysis," *American Political Science Review* 65, no. 2 (June 1971): 418-33.

18. Campbell and Ross, "The Connecticut," 110-125.

4

Aggregate Data Analysis

> That the novelty, though it be not rejected, yet be held for a suspect.
>
> *Francis Bacon*

WHAT ARE AGGREGATE DATA?

Aggregate data are data about collectivities. The 'collectivities' may be international organizations or nation-states or some subgroups within nation-states. In this sense, aggregate data differ from survey data which are about individuals. Hence, on the basis of aggregate data it is difficult to talk about individual behaviour. To infer individual behaviour from aggregate data would be fallacious ('ecological fallacy') just as it would be fallacious to infer collective behaviour from survey data ('individualistic fallacy').

There are two types of aggregate data: summed data and data about global or "syntality" variables. *Summed data* refer to such information as are based on aggregates of the subparts of a unit. These comprise the sum total of individual behaviour, and hence, they are not very dissimilar to survey data. The vital statistics of a country or the mean income of a group of people are examples of summed data. But there are situations when the whole is not simply the sum of its parts; it is either more or less than the summed parts. When one is dealing with such characteristics of nation-states as their constitutional forms, one is dealing with *syntality variables*. For instance, when we label a state as authoritarian, we imply that the totality of the state as a single unit is authoritarian. We do not imply that all the sub-units of that state or all the individual members of that state are authoritarian. Thus, the totality in this case is not a sum of the sub-parts. It is quite possible that most individual members of an authoritarian state are basically democratic. That is, the characteristics of the whole are its characteristics only when we consider the whole as a single entity. Thus, while the summed data can relatively easily be disaggregated, and their examination can be replicated at different levels, the data on the global or syntality variables cannot be so disaggregated.

Interestingly, the popularity of using aggregate data in empirical research varies according to countries. In the United States, for instance, survey data are more popular and usually preferred to aggregate data. American political scientists generally consider survey data as most desirable and aggregate data as only second best. There are several reasons for that. The survey data can be reduced to the level of the individual. The individual exists as a naturally available unit of analysis. Also, if one is taking the individual as unit, the range of inter-unit comparison becomes immense and lots of variance would be observable. Collectivities have a narrower range of variance. Further, in survey analysis an underlying assumption of the rationality of man is present. The survey analyst considers the individual to be a rationally and autonomously acting unit, whether or not he really is so. Hence, the survey analyst also assumes that one individual's views are as important as of anyone else. Because of these underlying assumptions, the use of survey data appears to be consistent with the North American political ideology of individualism.

Aggregate data, on the other hand, seem to be more popular among European scholars. They consider collectivities to be more important units of study. There is also the assumption that the collectivities (e.g., class) are not always reducible to individual preferences. Further, it is argued that the individual's behaviour may be significantly determined by the context. 'Catholic country', 'underdeveloped economy' etc., could be the significant variables in generating 'types of behaviour'.

Advantages of Aggregate Data Analysis

The use of aggregate data has several advantages over the use of survey data. Aggregate data are either about spatial units or about groups and collectivities. Thus while individual data (survey) have to be generated by the researcher himself, aggregate data would be more readily available, especially for those spatial units (e.g., nation-states) or groups (e.g., trade unions or chambers of commerce) who regularly document their activities. For instance, export-import data or price and production indices for nation-states, membership data of trade unions, etc., are available on a more or less regular basis for most nation-states and trade organizations. The researcher may just collect such data from relevant sources rather than himself gathering them. This is an enormous advantage for any researcher who suffers from either lack of finance and personnel or time.[1]

Secondly, in underdeveloped countries, collection of survey data sometimes poses insurmountable problems. As Dasgupta and Morris-Jones point out, over and above all the familiar uncertainties as to the meaning and reliability of responses in the case of data, "there might be fresh hazards in at least the early stages of the application of this technique (of survey research) outside the culture areas in which it had developed."[2]   Such problems can be avoided if one chooses to deal with aggregate data. Since in the case of aggregate data the analyst does not depend on others--most of the time on untrained interviewers and unaccustomed respondents in the case of underdeveloped countries, the problem of honesty or bias of the reporters does not arise.

Thirdly, as Ralph Retzlaff has pointed out,[3] aggregate data, being data on macro-units, help systems analysis, and also permit direct comparison at the level of macro-units. Besides, the use of aggregate data involves a deliberate commitment to quantification.

Finally, aggregate data are unobtrusive. They are not collected with a predetermined purpose of using them in specific research. Their collection, in other words, is independent of their use in research. Thus, when the census office collects information about land holdings or types of crop cultivated, they do so simply for the sake of gathering information. Their job remains totally uninfluenced by such future possibility that the data might be used by a social scientist to demonstrate, for instance, the bases of peasant communism. As a result, the use of aggregate data can avoid 'selective fallacy' (i.e., the tendency among scientists to selectively use only the evidence that supports one's hypothesis) as it can also avoid the observer-behaviour interaction (or effect of observation on the phenomenon studied, known also as "Hawthorne effect" or observer effect).

This does not mean that aggregate data are ideal; nor does it mean that one should look for aggregate data under all circumstances. This merely points out aggregate data have certain advantages over other types of data as the latter also have certain advantages over the former. In probing types of analysis aggregate data would be ideal. But there may be situations when one would need more exact data. Aggregate data would certainly be less than ideal on such occasions. Yet, sometimes the cost of improved exactness may not be worth the time of the political analyst. The most important thing, however, is to recognize the gains and the cost of each method.

SOURCES OF AGGREGATE DATA

Political Research and Analysis with quantitative data has a very short history in India. One can even say it has no history at all. Only recently one sees political scientists in India in search of quantitative data. But unfortunately, for most Indian political scientists interested in quantitative analysisAmerican political scientists have served as models (Almond and Verba's *Civic Culture* is a good example) and hence, the latter's preference for survey data has influenced their Indian counterparts very deeply. Those Indian political scientists who have an orientation towards quantitative analysis, in their over-enthusiasm for survey data (inspite of the known difficulties in gathering such data in this country) have generally neglected aggregate data which are easier to come by. As a result, historians and economists in India have more often taken advantage of aggregate data than political scientists. In the following paragraphs we mention some of the sources of aggregate data which political scientists can utilise very productively, especially for purpose of macro-quantitative analysis and cross-cultural comparison.

a.   *Census data*: Most countries conduct censuses at regular intervals in which comprehensive data are gathered on the entire population. The census technique entails the distribution of questionnaires to the entire population. Individual questions asked about the strength of each household, the age and sex distributions, educational and income levels, occupational information, place of residence (urban or rural etc.) and so forth. The responses are carefully tabulated and the results are printed and published by the census office. Sometimes, many countries also conduct mini censuses in-between the regular censuses in which similar data are gathered from carefully selected samples of the population. In the case of developed countries, such data are available for long time series. These data have been the first type to which researchers have turned when they found interest in using aggregate data for investigating political concepts.

Such census data are available in India from as far back as 1871 when the first census was conducted. While using them, one has to be careful about the data categories and bases, for they change from time to time. The census reports do not merely contain figures; there are also accompanying notes analysing in general terms the raw data as well as indicating the changes in data categories and bases. In India such data are available down to the level of the district. They can be very productively utilised by political scientists interested in analyzing problems such as urbanization, occupational changes, income distribution, spread of education, growth of working class etc., as well as in relating such macro data to political variables.[4]

b. *Governmental statistics*: In each country central statistical office as well as different government departments publish a lot of data on various matters of interest. Indian statistical abstract (*Statistical Abstracts British India* are available from 1865; they have been replaced since independence by *Statistical Abstract India*), *Indian Year Book* etc., fall in this category. The Annual *Economic Survey* which is placed before the Indian Parliament each year during the budget session and the state economic surveys are also of this type. The Information Ministry in India publishes a volume of summary statistics (titled as *India 1975*, for instance) each year. Besides, departments of agriculture, labour etc., both central and state, also publish lots of statistical information (*Indian Labour Statistics*, for instance). The Planning Commission's publications are also an important source of data on various economic and social indicators. The Indian Election Commission publishes electoral data by constituencies for every general election. These are in the nature of aggregate voting data. Very interesting analysis can be done by correlating these political data with socio-economic variables generated from census data.[5]The only problem in doing this type of analysis lies in the fact that Election Commission's electoral data are by constituencies while census data are available for districts. The problem can be solved by transforming constituency-based electoral data into district based data. In this connection, mention may be made of Craig Baxter's *District Voting Trends in India* in which he has converted constituency-level data to the district level for all the districts in India for the first five elections.

c. *Semi-Government and Private Statistics* : The statistics published by various banks, hospitals, and other associations about their activities are also very important sources of data. The quarterly *Reserve Bank of India Bulletin*, for instance, contains an enormous amount of very significant economic information. Similarly, the different chambers of commerce, or trade unions also publish regular statistics on their activities.

d. *Statistics Published by International Agencies* : Yearbooks and other statistics published by international agencies and organisations such as the UNO, WHO, UNESCO, ILO, World Bank, the IMF are also important sources of aggregate data.

e. *Data books* : Several books are available now on cross-national aggregate data. Bruce M. Russett, Hayward R. Alker, Karl W. Deutsch and Harold D. Lasswell's *World Handbook for Political and Social Indicators* (1964), and Arthur S. Banks and Robert B. Textor's *A Cross-Polity Survey* (1963) are particularly mentionable as early works in this category. Arthur S. Bank's *Political Handbook of the World* (1977), containing information on legislative structure, news media, official language, diplomatic representations, and social, economic, political and constitutional backgrounds of 163 independent nations of the world is another example of such early work in this group of materials.

USE OF AGGREGATE DATA

When one is using aggregate data, one is in the arena of macro political comparative research. A variety of macro-political research designs are possible. Two distinctive designs are longitudinal (overtime) and cross-sectional (over area at a single point of time).

Figure 4.1: Designs for macro- political comparison.

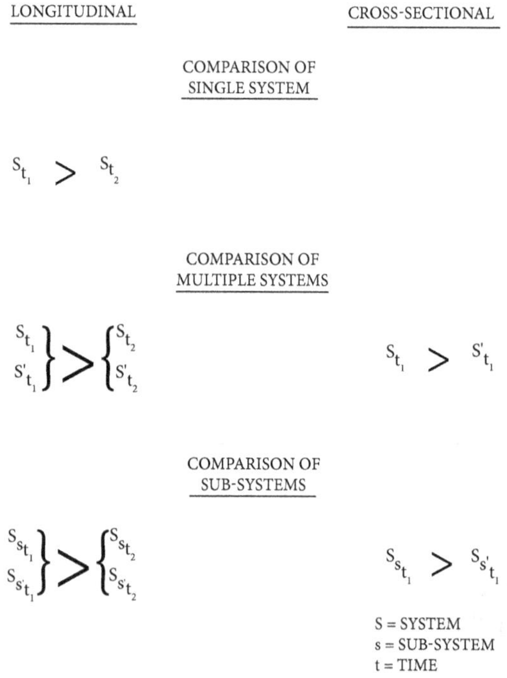

LONGITUDINAL   CROSS-SECTIONAL

COMPARISON OF
SINGLE SYSTEM

$$S_{t_1} > S_{t_2}$$

COMPARISON OF
MULTIPLE SYSTEMS

$$\left.\begin{matrix} S_{t_1} \\ S'_{t_1} \end{matrix}\right\} > \left\{\begin{matrix} S_{t_2} \\ S'_{t_2} \end{matrix}\right. \qquad\qquad S_{t_1} > S'_{t_1}$$

COMPARISON OF
SUB-SYSTEMS

$$\left.\begin{matrix} S_{s_{t_1}} \\ S_{s'_{t_1}} \end{matrix}\right\} > \left\{\begin{matrix} S_{s_{t_2}} \\ S_{s'_{t_2}} \end{matrix}\right. \qquad\qquad S_{s_{t_1}} > S_{s'_{t_1}}$$

S = SYSTEM
s = SUB-SYSTEM
t = TIME

Aggregate data analysis under longitudinal designs may involve either a single system or multiple systems. The former implies that the researcher is investigating the interrelationship of certain attributes and conditions in a single system over time.[6]That is, one is comparing existing state of the system with its prior state(s) or vice versa. Longitudinal design with multiple systems involves investigation of interrelationships of attributes and conditions over time in more than one system in a comparative framework. Such inter system comparison may be cross-national comparison or it may be comparison of sub-system or sub-units within one single political system.[7] Cross-sectional design, on the other hand, implies analysis of attributes and conditions of political systems and their comparison across national boundaries at one point in time.[8] However, cross-sectional designs may be applied to intra-system comparison as well. (Figure 2.1).

Longitudinal design permits deeper analysis than cross-sectional design. For the added dimension of time allows for greater variety and depth in the data. There is one difficulty however. It may be difficult to implement the longitudinal design if extended over long periods of time due to the lack ofreliable data over such long periods of time. Besides, with the passage of time, the collection of aggregate data becomes more systematic and sophisticated (that is to say, the Indian census data of 1871 may quite reasonably be assumed to be much less sophisticated than that of 1971 simply on grounds of technological advancement). Hence, reliability and comparability would pose serious problems for the analyst the more one goes back upon time. Only gross estimates may be used in the case of historical data.

Aggregate Data as Indicators

Whatever is the specific design followed, the idea in aggregate data analysis is to examine the interrelation of attributes (such as stability, integration, modernity, democracy etc.), and conditions (such as levels of economic or social development, social cultural homogeneity / heterogeneity etc.), of the units of analysis (such as nation-states, regions or groups within nation-states, supra-national organisations etc.). In measuring the attributes and conditions aggregate data are used as indicators. Sometimes we are interested in certain things simply because we are interested in them. But sometimes we may not be interested in certain thing as such; we may be interested in them because we see them as indicators of certain other things. For instance, we may be interested in the movement of mercury inside a thermometer not because of any abiding interest in the mercury itself, but because we take it as indicative of body temperature. Similarly, our interest in the G. N. P. (Gross National Product) values of certain nation-states may not be due to our interest in the G.N.P. per se, but because the G.N.P indicates for us the level of economic development of the units under study.

Indicators serve a number of purposes. For instance, they help to evaluate policies. The success of a labour policy aimed at achieving a high degree of satisfaction among the working class may be evaluated by using aggregate data on strikes as indicator of worker discontent. Similarly, the success of a literacy campaign may be evaluated by using the number or percentage of illiterates in a community for a number of years following the adoption of such a campaign and by examining whether it is increasing or declining.

The most important use of indicators, however, lies in their contribution to the clarification of concepts. Knowledge about interconnectedness of an indicator of a concept with another indicator helps one to develop a more refined idea about the concept itself. Thus, Daniel Lerner, while examining the critical function of mass media in the process of modernization, has found that

> modern media systems have flourished only in societies that are modern by *other* tests ...... the conditions which define modernity form an interlocking "system". They grow conjointly in the normal situation or they become stunted   severally.[9]

And what are these other conditions for modernization? They are urbanization, literacy and voting. That is, to be "modern," a society must be characterized by the presence of a media system as distinguished from an oral system of communication; at the same time, such a society must also be urban, literate and electoral. Lerner further finds that these four indicators of modernization are statistically highly correlated as well, and he points out that the high correlation coefficients (ranging from '61 to '91) "demonstrates that the relationship between the four sectors is systematic,"[10]. In consequence, Lerner has been able to develop a more complete model of modernization.

It is necessary to remember, therefore, that concepts and indicators are closely interlinked. This really refers to the problem of operationalization of concepts. The operationalizability of concepts depends on whether measurable indicators of it can be developed. We are not taking here the position that a concept is no good unless there are measurable indicators for it. Indeed, it is true, as Easton says, that "the task of theory is to point out what is necessary. As long as in principle it is possible to achieve, empirically, what is necessary, it becomes a *separate* although important matter to locate empirical indicators of theoretically important phenomena".[11] That is to say, the theoretician, while developing theoretically relevant concepts, need not bother much about the lack of measurable indicators. Yet it remains true that non-availability of such indicators would impose severe limits on concepts that are meant for empirical research.

It is no accident that there are numerous social science concepts for which no precise and measurable indicators are available. It is much easier to talk about developing and using indicators in an empirical research than to achieve them in fact. The process of operationalizing a concept involves several stages. An empirical researcher starts with one or more propositions or hypotheses which are statements about the relationship of certain concepts. Each of the concepts must then be very carefully analytically formulated (i. e., the components of the concept or the possible sub-variables of a variable must be straightened out). The researcher would then identify those components of the concept or sub-variables that are amenable to direct or indirect measurement. The next task is to compile the necessary data to work out the measurements for each of the components or sub-variables. These components or sub-variables would then constitute statistical indicators for the concept. Finally, the researcher would combine these indicators to construct an overall index of the concept. The following example from Robert Putnam's paper would help us to clarify this procedure.

Robert Putnam was interested in explaining military intervention in Latin American politics.[12] The literature suggested four broad categories of factors as causes of intervention or abstention :(1) aspects of socio-economic development; (2) aspects of political development; (3) the characteristics of the military establishment itself; and (4) foreign influence. The problem for him was to construct these propositions in such a way that it becomes possible to test them empirically. But before he could do that, it was necessary for him to develop an index for his dependent variable, i.e., military intervention. He constructed this index (the "MI index", as he called) by assigning a rating to each country (in Latin America) for each year of the decade 1956-65. This rating was based on the extent of military intervention in the political life of that country in each year. The rating was "on a scale from zero to three, from least to most intervention. Thus, for the decade, a country's MI score could be anywhere between zero and thirty" (Minimum =10 years x 0, and Maximum = 10 years x 3). These ratings were assigned by Putnam in the following manner:

"A rating of zero is given to a country in which the armed forces were essentially apolitical, their role restricted to that of a minor pressure group on strictly military matters. A country that was ruled by a military regime, either individual or collective, and in which civilian groups and institutions were reduced to supplicants or tools of the military, is rated three... A rating of two is given when a country was ruled by a military-civilian coalition in which the civilian elements had some real influence, or by civilians subject to frequent demands from a powerful military establishment, or by dictatorship (often of a paternalistic variety) based on force of arms but not solely responsible to the armed forces... A rating of one is given when a country was ruled by essentially civilian institutions with civilian power groups preeminent but with the armed forces still a significant political force in non-military matters."[13]

Similarly, before he could do correlational analysis between his independent variables on the one hand and the dependent variable on the other, he had to formulate the independent variables, and to construct an index for each of them. One of his independent variables, for example, was social mobilization. He identified five sub-variables to measure social mobilization: (1) percent of population in cities over 20,000; (2) percent of adults literate; (3) newspaper circulation per 1,000 population; (4) university students per 1,000 population and (5) radios per 1,000 populations. He, then, added together each country's (standardized) scores on these five indicators to form a single index of social mobilization which he called the "SM index."

Such examples can be multiplied.[14]But we hope the above two would give an idea of the procedure for operationalizing a concept through the construction of indices[15] and of how aggregate data could be used in the process.

Problems of Using Aggregate Data as Indicators

Several problems might beset the development and use of such macro-indicators in single-system or cross-national studies, and hence, it is necessary for the analyst to be aware of them. First and the most basic, is the problem of *reliability*. Reliability refers to the accuracy of the statistics: How accurate or reliable are the statistics in measuring what they are supposed to measure? If one is using crime rates in a community as an indicator of deviant behaviour, the statistics on crime must accurately report the number of crimes committed in that community. That is, to be reliable, the data must provide an accurate and realistic account of the phenomenon under study.

A number of factors might contribute to unreliable data. Lack of adequate training for the data gathering personnel is one. Secondly, over time, a data gathering agency may attain greater efficiency. For instance, an agency gathering crime statistics may become more efficient in collecting data over the years. Hence, increasing crime rates over time may reflect simply the agency's greater efficiency rather than real changes in the crime rate. Thirdly, social conditions may also affect data reliability. It is sometimes alleged, for instance, that the U.S. police systematically under record crimes by white men as compared with crimes by the Blacks. Such ethnic, caste or political biases among the society's law and order men are not quite uncommon in other societies as well. Similar accusations have been against Sri Lankan police in the 1980s regarding their stricter approach to Tamils compared toSinhalese. Under such conditions, police record on community crimes would be highly unreliable.

John Gillespie has suggested four ways to check data reliability.[16]To begin with, the researcher may use alternative sources for collection of information on the variables concerned. There are normally several alternative sources, both national and international, from which one may gather aggregate social and economic data. Only rarely the researcher would be faced with a situation when his data had a single source. For instance, when using the G.N.P. as an indicator of economic development, one may use the figures provided by the national government; but at the same time one may also look at the G.N.P. values for that nation either from some private domestic source or from U.N. or some other international agency's publication. The use of alternative sources would allow the researcher to cross-check and hence, to have greater confidence in the data.

Secondly, one may also look at other works using similar variables and compare them with his own. If the similarities and differences are along expected lines, the confidence in one's own data would be increased. Robert Putnam, while constructing his "MI" index mentioned above, found that Martin C. Needler had also constructed an index of the "normal political role of military" in Latin America. He took the opportunity of Needler's index and compared that with his own. While the comparison could not "prove" the accuracy of either, the concordance between the two assessments increased Putnam's confidence in his own index.[17]

Thirdly, the researcher should also examine the procedure through which the original data were collected. Same type of data (e.g., census data) for different countries may not be equally reliable because the efficiency of the different census agencies involved may vary a great deal. Again, tampering with statistics is a rather common thing in authoritarian and dictatorial regimes. Hence, whether one is using national or International sources, the researcher would be in a better position to assess his data if he examines as far as he can, the process of their generation.

Finally, the reliability of indicators, and also, by implication, of the basic data on which the indicators are constructed, can be tested by internal checks. While there are no set procedures for internal checks, one may, for instance, examine the inter-correlation of the sub-variables to see internal consistency of one's index. Thus, high level of inter-correlation among the modernization variables permits Lerner to assume that his modernization concept is internally consistent and "systematic."[18] Similarly, Putnam's finding that the indicators of his social mobilization index are highly inter-correlated (r = .81) allows him to have greater confidence in his "SM" Index.[19]

While through all these procedures, one may enhance the degree of reliability of one's data, it is necessary to remember that the question of data reliability is not absolute; rather it is relative to alternative procedures. The object is to use as reliable data as possible rather than to aim at the absolutely reliable data.

Next to reliability is the problem of *comparability* of data. Data comparability poses crucial problems particularly for cross-national research, though it is not totally absent from single system study. Thus, census data of two successive censuses for the same country may not be directly comparable, for the data categories might be different. Overlooking this simple fact might affect one's research very damagingly. Similarly, changes in the timing of observations (on the basis of which the data are collected) or the efficiency of the collecting agencies (discussed above) might also make two data series non-comparable.

The most serious problem regarding comparability in cross-national research arises out of the varying definition of a variable or lack of "uniformity of usage" of concepts. We have already pointed out the way in which Putnam constructed his "MI" index. That provides a good example of the essentially subjective basis of a lot of quantitative data in the social sciences.[20]This subjective element, which most often remains unavoidably present, creates problem for data comparability. Let us closely look at the following citation from Putnam again :

"A rating of one is given when a country was ruled by *essentially* civilian institutions with civilian power groups *preeminent* but with armed forces still a *significant* political force in *non-military matters....*" (italics mine.)

How does one define the italicized expressions in a comparative context? The concept of *non-military matters*, for instance, may vary greatly across countries. Again to be a *significant* political force, armed forces may have to engage in visible political activities in some countries while in some others it may become as significant a political force without engaging itself visibility in politics. Comparability, thus, would essentially depend on the solution of the problem of equivalence, that is, in answering whether one is comparing the "comparables".[21] The researcher should be very careful about it; for otherwise, he might be comparing non-equivalent data without knowing it and making fallacious inference.

The third crucial problem is using macro-indicators in aggregate data analysis is that of *validity*. Validity refers to the accuracy of the indicators in measuring the concept of our interest. If one is using crime statistics to infer social deviance, the question will be: how well does the crime rate represent social deviance in a particular society? Is there a better indicator? The problem of validity thus refers to the relationship between the concept and the indicator. Hence, part of the problem of validity is the problem of theoretical refinement of the concept. Valid indicators would be is easier to identify for a concept which has a high degree of refinement and operationalizability.

The problem of validity of indicators arises because of the fact that a concept may be measured through different indicators. In addition to the presence of multiple indicators there is also the fact that each indicator may have different dimensions. Thus, for instance, the concept of "political violence" may be measured through a number of indicators such as riots and demonstrations, government action against specific groups, sabotage, coups, political assassinations, civil wars etc. Again, each of these indicators are multi-dimensional: civil war, for instance, may be expressed in terms of its duration, popular participation, number of deaths, etc. Finally, in cross-national research, the same concept may have to be measured by different indicators in different countries. Thus, in one country political instability may have to be measured by the fall of cabinets, in another by the number of street riots.

The reverse of this is true as well; that is, the same indicator may have different degrees of validity in different countries. Thus, elections as an indicator of a participant polity will have different degrees of validity in India, United Kingdom and Pakistan. Which indicators would be more valid or which dimensions of an indicator should receive greater emphasis would essentially have to be decided by the theoretic problem at hand, and with the help of contextual knowledge. There cannot be any predetermined and prescribed formula for assessing the validity of indicators. It is only through a process of trial and error that the unnecessary or incorrect indicators can be identified and eliminated

Aggregate Data and Fallacy of Inference

Aggregate data, as we have already said, are data about territorial units and collectivities (groups, associations, national or sub-national social units etc...). Therefore, aggregate data deal with the mean values of attributes and conditions of such gross units rather than with the internal distribution of those values within the macro-units. One commits the fallacy of inference when one infers individual behaviour from a data on collectivities. This fallacy of inference is known as "ecological fallacy."[22]

ECOLOGICAL FALLACY

The problem of ecological fallacy becomes relevant as soon as our use of aggregate data moves beyond description and analysis of statistical relationships to that of inference. Failure to recognise this problem might result in completely wrong inferences from quite valid relationships.

Stated very simply, ecological fallacy means that correlatives of aggregated data for a group may not hold for individual members of that group. In other words, it will be invalid cross-level inference if we look at variables concerning social units and draw conclusions from them about individual behaviour or attitudes. W.S. Robinson in his pioneering article, "Ecological Correlations and the Behaviour of Individuals,"[23] brought the problem of ecological fallacy into focus. In his article, Robinson distinguished between "individual correlation" and "ecological correlation". In the former, the statistical object or thing described is indivisible, while in the latter the statistical object is a group of persons or a collectivity. The distinction is vital, for "the individual correlation depends upon the *internal* frequencies of the within-areas individual correlations, while the ecological correlations depend upon the *marginal* frequencies of the within-areas individual correlation." In as much as the marginal frequencies of a fourfold table do not determine the internal cell frequencies, there need be no correspondence between the individual correlation and the ecological correlation. Robinson, infact, demonstrated that not merely the individual correlation between the same variables will be widely different from their ecological correlation, but they may even change their directions (signs).

The reason why the two correlations are usually different is simple. In aggregate data analysis the regression line normally runs not through the raw data but through the mean numbers derived from raw data. For example, when different countries are plotted on a scatter gram the values for each country represent only the mean values, not the raw values for each individual in each country. That is to say, the regression line takes care only of the mean values, not of the internal structure of each mean value. In such a situation there may be cases when the internal structure fits in well with the regression line; hence there may be no 'group effect'. Theoretically this is possible. But from a practical standpoint, the only reasonable assumption will be that they do not fit.

The averages or summary statistics of two distributions as against individual observations that enter into the computation quite obviously reduce variability. And the larger the contexts for which units are aggregated, the more likely a significant difference between the individual and ecological correlations.[24]

Essentially, this is a problem of deduction. Each unit is made up of a number of sub-units and they may differ in their characteristics. Under such circumstances, deductions from our knowledge of any one unit to other units in either direction (i.e., from unit to sub-unit or vice versa) are liable to be fallacious. The danger of committing ecological fallacy is present when the unit to which the inference refers is smaller than the unit either of observation or of counting.

This does not, however, mean that ecological analysis should be abandoned. Within their limits, they are very useful; for we are interested in the behaviour of areas and collectivities too. In fact, interest in theoretically interpreting ecological correlations is increasing. The interpretation of the observed differences between 'total' (individual) and ecological correlations would also be theoretically very productive. What is important is to remember, as Robinson said, that "ecological correlation is almost certainly not equal to its corresponding individual correlation". With this in mind, there is no need to consider ecological correlation as an inferior substitute of total correlation based on individuals. In fact, a political scientist is more often interested in aggregate behaviour than in individual behaviour. In that context, study of aggregates can be highly useful.

Besides, individual political behaviour is very often affected by group characteristics. As Dasgupta and Morris-Jones note, "a particular mix of land system, occupational pattern, and demographic characteristics is likely to have a certain 'compositional effect' on individuals".[25] Ecological correlations are particularly helpful in analysing such group effect' or 'contextual effect' on behaviour.

ANALYSIS OF AGGREGATE DATA

Data analysis is the most difficult as well as exciting aspect of research. While how one analyzes one's data is always partly a function of the technology of the day, there remains an obvious danger in overusing technology. Indeed, data analysis can benefit much from a proper utilisation of technological developments as well as from developments in formal statistics, but the benefits can become productive only if the connections between technology and statistics on the one hand, and data analysis on the other are kept adequately flexible.

The basic objective of data analysis is to confirm or nullify, through a process of elaboration, certain hypothesized relationships among variables or phenomena. Its primary purpose has been very well stated by Tukey and Wilk :

> "..... to seek through a body of data for interesting relationships and information and to exhibit the results in such a way as to make them recognizable to the data analyzer and recordable for posterity. Its creative task is to be productively descriptive, with as much attention as possible to previous knowledge, and thus to contribute to the mysterious process called insight".[26]

According to the same authors, there are five specific objectives of data analysis: (1) to describe with greater specificity what is loosely known or suspected; (2) to identify unanticipated aspects in the data and to suggest unthought-of models for the summarization and exposure of the data; (3) to employ the data to assess (however tentatively) the adequacy of a contemplated model; (4) to provide both incentive and guidance for further analysis of the data; and (5) to keep the investigator productively stimulated while he absorbs the feel of his data and considers the steps to be taken next.

The above objectives suggest two major aspects of data analysis: summarizing and exposure. The 'summarizing' aspect involves an examination of the "fit", that is, the degree to which the actual data fit in with the hypothesized (predicted) relationship among variables. 'Exposure' involves an analysis of those portions of the data that do not fit in with the line of predicted relationship.

Any observation (data) consists of certain anticipated relationships (hence, 'explained') and certain unanticipated relationships (or 'unexplained'). Using technical expressions, one would call the former as "fit" and the latter as "residual". An observation can then be expressed as

observation = fit + residual

and residual can be expressed as

residual = observation - fit.

The 'fit' helps one to *confirm* that the relationship in the data is not the result of chance or accident while the 'residual' helps one to *discover* new relationships in the data. Thus, through summarizing and exposure the two essential objectives of data analysis, namely, confirmation and discovery, are met. In Figure 2.2 we have summarized the entire procedure described so far.

A glance at figure 4.2 reveals the centrality of 'fit' to data analysis. Through fit, we try to understand four essential things: the degree of *covariance* among variables, the *direction* of the inter-variable relationship, the element of *contingency* or spuriousness in such relationship, and the *stability* of the relationship across time or units.

Fitting may be done for several purposes. It may be used for pure description: for instance, to depict the way in which Y depends upon X. We are not, in such cases of pure description, concerned at all with the question whether such dependence is accidental or necessary.

Secondly, fitting may be used for prediction either of local or of global nature. In the case of local prediction, we would use the fit to predict Y, given X, "conditions remaining the same." In the case of global prediction, we would use the fit to predict Y, given X, far outside the range of our specific data (hence, depending considerably on "side knowledge").

Figure 4.2: Procedure for data analysis

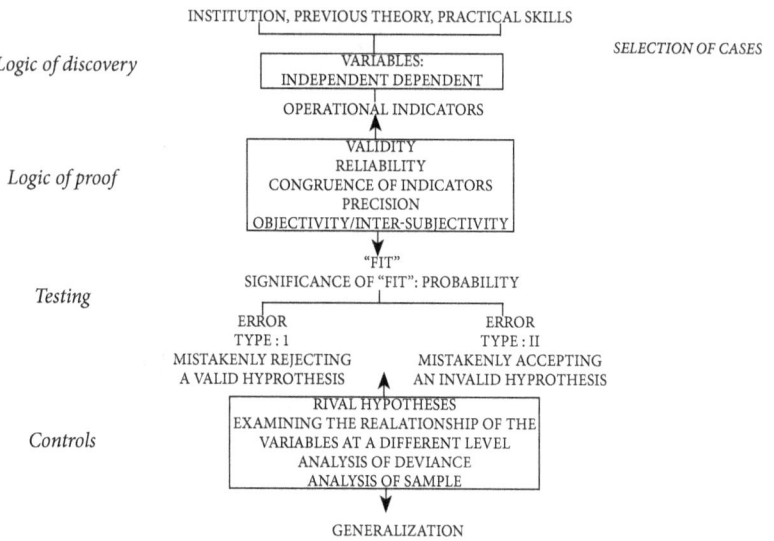

Similarly, the 'residuals' may also be severally used. First of all, the residuals may show a pattern by themselves and hence, may be analyzed in their own right and fitted separately. Secondly, the residuals would expose the inadequacy of the initial fit. Thirdly, the residuals might help identify the peculiarities in the data and hence, by suppressing them, the analyst might be able to strengthen the fitted relationships.

While there are various procedures through which aggregate data may be analyzed (some of them will be discussed below), Tukey and Wilk as well as Tufte[27] lay special emphasis on the examination of the goodness of 'fit' and analysis of residuals through regression procedures. They consider correlation coefficients to be both overworked and inefficient in certain respects (for instance, Tufte shows that quite different relationships between variables may generate the same correlation coefficients). Further, even in regression analysis, focusing only on tests of significance is inadequate, for, as Tufte, says,

> "probability levels and test statistics tell us very little about the strength and nothing about the substantive significance of a relationship ... what

to do with the relationships even if they are significant is never made entirely clear, and as far as we can see, it will be `up to the investigator to use his own judgement in appraising and weighing reports that show relations with conditions of observation. Perhaps it will never be possible to improve on individual judgement in such matters......"[28]

Hence, they suggest that regression line should be graphically presented through scatter-diagram which would expose the fit as well as the residuals and permit "some insight into the character and nature of the departure from fit."[29]

Having made these few preliminary remarks about the analysis of aggregate data let us now turn to some of the more specific procedures and ways in which the analyst can use such data. There are three major ways of handling aggregate data: First, the univariate analysis of data; secondly, bivariate analysis and thirdly, multivariate analysis.

Univariate Analysis

Univariate analysis is the most simple analytical technique. In univariate analysis, the analyst focuses upon single variables and looks at the distribution of cases or observations along different values of each variable. For instance, Russett et al., in their *World Handbook of Political and Social Indicators*, present their data for each variable in the form of a rank ordering; that is, by ranking the countries according to the values they score on each variable. Thus, on the variable 'Percentage of annual change in G.N.P. per capita', the country having registered the highest percentage change over the years under observation was given the highest rank and country with the lowest percentage change (this happened to be a negative score) was given the lowest rank.[30]

The primary purpose of such univariable analyses is description. One is not so much interested in exploring relationships among variables here as in exposing the various distributions of values of variables. Such analyses naturally demonstrate the existence of differentiation in the world. The univariate analyses thus serve as the first step toward more elaborate and penetrating research rather than the final one. A good example of such univariate analysis (and also of how univariate analyses can lead to bivariate ones, as the authors have explored certain relationships as well) has been provided by Mckinlay and Cohan in their article on "Performance and Instability in Military and Non-Military Regime Systems."[31]

The basic purpose of Mckinlay and Cohan in the paper was "to compare the performance of military and non-military regime systems" across five categories of variables. The variables they chose were the following:

A. Political Activity and Political Change Variables :

    (i)   Percentage of years the constitution is banned ;

    (ii) Percentage of years the legislature is banned;

    (iii) Percentage of years that political parties are banned;

    (iv) Mean percentage of cabinet posts held by military personnel;

    (v)   The number of constitution changes; and

    (vi) The number of main executive changes

B. Military Capability Variables

    (i)   Mean size of the armed forces per 10,000 population;

    (ii) Mean military expenditure as a percentage of GNP;

    (iii) The diversification of the armed forces measured in terms of the size of the navy and air-forces as a percentage of the total size;

    (iv) The rate of growth of the size of the armed forces; and

    (v)   The rate of growth of constant military expenditure.

C. Background Economic Variables:

    (i)   Constant per capita Gross National Product (GNP);

    (ii) Budget as a percentage of GNP;

    (iii) Gross domestic fixed capital formation (GDFCF);

    (iv) Primary production as a percentage of gross domestic product; and

    (v)   Number of doctors per 100,000 population.

D. International Economic Variables:

    (i)   Exports as a percentage of GNP;

    (ii) Imports as a percentage of GNP;

    (iii) International liquidity as a percentage of imports;

    (iv) Balance of payments position on private investment; and

    (v)   Balance of payments position on central government capital.

E. Economic Performance Variables:

(i)   Rate of growth of constant per capita GNP;

(ii) Rate of growth of cost of living index; and

(iii) Rate of growth of Exports.

The authors were interested in examining how the military and non-military regime systems score on these different sets of variables. The following table from their paper is a random example of how they find and present scores of the two regime systems for one set of variables:

Table 4.1: Military size and Expenditure by Regime Type*

Military size and Expenditure

Type of System	Military Size	Military expenditure as % GNP	Diversification	Rate of Growth of Size	Rate of Growth of Expenditure
MRS (Military Regime System)	47.9	3.21	11.64	8.10	8.80
NMRS (Non-Military Regime System)	56.4	3.15	16.42	5.64	9.60

* The table has been summarized to omit a third row giving the values for a control variable.

We need not discuss the substantive aspects of the findings presented in the Table above, although they appear to be very interesting. But we do get a good description of the relative position of the military and non-military regime systems with regard to the variable called Military size and Expenditure. Essentially, the authors here were interested in such description. While such descriptions are interesting as well as revealing by themselves, they also help generate relational hypotheses and identify dependent and independent variables and thereby take the analysis to a more advanced stage.

Bivariate Analysis

CORRELATION AND REGRESSION

As we have already indicated, univariate analyses, however useful, mark only the first step in political science research. As political scientists, we are normally more interested in exploring relationships among variables or indicators. One may be interested in figuring out whether her variables are associated with each other when paired; that is, she may try to answer the question whether any shift in the value of his variable x is associated with proportionate shifts in the value of her variable y. The standard statistical technique for measuring the degree of association between two variables is *correlation* and the measure of the association is expressed as correlation coefficient. The most commonly used correlational technique is Pearson's product-moment correlation or Simple (Pearson's) r. Symbol r ranges from + 1.00 to - 1.00. If two variables, x and y, are positively correlated perfectly, that is, if change in x is associated with corresponding change in y in the same direction, the resulting r will equal + 1.00. If change in x is associated with change in y but in the opposite direction (i.e., correlated perfectly but negatively), r will equal -1.00. And if change in x is not associated at all with change in y, r will equal 0.00, in which case we can say that the variables are totally uncorrelated or completely independent of each other (Figure 2.3). Normally, degree of association of paired variables will fall somewhere between + 1.00 and - 1.00.[32]

Figure 4.3: Possible extremes of two-variable relationship (correlation)

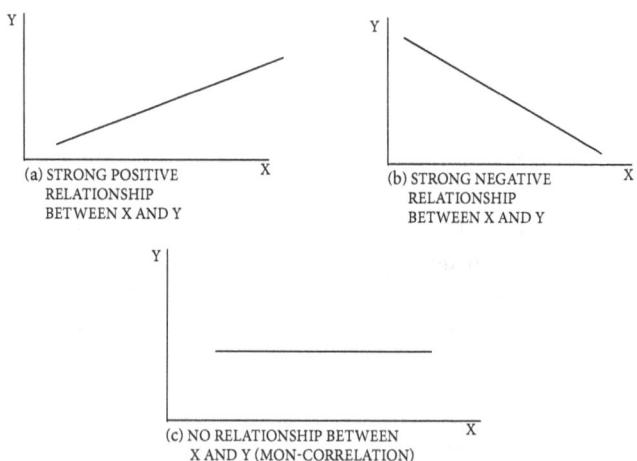

(a) STRONG POSITIVE RELATIONSHIP BETWEEN X AND Y

(b) STRONG NEGATIVE RELATIONSHIP BETWEEN X AND Y

(c) NO RELATIONSHIP BETWEEN X AND Y (MON-CORRELATION)

Simple correlation is a very widely used measure. As V.O. Key says, "whenever the data relative to a hypothesis can be put into the form of a number of paired variables, the technique of correlation may be used in reasoning about the relationships involved."[33] But there is one caveat that should always be kept in mind: correlation does not mean causation. If variables x and y are highly correlated, there is nothing in it which permits the inference that x causes y or vice versa.

The second thing to remember about correlation r is that it is a measure of linear relationship. Hence, r = 0 need not always mean absence of relationship between two variables. The variables concerned can have a perfect curvilinear relationship with zero r.

For the student of politics an understanding of the general mode of analysis and of reasoning involved in a correlation is vastly more important than the mastery of computational procedure. It is necessary to bear in mind that demonstration of degree of association between pairs of variables is not the end, but just the beginning of analysis. As V.O.Key rightly points out, "After the completion of the calculation the real work must begin."[34] Correlational analysis, thus, may be used to describe the strength of association between independent and dependent variables.

Secondly, as we have already indicated, correlation coefficients are used by analysts in examining the interrelationships of sets of dependent or independent variables or indicators, for by using them one can construct a composite scale or index. Finally, one may also use correlation coefficients as a stepping stone for more complex multivariate analysis (e.g. path analysis, factor analysis, multiple regression etc.,). Below, we present a hypothetical table to demonstrate how atypical tabular presentation of correlation coefficients would look like (Table 2.2).

Table 4.2: Pearson r Simple Correlation Matrix Among Ten Variables (Hypothetical)

	1	2	3	4	5	6	7	8	9	10
1	-	.47	.35	.27	.27	.21	.19	.24	.24	.23
2		-	.50	.36	.46	.19	.19	.27	.31	.24
3			-	.37	.45	.20	.18	.25	.23	.24
4				-	.36	.17	.17	.20	.21	.12
5					-	.14	.13	.18	.22	.22
6						-	.71	.64	.18	.10
7							-	.60	.17	.09
8								-	.22	.14
9									-	.38
10										-

While doing bivariate analysis one need not restrict oneself solely to the use of correlational technique. For, after all, correlation coefficients can merely suggest the *degree* of association between two variables; it says nothing about the *nature* or form of the relationship. It does not express itself in terms of specific unit change in one variable and its effect on the other in terms of unit change in the latter. This sophistication in analysis is possible if one applies the regression technique. Both the correlation coefficient and the bivariate regression coefficient are summary statements of the relationship between two variables. But in regression analysis one has to identify an independent variable (X) and a dependent variable (Y). The analyst is precisely asking here: if X changes by one unit, by how many units does Y change (rather than simply asking how strongly or weakly are X and Y associated)? The regression line is the least- square line or the line of the best fit between X and Y.[35] A two-variable linear regression equation will have the following form:

$Y = a + bx$

when a = intercept (i.e., the value of Y when X = 0)

b = slope (i.e., change in Y/change in X). It can be diagrammatically presented as:

Figure 4.4: Bivariate linear regression.

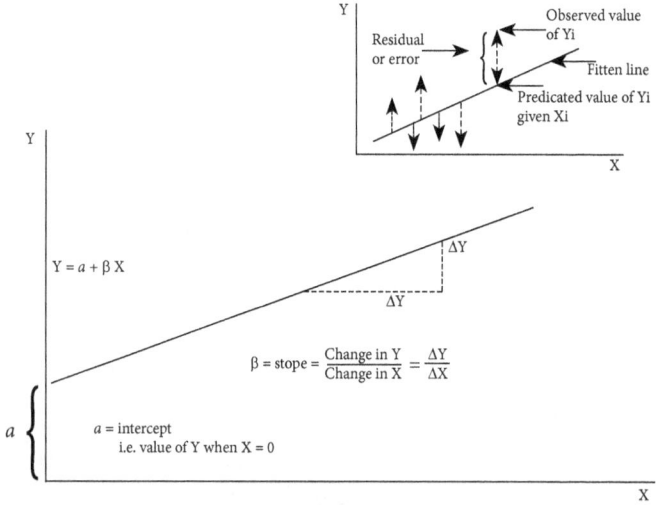

Analysts of aggregate data have frequently used bivariate linear regression. Edward Tufte, in one of his examples of two-variable linear regression technique, examines the relation between presidential popularity rating in America and the number of seats lost by the president's party in mid-term congressional elections between 1946 and 1970. An initial correlational analysis yielded a very high negative correlation (-.75) between these two variables. This suggested that the lower popularity rating of the president before mid-term polls (measured by the percentage of people approving the president in Gallup polls taken immediately before the mid-term elections), the greater the number of seats lost by the president's party in congressional elections. But obviously this does not tell the analyst "how much a decline in the approval rating is associated with a loss of how many seats." To calculate that, Tufte resorts to regression analysiswhich yielded a regression coefficient of -1.20. This implies that a one percent decline in the popularity rating of the President is associated with the loss of about 1.2 seats in the following mid-term congressional election. Through tests of significance and also by looking at the value of r^2 (square of correlation coefficient which expresses the percentage of variance explained by a regression line, also known as 'coefficient of determination') the analyst can further fortify his conclusions.

While regression coefficient is a more precise measure of the relationship between two variables and it may also be used for predictive purposes within limits, correlation coefficients are very useful measures in exploratory studies. Indeed, when identification of the important variables is the major problem, correlation coefficient is the most useful measure. It is true that sometimes correlation coefficient may be deceptive; for instance, when completely different forms of relationships among pairs of variables are hidden by exactly identical correlation coefficients or when a perfectly curvilinear relationship yields a zero coefficient.[36] But solution to such problems lies in a graphic presentation of the data through to scatter-grams, as both Tufte and Blalock emphasize, rather than in making pretentious use of regression equations.

Sometimes, correlation or linear regression may distort the true relationship between two variables. A look at the scattergram may demonstrate that a curve rather than a straight line is the best fit. For instance, Ted Gurr and Charles Ruttenberg in their study of civil violence find that the total magnitude of civil violence is low both for the poor and for the rich nations. Magnitude of civil violence tends to go up somewhere in the middle, when poor nations start developing.[37] One has to apply nonlinear regression equations to find out the best fitting curve for such data.[38] Thus, while both correlation coefficient (r) and regression coefficient (β) are good summary statements of the relationship between two variables, their limitations should be recognised. They fail when the relationship is nonlinear. They also fail when the data contain even single observation which is far from the mean, for in that case such an extreme observation will tend to determine the values of both r and β.[39]

One can also use the technique of rank-order correlation for bivariate analysis. Such qtechniques are used when one is dealing not with the absolute scores of the units (individuals, groups or countries, for instance) on the variables concerned, but with their ranks. One can compute the differences between the ranks on the two variables scored by each of the units and then, by using Spearman rank-order correlation technique, one can get a correlation coefficient (r_s) for the two variables.[40]

CROSS TABULATION

Cross-tabulation reminds one of the most commonly used techniques for bivariate (and multivariate as well) analysis. Cross-tabulation essentially means joint frequency distribution of cases according to two or more classificatory variables. While in correlation analysis the strength of association is measured by a single summary statistic, the coefficient(r), in cross-tabulation the degree of association is determined by examining the joint frequency distribution of two variables in tabular form. Cross-tabulation is a simple procedure. But in spite of its simplicity, it has great practical value and analytical utility in the disentanglement of relationships among variables. In cross-tabulation the display of the distribution of cases by variables takes a tabular form. A two-variable analysis of the relationship between caste and education (when each variable is dichotomized) can be presented in the following 2 X 2 table:

Table 4.3: Format of a 2 X 2 table

Education	Caste		
	Brahmin	Non-Brahmin	
Low	Cell	Cell	Marginal
High	Cell	Cell	Marginal
	Marginal	Marginal	

Even a quick look at the cell and the marginal frequencies of the table will give one at least a rough impression of the relationship between caste and education. It may be further illustrated with the help of a concrete example. Feierabend and Feierabend give an instance of how to use cross-tabulation with aggregate data.[41]They were interested in exploring the relationship between two variables, namely, social frustration and political stability. After defining their independent variable (social frustration) and the dependent variable (political stability), they cross-tabulate their cases (countries) in the following manner.[42]

Table 4.4: Cross-Tabulation of Two Dichotomized Variables

Degree of Political Stability	Index of Systemic frustration		Total
	High systemic frustration	Low systemic frustration	
Unstable	34	6	40
Stable	2	20	22
Total	36	26	62

The table (which has been summarised here) clearly demonstrates a relationship between systematic frustration and political stability. The unstable political systems are those that suffer from a high degree of systemic frustration while the stable ones show a low degree of systemic frustration. Thus, out of 36 countries suffering from high systemic frustration 34 are politically unstable. On the other hand, out of 26 countries indicating low systemic frustration only six are politically unstable while the rest show stability.

One can always introduce new variables to such cross-tabulational analysis. But then, obviously the cell frequencies will become smaller.[43]

Multivariate Analysis

In cros-tabulation analysis it becomes necessary to introduce 'control' variables, for such 'control' variables allow one to examine a bivariate relationship in depth as well as to discover new relationships. This, in general, points out the limitations of simple bivariate analysis. Very often, bivariate analysis would result in distortion or suppression of relationships due to the fact that in such analysis the important effects of third (intervening or conjoint) variables would remain hidden. For instance, one might find a strong positive relationship between urbanisation and electoral participation; that is, one might see that a significantly larger proportion of city-dwellers vote more regularly in elections than their rural counterparts. But closer scrutiny might reveal that a significantly higher proportion of literate people live in the cities than in the villages. Thus, the problem arises: is higher electoral participation by city-dwellers an effect of urbanization or of education? Indeed, we might find that they both affect participation in different degrees. All this calls for a method of analysis that can take into account more than a single independent variable. Such a method of analysis is called multivariate analysis. Since in the social sciences the enormity in the number of variables is a problem rather than their dearth, any serious analysis of social problems can hardly avoid multivariate analysis in some form.

MULTIPLE REGRESSION

We have already noted that multivariate analysis is possible through cross-tabulation. A more precise technique, however, is multiple regression. It is also a technique which is being widely used increasingly in the study of political and policy problems. While the two-variable linear regression allows the analyst to measure the linear relationship between an independent variable and a dependent variable, multiple regression allows one to examine the linear relationship between two or more independent variables on the one hand and a dependant variable on the other. The essential logic behind the bivariate regression and the multiple regression is the same. The basic idea behind multiple regression is to produce a "linear combination of independent variables which will correlate as highly as possible with the dependent variable."[44] In Tufte's example, discussed above (in connection with two- variable regression), it was assumed that the loss of seats by the president's party in mid-term American Presidential election was affected by the president's popularity rating. But in fact, the prevailing economic conditions might also affect the fate of the president's party.[45]Similarly, many other factors might be thought of as having significant effect on the party's election fortunes. Thus, the causal model behind multiple regression analysis would assume that there are a number of variables affecting the dependent variable rather than only one (Figure 2.5).

Figure 4.5: Causal Model of a Multiple Regression

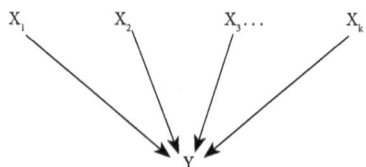

Multiple regression equation, which is an extension of the two-variable regression equation to include all the independent variables, would look like:

$Y = a + b_1X_1 + b_2X_{2+} b_3X_3 \ldots + b_kX_k,$

where a=intercept (i.e., value of Y when X=0).

$X_1X_2X_3 \ldots X_{K=}$ independent variables

Y=dependant variable

$b_1, b_2, b_3 \ldots b_K$ =regression coefficients of corresponding independent variables

The R^2 (in multiple regression it is called the 'coefficient of multiple determination') value will represent the overall explanatory power of all the independent variables (entered into the analysis) taken together in explaining variations in the value of Y (the dependent variable).

The multiple regression equation also yields the regression coefficients of individual independent variables (*partials*). The *partials* indicate the amount of change taking place in Y if there is one unit change in a specific independent variable (whose partial coefficient is being looked at), holding all the other independent variables constant (in a *statistical* sense).

It is necessary to point out one thing at this stage. Although there is always a causal model behind multiple regression analysis, the strength of the causal model depends on theory rather than on the demonstrated statistical relationship between the dependent variable on the one hand and the independent variables on the other. A good causal model will be the one that has a strong theory behind it and, at the same time, is consistent with the data.

As we have said, multiple regression analysis is increasingly gaining in popularity among political scientists. Availability of mechanical computational facilities further enhances its usability. Donald Zagoria's paper,[46] already mentioned, is an example of multiple regression analysis using aggregate Indian data. In the paper, Zagoria was interested in analysing the structural conditions that generate a favourable social base for Communism in India. With that in view, and taking the district as his basic data unit, he took the communist vote in 1957, 1962 and 1967 state legislative assembly elections in 285 districts of India (spread over all the Indian states except Jammu and Kashmir, and Nagaland) as his dependent variable and correlated it with 35 socio-economic and political variables computed from the 1961 census data and election data for all 285 districts.

While analysing the data, Zagoria found that "the most powerful explanatory variables associated with the rural communist vote were essentially two" : 'landlessness' (which was a composite of three elementary variables, namely, agricultural labourers as a percentage of all cultivators, tenants as a percentage of all cultivators, and holding of less than one acre of land), in combination with 'high rural population density'. He found that the 103 districts (out of 285) with high population density (i.e., more than 45 cultivators per 100 acres), landlessness explained 51.2% of the variance in communist vote (the three elementary variables of landlessness mentioned above yielded the following cumulative R^2 values respectively in a step wise regression: .416, .489, .512). Interestingly, he found that, considered separately, neither landlessness nor rural population density was highly correlated with communist vote. For instance, the composite variable landlessness yielded a cumulative $R^2 = .326$ only for all the 285 districts, much lower than the R^2 value for the select 103 high population density districts. This led Zagoria to conclude that "the most important key to the communist vote in countryside lies neither in non-ownership of land nor in dense rural populations but in some dynamic condition produced by the combination of the two."[47]

Stepwise regression is a powerful variation of multiple regression analysis which permits the analyst to choose from a number of independent variables a combination of a few select variables which will provide the best possible prediction. Suppose, one has 20 independent variables, and one wants to construct a prediction equation using only the best five of these 20. One solution is to construct more than 15000 combinations of these variables and to see which set of five is the best. But stepwise regression provides an easier alternative to such cumbersome procedure. In this method, the analyst first chooses the single variable which is the best predictor. The second independent variable is then added to the regression equation, and only that variable is chosen as the second one which provides the best prediction in conjunction with the first variable. One proceeds in this recursive fashion adding variables step by step until one exhausts the desired number of independent variables, or until the prediction equation has yielded the optimum value (i.e., no significant contribution comes from further addition of variables).[48]

Multiple regression, which is a precise and a very useful technique of data analysis, suffers from a serious problem. That is the problem of multicollinearity. The problem of multicollinearity occurs when two or more independent variables are highly intercorrelated. In such a situation it becomes difficult, if not impossible, to estimate the independent effects of each of the intercorrelated independent variables on the dependent variable. The presence of multicollinearity among independent variables implies that each regression coefficient carries not only the effect of that particular independent variable which has been put into the equation, but also of others with which it is correlated. The difficulty thus arises from the inability to disentangle or isolate the effect of a single independent variable from a number of other independent variables.

The near-impossibility of disentangling the independent effects of explanatory variables creates serious problems for analysis. Robert Putnam, while examining the relative importance of economic development and social mobilization as explanatory variables of military intervention in Latin American politics, finds that his explanatory variables show an inter correlation of 0.89.[49] In such a situation it is simply impossible to assess the respective weights of the two independent variables in explaining military intervention.

Dasgupta and Morris Jones face the same problem while explaining the percentage share of communist votes in West Bengal in 1967 elections with the help of a number of socio- economic variables which happen to be intercorrelated. In a stepwise regression, they first introduce literacy (X1) as independent variable and get a coefficient that is both positive and significant and also a reasonably high R^2 value (0.51). They next introduce urbanisation (X2) as an additional variable and find that the literacy coefficient is still positive and significant while the new R^2 value is 0.55 (i.e., again of 0.04). But they also find that "the coefficient for urbanization carries a negative sign, which is obviously wrong." They argue that this surprising result appeared because literacy and urbanization are highly correlated with each other (0.78); the former carries a good deal of the influence of the latter, and when both are introduced in the same equation as explanatory variables, their individual coefficients loose meaning."[50]

After adding three more explanatory variables to the equation, namely, per capita income, percentage of scheduled caste and tribes, and religious minorities, Dasgupta and Morris Jones get an R^2 value of 0.65, i.e., a gain of only 10 percent. But the regression coefficients of these new variables did not appear to be significant. On the other hand, even the coefficient for literacy now became statistically insignificant. Thus, as the authors point out, this is a "serious drawback of multiple regression analysis, that its individual coefficients are not meaningful when the explanatory variables are interrelated."

It may be assumed that the problem will be solved if one focuses on the difference between the two R^2 values as generated in two successive steps in a stepwise regression and takes the difference as the effect of the second variable.

This procedure would look like:

Independent variable		Dependent Variable
X_1	→	Y: Yielding R^2
X_1, X_2	→	Y: Yielding R'^2

$$R'^2 - R^2 = D = \text{Independent effect of } X_2 \text{ on Y.}^{51}$$

But then, the problem is that if X_1 and X_2 are highly inter correlated, their respective weights in explaining variance in Y depend on the order in which they are entered into a regression equation. As Bowles and Levin point out,

"By being related to each other, X_1 and X_2 share a certain amount of explanatory power which is common to both of them. The shared portion of variance which could be accounted for by either X_1 or X_2 will always be attributed to that variable which is entered into the regression first. Accordingly, the explanatory value of the first variable will be overstated and that of the second variable understated."[52]

Interestingly, this observation is corroborated by Zagoria's analysis as well. In his Tables 1 and 2, he reports the R^2 values generated by his three elementary independent variables (which together constitute the composite variable, "landlessness") in a stepwise regression. One finds there that the R^2 value generated by the variable entered into the first step of the regression equation is always much larger than the R^2 values generated by the latter two steps of the equation.[53]

Some of the symptoms of the presence of multicollinearity would be: (1) high correlation among independent variables, (2) a large multiple R^2 with statistically non-significant regression coefficients; (3) a very large R^2 generated by the first independent variable in a stepwise regression; (4) large changes in the values of estimated regression coefficients (sometimes even change of signs) as new variables are entered into the regression.[54]

There is, in fact, no way to solve this problem because, as Tufte rightly points out, "the fault lies basically with the data rather than with the method of analysis."[55] Multicollinearity implies shortage of data, or lack of information. Hence, one solution might lie in collecting additional data. Secondly, some of the variables causing trouble might be dropped from the analysis. For instance, if a bunch of four independent variables are highly correlated, one might take just one of them as representative of all them and enter that variable alone into the analysis leaving the other three out, or alternatively, one might combine the four variables by using the method of 'principal component analysis' and build a composite variable.

FACTOR ANALYSIS

Before we conclude the discussion on multivariate analysis, a brief reference may be made to the technique called factor analysis. Multivariate analysis is sometimes facilitated by the application of this technique. Factor analysis, or one of its variants, the principal component analysis, is essentially used to reduce complex multivariate data to certain manageable categories or factors. Thus, the distinctive quality of factor analysis lies in its 'data-reduction capability'. The technique of factor analysis may be utilized in several ways. First, factor analysis may be used for *exploratory* purposes: that is, for exploring whether any underlying patterns of relationships exist among the variables, and if so, what kind of conceptual and theoretical benefits may be derived from their exploration and analysis. Secondly, it may be used for *testing hypotheses* about the structuring of the variables. Thirdly, it may be used for *constructing composite indices* to be used as new variables in later analysis.[56]

Of these, the first one is the most exciting. But at the same time, it contains the greatest amount of risk. For, oftentimes, theoretical meaningfulness and statistical relationships are not overlapping. That is why some people suggest that the factors should be identified by numbers (e.g., Factor I, Factor II, etc.) rather than by verbal or conceptual labels (e.g., "Differentiation" factor, "Consensus" factor, "Sectionalism" factor etc.,). Even if they are so labelled, they should always be considered purely as 'artifacts' produced by the researcher.

The essential idea behind factor analysis is to see whether sets of intercorrelated variables cluster around a few uncorrelated factors.[57] While the ideal situation will be to find totally uncorrelated (orthogonal) factors, in fact, one may have to work with somewhat correlated (oblique) factors. If one's elementary variables show some degree of positive correlation among themselves, it would be unrealistic to search for absolutely uncorrelated or "orthogonal" factors.

There are two types of factor analysis : when the techniques of factor analysis is applied to examine the clustering of *variables*, it is called R-factor analysis; when, on the other hand, one applies it to examine the clustering of *units* (e.g., individuals, groups, countries), it is called Q- factor analysis.

Many political scientists have applied the technique of factor analysis when they have been faced with data covering either a large number of variables or of cases or units. Two easily readable examples of the application of both R-type and Q-type techniques of factor analysis to aggregate data have been provided by Gregg and Banks.[58] Following David Easton's concern in the *Political System* regarding the essence of political phenomena, Gregg and Banks in their paper, "Dimensions of Political Systems", have raised the question: is it possible to say that there are some basic dimensions that can be said to underlie the complex behaviour within political systems?

To answer the question, they factor analyzed 68 variables, all but 5 of which were derived from Banks and Textor's *A Cross Polity Survey*, and transformed these variables into seven factors "largely independent of each other". These seven factors accounted for 72 per cent of the total variance among 68 variables. Only 7 variables out of 68 failed to have a factor loading higher than +-.50 by at least one factor, and only three variables acquired loading higher than +-.50 by more than one factor. Gregg and Banks used conceptual labels for their factors. Their first factor reflecting "the degree of access to political channels" accounted for 24.6 per cent of the variance. The second factor reflecting "differentiation of political institutions within former colonial dependencies" accounted for 13.5 per cent and the third factor, "the degree of consensus and cooperation among participants" explained 13.2 percent of the variance. The last four factors labelled as "sectionalism," "legitimation," "interest circulation" and "leadership" accounted for 6.4, 5.4, 4.7, and 4.3 percent of variance respectively. These findings, they argued, "indicate that the political phenomena measured by the data do not occur randomly from one polity to the next; they occur in highly associated patterns or dimensions... basic dimensions do underlie the complex behaviour within political systems."

In their second paper, "Grouping Political Systems", Banks and Gregg illustrated the procedure for Q- factor analysis. Here they factor analyzed

115 independent nations on 68 variables and transformed the 115 cases into five factors (i.e., groups of nations). They labelled these five as "Polyarchic", "Elitist", "Centrist", "Personalist" and "Traditional" and found that together, they explain 88.7 percent of the variance.[59]

In this brief discussion on aggregate data and their uses we have merely attempted to scratch the surface. Some of the literature mentioned in the endnotes would constitute valuable "further readings." Use of the aggregate data in the analysis of political problems could be very promising. Almost all the techniques of analysis that can be applied to survey data, can also be applied to aggregate data. Although aggregate data have certain limitations when compared with survey data (especially the one arising out of ecological fallacy), their easy availability should make them more attractive specially to scholars in India (and perhaps in other developing countries as well) who have to do social science research without adequate funds or trained personnel. In the Indian context, aggregate data could perhaps even claim a higher degree of reliability than survey data.

Endnotes

1. This point has been very emphatically made by Dasgupta and Morris-Jones. BiplabDasgupta and W.H. Morris-Jones, *Patterns and Trends in Indian Politics* (Bombay: Allied Publishers Private Ltd.,1975), 2.

2. Ibid. 6.

3. Ralph H. Retzlaff, "The use of Aggregate Data in Comparative Political Analysis" in *Aggregate Data Analysis: Political and Social Indicators in Cross-National Research*, ed. Charles l. Taylor (Paris and the Hague : Mouton and Co., 1968).

4. A good example of such use of census data has been provided by Biplab-Dasgupta and W. H. Morris-Jones in their *Patterns and Trends*.

5. Dasgupta and Morris-Jones, Patterns and Trends; also, Donald S. Zagoria, "The Ecology of Peasant Communism in India," *American Political Science Review* 65, no 1 (March 1971): 144-60.

6. Philippe C. Schmitter's *Interest Conflict and Political Change in Brazil* (Stanford: Stanford University Press, 1971) is a good example of this type.

7. Daniel Lerner's *The Passing of Traditional Society:Modernizing the Middle East* (New York: The Free Press, 1958) is a good example of cross-national longitudinal comparison, while Zagoria's "The Ecology" and Dasgupta and Morris-Jones'*Patterns and Trends* are examples of longitudinal comparison of sub-units in a single system.

8. Ted Gurr and Charles Ruttenberg, *The conditions of Civil Violence : First Tests of a Causal Model* (Princeton University : Centre for International Studies, Research Monograph No.28, April 1967). The authors examine 119 countries for 1961-63 period. An abridged version of the paper has been reprinted in *Macro-Quantitative Analysis*, eds. John V. Gillespie and Betty A. Nesvold (Beverly Hills : Sage Publications, 1970), pp. 187-215.

9. Lerner, *The Passing*, 54-55 (italics mine).

10. Ibid. 63.

11. David Easton, *A Framework for Political Analysis* (N.J. Prentice Hall, 1965), 94 (italics mine). See also chapter 1 above for a discussion of the problem of operationalization.

12. Robert D Putnam, "Toward Explaining Military Intervention in Latin American Politics," *World Politics* 20, no.1(October 1967): 83-110.

13. Ibid, 89-90. The important point to be noted is the essentially subjective basis of the index which would be used for quantitative analysis. This, however, is not a unique problem with Putnam's index; rather it is a general problem for quantification in social science. Putnam has drawn the data for constructing his index from historical and political science literature on Latin America. See Ibid, Appendix I.

14. Karl Deutsch, "*Social Mobilization and Political Development*," *American Political Science Review* 55 no.3 (September 1961): 493-514 and Charles Tilly and Edward Shorter, "The Shape of Strikes in France,1830-1960," *Comparative Studies in Society and History* 13 no. 1 (January 1971): 60-86.

15. Operationalization essentially refers to the problem, first, of finding indicator for measuring a concept or a variable, and second, of reducing data by combining several indicators to a single measure. The process of achieving the latter through indexing, as described in the text, is the most simple procedure for summarizing data. Several other procedures such as scaling, cluster analysis, factor analysis are available for achieving the same end.

16. John V. Gillespie, "An introduction to Macro-Cross-National Research," in *Macro-Quantitative Analysis,* eds. John V, Gillespie and Betty A. Nesvold, 13-27,

17. Putnam,"Toward Explaining," 91.

18. Lerner, *The Passing*,63.

19. Putnam, "Toward Explaining,"93.

20. See n.13 above

21. For the problem of "equivalence," see the chapter on "Survey Research" below.

22. Ecological fallacy is the reverse of "individualistic fallacy." The latter ap-

pears as a problem in the analysis of survey data. See the chapter on "Survey Research" below for a discussion of "individualistic fallacy."

23. *American Sociological Review* 15 no. 3 (June 1950): 351-57.

24. Erwin K. Scheuch, "Cross-National Comparisons using Aggregate Data : Some Substantive and Methodological Problems," in *Comparing Nations : The Use of Quantitative Data in Cross-National Research*, eds. Richard L. Merritt and Stein Rokkan (New Haven : Yale University Press, 1966), 131-67; See also a rather technical discussion on the subject in Adam Przeworski and Henry Teune, *The Logic of Comparative Social Inquiry* (New York : Wiley Interscience, 1970), 57-73; for the computation of the "total" (individual) and "ecological" correlations, see Dasgupta and Morris-Jones, *Patterns and Trends*, 346-50.

25. Dasgupta and Morris-Jones, *Patterns and Trends*, 351.

26. John W. Tukey and M.B. Wilk, "Data Analysis and Statistics : Techniques and Approaches," in *Quantitative Analysis of Social Problems*, ed. Edward R. Tufte (Massachusetts : Addison-Wesley Publishing Co. 1970), 370.

27. Edward R. Tufte, "Improving data analysis in Political Science," in Tufte (ed.), pp.437-49. See also Tufte's *Data Analysis for Politics and Policy* (N.J.: Prentice Hall, 1974).

28. Tufte in Tufte (ed.), *Quantitative Analysis of Social Problems*, 439.

29. Tukey and Wilk, in Tufte (ed.), Ibid. 388.

30. Bruce M. Rusett, Hayword R. Alker, Karl W. Deutsch and Harold D. Lasswell, *World Handbook of Political and Social Indicators* (New Haven : Yale University Press, 1964), 160-61.

31. *American Political Science Review* 70 no. 3 (September 1976): 850-864.

32. For the statistical procedure for calculating the correlation coefficient (r) and for related statistical discussion, see chap. 13 below. Also, see V. O. Key, *A Primer of Statistics for Political Scientists* (New York: Thomas Y. Crowell, 1954), chap. 4.

33. Key, *A Primer*, 121.

34. Key Ibid, 125.

35. Tufte, *Data Analysis*, Chapter 3. H.M. Blalock, *Social Statistics* (New York: McGraw-Hill,1960), chap.17.

36. Blalock, *Social Statistics*,287, 311-17 and 351-54. Tufte, *Data Analysis*, 107.

37. Gurr and Ruttenberg, *The Conditions of Civil Violence*.

38. Blalock, *Social Statistics*, 311-317.

39. Tufte, *Data Analysis*, 101-103.

40. Blalock, *Social Statistics*, 317-19; Sidney Siegel, *Nonparametric Statistics for*

the Behavioural Sciences (Tokyo: McGraw-Hill, 1956), 202-23.

41. I.K. Feierabend and R. L. Feierabend, "Aggressive Behaviour Within Polities, 1948-62: A cross-national study," in Gillespie and Nesvold(eds.), Macro Quantitative,141-166.

42. Gillespie and Nesvold, Macro Quantitative, 152.

43. Cross tabulational analysis is extremely sensitive to the total number of
cases. This is all the more so if a large number of control variables are
used and the mode of analysis is multivariate rather than bivariate. Small
number of cases, in such a situation, would result in lots of empty or near
empty cells, thus taking a lot of weight and significance out of the analysis.
This might pose a special problem for the users of aggregate data as such
data are not collected by the users themselves. In other types of data, such
as survey data, the analyst intending to use multivariate cross tabulation
may begin with a large sample.

44. Norman H. Nie, Dale H. Bent and C. Hadlai Hull, Statistical Package for
the Social Sciences (SPSS) (New York: McGraw-Hill, 1970), 175; Blalock,
Social Statistics chap. 19; Key, A Primer, 147-53.

45. Tufte, Data Analysis, chap.4.

46. Zagoria, "The Ecology."

47. Ibid. 149.

48. Dasgupta and Morris-Jones, Patterns and Trends, 335 .

49. Putnam, "Toward Explaining," 94-95.

50. Dasgupta and Morris-Jones, Patterns and Trends, 332-33.

51. Tufte, Data Analysis, 154-55.

52. Samuel Bowles and Henry Levin, "The Determinants of Scholastic
Achievement – An Appraisal of Some Recent Evidence," Journal of Human
Resources 3(1968): 14-16, cited in Tufte, Data Analysis, 154-55.

53. Zagoria,"The Ecology," 141.

54. Tufte, Data Analysis, 152.

55. Ibid., 150.

56. Ibid.

57. Blalock, Chap. 21.

58. Philip M. Gregg and Arthur S. Banks, "Dimensions of Political Systems:
Factor Analysis of A Cross Polity Survey," American Political Science Re-
view 59, no.3 (September 1965): 555-578; Arthur S. Banks and P.M. Gregg,
"Grouping Political Systems: Q-Factor Analysis of A Cross Polity Survey,"
The American Behavioural Scientist 9, no.3 (November 1965): 3-5.

59. Sidney Verba and Norman H. Nie, Participation in America: Political De-

mocracy and Social Equality(New York: Harper and Row, 1972), chap. 4. Verba and Nie use factor analysis primarily for testing hypotheses about the structuring of the participation variables. They are basically interested in developing a typology of political participation. See also the note on cluster analysis in appendix F, pp. 390-402.

5

Survey Research: Data and Analysis

What is true of *relation* - of form and quantity - is often grossly false in regard to morals, for example. In this latter science it is very usually *un*true that the aggregated parts are equal to the whole.

Edgar Allan Poe

Survey research has developed as probably the most important method of empirical social research. Its importance is recognized not merely in countries with a strong empirical social research tradition such as the United States, but even in countries like India where empirical social research is relatively new. It may not be wrong to say that it is the most "popular" or "fashionable" research method in the social sciences now. Sometimes, while talking to young and aspirant social scientists in India, fresh from the university, one gets the impression that all they mean by research is conducting a survey, although a deeper examination might reveal that even the idea of survey is somewhat fuzzy in their minds. This reminds one of the so-called 'law of the hammer': give a child a hammer, he would feel everything around him needs hammering. Once a tool is there, there is a general tendency to apply it, sometimes without regard to necessity or benefits. This applies to India as well as to the United States, the birth place of survey research.

Be that as it may, the fact remains that there are some solid intellectual reasons for a large group of social scientists' preference for survey research. Survey research, by using standardized procedures, generates standardized and measurable data and thus makes possible not merely quantitative analysis and hypothesis testing, but replication as well. Furthermore, it can penetrate into society, much below the level of the nation-state. In fact, as through survey technique one gathers data about individual behaviour and opinions, one can thoroughly analyze variations *within* nations, or larger societies, by disaggregating such data down to the level of the individual. This, and the fact that by selecting her own sample and gathering her own data the researcher frees herself from the bindings and limitations of data already collected by some governmental or other agencies (as in the case of aggregate data) give survey technique some superiority over aggregate data analysis.[1]

Survey technique has also a high degree of exportability. It can be learnt and adapted easily and this accounts for the fact that it has travelled rather easily from country to country.

Survey research, in its cross-cultural variety, helps us to avoid pseudo comparisons and unfounded generalizations. Rather than developing a comparative politics on the basis of assumptions and untested hypotheses, it allows the researcher to gather data on identical variables across countries and thereby widens the possibility of a true comparative politics or comparative political sociology.

Survey research, then, is indeed a very powerful tool of social science research. It has already made major contribution to the study of political behaviour by greatly expanding our knowledge and understanding about such issues as voting behaviour, the process of political socialization and attitude formation, patterns of political competition etc. But that does not mean that the use of the method of survey research does not pose any problem. This chapter will be devoted to an explication of the survey technique, the strategy of survey analysis and the major problems involved in survey research. We will begin by defining survey research and giving a brief account of its origin.

DEFINITION, ORIGIN AND DEVELOPMENT OF SURVEY RESEARCH

Definition

In standard text books on methodology discussing survey research among other things one rarely finds a definition of this specific research method. While it is true that researchers seldom find it necessary to define the method they primarily work with and normally take a particular set of research techniques for granted, attempts to define the method may very well be worth one's while for such definition can indeed bring out its most characteristic features.

An attempt to define the survey method was done in an unpublished form by one of the foremost contributors to the technique, Herbert Hyman. He defined it as "a large scale systematic inquiry in a natural setting based on the procedure of questioning."[2] Building on this, Frederick Frey himself attempted to provide a definition. According to Frey, survey research is "a method (or the products thereof) for systematically obtaining specific information from a relatively large number of individual sources, ordinarily true questioning."[3] Such a definition clearly implies the essential features of survey technique. It implies, for instance, that survey data are individual data; that is, the basic units of analysis are individuals and their attitudes and behaviour. It further implies that the number of such units should not be small. To make the survey findings of any significance, the number of units should be *appreciably large*. Thirdly, it implies that the method of securing information from the individual units is through intrusive and direct questioning rather than through unobtrusive and indirect observation. And finally, it means that the data collection procedure should be systematic and as explicit as possible so that the possibility of personal bias and technical error in the data gathering process might be reduced.

Origin and development of Survey research

Stein Rokkan, in his contribution to the "trend report" on survey analysis, has very significantly pointed out certain social pre-conditions for survey research. He points out that some minimal level of *centralization and bureaucratization,* some amount of *literacy* in the population - at least enough to make it possible to recruit the required number of personnel for the tasks of questioning and information transmission, and the presence of enough *cross-local mobility* in the population to make it worthwhile to invest in information gathering of this type are the three crucial conditions "for the emergence of any system of standardized questioning and response registration."[4] Quite clearly, these are typical characteristics of modernizing polities and large-scale bureaucratic organizations, characteristics that differentiate them from the early kinship-centred "oral" communities.

Modernizing polities and bureaucratic organizations had to develop formal devices of information gathering, recording and control as usually these were too large and complex bodies to be adequately managed through the traditional methods of oral communication. The administrative questionnaire, the registration form and the census had been developed specifically for the management of the modern large scale territorial bureaucracies. Of these three, the census obviously marked the greatest advance in systematization. It was, as Rokkan says, "essentially an instrument of control and resource planning." The census was the most important step towards the development of sample survey.

While the census provided the method for collecting clear-cut, easily codable data on the entire population, its focus was on aggregated totals. The Sample Survey permitted the collection of information on a broader range of variables with coding in greater detail. At the same time, it was cheaper, could be administered more frequently and it permitted complete disaggregation of information up to the level of the individual.

Rokkan mentions two other important developments in this connection: the election and the referendum. Both of these are means for gathering information about individual choices. But the rules of secrecy prevent the social scientist from making full use of the vast mass of information generated by these methods, for the analyst cannot go beyond the level of the election district or the constituency to the level of the individual voter.

Interestingly, it was the election which directly enhanced the need for sample survey. For, with the extension of suffrage and the introduction of safeguards against bribery and intimidation, elections became very much a matter of chance and hence, it was attempting to develop methods which could predict the outcomes through mock elections or simulation like opinions polls before elections or 'exit polls' post elections.

No wonder, then, that the earliest attempts at predicting electoral outcomes through 'straw votes' etc., were made in the United States, the country where wide suffrage has existed for a long time. This was also facilitated by the American political culture marked by mutual trust, a willingness to communicate with others, wide freedom of political expression as well as by its institutional setup, namely, the Presidential form of government which made election to one single office the most important political event and thereby restricted the problem of popular choice to only a few candidates.

Large-scale survey of political opinion about elections began in 1916 with the *Literary Digest* polls in the United States. These "miniature elections" came to a "sad and dramatic end" in 1936 when Franklin D. Roosevelt collected 60% votes against the Literary Digest's prediction of only 40%.

The vacuum was filled in by new polling organizations set up by George Gallup and Elmo Roper. Their method was based on more scientific and precise sampling of the population, a method which could determine the extent of bias and at the same time, check the representativeness of the sample.

Very soon, a large number of such private organisations developed in the United States, England and France, and by 1950, even in some of the

Third World countries for political opinion surveys as well as for market research.

Government Agencies were also set up in most of these countries from the 1930s onwards for quicker and cheaper data collection. And finally came the academic survey organizations attached to universities. Academic survey made two contributions of fundamental importance to the method of sample survey: one was the introduction of 'multi-item test batteries' which could elicit responses to a wide range of items so that increasing statistical sophistication could be applied to the analysis of data. Secondly, it also introduced 'open-ended' interview as a tool for generating data which allowed the researcher to avoid artificial responses to 'fixed- alternative' questions. Parallel developments in linguistics, sampling and scaling procedures, statistical techniques, computer programming and communications research helped survey researcher to realise the contributions made by academic survey.

TECHNIQUES OF SURVEY RESEARCH (*or how to proceed*)

In this section, we shall try to make explicit the different steps that are involved in different stages of a survey research in a sequential manner and as clearly as possible. We shall conclude with a few words about data analysis, a detailed discussion of which will be undertaken in the following section of this chapter.

The following are the essential steps that a survey researcher must take while conducting a survey.

Specifying the problem

It is common knowledge that survey research is conducted through interviews and that generally, such interviews require a structured questionnaire which is thought out and clearly laid down beforehand. But drafting a questionnaire that will find out what people think about something or how they react to certain problems is not enough. The final report of the survey will not be meaningful at all unless there is an initial understanding of *why* is it important to find these out. In other words, it is important to know the purpose of the research for which it is necessary to know certain attitudes and opinions of the people or some aspects of their behaviour. A researcher can have a statistically perfect cross sectional sample, the best interviewers available and the most precise coding operation. But without a clearly defined purpose, the research will not be successful.

The purpose of the research or the problem must be specific. The problem of method can be naturally solved if the purpose of the research is specified and concretely stated.

Once the problem is known, the researcher must thoroughly orientate herself to the subject by means of a wide reading of the literature in that particular field. Normally, when a student of political science or of any of the social sciences goes to do a research on a problem, she has several years of formal academic training behind her. Generally, it is her background and her acquaintance with literature that lead her to certain research problems. But she may not yet have thorough knowledge of the past research in the specific area to which her own research problem belongs. Hence, she must do that now. If her problem belongs to an area which has its own terminology or vocabulary, she must try to learn them. For instance, if one is interested in studying the medical services, she must develop some acquaintance with medical terminology. That will help her both in drafting a more realistic questionnaire and in establishing easy rapport with the respondents.

Specification of the problem and a through acquaintance with the subject will place the researcher in a position when she can think about the tentative assumptions and hypotheses to be tested, the group of population in which she should be interested, the appropriate size of her sample and the specific methods to be applied. It is only at this stage that the researcher can write up a proposal. If she is looking for financial support, the proposal may be submitted to an appropriate body for considerations.

Drafting the questionnaire

Here the main issue obviously is how to construct a set of questions which will bring out meaningful responses for purposes of the survey. Meaningfulness of responses would depend on three aspects of the question: their content, approach and accuracy.

The *content* of the questions would depend on the purposes of the research concerned. No question is asked for nothing. Each question has a definite purpose: to reveal at least a fraction of the complex of opinions, attitudes or behaviour pattern of the respondents that is relevant for the research at hand. We do not intend to know everything about a person just as we do not wish to preclude anything that is relevant. Questions, then, must be subject relevant and purposive.

Approach is determined by the necessity of the survey. We need to know some of the opinions or attitudes of the people we have decided to interview. But we also know that people want to talk about themselves, about their opinions and attitudes provided they get good listeners. The interviewer must convince the respondent that she really wants to listen. For this, the question must be response evoking but at the same time casual, simple and as "neutral" as possible.

One must *not* begin either by asking personal questions (e.g., how many years of formal schooling did you have? What is your monthly income? etc.,) or questions that appear to test the respondent's information, knowledge or intelligence (e.g., do you know who is the chief minister of this state? or, do you know how many states are members of the United Nations at present? etc.). The interviewer must be careful not to offend or test the respondent by asking questions that may hurt his feelings or self-respect. The best way is to begin with an interesting question, one that most people have opinions on and will talk about freely. Further, the questionnaire must be such that the interview proceeds conversationally. The sequence of topics should be easy and natural and the wording must be as unambiguous as possible. It is necessary for a political or social scientist to remember that she is not interviewing any of her kind (unless she is really doing so) and that the common man may not be acquainted with his technical vocabulary and disciplinary jargons. (Thus, it will be futile as well as ridiculous to phrase questions like: do you think the principle of *ministerial responsibility* still holds in this country? or how would you describe the *power structure* within your factory? For, the italicized expressions may be totally unknown to the respondents even though they may well know the meanings they imply). The general rule to follow is: begin interestingly and proceed conversationally. To do this successfully, one must shelve the 'touchy' questions as well as those aiming at personal information till the end by which time the interviewer has established some rapport with the respondent and the latter has started to feel at ease.

The third vital the aspect of a questionnaire is *accuracy*. The obvious purpose in an interview is to get as accurate information as possible on the subject of research. The questions must be such that they elicit accurate and precise opinion rather than vague generalities.

For that, it is necessary that the questions should mean the same thing to all respondents.[5] Also, the respondent must understand the problem beneath the question before he tries to answer it. Therefore, the questions should be very clearly and simply worded. A vague question will always elicit a vague answer. The wording should be neutral and should avoid all possible bias. If carelessly chosen, words can 'load' a question and such a question cannot get an unbiased answer.

One should also be careful not to 'trap' the respondent into saying something that he does not mean or has never thought about before. To a series of questions on the issue of prohibition a respondent might have said that she/he supports it. Then, if in the next question, we ask him if he consumes alcohol, he is likely to say "no" for fear of being inconsistent or losing face. Again, the respondent may pick up answers to later questions from the phrasing of an earlier question. Thus, if one asks a bureaucrat whether he approves or disapproves of a number of ways (listed by the interviewer) to increase efficiency of his staff, and then, if in a subsequent question he is asked to name certain ways of increasing efficiency, he is likely to give back the information that the interviewer gave him in the earlier question. It may be difficult to completely rule out such unintended 'interviewer effect' on the responses. But an awareness of this may help and by carefully changing the sequence of questions such effects may be reduced considerably.

Pretesting

After the drafting of the questionnaire, the pre-test becomes the next most important step in survey research. Through the pre-test, it is possible to find out how appropriate our questionnaire has been in terms of its content, approach and accuracy.

Specifically, the pre-test has a number of functions. A pre-test, first of all, reveals the significant and insignificant aspects of the problem being studied. If, to a question or a set of questions, predominant number of the respondents answer in the same way, such a question hardly represents a problem and there is very often little to analyse. The fact(s) revealed by such question(s) is normally treated as a general characteristic of the group.

Pre-test also helps to discover new aspects of the problem being studied, aspects which were not anticipated at the planning stage of the research. That is why a pre-test questionnaire should have a large number of open ended questions, especially on issues (facts or attitudes) about which the researcher has a rather vague idea.

By implication, the pre-test also helps to 'close' open-ended questions. For instance, if after analysing responses to a set of open ended questions, the researcher can form a clear-cut and precise idea about the content of the answers, he can possibly split those answers into a few mutually exclusive alternatives, and transform his questions into 'fixed-alternative' ones in the final version of the questionnaire.

Fourthly, the pre-test helps to check whether the questions are really clear and easily understandable to the respondents and also, whether they are of a conversational sort. Sometimes, we draft questions on paper which are apparently very clear, concise and simple. But when we take them to the respondents and ask them, we observe an implicit lack of clarity. Words and phrases which to us are naturally understandable and have only singular meanings come to assume entirely different meanings in the ears of others. These problems can be taken care of through pretesting.

Finally, the pre-test also reveals the weaknesses, if any, in the original plans about the ways through which the interview was supposed to be conducted. For instance, it might reveal that the mail questionnaire method is unworkable, although originally maximum reliance might have been placed on it. Similarly, the pre-test helps perfecting the organization of the survey. A pre-test, being 'the final study in miniature', gives an idea about how much time the interview would take, what sort of materials would be required, how much money would be involved etc. Thus, it can be of great help for budgeting the study.

The Sample

If the attitudes, opinions and behaviour that we are interested in involve a large number of people, it may not always be possible to include all of them in our study. This entire group to which our study refers is called the 'universe'. It is essential to know this universe. The universe depends on the goal of the study. For instance, if we are interested in the voting behaviour of the people of West Bengal, our universe would include the entire adult population of West Bengal. On the other hand, if we are interested to know the voting pattern of the college-educated men in West Bengal, only the college educated males in the state of West Bengal would constitute our universe. Sampling techniques are necessary, for normally the cost of collecting information prohibits us from studying the entire universe. Through sampling procedures we select a smaller set of units for the data gathering operation. The basic requirement of any sampling procedure is to make sure that the sample is selected in such a way that the statements about this smaller (the sample) set is applicable, with known margins of error, to the total set (the universe).

While this correspondence between the sample and the universe is critical for any research based on survey, examples from medical research bring this out most vividly.

Once we have drafted and pretested our questionnaire, we need to be clear about the sample. There are different sampling procedures.

Since there is no way in which one can be certain that his sample truly represents the universe, one has to rely on probability. The 'probability' or 'random' sampling tries to eliminate the fallibilities of human judgement. Random selection means 'scientifically leaving it to chance'. This method of sampling presumes that we will select a good enough number of individuals or areas, as the case maybe, which reasonably would reflect most of the shades of opinion or patterns in the universe. It is also possible, in this method, to find out the amount of error (hence, the limit within which we can trust our findings) through the use of mathematical formulas based on the laws of chance.

"Probability" or "random" sampling may be of two types: simple random samples and stratified random samples.

SIMPLE RANDOM SAMPLES

Simple random sampling is like a lottery. Suppose we need to select ten individuals for our sample from a population of ninety. The name of each of the ninety maybe written in a slip of paper and all the ninety slips maybe thoroughly mixed in a bin. Then ten slips, representing our sample population of ten individuals, would have to be drawn successively from the bin, with a thorough reshuffling before each draw.

Social scientists normally do not obtain simple random samples through this lottery method. Mechanical procedures, like table of random numbers, are generally used. In such a case, list of all individuals in the population is prepared and a unique two-digit number is assigned to each individual. Then, by using a table of random numbers,[6] as many individuals as are necessary for the sample are selected.

In the case of sampling dwelling units (households) from a large area, one may adopt the technique of simple random sampling (or 'area sampling'). Under this procedure, the entire area is first divided into a number of smaller areas ('primary areas'). Then, from the total number of such "primary areas" a sample is drawn through the use of random number tables in the same way as described above. If the sampled 'primary areas' are still too big and unmanageable, they are further sub-divided into smaller spatial units and then a sample is drawn from these 'smaller units'. A list of all households within these sampled smaller units is then prepared, and from this list of total number of households, again, a sample is drawn. These sampled households or dwelling units are then approached by the interviewers.

Sometimes, interviewing any member from each of these households will be good enough. But sometimes, depending on the nature of the study, a particular member of the household (e.g., the head of the family) may have to be interviewed and no substitutions can be allowed. In such cases, the interviewer's task would become more demanding and several call-backs may be necessary.

Another variation of 'area sampling' is known as 'block sampling'. In this procedure, the 'primary areas' and the 'smaller units' are selected and sampled in the same way as mentioned above. But then, for each 'smaller unit', some general quotas of age, gender, employment status, education etc., are decided. The interviewer is required to fulfil the general quotas. For instance, in one 'smaller unit', the interviewer may be required to interview five women. For fulfilling this requirement, he need not stick to a number of pre-determined households. If no woman is available for interview in the first household he approaches, he can go to a second one and try his luck. Thus, no call-backs would usually be necessary in this 'block sampling' method.

STRATIFIED RANDOM SAMPLES

Stratified random sampling would be necessary when one is interested in a specific group, type or class of people. Such samples are selected by dividing the population into strata and then, selecting a random sample from each stratum. Thus, while studying labour unions, researcher may be interested in having a sample both of union leaders and of ordinary union members. The first thing the researcher has to do in such a case is to construct two separate lists, one of the union leaders and the other of the ordinary members. Then, by applying the procedures of random sampling, she can select her leader sample as well as the sample for ordinary members.

Collecting the data (or the interview)

There are several important ways of gathering data. In survey research the most frequently used one is personal or face-to-face interview. There can be three types of interview from the point of view of the respondents: structured, unstructured and structured open-ended.

A *structured* interview is of the sort of a check-list in which all questions are "closed" with fixed-alternative answers (generally these answers are precoded). The respondent is asked to select that particular alternative which best represents his opinion.

In the case of an *unstructured* interview, the respondent is asked to talk about any aspect of the subject. That is to say, the interviewer has certain broad questions which she pursues in her interview with the respondent without confronting him with a set of 'possible' answers as well. Thus, the question in an unstructured interview remains 'open-ended'. In this type of interview, an answer to a particular question may instantly generate father questions in the mind of the interviewer and the latter is free to ask them as follow-up questions.

Thirdly, the interview may be *structured open-ended*. That is the questionnaire may have some structured questions with fixed alternative answers and some open-ended questions. Open-ended ones would obviously be in areas where the interviewer fears that answers could be imprecise or could have too great a range of variance or the interviewer herself is not clear about the possible alternatives. The answer to such open-ended questions may, however, be "closed" later while analyzing the data by grouping them into certain precise alternatives and coding them at that stage.

From the point of view of the interviewer also, interview may be of three types: standardized, semi-standardized and unstandardized.

In the *standardized* interview, the interviewer strictly follows the specific order and wording of the questionnaire. She is not free to adapt her questions to the specific situation, or to change the order of topics or to ask follow-up questions as she feels necessary. In the *unstandardized* interview, the interviewer can develop each situation freely in whatever ways she thinks most appropriate for the purpose of the study. The *semi-standardized* interview, as the name suggests, stands in-between the former two: it permits the interviewer to freely probe a situation even though she always has a number of specific questions to start with.

It is probable, then, that the unstandardized and the semi-standardized interviews are also likely to be unstructured and/or structured open-ended sort of interviews while the standardized interview is likely to be structured interview. But such correspondence may not necessarily be true. For in areas like psychology, for instance, it is conceivable that a questionnaire may contain only open-ended questions, but the order of the questions or their wording may not be tampered with. Such a case will be an example of an unstructured yet standardized interview. What particular mode of interview will be adopted will largely depend on the purpose of research.

In fact, as Goode and Hatt point out, the structured interview was developed as "a solution to the problem of standardization."[7] Unless the questions are standardized, responses cannot be truly comparable. Thus, one of the basic canons of survey research is equivalence of stimuli. In the unstructured interview, it is difficult to maintain such equivalence. But, on the other hand, standardization is gained only at the cost of depth. Many interesting "leads" given by the respondents in answer to a particular question would have to be ignored in order to stick to the interview schedule. Unstandardized interview can be resorted to when the researcher is herself the interviewer or only a small group of interviewers are used who are highly skilled as well as well-versed with the purpose and substantive concerns of the study. It requires a very high level of interview quality. As Goode and Hatt rightly say, "with greater discretion, the interviewer must have great competence."[8]

One of the major problems for the survey researcher is to be aware of the possibility that the interviewer through his behaviour might bias the data. For our purposes here we may label it as the 'interviewer effect'.[9]The interviewer while taking the interview is engaged in an interaction process with the respondent. In his dress, manners, speech and in his general behaviour he will have to be 'acceptable' to the respondent. This is very crucial, for on this will depend whether or not he will be granted an interview or whether he will get only an evasive interview. But when we talk about the 'interviewer effect' we have something more in mind.

Generally, in order to encourage the respondent to respond, the interviewer has to do something. A totally non-committal attitude on the part of the interviewer may not help. But on the other hand, if he is overly demonstrative, if he too often shows approval or disapproval of the opinions and attitudes shown by respondents, he is more likely to 'dictate'his respondents to certain responses, and thus, bias the data. Perhaps the only way to avoid it is that the interviewer should maintain a permissive atmosphere and at the same time avoid making evaluative gestures and comments.

Organizing the data (or Code Building and Coding)

Once the data have been collected, one has to be concerned with the problem of organizing them so that the ideas, attitudes, opinions or information available in the data can be presented in a relatively concise form, through brief tables and summaries. Here, code building and coding are the essential steps prior to data analysis. These are also indispensable operations should the data be mechanically processed, as is the almost universal practice now.

Nowadays one cannot think about analyzing data, especially large volume of quantitative data, without the help of statistical packages developed specifically for this purpose. Some of the widely used packages are: Microsoft Access, Microsoft Excel, Statistical Package for the Social Sciences (SPSS), R (Language and environment for statistical computing and graphics) and Stata (syllabic abbreviation of the words 'statistics' and 'data'). Most of these packages require the data to be precisely and unambiguously coded. Coding procedure permits one to transfer the information from a questionnaire several pages long and in the linguistic mode to a numerical mode. Earlier it was done through the key-punch machines and punch- cards. Currently, with the onset and increasing popularization of appropriate software packages it is largely done with the help of personal computers (PCs). Once the data are coded it can be entered into the statistical packages to get finer and more detailed description of the data along with the sophisticated statistical analysis of its underlying nature and trends. For the present purpose we will discuss the coding procedure adopted in SPSS.

Questions, as we have already seen, can be of fixed -alternative answer type, or of the open- ended type. Both can be coded, although only the former can be pre-coded. Since in the fixed-alternative answer questions the surveyor already knows the number of possible answers to a question, he can put a number against each of the possible answers even before the question is in fact asked. For instance,

In your factory there are four unions; which one are you a member of? –

The INTUC... 1
The AITUC... 2
The CITUC... 3
The UTUC... 4
Not a member of any Union... 5

A question like this can be pre-coded, for the nature of the question limits the kind of answers we can get. After asking this question, the interviewer will put a circle on 1,2,3,4 or 5 depending on the answer. By doing so, the interviewer himself is doing the coding.

If the answer is "AITUC" in the above example, 2 is circled. Let us illustrate the coding procedure of this response in SPSS. Opening the SPSS in a computer one will find the window named SPSS data editor. This has two views: the Data view and the Variable view. To code the different values of a variable one need to open the variable view which looks like the following. It can be seen that there are 10 columns in the data editor. The first of these is 'Name'.

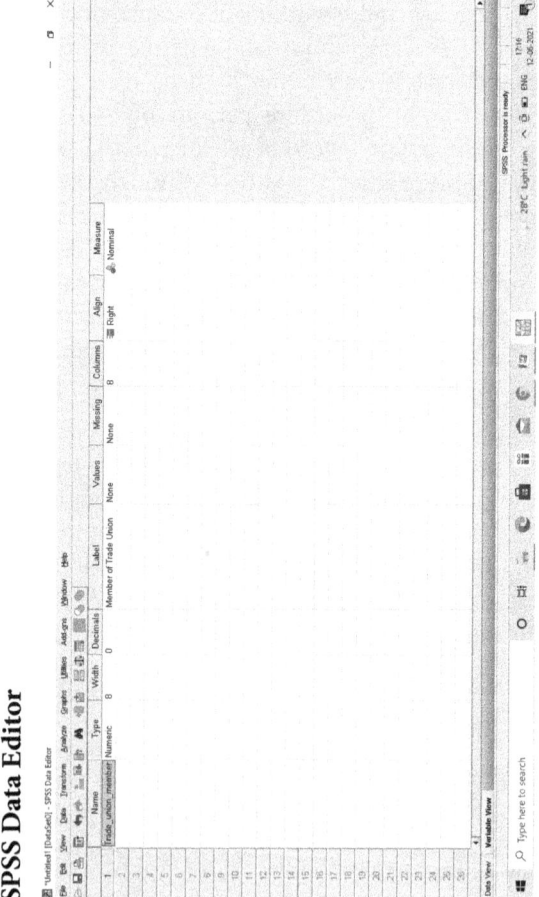

Here we have to give a suitable name to the variables we are trying to measure. In our case let it be trade_union_member. The next column is 'Type' of the variable. SPSS allows several options like the following:

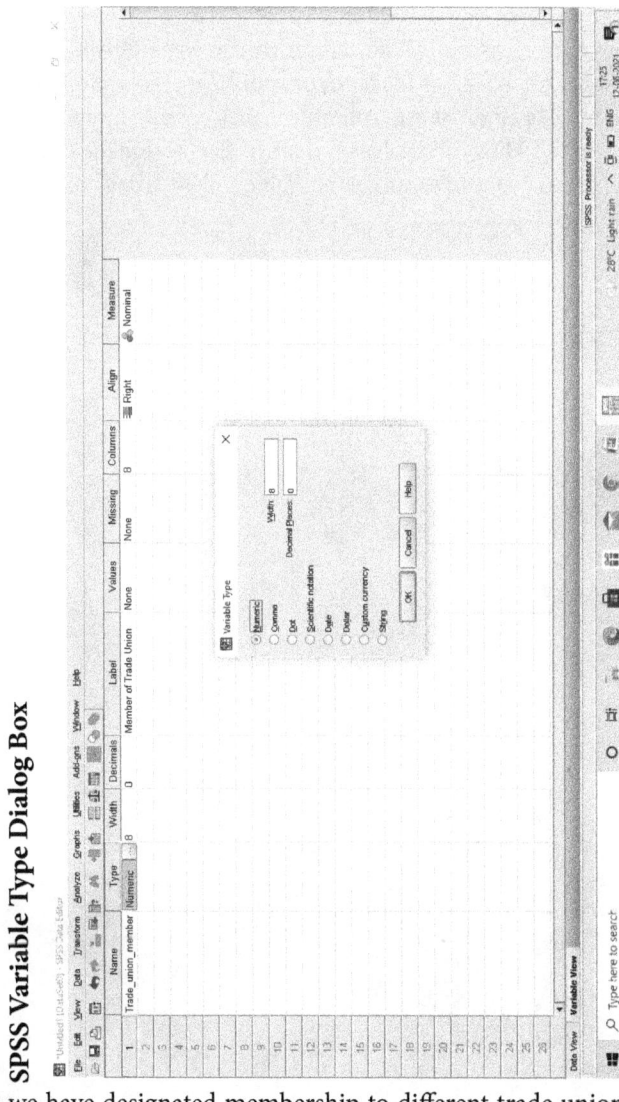

SPSS Variable Type Dialog Box

As we have designated membership to different trade unions in terms of numbers, so, here we would select 'Numeric' as the type of the variable. The width of the variable column along with its decimal places can be specified here in this dialog box, or else these can be specified in the next two columns, as well. The width is concerned with the number of digits the value of any variable can take and decimal places fixes the point after the decimal the value of any variable can assume.

The next column in the data editor is 'Label'. Here we can write details about the variable we are measuring. For example we can write 'Of which of the four unions are you a member?' as the label, or simply, 'member of trade union' as is shown in the data editor above. After the 'Label' column there is the 'Values' column. Basically coding of variables is done here. Clicking the cell just below the column named 'Values', we can get the 'Value Labels' dialog box as following:

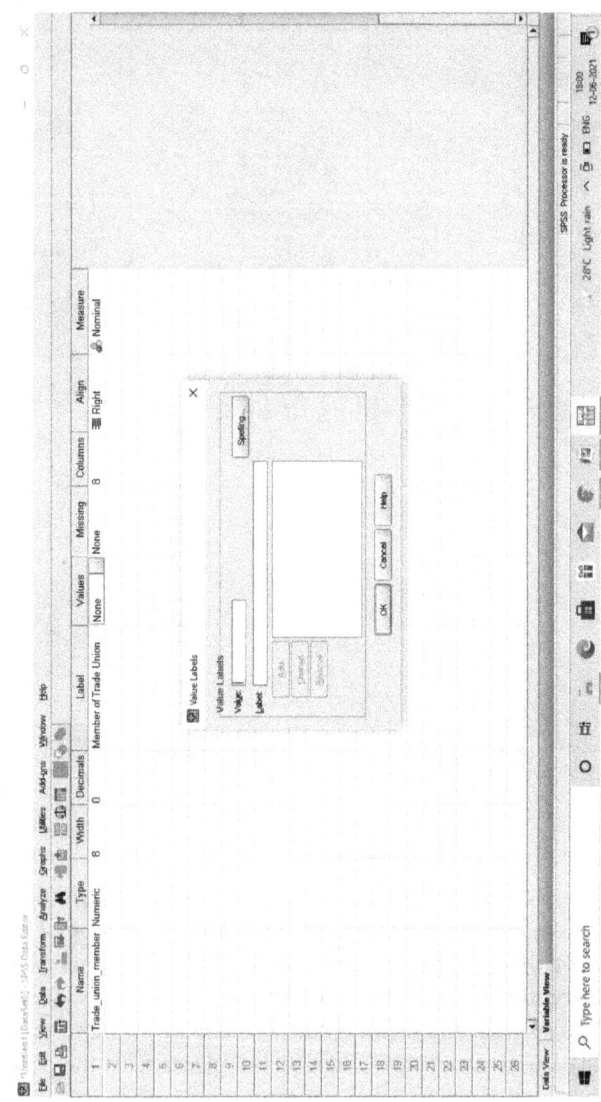

SPSS Value Labels Dialog Box

Here in the empty box titled 'Value' we need to enter the numerical codes of the variables. For our present case, we will enter 1 here and write INTUC in the empty box just below it, marked as 'Label'. Once we do this, the 'Add' button below will be activated. Clicking on 'Add' we will enter the code of 'INTUC'. Similarly, we will enter the codes of other trade unions, viz. 'AITUC', 'CITUC', 'UTUC' and 'Not a member of any Union', respectively. Hence, the dialog box will look like the following:

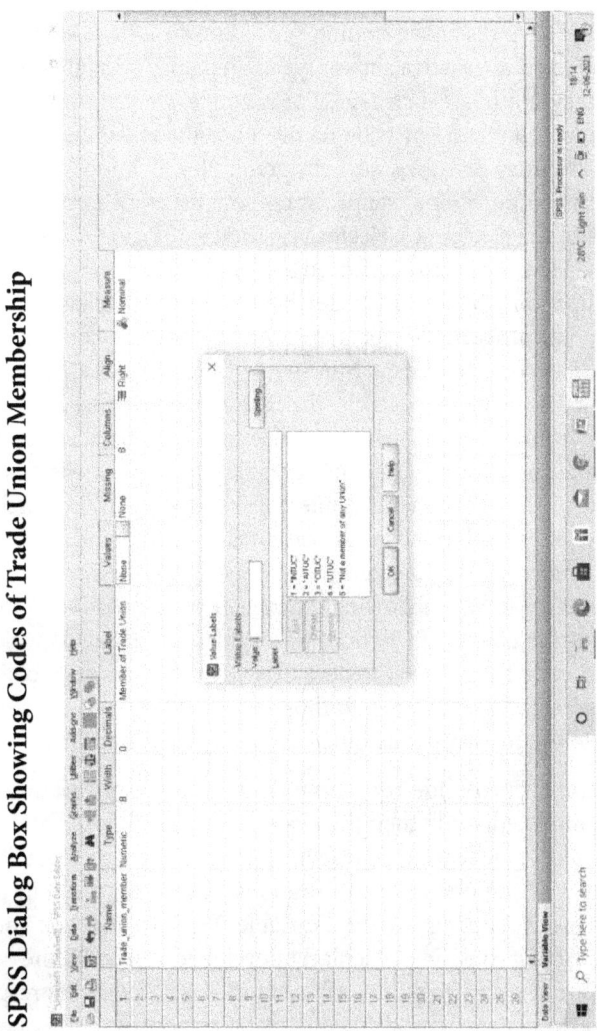

SPSS Dialog Box Showing Codes of Trade Union Membership

Clicking the 'OK' button now will enter the codes of all the trade union membership into the package.

While entering the data of the variable 'trade_union_member' (as we have named it), one just needs to enter the code '2' for the respondent who is a member of AITUC in the data view of the SPSS Data Editor. SPSS will decode this code '2' to denote membership of AITUC. Similarly, to enter the data of other respondents who are members of the other trade unions, we need to enter their respective codes.

So far we have discussed coding procedure in SPSS for the responses which are of fixed-alternative answer type. There may be situations when the responses may not be of such type. For example, we can mention here the case of respondents' caste or tribe name. Since the respondents can belong to numerous castes or tribes, so here pre-coding is impossible. The same can happen to occupational status, important issues determining electoral preferences of the electorates, electorates' choice of Prime Minister or Chief Minister etc. Here the researchers need to prepare exhaustive list of the castes, tribes, occupations, important issues having electoral relevance, probable names of political leaders or personalities who can be considered by the electorates to become the Prime Minister or Chief Minister. After preparing the lists as exhaustively as possible, the researchers need to assign codes to each of the enlisted castes, tribes, occupations etc. Needless to mention, preparation of such lists requires considerable effort and intellectual exercise on the part of the researchers. While collecting data the researchers/field investigators only need to record the caste/tribe name of the respondents on the questionnaire. During data entry the codes of the respective caste/tribe should be entered in SPSS following the same process described above. Here, if any caste/tribe appears in significant number, the name of which is not there in the code list, the researchers may list it and assign a code to that also. The researchers can also club those caste and tribes, with very minor representation in the sample, as 'others' and assign a code to it.

In the case of open-ended questions, coding has to wait till the interview is almost completed. Only then the answers can be analyzed and the basic ideas extracted. Codes can be built against these basic ideas. IN SPSS to enter the responses of the open-ended questions, which are often in linguistic mode, we specify 'String' in the 'Variable Type' dialog box mentioned above. The 'String' type is particularly developed to record the responses which are not in numeric mode. After entering data of all the respondents the SPSS package can show all the linguistic responses of the open-ended questions systematically. A critical scrutiny of all the responses may reveal the basic ideas to be extracted from these. Depending on the core themes of the responses codes can be assigned to those. This will help in reorganizing the responses of the open ended questions for better comprehension and analysis. Obviously, this is of much help to make sense of qualitative data.

Sometimes, some answers are just irrelevant to the question. Such answers should be grouped together and labelled "irrelevant." They need not be coded, as they cannot be included in tabulation.

Building codes after extracting the basic ideas from an open- ended questionnaire may appear to be very easy. But in fact, it is not so. The problem of semantics is not easy to solve. People use words and phrases which are popular and in most cases, they mean quite different things by the same words. It requires considerable amount of interviewing skill to be able to "tie the person down" so that he is forced to abandon popular phrases and find exact words to express his thinking. It is the interviewer's task to get each respondent express his ideas as clearly and relevantly as possible, and to clarify the un-codeable ideas. For that, the interviewer has to be very clear in his own mind about the purpose of the question concerned.

SURVEY DATA ANALYSIS

As it has already been emphasized, the data in survey research are collected with reference to some problems, the idea being that the information gathered would enable one to analyze the problems and enhance one's understanding of them. One may pre-formulate certain hypothetical relationships among different aspects of the major problem(in the form of factors or variables), and with the data in front, one may start testing the validity of these pre-formulated hypotheses. Alternatively, one may also start with the data and enter into post-factum analysis. The strengths and weaknesses of the latter procedure have already been discussed in an earlier chapter.[10] Let us now look at the procedure of hypothesis testing.

Hypothesis Testing

We have already noted that there may be descriptive as well as relational hypotheses. While the former are important, as social scientists, we are more interested in the latter and we use the former in order to build up the latter. We may, for instance, have a descriptive hypothesis, such as: 'the majority of Indian citizens would reject a nuclear weapons programme'. Hypothetically, the responses in the data could look like:

Supporting a N- weapons program 45%

Rejecting   "   "   50%

Undecided   "   "   2%

Don't know   "   "   3%

Such information is good as far as it goes. But in fact, it raises more questions than it satisfies. For instance, we would like to know which respondents are the supporters and who constitute the opposition. Does the *social class* of the respondents have anything to do to with their attitude towards nuclear weapons program? Or, does the *level of education* of the respondents have any relationship with their attitude to a nuclear weapons program? What about their general *political orientation* (for instance, ideological position of the respondents)? Does the *regional distribution* of the respondents have any bearing on their attitude to the question? In other words, we are interested in identifying certain important variables and in exploring their relationship to the attitude of the respondents to a nuclear weapons program. That is to say, we are interested in testing relational hypotheses.

Scientific knowledge advances through what Carl G. Hempel calls " the method of hypothesis;" that is,"by inventing hypotheses as tentative answers to a problem under study, and then subjecting these to empirical test."[11] This method is also of great importance in survey research. Yet, narrowly conceived, hypothesis testing would be self-defeating. For, after all, hypotheses are guesses that are invented to account for observed facts and even extensive testing with "positive" results would not establish a hypothesis conclusively, but provide only more or less strong *support* for it.[12]

For example, one may hypothesize that women are less capable of intellectual activities than men, and the data on gender distribution of intellectual elite in a particularcountry might support the hypothesis. Yet the underlying theory, i.e., that gender determines the capability for intellectual activity might be wrong, for the relative success of men may not be due to their gender, but rather to certain other advantages and opportunities that are more open to them than to women. Thus, one may be right for the wrong reasons.

This also points out that hypothesized relationships maybe spurious or may be due to the other unchecked extraneous or intervening variables.

Therefore, while testing a hypothesis, a researcher should keep his eyes and ears open, and carefully check whether the relationship that he finds is indeed true.

There are ways in which one can check against "spurious" relations or against the unobtrusive operation of extraneous or intervening variables. For instance, one can introduce a third variable as a control variable in a bivariate relationship. Sometimes, relationship between two variables may be entirely a function of a third variable which is independent(casual) to both and when the latter is controlled, the relationship between the former two vanishes altogether. Thus, to give a very simple example, one finds a strong correlation between increase in shoe size and clarity of speech among the children, but the " spuriousness" of such a relationship becomes clear when one introduces age as the third variable: It is increase in age that is responsible for both increasing shoes size and clarity of speech rather than shoe size causing clarity of speech or vice versa.

There are other cases where the introduction of a third variable may strengthen, weaken or modify the original bivariate relationship. While examining the relationship between caste and political participation, Verba et al.,[13] find that the 'Harijans' in India participate in *voting activity* as much as the caste Hindus while their participation in *campaign activity* is less than that of the caste Hindus. By introducing the place of residence(urban/ rural) as a third(or control) variable, they find that in terms of voting, the two groups participate equally in urban as well as in rural areas(thus, the original relationship is strengthened). In terms of campaign activity, on the other hand, 'Harijans' are less participants only in urban areas, but not in the rural areas. Therefore, the original relationship between caste and campaign participation is clearly *modified* when one controls for place of residence.

Durkheim, in his famous study *Suicide*, for instance, finds that the unmarried persons are more likely to commit suicide than married persons. But when he brings in age as a third variable, he finds that the relationship is reversed for certain age groups (e.g., in cases of early marriage). By adding more variables(e.g., gender, region etc.,) he further enriches his analysis.[14]

A researcher may enrich the analysis of a two variable relationship by further examining the possibility of the presence of component and intervening variables as well as of conjoint influences. Let us take a hypothetical example. One may examine the relationship between social class and voting and find that the upper class people vote more regularly than lower class people. But social class is a broad category and it may be conceptualized as consisting of education, income, type of occupation, ownership of property etc. Therefore, one may be interested in further examining the relationship between each of the components of social class and voting (Table 3.1).

Table 5.1 (a): (Hypothetical) a. Social class and Voting (in Percentages)

Frequency of Voting	Social Class	
	Upper	Lower
Regular	80	22
Occasional	20	78
Total %	100	100

Table 5.1 (b): Social class and Voting, Controlling on Education (in Percentages)

Frequency of Voting	Social Class			
	UPPER CLASS		LOWER CLASS	
	High Education	Low Education	High Education	Low Education
Regular	90	25	78	5
Occasional	10	75	22	95
Total %	100	100	100	100

The first half of the above Table (5.1.a) examine the relationship between social class and frequency of voting and shows that the two are strongly related positively. That is to say, upper class people are markedly more regular voters than the lower class people.

In the second half of the Table (5.1.b), one of the components of social class, namely, education, has been extracted and separately examined in relation to voting frequency. Very interestingly, the second half shows that voting frequency depends not so much on social class per se, as on education. People with higher education are likely to vote more frequently than those with low education irrespective the social class to which they belong.

Similarly, one may examine whether the relationship between social class and voting is mediated by some intervening variables. For instance, lower class people may vote less frequently not so much because they belong to the lower class as because they lack a sense of political involvement. That is, if the sense of political involvement as a variable is controlled, the relationship between social class and voting would weaken. In other words, one may find that original relationship between social class and voting is strengthened when it is mediated by a sense of political involvement (Figure 3.2).

Figure 5.1: Elaboration of relationships among variables

Social Class   →   Voting

Social Class   →   Sense of Political Involvement   →   Voting

Finally, examining the conjoint as well as separate influences of a set of independent variables on the dependent variable is also important. For instance, one may find that social class influences voting; but similarly, place of residence (urban/ rural) may also affect voting behaviour. One would be interested to know whether place of residence has any effect on voting *independent* of social class, and if it has, which one of these two independent variables is more important in influencing voting behaviour. That is, one may explore both their joint effect as well as their separate or independent effects on voting. There are statistical methods, such as crosstabulation and partial correlation, through which independent effects of each of the independent variables may be checked.[15]

Verba et al., for instance, in their study of *Caste, Race and Politics*, examine the independent effect of caste on different modes of political participation, controlling on the effect of socio-economic status (the authors' version of social class) variable. They find that when the socio-economic status variable is controlled, the effect of caste is reduced to nearly zero. That is to say, whatever effect caste appears to have on political participation(and it is not very great to start with as the simple correlations presented in the book show), it is due more to the fact that a lower socio-economic status is associated with 'Harijan' caste than to the caste factor alone.[16]

The purpose of the preceding paragraphs is to suggest that the analysis of survey data does not merely consist of testing pre-formulated hypothetical relationships between two variables. It is just the beginning, not the end of analysis. While analyzing the data, the analyst should think of all possible causal chains. Indeed, it is impossible to test the complete casual sequence. But by specifying and introducing more and more variables--extraneous, component, intervening or antecedent, it is possible to make analysis more complete, exact and insightful.

It is not merely important that the analyst should weave around the hypothetical relationship, but he should also have a willingness to move towards unexpected paths and unhypothesized observations. The idea is that he should be ready to follow all the explicit and implicit 'leads' that are available in the data with the mind of an explorer. History of science is full of examples where the scientist 'invented' things which he was never looking for or only faintly expecting to find. The alertness of mind that helps one to see the unforeseen or to find the unexpected is an essential quality of a true investigator.

PROBLEMS AND LIMITATIONS OF SURVEY RESEARCH

Survey research is a major technique for comparative analysis. Since it is based on individual data, it permits an enormous range of comparison. One can compare the responses between individuals, between groups of individuals, and in cases of cross- national samples, between nations. While it is, thus, a very powerful tool for comparison of attitudes, opinions and behaviour of individuals and collectivities, it suffers from several problems some of which are unique to it alone, and some of which it shares with other methods of data gathering and analysis. The major problems that survey research suffers from can be grouped under validity and equivalence, keeping in mind, however, that these two are related.

Validational Problems

Problem of validity may arise due to faulty indicators, mistaken measurements and fallacious inference. While some or all of these may affect other types of data analysis as well (e.g., aggregate data analysis), in the case survey research the specific forms they take may be different.

Indicator and measurement problems are very closely related. We need to have precise indicators in order to make quantitative measurements. If indicators are faulty, they cannot give us proper measurements.

An indicator may be faulty due to technical or conceptual reasons. An indicator is technically faulty if it is not properly constructed. For instance, a temperature chart would not indicate body temperature properly if the thermometer was defective or if it was wrongly administered. Similarly, if one is taking an exceptional year rather than a normal one as base year for indicating trends in industrial production or labour unrest the indicator would be faulty. Again, if one is taking the yearly number of riots as an indicator of the degree of domestic political instability for several countries, one must be sure that such riot statistics have an identical coverage in all the countries concerned. Otherwise, comparison would be invalid due to technically faulty indicator.

But an indicator may be faulty for conceptual reasons as well. An indicator is conceptually faulty when it does not measure the thing that we want it to measure. One would be wrong, for instance, to use temperature chart as an indicator for one's state of health (although it is a valid indicator of one's body temperature). Similarly, it would be wrong to use the rate of industrial production as an indicator for employer-employee relationship in industry. That is, an indicator may not measure what we wish it to measure if the items on which it is based are not relevant for the theoretical concept we want to examine.

This brings us to the question of mistaken measurement. Survey research is particularly prone to this because it uses questions (in some language) to elicit responses. The same word may convey different things to different people. The problem is compounded when one is dealing with more than one linguistic area. Thus, a question like 'what would you do if you were the governor of a state where the government had lost majority in the legislative assembly?' may measure a respondent's empathy or his ability to place himself in a different political role (i.e., the role of state governor) or it may measure his political knowledge about the powers of a governor. Neither the interviewer nor the analyst would know which one was she in fact getting.

There are two other situations where mistaken measurements may take place. We will call these as arising out of 'interviewer effect' and 'community norm effect'. The 'interviewer effect', what Frederick Frey calls "courtesy bias," takes place when the respondent, while considering and answering questions, is moved by a paramount concern "to please the interviewer or the authors or sponsors of the survey. He repeatedly says what he thinks his interrogators will want to hear". Thus, rather than opening his mind, he starts to agree with whatever assertion is made to him.

'Community norm effect' takes place when the respondent tries to make all his opinions consistent with whatever is socially desirable. This refers to a very general tendency. For instance, if taking dowry in marriage is socially condemned, there will be a general tendency among respondents to conceal his real opinion or behaviour with respect to this issue and to try to conform to community norms in his responses. In both of these situations, valid measurement would be impossible.

Finally, validational problems also arise out of fallacious inference. The fallacious inference that survey analysis suffers from has been called 'individualistic fallacy' (which is the opposite of 'ecological fallacy' discussed in the preceding chapter on aggregate data analysis). Survey data are individual data; but sometimes these are used for macro-political statements. 'Individualistic fallacy' takes place when statements are made about *social* units on the basis of measurements based on *individuals*. Stated simply, the problem is that what is true for individuals may not hold for collectivities of which they are members. For example, if a cross-section population sample shows that the individual respondents reject personalism in administration, one cannot validly infer that such a phenomenon is absent from the society to which these individuals belong. There are societal variables, such as social /political structure and culture, which mediate between individual responses and collective behaviour. As Hayward R. Alker noted, for instance, that "to assume that competition among individuals will universally produce industrious citizens does not mean, *necessarily*, that the nation with the most competitors will be the most industrious."[17]

The Problem of Equivalence

Whatever is the specific method followed, the problem of equivalence is a fundamental problem in any comparative social research. The procedures of survey research (especially when it is cross-cultural or cross-national) help bring out this particular problem in sharper focus. The question that arises is whether we are comparing equivalent things (or things with *known* non-equivalence) or not. Can, for instance, voting in one country be compared with voting in another country? Or, can we compare frequencies of organizational membership from one country to another? Or, again, can we compare people's attitude towards workers' strikes across countries, or even across sub-cultures within a single country? In other words, are we comparing things that are comparable; or even more intricate, do we know what are comparable and what are non-comparable phenomena?

The problem of equivalence is,in a sense, a phenomenological problem. For not only is equivalence difficult or nearly impossible to achieve; in all probability, we would not know even if it is really achieved. This has led some to believe that we make too much of the notion of equivalence. Federick Frey argues, and indeed rightly, that equivalence is not absolutely vital:" What is absolutely vital is for the researcher to understand the full meaning of his operations, not for those operations to be totally equivalent even in a functional sense in all countries.".[18] While Frey admits that equivalent data "permit more sophisticated and powerful inference than non-equivalent data," yet he believes that non-equivalent data may also be of interest and importance provided the researcher understands the nature of non-equivalence. But as we have already said, understanding the nature of non-equivalence in specific data sets is no less tricky than establishing equivalence.

In survey research, we compare the responses of the respondents to survey questions. But the responses of different respondents can be compared only if the stimuli to which they are exposed are identical. For, the aim of the researcher is to observe how different respondents react to equivalent stimuli. The idea is to compare and analyse the differences in the responses of the sample population holding the stimuli constant so that one can take it for granted that such differences as are observable are not due to difference in stimulus. Hence, the problem of equivalence lies in establishing that the stimuli had been constant or equivalent. There are three problems that make such equivalence difficult to achieve. The first one involves interview- setting, the second one the problem of language, and the third one the problem of concepts.

INTERVIEW-SETTING

By interview-setting we refer to the general area of interviewer-respondent relations. In order to make the responses comparable, the interview-setting must be the same in each case. But when interviews take place under different cultural and social-structural conditions, non-comparable elements enter almost inevitably into the interview-setting. Societies differ in terms of stratification and patterns of cleavage. Sometimes, regions within the same society may also have such differences. Interviews are affected by the relative social statuses and positions of the interviewer and the respondent. It is now well known, for instance, that Black respondents in the United States reply quite differently to Black and White interviewers.

Similar information regarding interviewer-respondent relationships, when they belong to different castes, for instance, is not so readily available in India. But it is likely that a high caste interviewer may not do very well in interviewing Dalit respondents especially in areas of caste-Hindu/Dalit tension. Similarly, a Hindu interviewer is likely to have certain difficulties in interviewing a Muslim respondent which she need not face while interviewing a Hindu respondent. This is especially so if one wants to have opinion on touchy subjects. Similarly, the dress, manners or even styles of pronunciation of the interviewer may make her quite acceptable to some respondents but unacceptable to others not sharing her ways. That is to say, identical dress, manners and pronunciation styles may cause different kinds of stimulation for different respondents. Thus, racial, caste, religious or class characteristics of a society create lines across which uninhibited social intercourse might be difficult. It may not be possible for someone engaged in cross-cultural or cross-national survey(or even in surveys of cross-sections of a single population) to match each respondent with an interviewer of the same social characteristics.[19] The risk of taking non-equivalent data as equivalent would thus be present.

Similarly, some respondents may have greater inter-personal trust(as either his personal or social characteristic) than others. The way one responds to interview questions or the range of questions(especially in personal and private matters) that one may entertain would certainly be affected by such characteristics as these and therefore, would inject quite undetected non- equivalence in the data. The differences in the degree of one's familiarity with survey and interviews would create similar non-equivalence in data(this, for instance, would make U.S. and Indian data sets quite uncomparable; for it may be expected that an American respondent who is generally used to being interviewed personally or over the telephone would behave quite differently in relation to an interviewer than his Indian counterpart).[20]

Thus, the interview setting may itself become an independent variable capable of explaining a lot of variation in the response sets.

LANGUAGE PROBLEM

The language problem again is generally present in all comparative cross-cultural research, whether or not the specific method of field survey is being followed.[21]But it is in survey research that the problem becomes most manifest and unavoidable. A survey researcher, whenever she is interested in cross-cultural comparison(involving a single multilingual nation or a number of nations speaking different languages) has to deal with more than one linguistic group.A Bengali political scientist who is interested, for instance, in interviewing students or local political or trade union leaders or workers in Bengal, Maharashtra and Tamil Nadu, would have to solve the problem of translating his questionnaire from the original language. Similarly, when an American or an Indian scholar is studying the voting behaviour in these two countries through the method of sample survey, he faces the same problem. Two questions are involved here: one, whether a literal translation of the questionnaire is possible, and second, whether the literal translation is adequately meaningful.

Sometimes, a literal translation of a word is just not possible. An emotional state which is well recognized in one culture may not have a linguistic equivalent in another culture.Take a Bengali word like *abhiman* or *udas* for example. They refer to states of mind whose meanings are clearly understandable to any Bengali, but they do not have their exact English equivalents. One has to use longer and more involved expressions as a way out, but they may not always solve the problem.

As a solution to the general problem of finding out the 'more exact' linguistic equivalent, different techniques of translation are suggested. One of these is a 'blind translation' from the original to the new language followed by a blind retranslation back into the original language. That is, if the original questionnaire was in Bengali, then it would be necessary, according to this procedure, to translate it into, say, Tamil by someone who was not connected with the framing of the Bengali original (hence 'blind'), and then, to retranslate it by someone else again back into Bengali. One can now compare the original Bengali questionnaire with the retranslated Bengali questionnaire and see whether, after translation, the meanings conveyed by the original questionnaire are *retained* within safe limits (Figure 3.3).

Figure 5.2: procedure for "blind transaction"

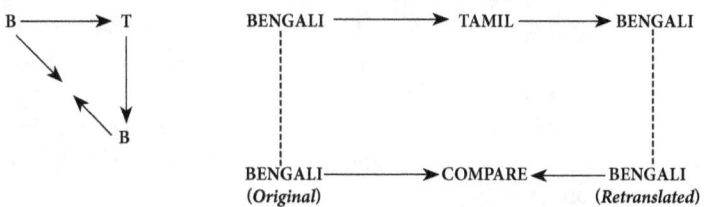

But, as Verba reports, research conducted by the Institute of Political Studies at Stanford and the Survey Research centre at Berkeley, California in collaboration with University groups in four other Nations has found this method to be rather inefficient.[22] It has been found that this technique of 'translation-and-blind-retranslation' does not tell us much about the equivalence of the final products.

As a more effective alternative, a 'parallel blind' translation technique is sometimes recommended. In this procedure, two independent sets of blind' translations are made from the original into the new language and then, these two versions of the translation compared (Figure 3.4).

Figure 5.3: "Parallel-blind" translation.

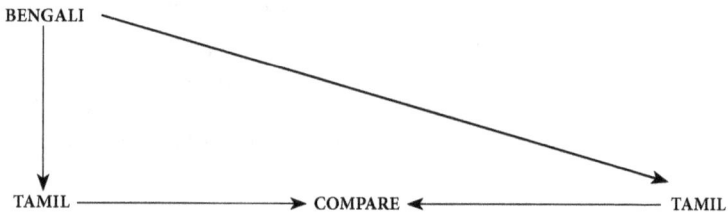

To enhance reliability, Verb suggests, this parallel "blind translation technique" should be " coupled with intensive discussion of the meanings of the items" in the questionnaire among the several translators and the drafters of the original items.

This last point suggested by Verba is very important. For literal translations, carefully done and compared, are relatively less important in establishing equivalence. The more important problem is to know whether the translation is equivalent to the original in terms of *meaning*. A single word may have multiple meanings in one culture but not in another. In one culture a word may have a very specific meaning; in another, it may have very wide connotations. Take the word 'religion' for example. In English, it refers to a relatively specific phenomenon. When translated in an Indian language, it becomes *dharma*. Now, the word *dharma* has multiple meanings in Indian culture. It indeed means religion, as in English. But it also means "role" (e.g., *dharma* of a Brahmin as opposed to that of a Kshatrya), and nature (*dharma* of a snake, for instance). In Japanese language, Frederick Frey points out, "translation of 'light' (*Karu-i*) refers only to weight and not too illumination, as in English."[23]

The problem of meaning can, perhaps, best be solved by identifying clearly the dimension of a phenomenon that one is interested to explore. Once one can identify the dimension, the problem would be reduced to one of finding out the most effective indicators of that dimension in different cultures. Thus, if one is interested in understanding and exploring political participation in two different cultures, one simply has to find out most effective indicators in respective cultures. In one culture (or society), voting maybe the most effective way of political participation; in another, it may be party membership. One can then treat voting and party membership (which are apparently non-equivalent) as equivalent indicators (in the sense of being the most important indicators) for political participation in these two different cultures and compare political participation in these two countries in terms of voting and party membership respectively.

It is in this sense that Frederick Frey is right when he says that "equivalence is not identity."[24] Equivalence is never total, and because it is never total, one must specify the dimension for which equivalence is sought. Thus, one may look at the major social classes in one society, the major racial groups in another and the major religious affiliations in a third society if she is interested in a *single* dimension of these three societies, namely, the major patterns of social cleavage. That is to say, one can look at apparently *non-equivalent indicators* in different societies or culture-areas in order to explore an *equivalent dimension* of life in these societies and culture areas. In other words, the most adequate and effective indicators of the same dimension in two different societies may assume quite different forms.

The survey questions used by Verba, Ahmed and Bhatt in their comparative study of India and the United States illustrate the point somewhat. The authors were interested in exploring a number of identical dimensions of life of the major deprived groups in these two societies, namely, the Blacks in the United States and the 'Harijans' in India. But they have used *two differentsets* of questionnaire with some identical and some non-identical questions for their American and Indian samples.[25] For example, in order to explore the level of 'Exposure to Mass Media of Communications', they asked their American respondents the following questions:

"(1) How often do you to watch the news broadcast on television - everyday, a few hours a week, about once a week or never?

(2) How often do you read newspaper-- everyday, a few times a week, about once a week, or never?

(3) How often do you read magazines - everyday, a few times a week, about once a week, or never?"

For the same item (i.e., 'Exposure to Mass Media of Communications') they ask their Indian respondents somewhat different questions:

"(1) Do you ever read the newspaper or have someone read it out to you - about how often?

(2) Do you ever go to the cinema?

(3) Do you ever listen to the radio?"

Thus, in order to generate equivalent, and hence, comparable response, the authors found it necessary to administer non-equivalent stimuli. Indeed, the book itself is a substantiation of the point that one may justifiably-- sometimes even indispensably, compare non-identical phenomena(e.g., ethnic group vs. caste group) for the understanding of an identical problem (e.g., political behaviour of deprived groups) in two different societies. This essentially leads us to the third aspect of the equivalence problem, namely, the problem of conceptualization.

PROBLEM OF CONCEPTUALIZATION

The most tricky aspect of the problem of equivalence is "conceptual" or "meaning' equivalence. It refers to the fact that the same act performed by different individuals may assume different meanings in different cultures or societies. That is, while the act we look at or examine or measure is nominally the same, but it differs in terms of its implied concepts or meanings or motives from culture to culture or person to person. Quite obviously, unless the concepts, meanings or motives behind the act are clearly understood, any comparative analysis across societies and cultures would be misdirected.

Let us take the act of voting which has been very frequently studied by the students of comparative political behaviour as an example. Individuals may vote for quite different reasons. For some, it may be an exercise of the right of citizenship; for others, it is a means for throwing somebody out of power whom they do not like, or for bringing some individuals or a party in power that they like; for still others, it may be just a ritual, or simply an act of conformity to law or maybe, even a way of earning some money. Thus, it would be quite naive to compare the rates of voting in the U.K. with those in Belarus; or to treat as equal the act of voting by a young educated urban Indian having a strong sense of political efficacy and clear ideas about party preference and by an old, illiterate, thoroughly apolitical housewife from a remote village. The act of voting is the same, any yet it is different. It is different because it means quite different things for the two different systems or for the two different individuals mentioned above.

The problem that we are here up against is, as Przeworski and Teune suggest, one of inference, and not of direct observation.[26] In the above example, for instance, both the politically aware urban youth and the senior village housewife perform an identical act (voting). And their ballots, if validly cast, will have equal value in deciding the fate of the candidates concerned. Yet, they are not equivalent if we want to *infer* from the act of voting the voter's sense of political efficacy. While the act is the same, in one case it does represent the voter's sense of efficacy, in the other it does not.

Almond and Verba in their *Civic Culture* study found that a much higher proportion of Americans watch news broadcast on television than Mexicans. It does indicate a real difference in the behaviour of Americans and Mexicans, and as an observation, it is indeed of interest and importance. Yet, Verba himself raised the question, can one validly infer from this that Americans are more interested in politics and in governmental affairs than Mexicans?[27] Surely not, simply on the basis of this indicator. Contextual differences are very important here. While the Americans may have greater access to television, the Mexicans might be using alternative channels for gathering political information.

Such differences in meaning affect not merely explicit acts but also attitudes and opinions, and even social implications of individual attributes such as age, education, income or occupation. Thus, for instance, while it is easier to measure the level of education of the respondents belonging to two different cultures or societies in terms of the number of years of formal education, it is immensely more difficult to know what education means in these two cultures or societies. In one, an individual with higher education may not mean much; in another, a university degree may be enough to place one among the intellectual elite. Similarly with occupation. Two lathe operators in two societies may be said to belong to the same occupation: yet the occupation itself may have entirely different prestige ratings in these two societies. As for age, for instance, somebody at the age of 25 in one society maybe citizen with an independent family of his own, while in another he may still be looked upon as a dependent child. Such non-equivalence in the meanings of apparently similar phenomena in different societies make it very difficult to directly compare them across societies or even across sub-cultures within a single society.

CONCLUSIONS : SOME SOLUTIONS TO THE PROBLEMS OF SURVEY RESEARCH

The above discussion on the problems of survey research makes one thing clear; survey data being based on the individuals, there may be a tendency on the part of the researcher to abstract these individuals from their contexts and to consider their responses as independent of time and place. Also, there may be an assumption that the respondents differ among themselves only quantitatively, not qualitatively. These create much less problem when the researcher is dealing with respondents belonging to her own (researcher's) class or culture. It is likely that a number of qualitative factors would be naturally controlled in such a case. But as one leaves one's own society or class and moves toward the study of other societies or toward comparative cross-cultural research, increasing complications would be created by such naive assumptions regarding qualitative equivalence or non-relevance of the context.

The way to solve this problem, then, is to add the contextual dimension to the individual data generated by survey research. Whether one is dealing with different societies and political systems or with different classes or groups with subcultures of their own in one single society, one must try to develop deep familiarity with the substantive aspects of these societies, systems or subcultures, and to try to capture as much of their uniquenesses as possible. An excellent example of how, without such familiarity, one maybe misled in interpreting one's data was provided by the *Time* magazine's international survey of 1948.[28] The questionnaire for that study contained an item asking people to choose the two most important civil rights from a list of five such rights. The analysts found to their surprise that while in Sweden 52 per cent selected the right to free speech and writing and 75 per cent selected the right to vote in free and fair elections to choose who shall govern, in Switzerland, 55 per cent chose "free speech" and only 41 per cent selected the "right to vote". The question was, how is it that in Switzerland, which happens to be one of the most well founded democracies of the world, "the right to vote" was considered so unimportant?

The answer to the riddle lay in the fact that the Swiss system was based on frequent use of the referendum. Thus, when the Swiss people could themselves decide every important issue through the instruments of direct democracy, they did not mind much about who were elected into office. Without this piece of information about the substantive aspects of the Swiss political system, the data were simply unintelligible. It is, therefore, clear that a thorough knowledge of the institutions, practices and mores of a society or culture is an essential precondition for meaningful behavioural research.

This also points out another limitation of Survey research. One would be better off with some other method than survey when one is dealing with a completely new area of investigation. Survey technique is most productive when considerable amount of impressionistic information is already available through other methods (namely, case study, participant observation, etc.,).

Through an intelligent interrogation strategy, however, one can generate contextual information even in survey research. In one's questionnaire, for example, one can ask questions about actions or behaviour and at the same time she may have some further questions on the subjective meanings of those very actions or behaviour to her respondents. That is to say, one can use the questionnaire to gather both objective and subjective information. Thus, one can ask her respondent about his income or occupation and at the same time, let him say what it means to belong to that income group or occupational category in his society. Similarly, rather than simply measuring the frequency of voting activity, the analyst can also try to know her respondent's understanding of the meaning of elections in his own country.

Such an interrogative strategy would also be most helpful in assessing the relative usefulness and comparability of indicators across cultures. If, in the *Time* magazine international survey mentioned above, a question about the meaning of vote had been put to the Swiss respondents, their answer would have clearly demonstrated that, as an indicator of the degree of attachment to democratic institutions, voting in a general election in a country with instruments of direct democracy is not comparable with voting in other countries without such elements of direct democracy. For, in countries of the former type(for example, Switzerland,) other and more important channels of political participation and control than voting are available, and hence, in such situations the rate of voting can at best only partially indicate the degree of democratic commitment.

The questions in a survey questionnaire should also be very precise, and they should have, as we have noted already, a single frame of reference. Validational problems would arise not merely out of the possibility that the respondents might use multiple frames of reference but also out of unstable or inconsistent and superficial answers by the respondents. To avoid such instability and superficiality of responses, questions must be so framed that they can *involve* the respondents. That is to say, the questions must be posed in an idiom known to the respondents. The use of different indicators for measuring a single variable in different contexts is also helpful, and sometimes necessary, for avoiding the danger of misleading comparisons.[29]

Survey analysis may further be strengthened if survey data are supplemented by aggregate data. The latter may be generated by sampling social units in addition to individuals, as well as by analyzing such ecological data as census data, voting data or such other relevant information as are available in public documents etc. This will help the analyst to place her individual data in macro social context.

In cross cultural studies, 'second order' comparisons would also help one to preserve the contextual characteristics. That is, rather than comparing *variables* directly across systems or cultures, one can compare the inter-variable *relationships* in different systems. Thus, for instance, instead of comparing voting frequencies in India and the U.S. directly, one may compare the relationship between education and voting or social class and voting in these two countries. That is to say, through such comparison one would want to say if there is a relationship between these two variables in both countries and if the direction of relationship or the degree of relationship is similar or different in them. In such second-order comparisons, one is not so much interested in comparing the absolute frequencies of the variables as in finding out the patterns or trends in the relationships among variables across systems or cultures. Such a strategy would focus on system interference rather than suppressing or concealing it, and thereby would help one to further investigate the contextual or system characteristics.

There is an obvious anomaly in what we have suggested above as solutions to the problems of survey research. The suggestions, if followed, would make the analyst even more conscious of the elements of non-equivalence when his problem was to establish equivalence. But this is unavoidable as there is no simple answer to the problems of survey research (and as we have already indicated, most of these problems affect other research methods as well). Survey research has the logical potentiality of making and validating a-historical generalizations, provided empirical conditions permit that. But that is never achievable by ignoring the historical background and the specificity of the units studied. Survey studies can contribute to the understanding of behaviour, whether of political systems or of individuals, only when they are grounded firmly in the patterns of historical development. Thus, the goal need not be, as Przeworsky and Teune point out, "to eliminate system interference altogether, but rather to reduce it to tolerable proportions."

Before we conclude, we will make two other points regarding this method of research. We have already mentioned that survey research, at least in its currently used version, is of American origin. Also, American scholars have most frequently used this method especially in the first few decades following the Second World War. There were certain reasons for this. Survey research involved interviewing individuals, most of the times, hundreds, if not thousands of them across a country or in more than one country. For efficient processing and accurate analysis of data, survey research necessitated some amount of technological competence as well as easy availability of machines such as computers. Survey research permits a more thorough cross-system comparison than aggregate data analysis and at the same time, it is less time-consuming than cross-system comparison through participant observation. Hence, it attracted American political scientists of the post World War II generation, a large section of whom were experimenting with the new "science" of comparative politics. Further, survey research, whether done in one's own country or(and all the more so) across cultures, poses great problems of organization and finance.[30]These were some of the issues which prevented even the European political scientists, not to speak of scholars from the Thirld World, from adopting survey research as a major method of study in those early years. Much of these early advantages the American political scientists enjoyed in the past decades have now disappeared with the coming of the internet and the Personal Computer (PC). The Statistical Package for Social Sciences (SPSS) and many other similar packages and their wide popularity and use all over the world have removed the early disadvantages of lack of technological competence and cost. These have made survey research a vastly used method for various types of investigation, academic or otherwise, all over the world.It may still be remembered that using methods other than survey need not necessarily result in poor political science, as survey method by itself does not guarantee easier attainment of scientific truth. This, however, is no counsel to reject survey research as unusable.

Secondly, for successful use of the survey technique in gathering information, it is necessary to develop a favourable popular attitude to survey. That indeed depends on how frequently surveys (for whatever purposes) are conducted in a society. While that is important, a conscious effort on the part of the survey organizations and interviewers would also help reduce 'interviewer-shyness' of the respondents. One way to do it, for instance, is to emphasize that opinion surveys are not intelligence operations. Besides, a society in which the leaders of the government and other important organizations frequently lend themselves to be publicly interviewed and cross-questioned, is more likely to have an atmosphere favourable to opinion surveys.

Endnotes

1. The word "superiority" has to be read with caution: it strictly means methodological superiority. It does not mean at all that micro-level research, conducted through survey method, is in any sense superior to macro level research.

2. Federick W. Frey, "Cross-Cultural Survey Research in Political Science," in *The Methodology of Comparative Research,* eds. Robert T. Holt and John E. Turner (New York: The Free Press, 1970), p. 385(n.1).

3. Ibid. 175-76.

4. Stein Rokkan, "Cross-National Survey Research: historical, analytical and substantive contexts," in *Comparative Survey Analysis* by Stein Rokkan, Sidney Verba, Jean Viet and ElinaAlmasy (The Hague : Mouton, 1969), 5ff.

5. This touches on the very serious problem of equivalence in survey research. It has been discussed in detail below. See also the chapter on "Participant Observation" below.

6. Tables of random numbers are usually appended to standard statistics textbooks.

7. William J. Goode and Paul K. Hatt, "The Interview: A Data Collection Technique," in *The Conduct of Political Enquiry,* eds. Louis D. Hays and Ronald D. Hedland (New Jersey: Prentice-Hall, 1970), 116-117.

8. Ibid. 117.

9. It should be noted, however, that the 'interviewer effect' in this sense is somewhat different from the 'observer effect' discussed in the chapter on "Participant Observation" below. While the 'observer effect' results from the *act* of observation itself, the 'interviewer effect' in the present sense could arise out of the *manner* in which the interviewer would conduct himself during the course of the interview.

10. See chapter 1 above.

11. Carl G. Hempel, *Philosophy of Natural Science* (New Jersey: Prentice Hall,1966), 17.

12. Ibid. 18.

13. Sidney Verba, Bashiruddin Ahmed and Anil Bhatt, *Caste, Race and Politics: A Comparative Study of India and the United States* (Beverly Hills: Sage Publications, 1971), 121 and 155.

14. Durkheim, *Suicide* (New York: The Free Press [paper], 1951), 175-79.

15. As the use of some of these statistical techniques have already been discussed in the preceding chapter we omit further discussion here. For more on the issue see Part 2 of this volume.

16. Verba, Ahmed and Bhatt, 163.

17. H.R. Alker, *Mathematics and Politics* (New York : The Macmillan Co.,1965), 103, cited in R.L. Merritt, *Systematic Approaches to Comparative Politics* (Chicago: Rand McNally and Co., 1970), 14; E.K. Scheuch, "The Cross-Cultural Sample Surveys: Problems of Comparability," in *Comparative Research Across Cultures and Nations*, ed. Stein Rokkan (Paris: Mouton, 1968).

18. Frey, "Cross Cultural Survey," 232-33.

19. For certain reasons it may not always be desirable to do so either. For instance, sometimes we talk more freely about different aspects of our personal and social lives to someone who is an outsider to our culture than to one who belongs to it.

20. Lloyd I. Rudolph and Susanne H. Rudolph, "Surveys in India: field experience in Madras," *Public Opinion Quarterly* 22, no. 3 (Fall, 1958): 235-44. The authors believe that certain problems which are amenable to survey method in the West can be better handled by the methods of the anthropologists in developing countries. The paper, though somewhat dated, is still relevant.

21. Thus, the anthropologist John Beattie while writing on the Bunyoro recognizes this very problem and says that "many of the categories of Nyoro kinship terminology have no exact equivalent in English," and that translating them in English kinship terms "may lead to serious misunderstanding." John Beattie, *Bunyoro: an African Kingdom* (New York: Holt, Rinehart and

Winston, 1960), pp. 7-8; cited in Verba, "The Uses of Survey Research," in *Comparative Survey Analysis*, eds. Stein Rokkan et al., 65.

22. Verba, "The Uses of Survey Research," in Rokkan et al., *Comparative Survey*, 63.

23. Frey, "Cross-Cultural Survey," 269.

24. Ibid., 240.

25. Verba, Ahmed and Bhatt, *Caste, Race and Politics*, Appexdix B and C, 252-264.

26. Adam Przeworski and Henry Teune, *The Logic of Comparative Social Inquiry* (New York: Wiley-Interscience, 1970), 118.

27. Verba, "The Use of Survey Research," in Rokkan et al., 72.

28. Frey, "Cross-Cultural Survey," 257.

29. Przeworski and Tune have argued that system-specific indicators can very well be used for establishing equivalence and that such a strategy of using system-specific indicators is certainly better than using "common" (in appearance) but non-identical (in meaning) indicators. Thus, membership of political party in Poland may be equivalent to voting in election in Chile in indicating the degree of political participation in these two systems. See Przeworski and Teune, 117-130. For further discussion on the problem, Stefan Nowak, "The Strategy of Cross-National Survey Research for the Development of Social Theory," in *Cross-National Comparative Research--Theory and Practice*, eds. Alexander Szalai and Riccardo Petrella in collaboration with Stein Rokkan and Erwin K. Scheuh (International Social Science Council, Oxford: Pergamon Press 1977), 34-44.

30. Anil Bhatt, "Some Social and Human Aspects of Conducting Large Scale Field Surveys in India," *Political Science Review* (Jaipur) 17, no. 1-2 (January-June 1978): 30-48. The author has lucidly discussed some inter-personal and social problems in organizing surveys in India.

6

Content Analysis

Analyzing texts in the contexts of their uses distinguishes content
analysis from other methods of inquiry.

Klaus Krippendorff

Content analysis (CA) as a technique of **textual analysis** seeks to make
sense of the content of often unstructured and voluminous messages,
and to determine the **meaning and intent of a body of texts**. As Robert
Weber[1] defines it, CA is a research method which has both **quantitative
and qualitative** versions uses a certain set of procedures for making valid
inferences from the text. Thus following this technique one could try to
assess how much salience economic issues received during the run-up to an
election by scanning the campaign speeches of major party leaders. There
are of course several other methods that explore textual material such as
conversational, rhetorical or discourse analysis to uncover its meanings and
motives. But CA is distinct in the sense that, to quote Klaus Krippendorff[2],
it aims at making **replicable and valid inferences** from texts with reference
to their contexts (which would be elucidated later). In other words, CA is
marked by its inferential nature:

➢ It seeks to answer specific research questions

➢ by making inferences from certain premises and sample,

➢ following a set of guidelines and procedural rules

➢ derived from existing theories or previous research.

Moreover, this process duly takes into account the **contexts** within
which the messages are embedded for the same phrase or picture might
attain radically different significance in different settings.

Content Analysis as Summarizing: CA involves **data reduction**, i.e.
converting a huge volume of textual data into a more manageable and
informative set of statements. As Kimberley Neuendorf[3] observes, CA is
essentially a summarizing activity which condenses the details pertaining
to a message set. This needs to be differentiated from micro-documenting
exercises often undertaken, for example, by historians that produce very

precise, fully explicated analyses based on textual resources. Thus, a historical account of Bengal during the famine of 1943 could very well be culled out by consulting the contents of Bengali newspapers/fictions. But these works have a tendency to collect detailed data about varied and huge number of units of analysis instead of concentrating on a few select units and summarize the *characteristics* of the messages, and hence cannot be considered as examples of CA. Again, some scholars often pick up quotations, excerpts or examples from various texts to support certain observations or conclusions. Others cite various statistical measures related to farmers' suicide or campaign spending from official or unofficial reports to illustrate their own research findings without modifying these figures in any appreciable manner. CA is different from these popular modes of analysis in that **it seeks to develop *numerical* measures from extensive non-numerical records**. Thus, one can survey the coverage of Covid-related news in the print media to find out which of different theories offered to explain the intensity of the virus attack has found maximum exposure in the media. It would call on the researcher to convert hundreds of newspaper features and articles into a handful of numerical indicators related to the relative popularity of various theoretical positions. Janet Johnson and Richard Joslyn[4] (following Kenneth Bailey) describe the **steps involved** in this transformation of a verbal non-quantitative material into quantitative data thus: A researcher

> ➤ 'first constructs a set of mutually exclusive and exhaustive categories that can be used to analyze documents,

> ➤ and then records the frequency with which each of these categories is observed in the document studied'. (These procedures would be elaborated afterwards.)

Content Analysis - Qualitative and Quantitative: What Johnson and Joslyn depict of course is **quantitative** content analysis which emerged (during and) after the Second World War as an objective and systematic method to analyze the fast expanding volume of communication, emanating from both governmental as well as non-governmental sources. But as already noted, CA has its **qualitative** variant as well, and Sandra Halperin and Oliver Heath[5] differentiate between the two thus:

> ➤ Quantitative CA seeks to make inferences about the meaning and intent of a text

> ➤ through an analysis of usage and frequency of words and images and

the pattern they create within the text

➤ Qualitative CA is more interpretative in nature, and

➤ is more sensitive to the context in which texts are produced.

Indeed, the difference between the two largely flows from a distinction often made between **manifest and latent contents** of a text.

➤ Manifest content resides in the surface of a communication, easily observable, which quantitative content analysts count in terms of 'how many' or 'how often'.

➤ Latent content or the 'meaning' of a text which underlies the manifest content can be accessed by 'reading between the lines, the task of qualitative content analysis.

Thus, a study of the manifest images of women in advertisement might take into account the different roles they are portrayed in – cooking, washing, feeding children or taking care of husband. But viewed in a wider context, all this might be viewed as instances of a single concept or idea – gender stereotyping – the latent or hidden meaning underlying these messages. Though both manifest and latent contents require interpretation, these interpretations vary in terms of depth and level of abstraction.

Points to remember:

• CA is a mode of textual analysis which seeks to derive valid inferences regarding the meaning and intent of a body of text.

• CA aims at data condensation by converting texts into numerical terms.

• CA has both quantitative and qualitative forms which roughly overlap with studies of manifest and latent contents of texts respectively.

This chapter begins by outlining a brief history of the evolution of the method taking into account the shift from its quantitative to a qualitative phase, and the possibilities opened up by computer-based analysis. Next, it elucidates the definition and nature of the technique combining the features of qualitative and quantitative perspectives. Thirdly, it describes in detail the steps and sequences involved in the application of CA duly illustrated by summary of two research works that followed. A separate section has been dedicated to summarily capture the differences between quantitative and qualitative CA. The chapter concludes with an assessment of CA as a research tool.

History[6]

CA, as a systematic research technique of textual analysis found an identity of its own in the 1940s. An immediate impetus came from the US government which, **during World War II**, sponsored a project to weigh up enemy propaganda headed by political scientist **Harold Lasswell**. The project received liberal funding and the methodology devised for its execution was largely adopted by the future – first generation – practitioners of this method. The project, among other things, produced a volume titled *Language of Politics* (**Lasswell et al**) which counted among the early milestones in CA literature.

At first, the technique concentrated on counting the **frequency of occurrences of identified words** while drawing inferences from examination of texts. This, however, was considered inadequate for surveying large texts/ texts other than written documents as well as for undertaking complex investigations. Since the 1950s therefore, **CA became more sophisticated** as its practitioners started dealing with concepts and themes (rather than words), identifying patterns and relationships (instead of counting numbers), and also took into account contextual factors in understanding the meaning of texts. This facilitated **application of CA to a diverse range of texts** including books, newspaper articles, historical documents, political speeches, party manifestoes, medical records, television programmes, Websites, sketches and cartoons, interviews and informal conversations among others. Popularity of the technique also increased manifold as was evident from its **wide application in a range of fields and disciplines** such as marketing and advertising, literature and rhetoric, media studies, anthropology, culture/ gender studies, sociology, political science, psychology and religious studies.

Again, the technique initially was carried out **manually** which not only subjected it to time constraints but also exposed it to human errors. **Reliance on computers** and availability of appropriate software packages has helped the analysts overcome these difficulties. It allowed them to scan large quantum of material with relative ease, and crosscheck their findings with conclusions drawn by other scholars using different data bases and techniques of analysis. As a result, it is now widely recognized that thorough and careful exploration of communication content and the resulting patterns through the application of CA has amply expanded the knowledge of social scientists about individuals, groups, organizations, institutions and the wider society in which they are embedded.

Highlights:

- CA initially stressed counting frequency of words and sentences in reading texts.

- Since the 1950s CA resorted to more sophisticated treatment of textual material by focusing on concepts and themes, looking for patterns and relationships and taking contextual factors into account.

- Evolution from manual scanning to use of computer-based analysis added to the efficiency of CA in more recent times.

Definition and Nature[7]

Bernard Berelson, one of the pioneering CA scholars defined it (quoted in Neuendorf as a research technique for the objective, quantitative, systematic description of the manifest content of communication, which locates CA within the positivistic-scientific tradition of research. This legacy was carried forward by **Neuendorf** for whom CA had to meet the criteria of scientific method including objectivity, hypothesis-testing, a priori design, quantification, reliability, replicability, validity, and generalizability. Following him, we can take brief note of these features of CA. (**Krippendorff** of course expressed his reservations about a couple of these features, especially those regarding the use of a research design developed in advance, and emphasis on quantification at the cost of qualitative reading of texts, but first we note the areas of agreement.)

➢ **Objectivity/inter-subjectivity**: CA aims at attaining objectivity – description and explanation free from the researcher's personal biases – or, alternatively, inter-subjective agreement regarding its findings.

➢ **Hypothesis testing**: CA can be used as a tool of hypothesis testing.

➢ **A priori design**: CA should function with a preconceived research design based on various decisions as to the variables to be studied, their measurement, and coding protocols before data collection begins.

➢ **Quantification**: CA involves counting of key categories and measurement of the amounts of all variables e.g. to count how many times a phrase or image occurs in a particular communication.

➢ **Reliability**: The counting/measuring procedures in CA employed repeatedly should produce the same results.

➢ **Validity**: There should be an appreciable degree of correspondence between measures used in CA and the concepts they seek to represent, e.g. GDP and economic development.

➢ **Replicability**: Application of CA has to be governed by a set of explicit rules in order to ensure reproducibility of its findings.

➢ **Generalizability**: The findings of CA research need to be applicable to other similar situations.

Nevertheless, while **Krippendorff** more or less agrees with the above features of CA, he **strongly disapproves of the positivistic fascination** with 'description of the manifest content of communication' as it appears in Berelson's definition. This statement, he notes, implies that content is *contained* (or inherent) in the text which is to be examined *in isolation from* its form or the milieu within which it originates. Rather Krippendorff sides with Ole Holsti's efforts to understand the content of communication in the light of the **sources and context of the analyzed texts**. The content analyst, Holsti maintains, should describe the characteristics of communication in terms of 'what', 'when' and 'to whom', in order to infer their antecedents in terms of 'who' and 'why' and their consequences in terms of 'with what effects'. **Devi Prasad** following this lead **divides the purpose of CA under three heads and also spells out the corresponding questions and research problems as under.**

Table 6.1: CA - Purposes, Research questions and Research problems

Purpose of CA	Questions	Research Problems
To describe the characteristics of content	*What?*	To describe trends in communication content. To relate known characteristics of sources to the messages they produce. To check communication content against standards To analyze techniques of persuasion. To analyze style.
	How?	To relate known characteristics of audiences to messages produced for them To describe patterns of communication
	To whom?	

To make inferences about the causes of content	Why?	To secure political and military intelligence. To analyze psychological traitsof individuals. To infer aspects of culture and cultural change. To provide legal evidence To answer questions of disputed authorship
	Who?	
To make inferences about the effect of content	With what effect?	To measure readability. To analyze the flow of information. To assess responses to Communication.

It follows from the above that the **first task of CA** is to describe content characteristics along three dimensions: (a) what is being communicated (e.g. identify the patterns emerging from the message content); how it is being purveyed (to look at the technique and style of communication); and (c) for whom the message is meant (the target audience of the communication). The **second aspect** of the content analyst's task takes us into the realm of explanation/ understanding of the message by asking questions relating to (a) who has transmitted the message (which also calls for an inquiry into who the 'real' author of message is); and (b) why the message has been conveyed (e.g. to analyze a policy, garner support for a poll candidate, seek justice or defame a public figure). **Finally,** there is an attempt to assess the consequences of the communication – how far it attained its intended object – by ascertaining the responses to the message.

But **Krippendorff** contends that capturing the communicator's intent ordains us to **move beyond this sequential, objective framework** drawn up at the outset of the analysis based on inputs from existing theories and research. In addition, he proposes that the analyst should get *immersed into the message content* with an open mind ready to take account of new ideas and concepts likely to emerge from this intimate engagement with texts. Through this exercise, which Krippendorff calls 'ethnographic content analysis', the analysts can make their own conceptual contributions to the appropriate reading of a text. This also brings us to the **distinction between quantitative and qualitative content analysis** which we would summarize after presenting an outline of the CA technique along with some of its examples.

To summarize:

- From the classical positivistic standpoint, CA has to concentrate on descriptive and explanatory study of explicit textual content.

- In an evolved understanding, CA has three components: descriptive (the *what*, *how*, and *for whom* questions); explanatory which focuses on the sources of and intent behind message transmission; and evaluative i.e. whether the message has created the desired response or impact.

- 'Ethnographic content analysis' (to use Krippendorff's terminology) discards the idea of using a ready research design and stresses instead on the investigator's creative contributions to development of concepts based on a thorough reading of message contents.

Description of the Technique[8]

While CA could be more quantitative or qualitative in thrust, the steps involved in executing it and the procedures followed in collecting data remain by and large similar. In case of CA, as in most other techniques, the researcher has to take some basic decisions at the outset such as selecting the relevant population of texts, pinpointing the content needed to be examined along with its rationale, and identifying (or generating if necessary) the requisite data. More specifically, **four steps** are involved apart from data analysis – selection of textual content and sample; development of content categories; finalization of the units of analysis; and drawing up of a coding schedule.

This sequence is of course prefaced by **identification of the relevant concepts and formulation of research questions/ hypotheses** which prevent the content analytical exercise from turning into pointless 'word crunching'. Thus, a CA-based study of the print media's coverage of foreign policy issues/events in India sought to explore three roles of the press: as 'observer' (or informer), 'participant' (in the foreign policy process through editorial responses) and 'catalyst' (of public opinion vis-à-vis foreign policy). These roles were sought to be understood with reference to three crisis situations in India's external relations – India-China (1959-63); India-Pakistan (1970-72) and India-Sri Lanka (1987-89). Some of the research questions it asked included: (a) Is the coverage of foreign policy news objective? (b) How to characterize the disposition of newspaper editorials towards the substance and conduct of Indian foreign policy? (c) Does the press act as a forum for foreign policy-focused public debate? These questions emanated from existing theories and previous research, and imparted substance and direction to the whole exercise which otherwise would be tantamount to 'counting for the sake of counting' unable to yield any meaningful results.

This brings us to the first step, i.e. **selection of the textual material** (e.g. documents/ newspaper reports/ films/ photographs/ conversations) that would serve as the basis of analysis, and also known as *population*. The selected material is expected to furnish answers to the research questions or evidence for testing the hypotheses the researcher has framed. If the researcher is interested in studying political values of those contesting parliamentary elections, party manifestoes or campaign speeches could form the population. If the researcher intends to measure the presence of gender bias in a society, the population of texts might include novels, films or television soaps. The researcher might include textual data that falls into a single semantic domain (e.g. campaign speeches) or cuts across different domains such as interviews given by political leaders to newspapers, and videos made for campaigning purposes. It is important, however, to ensure that the identified material is actually available or accessible to the analyst, especially if running records such as a decade's legislative proceedings constitute the population – otherwise an element of bias might creep into the analysis. It also needs to be checked if the chosen material is available in existing archives (government archives, public libraries, online databases) or needs to be collected separately for the purpose of research.

Again, if the researcher finds it manageable to cover the entire population of texts relevant for answering the questions, then **sampling** issues do not arise. But in most cases, the population appears too large for intensive investigation; and the researcher has to settle for analyzing a representative sample. Thus, taking the population as the *samplingframe*, a sample could be selected using probability (e.g. random, systematic, stratified, cluster) or non-probability (e.g. convenience, purposive, quota or expert) sampling techniques. Recourse to probability sampling would enable the researcher to generalize the research findings; non-probability sampling would suffice if the researcher does not aim at generalization, or application of such techniques is found impracticable. The study of the press's response towards foreign policymaking in India took the English language newspapers published from India as its 'population'. It was based on the assumption that the 'elite' English press attracted more attention from India's policymaking community, especially the makers of Indian foreign policy, than the vernacular press. Four newspapers – *Times of India, Statesman, Hindu* and *IndianExpress* – were included in the sample chosen for executing the research work, keeping in mind places of publication, circulation figures, popular standing and so forth. Further, of the three roles of the press identified above, the 'participant' and 'catalyst' roles were examined in terms of the whole population of editorials and letters to the editor respectively, published during the chosen time frames. However, a sample of news reports, too voluminous to study in full, was drawn up corresponding to a set of events pertaining to each of the three external crises based on multiple considerations. Thus, they all constituted *significant* events going by the extant literature on the crises; each event generated front page banner headlines in all the sampled newspapers for three consecutive days; and each generated more than one editorial in all the papers concerned.

Once the population/ sample is selected, the researcher has to decide precisely what she would be looking for in the texts – her topic of interest – formally called *content categories*. **Content categories** could be understood as compartments or pigeonholes into which the units of content the researcher seeks to measure are coded for analysis. Content categories follow immediately from the research questions, but are ultimately derived from a review of the literature relevant for the research theme. A study of portrayal of women in television soaps might measure the personality traits of the female characters in terms of categories such as strength, warmth, integrity, humility and wisdom. Similarly, the level of popular support for a prime minister halfway through her term could be ascertained with reference to five categories: greatly dislike, moderately dislike, indifferent to, moderately like, greatly like. The study of the Indian press's appraisal of foreign policy issues sought to assess the 'objectivity' of foreign policy news in terms of the two categories of 'factualness' and 'neutrality'.

Appropriate content categories could be borrowed from prior research work relevant for one's own investigation. To devise categories independently, however, the researcher needs to indulge in experimentation – a trial and error game – and a pilot study is often of much help. But either way, category development remains of crucial significance for the content analyst as far as the validity and reliability of the research is concerned. Hence Berelson, author of one of the classic CA texts, observed that content analysis stands or falls by its categories. To be useful, the categories must be thoroughly and completely defined so as to make it abundantly clear what kind of observations could (or could not) be accommodated by them. In other words, the categories must be mutually exclusive and exhaustive so that they do not overlap – no sentence or movie scene under the analyst's scanner, for example, falls between two categories – and all observations are ultimately assigned to the 'right' category. Thus, definitions of the categories need to be operationalized, and clearly formulated before coding starts.

In our above example of press appraisal of India's foreign policy, 'factualness' was attributed to a news report which dealt with events and statements amenable to checking against sources, and presented free of the reporter's comments. Similarly, 'neutrality' referred to *balanced reporting*, i.e. allotment of equal or proportional space or emphasis as between opposite points of view in a news report. Finally, to measure the press's perceptions of India and its bilateral counterparts – for example, China during the Sino-Indian tensions of late 1950s and early 1960s that precipitated a war in 1962 – as reflected in mere *description* of their behaviour, two sets of categories were developed. As far as India was concerned, these included terms such as 'Humane', 'Firm', 'Flexible', 'Peace-loving', 'Discreet' 'Vigilant', 'Militarily weak'; while China's posture was sought to be captured through categories such as 'Intruder/ Aggressor', Imperialistic', 'Deceitful' and 'Devious'.

The next task is to choose the **unit of analysis** or the segment of the text that will contain what the researcher is looking for. It is indeed the smallest unit of content that is coded into content categories. For example, from a given text, the researcher may opt for coding each word (e.g. words that convey particular value positions), sentence, paragraph, theme (a single idea or 'a single assertion about some subject', relevant for studying, for example, propaganda or beliefs and attitudes), character (e.g. from a fiction or film), or an item in its entirety (book, newspaper report, radio programme, TV commercial or Web page). Thus, to measure the tone of news coverage – one of endorsement or otherwise – in news magazines towards contending chief ministerial candidates during the run up to an assembly election in an Indian State, a paragraph could be selected as a unit of analysis. Again, to find out the amount of attention focused on the national economy in television news, a story could serve as a unit.

Units of analyses may be divided into (a) recording unit and (b) context units. The recording unit, as already noted, refers to the specific slice of content in which the observation of a particular fact is counted. Thus, the unit may be a single word such as 'constitution' and the number of references to it found in the text could be counted. However, if the unit is 'attitude to constitution', it cannot be determined by looking at the word alone – it would call for identifying the context within which the word occurs and draw our attention to the context unit, a larger chunk of content that may be examined to characterize the recording unit. Thus, a sentence or paragraph could form the context unit for a word/word cluster (such as 'attitude to constitution') and indicate whether the text emphasizes adherence to the constitution or calls for its defiance.

A researcher may choose to divide the text into smaller components or have preference for smaller content units such as words or sentences; or favour studying documents in entirety. If the category is too small (a word), it would be easily identifiable and facilitate the coder's job; but it would at the same time make it difficult to find an appropriate category for each case under consideration. If, on the other hand, the unit is too large, it may not encompass the categories being investigated – a paragraph may contain too many ideas which would make consistent coding of the text into a single category problematic – and thereby make the coder rely too much on subjective judgment. In fine, it is difficult to suggest any rule of thumb for unit selection: it depends largely on the research questions and the variables that need to be measured as well as the textual matter that is being coded. No wonder, it often involves trial and error, compromise and adjustments in pursuit of measures that effectively capture the content of the material being coded.

The next important step – which takes place almost simultaneously with developing content categories and finalizing the units of analysis – is to identify, and mark the presence in the units of analysis of, the content categories. This involves three things: creating a **coding protocol**; working out a **coding schedule**; and **coding** the unit of analysis into a content category. Coding protocol refers to a set of rules, a system of enumeration for the content being coded. This takes care of the question of reliability of coding and ensures that the items are coded consistently into a content category, throughout the text and in the same way every time.

An important choice in this connection relates to that between 'a priori coding' and 'emergent coding' (or what Mayring calls 'deductive category application' and 'inductive category development'). In a priori coding, the categories are determined before the analysis begins and derived from research questions/hypotheses; existing theories/previous research; or even from content analysis dictionaries which are available to support examination of texts. Further, opinions of professional colleagues are sought before finalizing the inventory; it is also piloted and applied to data; and revisited and revised if necessary. Using pre-set concepts and categories allows the researcher to only look for very specific things, somewhat anticipated, while going through a text. In emergent coding, on the other hand, a tentative set of categories is established to start with, based on a preliminary examination of textual data; but the list keeps on expanding as new categories are deduced step by step even during the data analysis stage. While going through the data, the researcher is always on the lookout for new themes, and once s/he comes across one, s/he carefully assesses whether it fits the definition of any of the existing categories; if not, it is placed into a separate category. This flexibility allows incorporation of new, pertinent material into the coding process which the researcher is not really expecting and yet which has important bearing on the findings of the analysis.

A second important decision is whether to code for a given word only or also for its meaning equivalents because words often appear in different forms while carrying the same meaning. Thus, 'agree', 'agreeing', and 'agreement' might carry the same implication in a particular text, and the researcher could bring them all under the umbrella category 'agreeing words'. Similarly, 'Jawaharlal Nehru' could also be referred to in a text/ body of texts as the 'the first Prime Minister of India, 'Pandit Nehru' or simply 'the Prime Minister' or 'Panditji', all of which could be coded into the same category.

Counting or quantification of the units follows several enumeration methods, e.g. space/time; frequency or intensity/direction. The significance of a unit or a topic could be measured in terms of the space (column inches) devoted to it in a written document or time (minutes/hours) spent on it in a radio or television programme. Frequency counting implies keeping a record of the number of times a particular word or theme occurs in the body of a text. Again, measuring the intensity or direction of a message may involve capturing its orientation in terms of a 'favourable-unfavourable-neutral' spectrum.

Framing the **coding protocol** is followed by the preparation of the **coding schedule** which resembles a survey questionnaire and records the details of the codes applied to the data during the coding process. **Codes** are abbreviations or tags for segments of text, more precisely, of the content categories. The aforementioned work on press perceptions of India's foreign policy, which sought to assess the objectivity of news reports in terms of explicit mention of news sources, space provided to news emanating from 'adversarial' sources, and news presentation free of journalists' comments, the following codes were developed:

Governmental source: (1) Non-governmental source: (2) Both: (3)

Indian source: (3); Chinese/ Pakistani/ Sri Lankan source: (4)

Number of (a) Descriptive sentences (1) (b) Judgmental sentences (2) (c) Unsupported conclusions (3)

In other words, to code a particular item into a certain category, it assigned the numerical value (1) to a news item that used governmental source; while a report which combined governmental and non-governmental sources was labeled (3), and so on.

Assigning the unit of analysis into a content category is called **coding** which helps summarize the data and enables the researcher to easily retrieve information, compare cases and arrive at conclusions. Coding may be done by the researcher but depending on the volume of the material, multiple coders may be employed leaving the researcher to supervise the overall consistency in the execution of the coding scheme. Success of coding of course depends on making the coding rules as unambiguous as possible so that every individual coder would categorize or label the units in one and the same way. To ensure this, the coding scheme needs to be piloted, i.e. applied on a randomly selected data set to detect in advance its problems, if any, and plug the loopholes in time. Holding a training session for the coders is also advisable before actual coding begins, where they interact and make sure they have the same ideas and protocol to start with.

This brings us to the issues of applying measurement standards, of **reliability and validity**. Coding is often done manually and is therefore prone to human errors. If such errors are random, they would be mutually cancelled out when many observations are taken into account. But systematically coding a unit incorrectly implies repeated error and introduces a bias. To avert this possibility, CA must pass the twin test of reliability and validity so that its results become trustworthy.

The reliability criterion seeks to ensure that coding results are the same, i.e. replicable, when different persons execute a coding manual. To ascertain that this was the case, several measures of inter-coder reliability, i.e. the degree to which different coders get the same results, have been recommended. One such measure is percentage agreement which is obtained by the following formula: PA=A/n X 100 in which PA=percentage agreement; A=number of agreements and n=number of segments coded. However, the problem with this measure is that there is no consensus on what constitutes an acceptable level of reliability. More sophisticated statistical measures of reliability include Scott's pi, Cohen's kappa or Krippendorff's alpha.

Validity refers to the extent to which a measuring procedure captures the intended – and only the intended – concept. The key question asked here is whether we are really measuring what we claim to measure. One test of validity takes place through triangulation, i.e. recourse to multiple data sources and analytical techniques to establish credibility of the findings of CA research. Krippendorf recalls two studies which suggested allied validational techniques: Janis maintained that the results of mass media content analyses should be correlated with the media audience's verbal reports or observed behaviour (e.g. voting or opinion polls). Similarly, Gerbner and his colleagues argued that the quantum of violence visible on television needs to be crosschecked with survey data on the perceptions of audience members' of how violent the world around them 'really' is.

To turn to assessment of validity without triangulation, one could ask whether the findings are generalizable, i.e. they could be extrapolated to other settings or times? Again, some validity issues relate to the coding scheme, e.g. whether adequate number of variables has been included to tap into the full content or whether the categories have been exhaustive or unambiguous; and defined operationally? The final requirement perhaps is that the data and raw material used in the analysis should be made available for verification: the coding manual (including coding rules) as well as a detailed account of the coding protocol should be made public. After all, all research needs to clearly state how it was carried out, and how the complex reality was subjected to analysis through use of sophisticated procedures.

Steps in doing CA: a summary

• Identifying the texts for study and developing a sample

• Choosing the content category or whatever the researcher seeks to study in the text

- Defining the unit of analysis or the smallest segment of the text to be assigned to content categories

- Developing a coding protocol or a set of rules for coding or assigning the units to the categories

- Engaging in coding – the core of CA – or reduction of data which helps the researcher to arrive at findings

- Applying reliability and validity checks to the research process

Examples

Elizabeth Monk-Turner[9] and others undertook a quantitative CA of movie violence in the United States. The American people, they argued, are rightly concerned about the violent imageries often carried by movies for this might not only desensitize viewers towards violence but also instigate imitative antisocial behaviour. The authors opted for studying war movies which in their view contain violence that is regarded as by and large socially acceptable. They aimed at studying evolution of the nature of violence showed in war movies and their hypothesis was that more recent films are more violent and gory compared to films of yesteryears. This hypothesis was rooted in previous research which suggested that exhibition of violence in movies not only generates a sense of addiction among the moviegoers but also makes violence more socially acceptable and thus boosts the demand for movie violence. The study published in 2004 rested on a survey of select top-grossing American war movies released between 1970 and 2002. The 'population' or the sampling frame was drawn up from the websites www.worldwideboxoffice.com and www.suncoast.com. From this master list, a sample of 12 – three films from each decade – was randomly selected for the final execution of the project.

The researchers began by watching one of the latest movies *We Were Soldiers* (2002) to determine the content categories, and also to assess the level of inter-coder reliability at the pre-test stage. Four categories – implements of violence, the ratio of battle scenes to the duration of the movie, gore, and violence other than soldier to soldier (noncombatants) – were devised for the purpose of the study. Again, implements of violence were coded into six categories: by hand, blades, primary weapons, small arms, artillery, and explosives/bombs. Precise definitions were sought to be developed for each: thus, violence included hand-to-hand combat, using the butt of the gun, shipping, and torching. For each movie, the researchers counted each time any one of these acts occurred. Similarly, the time duration of each of the battle scenes was counted, and finally added up in order to calculate the ratio of the battle scenes to the running time of the movie. Thirdly, gore – defined as a bloody wound resulting from an act of violence – was coded in two ways. Thus, specific instances of gore were identified and coded which in turn were assigned to a five-point scale ranging from one to five representing the whole spectrum of the least gory to the goriest incidents. The final area of violence involving noncombatants was classified into four categories – children, women, animals, and civilian structures. Each act of violence directed at noncombatants was counted and tallied at the end of the film.

The findings corroborated the authors' hypothesis that violence and gore increased in movies produced since 1990 compared to those released between 1970 and 1989. Going by the mean differences, for example, for the later period, there was a mean of 22.2 minutes of battle time compared to 11.7 minutes in earlier films. The gore ratio also increased in later films that had a mean gore ratio of 2.93 compared to a mean gore ratio of 1.68 in earlier war movies. Similarly, there was more violence among the noncombatants in the later films though the count of violence directed at noncombatants did not vary much between the two time periods. The authors acknowledged of course that concentration on war-related violence alone which in any case seemed to have greater social legitimacy together small sample size imposed evident limitations on their study. The task of ascertaining the reasons behind the rise in violence levels observed in the later movies – whether it was to be attributed primarily to the preferences of the audiences of perceptions of the film-makers – had also been left to the future researchers to pursue.

Our second example, a study of the print media undertaken by **Chatterji and Basu Ray Chaudhury**[10] focused on the Indian newspaper press's perception of China during 2012-2015. The three year period was selected in view of the rise of new leaders in the two countries who affirmed their resolve to strengthen bilateral relations though outbreak of border skirmishes continued especially during high level visits. Using the newspaper websites, three premier national level English dailies – *Times of India, Hindu* and *Indian Express* were selected for executing the study. Further, two papers primarily known for their economic content – *Economic Times* and *Financial Express* – were also included in the sample, given the increasing importance attached to trade relations between China and India at that time. The editorials of the papers constituted the unit of analysis, and they were analyzed both qualitatively and quantitatively though we would be covering only the quantitative dimension here. Four content categories were developed by the researchers for scanning the editorials: length, degree of attention paid to China, number and variety of themes addressed, and nature of perception of China.

Out of 187 editorials consulted by the researchers, 122 or 73 per cent contained more than 350 words and only 45 (27 per cent) were of a lesser size which brought out the conviction in the Indian press that India's relations with the China, despite periodic fluctuations, called for elaborate treatment. Moreover, while most of the longer editorials appeared in the general interest papers, the financial press, though   representing one-fifth of the sample, contributed about one-third of the longer editorials. Further, these papers did not restrict their editorials to bilateral economic issues alone but covered political developments as well which could have 'upset the economic applecart' and thus attested to the importance attached by the Indian press to the economic component of bilateral ties.

Further, to look closely at the degree of attention paid by the press to China, 'attention score' was computed for each newspaper. For this purpose, the number of editorials published by each every 365 days for these three years was multiplied by 100 to get a standardized score (i.e. number of editorials divided by 365 multiplied by 100). In terms of this scale, if a paper published one China-related editorial on each day for 365 days, it would get a score of 100; and it would score zero if it did not carry any such editorial during that year. The 'attention score' brought out the interest shown in China by each paper in comparison with the other four. The aggregated scores for three years, however, did not reveal any clear pattern as far as the attention of the papers in China-related issues was concerned.

Thirdly, the researchers went through the selected editorials and identified four major themes covered by the papers – India-China border issues, China-Pakistan relations, China as a rising power, and Chinese domestic issues – with other sundry themes categorized as 'Others'. Of the four themes, editorial concerns were dominated by 'China as a rising power' – indeed the number of editorials dealing with this theme more than doubled during 2012-2014. This was undoubtedly a reaction to China's increasing assertiveness in world politics especially with Xi Jinping's emergence as its new helmsman in 2012. Curiously, China-Pakistan ties appeared relatively unattractive as an editorial theme. Coverage of India-China border question also fluctuated in keeping with the reported incidence of border skirmishes. Interestingly again, some of the issues classified under the residual 'Others' head – such as investment and balance of payment issues on one hand, and connectivity and tourism-related issues on the other seemed to call attention to new vistas in bilateral engagement.

Finally, the newspapers' overall perception of China was sought to be measured through a 'positive-negative' binary: a positive assessment implied China was perceived as cooperative and trustworthy, and vice versa. On the whole, 42.5 per cent of the editorials showed a positive evaluation of China while 57.4 per cent had a negative disposition towards it. However, of all the papers, more than 61 per cent of the editorials published by *Hindu* had a positive tone – perhaps under the influence of its known ideological predilections. All the papers other than *Hindu* seemed to project China largely in a negative light. On the other hand, the gap between negative and positive evaluations of China remained relatively insignificant for the economic newspapers compared to the others. That these papers dealt with more mundane and less value-laden economic/financial issues – compared to more emotive issues such as border dispute prioritized by the general interest papers – perhaps accounted for this trend.

The authors concluded with a few major lessons learnt from their study regarding India-China ties: First, the Indian press's interest in China not only remained substantial but also steadily growing with new issues including China's domestic developments capturing their attention. Second, the overwhelmingly negative perception of China was being balanced by a section of the press, especially the economic newspapers, confidently pointing towards areas where cooperation was attainable. Lastly, despite emerging areas of potential cooperation and mutual trust, steady advances in bilateral exchanges still called for successfully addressing the border question.

Table 6.2: Lessons learnt from the examples

Example 1	Example 2
Focus of interest: Movies	Focus of interest: Newspapers
Rationale of choosing samples explained	Rationale of choosing samples explained
Content categories defined, coding protocols explicated	Content categories defined, coding protocols explicated
Quantitative in thrust	Combined quantitative and qualitative CA
Tested hypothesis	No hypothesis
Explanation skipped	Offered tentative explanations of findings

Quantitative-Qualitative Continuum in CA[11]

In this section we take up the discussion – which we had postponed– following **Niels Gheyle and Thomas Jacobs** on qualitative and quantitative versions of CA and their interface. Early CA, as already noted, adopted a 'list-and-count' approach. It all started with coding of newspaper data into explicit predetermined categories, and their characteristics described with the help of statistical measures such as cross-tabulation, or more sophisticated correlation and regression analysis. The major elements of this scientifically inclined quantitative CA, as already mentioned, consisted of generation of hypothesis, sampling of data and an a priori coding scheme.This involved a deductive approach: exhaustive content categories are devised in the beginning; unambiguous coding rules are formulated for assigning the data into appropriate categories; and then statistical tools are employed to analyze the results with an eye on their reliability/ replicability, validity and generalizability.

Qualitative CA shares with its quantitative counterpart a number of features such as hypothesis testing, sampling, category development, and coding content into categories. It also uses descriptive statistics (percentages and cross-tabulation) to report findings, and standard measures (such as transferability or confirmability) to establish the trustworthiness of the findings. **However, its major differences with quantitative CA relate to (a) categorization and coding and (b) sensitivity to the meaning behind the text.** The early stage of Qualitative CA is more *inductive*: the researcher can start out with some predefined content categories, but these are yet to take any final shape and thus keep the research outcome rather open-ended. The researcher goes on constructing categories (that appear for the first time) as she scans a text. Similarly, instead of having an a priori coding scheme, coding and analyzing also take place simultaneously. This can lead to a review of the research questions as well – indeed evidence becomes as important in guiding the research as the initial questions. Krippendorff calls this process of constantly re-contextualizing and redefining research a 'hermeneutic loop'.

Moreover, quantitative CA, instead of focusing only on relevant words or phrases, takes interest in relationships among them and thereby unearths the meaning behind texts. It goes beyond mere counting of words or column inches, to quote Weber, by categorizing chunks of texts similar in meaning. These categories also go beyond manifest content – the themes and main ideas of a text – and include latent content or inferred communication, often by reading the text with reference to its context. Thus qualitative CA essentially involves subjective interpretation of textual messages through a flexible coding system and identification of themes and patterns. Hence Philipp Mayring contended that qualitative CA aims at preserving the advantages of quantitative CA and moving beyond it by paying greater attention to the theory behind the construction of categories. This brings us close to Krippendorff's observation: 'Ultimately all reading of texts is qualitative, even when certain characteristics of a text are later converted into numbers'. This leads Gheyle and Jacobs to conclude that CA comprises a range of methods along a continuum of deductive-quantitative to inductive-qualitative. 'In practice, research is often somewhere on this continuum, with some sense of theories and categories beforehand, while also being open to and informed by evidence'.

Table 6.3: Quantitative-Qualitative Continuum in CA

Similarities	Differences
Sampling Hypothesis testing Category building Content coding Confirmation checks	In qualitative CA, categories are tentative; coding scheme far from final; category building, coding proceed alongside analysis In qualitative CA, focus not simply on quantification of manifest content (words or phrases) but search for meanings, which involves 'inferred communication' and relating text to its context

Assessment[12]

CA is a **flexible technique** applicable to a varied body of text sources. It gives researchers **access to research subjects** who remain physically inaccessible – either because they are difficult to contact or no more. CA is, further, considered a safe method in that the **researcher can always revisit the text to address the problem of missing or wrongly coded data** which gives it an edge over survey or experimental research. It also **enables investigators to study larger populations** than would be possible through observation method or interviewing which have to depend on samples of limited size. CA can deal with volumes of data limited, as Krippendorf argues, only by 'what a researcher can read reliably and without losing track of the relevant details'. The task of data processing, though somewhat laborious, has been rendered much easier with the availability of computer software programmes. Indeed, the procedures involved in the method, if stated explicitly and clearly, facilitate repeated application by multiple coders or computer software. While it is true that practitioners of CA often have to work with small samples due to time or fund constraints, Krippendorf holds that this prevents the exploitation of the full potential of the technique.

Secondly, CA has the **advantage of combining quantitative and qualitative procedures** that sets it apart from other popular research techniques. It **goes beyond impressionistic expressions** about a phenomenon and helps make specific, quantitative statements in terms of number and percentages. At the same time, CA is also **context-sensitive** and can therefore capture qualitative content and **deal with textual data that is meaningful**, significant, and informative. As Krippendorf notes, surveys, structured interviews, experiments under laboratory situations or statistical analyses do not take contextual factors into account. Practitioners of these techniques are often found to make disembodied observations, treat complex and contiguous events as unitary, and take single words in isolation from other parts of the text. Context-sensitive methods on the other hand keep in mind the inter-textuality of data, i.e. data are meant to be read and made sense of by others with reference to their contextual underpinnings. This particular feature helps content analysts, as seen in our above example, to understand why the theme of 'China's emergence as a major power' dominated the Indian press or the economic newspapers exhibited a slightly more positive perception of China.

Thirdly, CA, unlike survey or interview, is an **unobtrusive technique applied in a non-reactive way** which goes a long way towards making research bias-free. Both the interviewer and interviewees may come to the interview setting with their own biases and prejudices which is likely to tamper with the interview sequence and results. Again, research subjects may react to research techniques in several ways: thus the interviewee may try to respond to questions in a politically correct manner, to say what the interviewer supposedly wants to hear; or to suppress the truth either because of lack of knowledge or she is too embarrassed to share it. Similarly, research subjects may also be susceptible to the Heisenberg Effect', i.e. the very consciousness of being observed might change their natural behaviour which in turn would contaminate research findings. CA as a non-invasive technique can largely sidestep these issues: no one needs to be interviewed, fill out lengthy questionnaires, or is required to encounter artificial laboratory conditions. Rather, the researchers deal with newspaper accounts, public addresses, libraries, archives, and similar sources all of which constitute non-reactive material.

Again, CA is **especially useful in investigating a topic longitudinally** – to study processes that occur over long periods of time or reflect societal trends – through the examination of contemporary texts. We have already cited one example where the researchers sought to study the changing nature of violence displayed in American war movies during the last three decades of the twentieth century. Again, many researchers have used this technique to trace the evolution of the images of women through time in literature, films or media in general. Finally, CA is a cost-effective technique since it is largely labour-intensive and requires minimum capital investment. The materials required for conducting CA are easily and inexpensively accessible so much so that even college students can resort to this technique relying on their own resources. On the contrary, conducting a survey effectively and credibly might be quite costly in terms of staff, time and money.

On the downside, sampling and coding might give rise to significant **reliability and validity issues.** Document availability and sampling process could become sources of implicit bias. Again, symbols are processed and coded according to the attribution of the researcher/coder though it could very well be different from the meaning conveyed by the sender. Again, CA becomes problematic when confined simply to counting the individual units and frequency of their occurrence. Abstraction of content, e.g. development, from its context fails to capture the meaning and significance with which it has been imbued in the text. In fact, since the inferences of content analysts are limited to the text itself, they often to ignore unobtrusive messages. At times though, silences could become more meaningful and significant than the express content of the text. Last but not the least, CA is not an effective tool to test causal relationships between variables. While it is very useful in capturing socio-political trends across time, the explanations one proposes for the same cannot be substantiated with reference to the textual matter. This precipitates the broader but unresolved question of the extent to which documentary analysis furnishes a key to the world beyond the text. More than criticism of CA, it constitutes a caveat against assuming a simple correspondence between the text and the external world.

Table 6.4: Assessment of CA

Strengths	Weaknesses
• A flexible technique, effective in dealing with large volumes of data and physically unreachable research subjects	• (Un-)availability of documents can introduce incipient bias.
• Prospect of combining qualitative and quantitative analysis/search for generalization and quest for meaning	• CA when confined to 'list and count' exercise detached from context creates problems of interpretation
• A non-invasive technique capable of avoiding researcher bias and respondent reactivity	• Little scope for testing causal relationships among variables.
• A low-cost technique that helps longitudinal study or examination of long-term processes and trends	• Difficult to accept the correspondence between the world of text and the world beyond at face value

Endnotes

1. Robert Weber, *Basic Content Analysis,* (Thousand Oaks: Sage, 1990).
2. Klaus Krippendorff, *Content Analysis: An Introduction to Its Methodology,* (Thousand Oaks, Sage 2004), 18.
3. Kimberley A. Neuendorf, *The Content Analysis Guidebook,* (Thousand Oaks, Sage 2002), 15.
4. *Political Science Research Methods,* (New Delhi: Prentice Hall India 1989), 207.
5. Sandra Halperin and Oliver Heath, *Political Research: Methods and Practical Skills,* (Oxford: Oxford University Press 2012), 319.
6. B. Devi Prasad, 'Content Analysis: A Method in Social Science Research' in Lal Das, D.K and Bhaskaran, V (eds.), *Research Methods for Social Work,* (New Delhi: Rawat 2008), 1; Lavinia Stan, 'Content Analysis', in A. J. Mills, G. Durepos and E. Wiebe (eds), *Encyclopedia of Case Study Research,* (Thousand Oaks: Sage 2010), 226.
7. Neuendorf 10-13; Krippendorff 19-21; Devi Prasad 3-4.
8. Susan Rose, Nigel Spinks, Ana Canhoto. *Management Research applying the Principles,* Oxon: Routledge, 2015 (Expanded content to Chapter 6 file:///C:/Users/HP/AppData/Local/Temp/Quantitativecontentanalysis-1. pdf, 3-6; Niels Gheyls, and Thomas Jacobs. 'Content Analysis: A Short Overview' http://www.researchgate.net/publication321977528; Krippendorff, 6-11; Devi Prasad 9-16; Partha Pratim Basu, *Press and Foreign Policy in India,* (New Delhi: Lancers 2003) passim.
9. Elizabeth Monk-turner et al. 'A Content Analysis of Violence in American War Movies', *Analyses of Social Issues and Public Policy,* (Vol. 4, No. 1, 2004) https://devl1980.files.wordpress.com/2011/05/content-analysis-on-movies.pdf
10. Rakhahari Chatterji, and Anasuya Basu Ray Choudhury. *Indian Media's Perceptions of China: Analysis of Editorials,* (Kolkata; Observer Research Foundation 2016).
11. Gheyls and Jacobs, 2-3.
12. Devi Prasad 5-8; Rose and Spinks 7; Krippendorff 40-42.

7

The Logic and the Practice of Participant Observation

Social facts do not reduce themselves to scattered fragments. They are lived by men, and subjective consciousness is as much a form of their reality as their objective characteristics.

Claude Levi Strauss

The behavioural movement in political science has turned the attention of the political researchers from formal structures and institutions of political systems to individual political actors. As Harold Lasswell and Abraham Kaplan claimed, persons and their acts have assumed centrality in political research. Instead of speculating about the normative aspects of political life, the political scientist is more interested today in observing what people actually say and do.

But as soon as one conceives of politics in terms of action, one confronts the problem of understanding the meaning of actions. As long as the scientist conducts research in her own society and among people belonging to her own culture-area, the problem of understanding the meaning of action does not surface itself in all its complexities. For then, the scientist can easily capture the meanings of actions as she is sharing along with her respondents a common context of meaning. But once the researcher steps out of her own culture-area, either within her own larger society (for instance, a Bengali social scientist doing research in Tamil Nadu or Kashmir) or while studying other societies (an American social scientist studying India, for instance), the problem of understanding the meaning of action becomes enormous.

This problem was particularly encountered by the perceptive practitioners of survey research working in the area of cross-cultural comparison. To them it appeared as the problem of equivalence; that is, whether the same act performed in two different social and cultural contexts would have an identical meaning. For instance, elections may be quite common to most political systems; yet the act of voting may have completely different meanings in different political systems and under different social and economic conditions. Even within the same system, two individuals may perceive the meaning of voting in quite different ways. As Verba remarks,

> "Activities which receive the same label and which appear on the surface to be the same kind of activity in two nations may, due to different contexts in which we are measuring the particular behaviour, differ sharply from each other."[1]

That is, the meanings of actions are highly dependent on the context of their performance. Verba suggests a "contextual research design" for the survey researchers which would take as much care of the context as possible, both in collecting and analyzing the data, through such techniques as the use of "self-anchored" scale (which allows the respondents to define the meanings of actions in terms of their own perception) and "second-order-comparisons" (i.e., rather than comparing the variables directly across cultures, one may compare the structure of relationship of variables; for instance, instead of comparing the rates of voting in two societies, one may compare the relationship between voting and education in each society with one another). While this could help, it would not solve the problem of understanding altogether. Verba himself recognized the limitations of the survey method in this regard when he pleaded that the survey researcher "must found his work in the historical background of the system he studies...... survey analysis alone cannot be expected to encompass the variety of approaches and materials needed for the understanding of political system..."[2]

Another exponent of cross-cultural survey research, Fredrick Frey, also recognized the problem of understanding the meanings of attitude and behaviour. Thus, he argued that to ensure equivalence in comparative research, the scientist must not only know that her respondent engages himself in a particular behaviour, but she must also know the meaning of that behaviour for the respondent himself; that is, the respondent's *own perception* of the meaning of his behaviour must be understood. In other words, the scientist's task would be to know an action or behaviour both objectively and subjectively.

Frey himself illustrates this point from his own work on Turkey. While surveying the value system of secondary school students in Turkey, he asked whether the students, regarding their personal future, feel "enthusiastic, hopeful, indifferent, resigned or embittered?" His expectation was that the Turkish students would understand the sequential arrangement of the choices in terms of descending order of optimism. But the ranking, which was rather obvious in terms of western culture, was not so for the Turkish students. While presenting the item, Frey came to realize that in terms of Turkish culture, "being indifferent to one's future was worse than being embittered."[3]

This leads Frey to suggest that survey research should be backed by contextual or configurational analysis through a "multi-stage sampling" since the latter would help locate the individual respondent "in the social and cultural setting which surrounds him and gives shape to his attitudes and behaviours."[4] Indeed, Frey repeatedly suggests that the researcher must have a "deep familiarity" with the substantive matter which she is investigating and that the research must be grounded in "sophisticated knowledge of each country's mores and practices." He even warns that it is "rarely appropriate to start a completely new area of investigation with a survey. Ordinarily, the survey technique is most productive if employed only after considerable impressionistic and case study information has been collected."[5]

Our purpose here in this chapter is less to point out the limitations of survey research than to focus on the problem of understanding and comprehending the context of meaning of actions. In fact, even a contextual research design based entirely on an analysis of aggregate data would not solve the problem, for aggregate data could well provide the quantitative aspects of the context leaving aside its subjective dimensions. The question of how to understand the meaning of actions thus remains open for the political scientist who takes action as her basic unit of analysis.

In what follows, an attempt will be made to examine briefly how the problem of understanding the meaning of actions has been faced and tackled by two other social sciences, namely sociology and social anthropology and also to what extent the solutions devised by these two sister disciplines arerelevant for political science research. In the second half of this chapter, a thorough examination of the techniques of conducting participant observation will be undertaken.

MEANING UNDERSTANDING AND SOCIOLOGY

In sociological literature the problem of understanding the subjective meaning of social action has been debated for quite some time so much so that two opposing sociological schools have emerged with reference to this particular problem. These two schools may loosely be labelled positivistic-naturalistic school and the humanistic-culturalistic school.

The debate between these two polar positions does not merely involve the issue of subjective understanding. It involves, by extension, the very nature the of social science - that is, whether the social sciences are at all different from the natural sciences or whether both could be developed on the same model, and also their goals-- namely, the question whether the social sciences should be regarded as idiographic or nomothetic.[6] Leaving aside the absolutely polarized hardliners within both groups, an area of overlap can indeed be discovered among the softliners of these two schools. Standing in this area of overlap, the softline positivist admits the importance of subjective understanding in the social sciences, especially in generating hypotheses if not in confirming them and the softline culturalist recognizes the need for using the scientific method (i.e., observation of social facts and their verification) though to a limited extent. Such softline positions may be said to represent the most realistic approach to social science problems, and a very systematic statement such an approach was given by Max Weber.

For Max Weber, the social sciences are indeed different from the natural sciences and in the former "we can accomplish something which is never attainable in the natural sciences, namely, the subjective understanding (*verstehen*)[7] of the action of the component individuals." Unlike the natural science objects, social collectivities permit us "to go beyond merely demonstrating the functional relationships and uniformities," and to look into the meanings.[8] This meaning of man's social action is derived from the fact that such action is always related to an "intended purpose."

Weber talks about two types of understanding in this connection. First, there may be direct observational understanding of ideas and actions (for instance, understanding the meaning of the proposition 2 X 2 = 4 or understanding the action of a woodcutter). Secondly, there may be explanatory understanding (for instance, understanding whether somebody is using the proposition 2 X 2 = 4 to balance a ledger or to make a scientific demonstration; similarly, understanding the reason behind one's cutting a wood). Such explanatory understanding is derived from one's "rational understanding of motivation which consists in placing the act in an intelligible and more inclusive context of meaning."[9]

For Weber, this explanatory or subjective understanding is the most peculiar characteristic of sociological knowledge. Such understanding in the social sciences as against the natural sciences, is, however, achieved at a cost: social science findings assume a "hypothetical and fragmentary character" to a greater extent than their natural science counterparts. To minimize the cost, Weber suggested that subjective interpretation should be verified by comparing it with the "concrete course of events," that is, by checking the "statistical probability" of the correctness of the subjective interpretation. An adequately meaningful action ("adequacy on the level of meaning"- Talcott Parsons) will merely remain a "peculiarly plausible hypothesis" unless it is, in addition, statistically verified and established as "causally adequate." Thus, to counter the problems of motivational analysis and to attain "a correct causal interpretation of a concrete course of action," Weber suggested that both the overt action and the motives should be correctly apprehended and their relation should also become meaningfully comprehensible.[10]

Weber's statement on *Verstehen*(i.e., the role of subjective understanding in the social sciences) reopened rather than resolved the issue of understanding the meaning of action. While some tried to demolish it all together by claiming that it was a useless procedure for scientific investigation of social behaviour[11] others, like Peter Winch, attacked Weber for conceding too much to statistical verification.[12] More often, however,social scientists recognized the necessity of interpretative understanding and attempted to accommodate *Verstehen*in an otherwise positivistic framework of knowledge.[13] For our present purpose, however, it is not essential to enter into a discussion of the various shades of opinion on the necessity of *Verstehen* in social studies among philosophers of science. The crucial question for us is: given the necessity for subjective understanding of social action, how would one achieve such understanding?

Critics of Weber's *Verstehen* concept have maintained that such understanding is possible only through "the application of personal experience to observed behaviour."[14] In other words, attainment of interpretative understanding is possible through the application of a psychological technique which consists of "putting oneself in the other fellow's position." In fact, however, Weber rejected such "imaginative role-playing" as a means for achieving subjective understanding: for him, "One need not have been Caesar in order to understand Caesar."[15] Weber's emphasis, rather, was on "sympathetic participation." It was through such an act of participation that one could "adequately grasp the emotional context" of the action. In this connection, Weber made a statement which is of crucial significance for us. He said that the importance of such sympathetic participation is all the greater when the observer is attempting to understand actions of peoples whose ultimate values radically differ from his own.[16] That is to say, sympathetic participation and empathy are indispensable tools for understanding particularly when one is dealing with actions of groups or peoples other than the ones to which he himself belongs. We will come back to this point later.

Even though Weber talked of "sympathetic participation," any discussion of his idea of *Verstehen* leads, time and again, to a discussion of the "psychological technique" for its attainment simply because of Weber's point regarding "rational understanding of motivation." If *Verstehen* is identified with the understanding of motives behind actions, then some sort of psychologism would be inevitable.

But, in fact, while Weber put emphasis on the psychological variables, he did not believe in psychological reductionism. It is true that his "explanatory understanding" did involve "grasping the motive of an individual actor;" yet he was aware of the diversity of motives and, as Neil Smelser points out, "Weber did not conceive of them in a narrow psychological sense."[17]

Parsons has also brought out this point while discussing Weber's methodology.[18] According to him, Weber did distinguish between two meanings of *Verstehen*, one implying "elements of concrete motivation," and the other referring to "an atemporal world of meanings in abstraction from concrete motivation." Accordingly, actions could be looked upon either as motivational, or as symbolic.[19] While this latter meaning of *Verstehen* is quite discernible from Weber's empirical works, in his theoretical discussions *Verstehen* was nearly identified with imputation of motives.

It thus appears that any attempt to answer the question, how could one achieve subjective understanding of action, will beg another crucial question: what, after all, do we exactly mean by subjective understanding? Weber's discussion of the subject leaves quite a few questions open. This necessitates a restatement and elaboration of the idea of *Verstehen* since it is so essential for the understanding of social behaviour. Such a restatement has been very fruitfully done by Murray Wax.[20]

Wax lamented the fact that in his theoretical discussion on the subject Weber, instead of analyzing the different meanings of *Verstehen*, transformed the issue "into the specialized problem of imputing motive to the actor." Thus, important gaps remain in our understanding of *Verstehen* which makes it necessary that its possible meanings be explicated. According to him,

Verstehen, or "subjective understanding," can have four possible meanings. It may mean, first of all, "extra-cultural" or "extra-species" understanding (as, for instance, man's understanding of the behaviour of animals). Secondly, it may be used in the sense of "intra-cultural" understanding (namely, the understanding of an alien culture developed by an "outsider" as is common in the case of ethnographic field research). Thirdly, it may mean "pattern analysis" (as, for instance, "delineation of patterns in historical societies"). Finally, it may be used in the sense of "inter-personal intuition" (that is, imputation of motives). Of these four possible meanings, Wax believes that the second one is the most useful and appropriate meaning.

Intra-cultural understanding, for Wax, is best conceived not as an "operation" or instrument (as Theodore Abel would like to see it), but rather as a "precondition for research," It is something to be "acquired" in relation to the subject of study rather than "applied" to it.

But what exactly does Wax mean by "acquisition of *Verstehen*" in its intra-cultural sense? Whether in relation to historical investigation or learning a new language, or studying a strange people *Verstehen* would imply acquisition of contextual knowledge as a key to understanding. Thus, in all these cases, the scientist starts as an "outsider" to the interaction process: the historical documents he is examining appearing as meaningless information, or the language he is confronting appearing as mumbo-jumbo without any pattern, or strange society he is encountering appearing as thoroughly unstructured bundle of interactions. But gradually as he acquires familiarity with the historical period concerned or with the phonemes of the new language or with the kinship structure, the cultural characteristics and historical background etc., of a strange people, patterns begin to emerge before his eyes. The structure and meaning of what first appeared as totally without any shape or form gradually become apparent and allow themselves to be grasped by the scientist. The researcher who was an outsider in the beginning is transformed into an "insider" through the acquisition of *Verstehen*.

But how does this process work? That is, in other words, how is such contextual knowledge acquired? Socialization is, for Wax, the answer to this question. It is through socialization, or in Wax's words, "participation in the cultural dynamic" that one acquires the much needed contextual knowledge. Indeed, one has to be socialized into one's own society and culture. This is what is called primary socialization. It is through primary socialization that a child learns the dialect of his people, internalizes the mores, customs and traditions of his society and culture. There are two main characteristics of such primary socialization. First, such socialization and understanding (*Verstehen*) derived from it are available only to the natives of a culture. Secondly, primary socialization operates in such an unobtrusive manner that the natives remain almost unaware of the resulting *Verstehen*. That is the reason, according to Wax, why a sociologist conducting research in his own culture-area often fails to perceive "the vast background of shared meanings" between himself and his subjects of study that his research techniques simply take for granted. A perceptive eye can easily detect the underlying *Verstehen* expressed in the phraseology of a survey questionnaire or the use of words and concepts in describing an event.

But the situation is different when one is studying an alien culture. We have already referred to the point made by Weber that the need for *Verstehen* is all the greater when one is studying a people or culture whose ultimate values differ from one's own. Weber is right in the sense that in studying alien peoples or cultures the acquisition of *Verstehen* has to be conscious as well as an intrusive process. Not being a native, the observer here is deprived of the advantages of primary socialization. The only course to her is secondary socialization. It is of course true that secondary socialization, however "intimate and extensive," cannot give the observer as authoritative an experience as that of the native. Yet, as Wax says, "...because culture is a dynamic system maintained and modified by its members, participation is the most efficient way to as near a total grasp of it as is possible for the alien."

Secondary socialization through participant observation of the actions and behaviour of an alien people allows the scientist to achieve an insider's view. No sample survey, no structured questionnaire can enable the observer to come as close to the alien culture or to grasp as neatly the cultural heterogeneity of a people as is possible through participant observation.

Thus, Wax while admitting that *Verstehen* is capable of assuming four clear different meanings, has particularly insisted on its intra-cultural sense. This, for practical purposes, implies the significance and necessity of acquiring contextual knowledge of given events or phenomena. He has further suggested that such contextual knowledge may be achieved through participant observation.

MEANING UNDERSTANDING AND SOCIAL ANTHROPOLOGY

From the foregoing examination of Wax's interpretation of intra-cultural *Verstehen* it should appear as no wonder that Wax happens to be a professor of Anthropology. Almost from the very beginning, social anthropologists have faced the problem of understanding the meaning of actions and behaviour of strange peoples and since the beginning of the last century they have found the solution to the problem in participant observation. It was simply unthinkable for a social anthropologist in the last quarter of the twentieth century to repeat the reported gesture of Sir James Frazer and say "God forbid" when asked had he ever lived amongst the savages.

All the great social anthropologists of the last century, whether they thought of the discipline as nomothetic or idiographic, were centrally concerned with the problem of understanding the meanings of beliefs, customs and behaviour of the people they studied. It was this central concern of the social anthropologists that led them to realize the significance of contextual knowledge and as a result, they all insisted on looking at life as a whole. Thus, Radcliffe Brown, who accepted a natural science model for anthropology and believed that it should be aiming at the discovery of "general laws and adapting to its special subject matter the ordinary logical methods of the natural sciences,"[21] did not fail to point out that the concern of the "newer anthropology" was with the "meaning of various elements of culture" and that such "meaning of an element of culture is to be found in its interrelation with other elements and in the place it occupies in the *whole life of the people.*"[22]

Similarly, E.E. Evans-Pritchard, Radcliffe-Brown's successor at Oxford--but who, unlike his predecessor, believed that social anthropology is best regarded as an art and not as a natural science,"[23] also insisted that the anthropologist must study social life as a whole for "it is impossible to understand clearly and comprehensively any part of a people's social life except in the *full context of their social life* as a whole."[24]

Robert Redfield, who laid great emphasis on "understanding human communities and said, understanding and her apotheosis, wisdom are the true gods within the temple,"[25] pointed out the need for recognising the "human whole" for such understanding. An anthropologist, for Redfield, "seeks to understand the relationships of the parts to one another within that whole."[26]

Finally, Bronislaw Malinowski, who was such less concerned with theory than with field work, was equally emphatic about the problem of understanding the meaning of actions and argued equally forcefully that such understanding could be achieved only through placing actions in their extract context. Thus, while Malinowoski was centrally concerned with the economic activity of the Trobriand Islanders, with their commercial enterprise and trade and exchange (*Kula*), he found it necessary to deal "with the totality of all social, cultural and psychological aspects of the community, for they are so interwoven that not one can be understood without taking into consideration all the others."[27] Sir James Frazer quite correctly said that "It is characteristic of Dr. Malinowski's method that he takes full account of the complexity of human nature. He sees man, so to say, in the round, not in the flat."[28]

Thus, social anthropologist, even if concerned only with a specific aspect of people's life, must try to know the entire context within which that particular aspect of its life unfolds itself. While writing about them she may not, of course, use all the information about their entire life process; yet the specific aspect that she would be dealing with must be analyzed and explained against the background of the totality of their existence. In social anthropology, such contextual knowledge of social reality is required as a necessary condition for understanding. As Professor Raymond Firth put it,

"In his study behaviour the anthropologist works by *contextualization*. He assumes that if he grasps the context adequately, he can apprehend the *meaning* of the behaviour. The context of associated circumstances allows him to see the end of the activity and the value attached-- that is, the quality of the relationship inferred."[29]

The acquisition of contextual knowledge is, thus, a matter on which social anthropologists of otherwise different philosophical viewpoints seldom differ.

The other point, which is a corollary to the above and on which modern social anthropologists of different philosophical inclinations also agree, is that to know a part in the context of the whole or to know the whole itself in the context of the interrelationships among its parts (the latter particularly has been the purpose of "little community" studies), one has to participate while observing. Participant observation is considered an adjunct to "contextualization." Establishing "ties of intimacy" with the people one studies or, to use Malinowski's expression, "plunging into the life of the native," and communicating with them in their own language as far as possible have been the two basic requirements in modern social anthropological studies. Only these can help develop the quality of "intellectual and emotional appreciation"[30] so necessary for understanding.

Bronislaw Malinowski was the first anthropologist to conduct his research among the Trobriand Islanders in the native language and it was primarily due to his works that the superiority of using the native language came to be recognized. Margaret Mead, in a very interesting paper on "Native Languages As Field Work Tools,"[31] delineated the necessity as well as the nature of knowledge in native language that an anthropologist should possess. According to Mead, such knowledge is necessary primary for three purposes: (i) for asking questions correctly and idiomatically; (ii) for establishing rapport; and (iii) for giving instructions. Mead put emphasis on "using the language" rather than on "speaking" it. By this she meant that what was essential for the anthropologist interested in unravelling the actual way a society works was not linguistic virtuosity but a working knowledge of the native language which would enable her to understand "the cultural usage as a whole.". In Mead's judgement, between two researchers, "one with an intimate knowledge of the local scene, the formal and the casual interrelationships between individuals, the recent events of interest and but an indifferent knowledge of the language, the other with a fine analytical knowledge of the language and a much larger general vocabulary, but with a slighter knowledge of the local scene, the former will understand much more of a general conversation."[32]

Thus, the knowledge of the language that is necessary cannot be satisfactorily attained in the language laboratory; rather it has to be attained the "field." For what is important is not richness in the technicalities of the language but an "attention to cultural usage as a whole." Encountering the culture itself is, then, an imperative.

Radcliffe-Brown's *The Andaman Islanders* and Malinowski's *Argonauts of the Western Pacific* are the two classic demonstrations of the fruits of such direct encounter with the cultures under study. They have clearly demonstrated the virtues of participant observation or the enormous advantage of observing the daily activities of societies from within. To know the actual working of a society it is necessary that one is "physically and morally a part of the community" as far as possible. To be, in this sense, a part of the community, the anthropologist should not merely observe; it may also be necessary for him to perform. Research, for the anthropologist, means, as Professor Firth says, "a process of learning and practising new modes of personal behaviour. He is adopting for much of the time *their* pattern of living, greeting, eating and perhaps, even of *participation* in ceremonial life."[33]

The meaning of such sympathetic participation through participant observation has been excellently expressed by Evans-Pritchard:

"An anthropologist has failed unless, when he says good bye to the natives, there is *on both sides* the sorrow of parting. It is evident that he can only establish this intimacy if he makes himself in some degree a member of their society and lives, thinks, and feels in their culture since only he, not they, can make the necessary transference."[34]

The necessity and significance of participant observation is thus apparent. If by subjective understanding one primarily implies understanding the symbolic meaning of action and behaviour, then such understanding can best be achieved by placing the actions and behaviour in their proper context. Participant observation appears to be an efficient means for such contextualization.

PARTICIPATION AND UNDERSTANDING THE POLITICAL PROCESS

For the political scientist, the important thing to note is that the superiority of this anthropological method of participant observation is clearly borne out by the anthropologists' study of even the political process. To demonstrate our point, we will only refer to two distinguished works by two eminent anthropologists: first, the classic work of Evans-Pritchard, *The Neur- A Description of the Modes of livelihood* and *political institutions of a Nilotic people*, and second, F.G. Bailey's work on India, *Politics and Social Change-- Orissa in 1959*. The first contains an attempt to understand the static political process of a simple and segmented society through the "fission and fusion" model; the second makes an effort to capture a dynamic political situation in which a simple traditional society is confronted with an emergent state of affairs which assumes complexity. In both cases, the anthropologists concerned spent a considerable period of time with the communities understudy and tried to make the "necessary transference."

David Easton, in his critic of the state as a key orienting concept for political research, has drawn our attention to the fact that the 'political' is not necessarily coextensive with the state. Accusing political scientists of a certain inattention to the anthropological data about political life among primitive and non-literate peoples, Easton points out that "where there is any kind of organized activity, incipient as it may be, there, what we would normally call political situations, abound."[35] Thus, in societies where the state is non-existent, there may be "excellent material for a general understanding of political life."[36]

For a political scientist with his typical disciplinary training it is easier to accept Professor Eatson's point than to practice it in real research. The obvious problem for him would be one of method. It is not enough merely to recognize, following social anthropologists, that the organized life of the primitive and non-literate people is imbued with political interactions. It is necessary to know how to penetrate these interactions, gather first-hand data and develop an understanding of their political processes.[37] The two writers mentioned above -- Evans Pritchard and Bailey - clearly demonstrated that these can be achieved by an application of the anthropological method of contextualization through participant observation.

To an outsider, the cattle raids between the Nuer and the Dinka, the frequent intra-tribal and inter-tribal feuds and occasional "blood-feuds," the peculiar way of settling "blood-feuds" through the elaborate negotiations on the acceptance of cattle, the role played by the chief in these negotiations, the relation between the extent of difficulty in settling a feud and the size of the group etc., will simply make no sense at all. To understand these essential components of the Nuer political system one has to know the tribal structure of the Nuer, the personality traits of the Nuer and the Dinka, the kinship system of the Nuer tribes, the importance of structural distance between different tribal sections among the Nuer, the minor authority enjoyed by the chiefs in non-ritual matters, the essential equalitarian upbringing and democratic orientation of the Nuer etc. That is to say, only through a holistic approach and contextual analysis through participant observation that Nuer political life could be traced and understood. As Evans-Pritchard remarks, the Nuer state is

"anacephalous kinship state and it is only by a study of the kinship system that it can be well understood how order is maintained and social relations over wider areas are established and kept up. The ordered anarchy in which they live accords well with their character, for it is impossible to live among Nuer and conceive of rulers ruling over them."[38]

It is needless to say that the last part of this statement can hardly be made by anyone who has been unable to make the "necessary transference" through sympathetic participation.

Bailey was encountering a situation which was substantively quite different from that of Evans-Pritchard. It was a situation characterised by change rather than stability. Hence, instead of Evans-Pritchard's "fission-fusion" model, he adopted an interaction approach in his analysis of the three different levels of politics in an Indian state: the village, the constituency and the state. Yet, it was only through contextualization and participation, or in other words, by adopting *their* respective points of view that Bailey could bring out the full implications of the relationship between the politicians (the elite) and the villagers (the masses) as well as the significance of the electoral constituency in this relational context. In his brilliant analysis of the quite different political processes within his two villages, Bisipara and Mohanpur, Bailey has demonstrated how important it is to grasp the meaning attached to their socio-political universe by the villagers themselves.[39]

PARTICIPANT OBSERVATION: HOW TO PRACTISE IT

The discussion so far has made it clear, we hope, that contextual knowledge is necessary for understanding the meaning of action or behaviour and that such contextual knowledge is to be acquired, for an outside observer, by means of secondary socialization through participant observation. Inasmuch as a political scientist is interested in understanding the meaning of political action and behaviour the necessity of contextual knowledge and the relevance of participant observation apply to her too. But we have not said so far exactly how can one participate while observing. The task of this section will be to clearly and precisely delineate the alternative possibilities that one may have while practising this particular mode of research.

Some specific discussion on the method of participant observation or "field-work," as it is more generally known among social anthropologists, has been done by Malinowski in the first chapter ("Introduction") of his *Argonauts of the Western Pacific* as well as by Radcliffe-Brown in his address on "the Present Position of Anthropological Studies."[40] E.E. Evans-Pritchard, in his *Social Anthropology*, has briefly discussed the "essential rules of good field work" in addition to giving a short account of the way in which a social anthropologist is trained at the University of Oxford.[41] Further, there are two excellent volumes, one edited by A.L. Epstein[42] and the other by M.

Freilich[43] in which the field work method has been discussed. To these was added yet another volume, edited by Andre Beteille and T.N. Madan,[44] in which a number of anthropologists-- most of them working on India, have presented rich personal reflections on their own field work experience.

While these constitute a highly illuminating as well as indispensable body of literature for training in participant observation, for a beginner, especially with political science background, a more precise formulation of the method of participant observation would be helpful. Michael Martin, following Becker and Geer, has attempted to present such a formulation.[45] With Martin's paper as our starting point we will elaborate below the different modes through which participant observation may be practised.

Modes of Participant Observation

Martin has distinguished three different possibilities that may be open to a social scientist intending to be a participant observer. First, the scientist may become a participant observer by *being a member of the group* he is studying. Secondly, the scientist may simply *pose as such a member* without in fact being so. Thirdly, the scientist may adopt the *role of an observer* rather explicitly.

"POSING" AS A MEMBER

Of these three, the second one is the most vulnerable. "Posing as a member" of the community one studies implies that the observer would go to the community and simply start living in it without revealing his purposes for doing so. Obviously, this is quite impractical as well as problematic. Assuming that the scientist is studying an alien society, how could he hide his own alien identity or "foreignness" in terms of his racial characteristic, language, dress and manners etc.? Could it have been possible for Malinowski to simply pose as one of them among the Trobriand Islanders or for Evans-Pritchard among the Nuers?

The problem is no less real even when an anthropologist goes back to study his own community as a participant observer. For if someone is staying outside his community for some time and then goes back to live in it temporarily, he has to do a good bit of explaining for his 'retreat'. And it would be well-nigh impossible for the scientist to continue his investigations and at the same time, hide the fact while offering explanation for his 'retreat'.

Besides, as M. N. Srinivas makes it very clear in his monograph,[46] even when the scientist goes to study a village in the region where his ancestors once lived, as Srinivas himself did, he need not expect an easy and automatic acceptance of himself by the native community. It is true that Srinivas did not attempt simply to "pose" as a member of the community without revealing his intentions. But the account of his encounter with the villagers shows rather unmistakably that he would have failed had he wanted to do that. For he was very *different* from the villagers and even such private habits and manners of his as eating a raw tomato as part of his lunch (the villagers are not used to eating salads and only the children are in the habit of eating raw vegetables when they are being sliced by the housewives for cooking) or having a shave after rather than before his bath or preferring to have his bath in an enclosed booth rather than out in the open aroused curiosity, questions and disapprovals among the villagers.

The fact is that the scientist is always different in some important senses from the people he is studying and this makes it impossible for him to *pose* as one of them. This fact that the scientist is different from the people he studies is relevant not only when one studies a spatially bounded community such as a village, but also when special groups such as factory workers or 'street corner boys' are the subjects of study. Can a scientist, studying factory workers, simply pose as one of them? Would it have been possible for a Harvard graduate like William F. Whyte to pose as one of those slum dwelling gangs of unemployed boys found regularly in street corners whom he wanted to study?[47]

Besides, there is also the problem posed by the 'gatekeepers' of social research and it is not easy for the scientist to entirely escape them and enter into direct relationships with the people he will be studying.

This point needs some elaboration. According to Professor J.A. Barnes,[48] social science research has four components : the scientist, the citizens,[49] the sponsors, and the gate-keepers. By this last mentioned term Barnes means those individuals or organizations who control necessary access to the 'citizens': for example, the management whose permission must be sought before one enters a factory and approaches the workers for information for research. These 'gate-keepers' play a very crucial role and without letting them know her purpose and intentions, it is nearly impossible for the scientist to get to the citizens. How could Srinivas, for instance, bypass the Deputy Commissioner of Mysore District and still gain access to the documents concerning the village, or avoid the village headman and still enter and stay in the village posing as one of the villagers? Similarly, Whyte learned early in his Cornerville period the crucial importance of having support of the 'key individuals' of the groups or organizations he was studying and while he was willing to give information regarding his research to anybody it was only with the group leaders that he "made a particular effort to provide really full information."[50]

Finally, apart from these practical though very crucial difficulties, there is yet another problem of a more serious nature. Suppose that a scientist goes back to his own community or to any community and succeeds in posing as a member of that community without revealing his purpose. This will mean that gradually he will be absorbed into the life of the community and that the natives will allow him to know many of their private affairs without knowing that the scientist "would destroy the prized privacy of domestic life by rendering it public." This will naturally create, as it did for T.N. Madan,[51] a serious ethical problem for the conscientious scientist: whether and to extent he ought to use the material thus gathered?

A classic example of this essentially ethical problem was the Wichita Jury study of 1954 which was a part of the University of Chicago Jury Project. Under a grant from the Ford Foundation, a group of researchers of the University of Chicago Law School undertook an inquiry into the American jury system. As a way of gaining direct experience of actual jury deliberations the researchers decided to secretly tape such deliberations in a number of civil cases. After a long negotiation they persuaded the local judges to grant permission and it was decided that all marks of identification of persons and places would be carefully eliminated from the transcripts. But very soon the matter became public when an edited version of some jury deliberations were presented in a conference of lawyers, and immediately it created a serious controversy. The United States Senate intervened and a bill was enacted by which the recording of the deliberations of any federal jury was prohibited by law.

This is a situation which is very similar to, though not exactly identical with, "posing as a member" of the group. Here the researchers could not have the opportunity to pose as a member of the jury. But essentially the same tactics - that is, collecting necessary information without letting anybody within the group know - was applied by deciding to 'bug' jury deliberations.

The ethical questions involved in this case are clear: is it morally right to allow the jurors to think that they are acting in privacy when in fact they are not? And also, is it right to expose the jurors to the danger that what they individually say during deliberations might, in spite of all precautions by the researchers, become publicly identifiable?[52]

It is thus clear that participant observation, when it means collection of information in secret and under pretense, involves a number of practical and ethical problems. Hence, it might be best to avoid such a course in one's conduct of inquiry.

"BEING" A MEMBER

We now come to the meaning of participant observation in the first of the three senses mentioned at the beginning of this section, namely, 'being' a member of the group or community one is studying. According to Martin, 'being a member' of the group may have three distinguishable meanings. First of all, it might mean being a member of the group in the same sense in which a native is a member of the group ("native sense"). Secondly, one can be a member of the group simply by living in the group ("living-in" sense). Thirdly, living-in may sometimes mean that while the observer lives in the community under study, he also assimilates within in himself some of the characteristics of the group ("assimilation" sense).[53]

Native sense: Martin's discussion of being a member of a group in the "native sense" implies that only the natives can be members in that sense. Such a formulation, it appears, is not very helpful. The natives, though they are always members of their own group and participate in their group life unless they are physically away, can hardly be called 'observers'. For normally, a native does not observe her group life for the deliberate purpose of studying it (except in the sense that every self-reflecting person studies herself and her immediate surroundings carefully; but to bring participant observation down to that level is to entirely lose the meaning of the term as a research technique). On the other hand, when a native has, as her formal purpose, studying her own community, a process of 'distantiation' supposedly takes place between her and her community which distinguishes her from the other natives. About this latter point more will be said latter.

The point to be noted here, however, is that the native is either not an observer or when she is an observer,she ceases to be a native in the ordinary sense. Thus, Martin's idea that the "native sense" of being a member of the group is applicable only to the native is not very meaningful. It will simply be another way of saying that the natives are natives. If we are to retain this category at all, we have to apply it to all those observers who try to live as the natives to do with regard to a particular community.

But even in this sense, the "native sense" of being a member runs into difficulties. For what we have already said regarding "posing" as a member of the group also applies here. We have said that the scientist is different from the "citizens" (to use Barnes' expression) i.e., his respondents in some very important senses and that these differences are quite independent of whether the scientist shares the citizen's language, culture etc., or not. Thus, John Beattie, an English anthropologist, could not become a member in the native sense of the African Bunyoro community which he was studying because of the sharp differences between his own cultural background and that of the Bunyoro.[54] But neither could T. N. Madan become a member of the group of Kashmiri Pandits in the native sense in spite of his being himself a Kashmiri Pandit. Nor could M.N. Srinivas become a member of the village of Rampura in this sense even though he spoke the language of the villagers and shared their cultural background in a general sense. Thus, being a member of the group in the native sense does not carry us very far and hence, this need not be aimed at by the participant observer.***

Living-in Sense. There is, as we have already mentioned, a second sense in which the scientist can be a member of the group he is studying. This is the "living-in" sense. Simply, this implies that the scientist as participant observer lives in the community under study. Such "living-in" may ordinarily mean that the scientist lives in the community in the same way as he lives in his own community (though that may not exactly be possible). But it may also mean that while living in the community under study, the scientist emulates the ways of the natives: he attempts to share the beliefs and values of the natives and practice some native customs and rituals even though temporarily.

"Living-in" in this latter sense maybe distinguished from "living-in" in the ordinary sense and it may be termed as being a member of the group in the "assimilation sense." We will come to it in a moment.

Even in the ordinary sense, "living-in" does not mean that the scientist, while in the community under study, will be able to conduct himself in the same way as he does in his own society. That is, if he wants to live in the community under study, he will have to depart in some ways from his usual pattern of living. Thus, adaptation, if not assimilation, must take place in some form. To what extent the participant observer will adopt the ways of the natives leaving temporarily those of his own will depend on the scientist himself as well as on the society he is studying. For instance, Malinowski, while living among the Trobriands, deliberately isolated himself from the white men living there, took residence in the village, ate native food, sought out native entertainment and conversation through the native language. Yet, as his *Diary*[55] makes it clear, he could not completely share the customs and values of the natives nor did he seek emotional identification with them (the life of natives remained "as remote from me as the life of a dog").[56] For American or European women anthropologists and anthro-historians coming to India, the adoption of the native dress (sari) is rather common.

The fact that the nature of "living-in" depends much on the society itself becomes very clear if one considers Evans-Pritchard's encounters with the Nuer and the Azande. To study the Nuer, Evans-Pritchard had to participate in the everyday life of the Nuer community and to submit to Nuer custom. In fact, to overcome his initial difficulties and to feel himself as a member of the community, Evans-Pritchard even had to acquire a few cattle. But the Azande would not permit anything of the sort. In the words of Evans-Pritchard himself:

> "Azande would not allow me to live as one of themselves; Nuer would not allow me to live otherwise. Among Azande I was compelled to live outside the community; among Nuer I was compelled to be a member of it. Azande treated me as superior: Nuer as an equal."[57]

Assimilation Sense. To be a successful participant observer, simple "living-in" may not, however, be adequate, and some sort of assimilation may be necessary. This makes "living-in" in the assimilation sense important. For what is essential is not merely to live in the community one is studying but to live there with "ease, comfort, and familiarity." One must develop a 'feel' for the people one is studying and be able to generate responses among them. As Martin says, "...... to be a participant observer is to utilize a certain social know-how while living among the natives."

Assimilation with the community and developing this social know-how are the two sides of the same coin: one helps the other. One develops this social know-how with reference to a particular community through his assimilation with that community; on the other hand, one can successfully assimilate *for purposes of research* to the degree one has the social know-how necessary for that particular community. The expression 'for the purposes of research' in the above sentence is important for we are assuming that however much the scientist assimilates with the community, he does so for the specific purpose of understanding the community through participant observation. It is understanding that he aims at, not assimilation per se. There are cases, though rare, of anthropologists who become so much emotionally identified with the natives that they decided not to publish their data at all and preferred to live with the natives permanently.[58] But from our point of view, by such actions, they also cease to be participant observers.

That is to say, for acquiring the necessary social know-how, some sort of assimilation, though not complete identification, will be necessary. What this 'some sort of assimilation' exactly means will depend on the situation. Knowing the language would be one of the very first things. Besides, adoption of some of the customs and practices of the groups would also be necessary. Adoption of the *beliefs, goals or attitudes* would not be necessary for assimilation though occasionally, the scientist may have to pose as if he has in fact adopted them (for instance, when one deals with exotic peoples who would not otherwise permit the scientist to be with them at all). But, as we have said, it will be a matter of situational decision. Thus, for instance, acquisition of a few cattle was necessary for Evans-Pritchard for assimilation with the Nuer. Similarly, the spirit of assimilation led Whyte to organize a march on the city hall by the street corner gangs demanding better living conditions.[59] But, when Whyte used the slum language "to enter into the spirit of the small talk" while walking with some corner boys, "the walk came to a momentary halt as they all stopped to look at me in surprise. Doc shook his head and said, "Bill, you're not supposed to talk like that. That doesn't sound like you."[60]

Thus, the scientist has to decide where to draw the line in each case. Failure to do so might create misunderstanding or even bring hostility and ridicule.

The above discussion of the ordinary "living-in sense" and living-in in the "assimilation sense" of being a member of the group shows that these two senses cannot really be distinguished except in their simplistic meanings.[61] "Living-in" would surely include some amount of assimilation if it has to be meaningful. Thus, the one shades off into the other.

ADOPTION OF "OBSERVER ROLE"

The curbs on the attempts at assimilation by the scientist discussed above bring us to a discussion of the third possibility open to the scientist as participant observer, namely, the explicit adoption of the role of an observer ("Observer-role" sense).

Participant observation in this "observer role" sense would imply that the scientist would join the group she wishes to study as an observer, and once she joins the group she will promptly let it be known that she is there to study the group for research purposes. The most obvious case was that of John Beattie who went to the Bunyoro village in Africa as an observer. On his arrival, he announced to the villagers:

> "I have come to your country to learn your language, and about your history, your traditions and your customs and the way you live. I have come from a big school in Europe where grown-ups are taught, including some who come to Africa...".[62]

This placed Beattie in the observer role.

The adoption of such observer role does not mean that the scientist can no longer be a participant observer in the "living-in sense" or in the "assimilation sense" discussed above. There is nothing to prevent such an observer either to live in the community or to adopt some of the customs and practices of the people under study. In fact, in most cases, the holder of the observer role does both. Indeed, John Beattie himself, while assuming the observer role, was also a participant observer both in the "living-in sense" and in the "assimilation sense". But the "observer" has a choice. The scientist in the observer role may not try to assimilate at all; he may not even live in the community and opt for occasional visits. Besides, very often adopting observer role and restricting oneself to occasional visits may be the only means for participant observation (for instance, when one is studying such spatially scattered groups as factory workers in a city or middle class working mothers etc.). Thus, the observer-role sense is logically as well as practically distinguishable from the "living-in-sense" and "assimilation sense" of being a member of the group.

But Martin also believes that the participant observers in the latter two senses too have a similar choice: that is, participant observers in the "living-in-sense" or in the "assimilation sense" may not necessarily take on the "observer role". It seems difficult, however, to accept this position. The observer role is more universal and compelling than Martin believes.

First of all, it is doubtful whether any such announcement as the one made by Beattie really conveys to the natives what the scientist would want it to convey. How meaningful is it to the Bunyoro villagers that a white man from Europe has come to *observe* their way of life? They understand little of the meaning of observation in this sense and therefore, develop their own meaning of the scientist and her activities.

Whyte also found, while he started to hang about Cornerville, that he needed some explanation for himself and for his study and he began with rather elaborate explanation. But as he soon discovered, while the explanation was quite pleasing to himself, "nobody else seemed to care for it...... it was .apparently too involved to mean anything to Cornerville people .... I soon found that people were developing their own explanation about me...."[63]

This is what commonly happens. The community under study maybe completely alien to the scientist or it may be the one to which he ultimately belongs. In either case, the scientist will always have a role in the community; whether he likes it or not, it will be cut out for him by the community itself. Thus, Srinivas was not merely a Brahmin, but a "respected outsider and guest" in the village of Rampura. Such a role did not always suit him. For instance, even those people who became particularly close to him and served as very good informants kept him away from unpleasant facts about the village as such things ought not to be revealed to an outsider and guest.[64] Thus, the role he was asked to play made it hard for him to gather reliable information particularly regarding sex and money matters. But he hardly had any option.

This assignment of role by the community is important and no matter whether the scientist decides to become a member of the group in the "living-in sense" or in the "assimilation sense," she will, in addition, surely have to assume the observer role. The important thing for the scientist then is to try to understand what role she has been assigned to by the community she is studying and what does such assignment imply for her relationship with the members of that community. For it is on the basis of an understanding of this assigned role that the scientist will have to regulate her subsequent conduct and structure her future expectations.

The universality and compulsiveness of this assigned role has been brilliantly portrayed by McKim Marriott.[65] Having arrived in KishanGarhi, a village in Uttar Pradesh, just before the Holi he decided, as a true participant observer with Malinowski's advice in mind, to stay in the village and directly observe what goes on. It was no problem for the villagers to assign a role to this inquirer coming from a faraway land. Doused with pail of buffalo urine early in the morning by the wife of the barber, so far the most quiet and deferential lady in the neighbourhood, the anthropologist was welcomed in to the festival. In the afternoon, he was cleverly drugged with bhang (marijuana) by his so far constant benefactor, the village zaminder, which helped him to float that afternoon towed by his hosts. In the morning next, back to his senses, the anthropologist, by looking at his drenched clothes, vermilion-red face and orange hair, could only guess what went over him in the previous evening.

It took Marriott a whole year to understand the meaning of this riotous pandemonium of North Indian Holi and the role the village had assigned to him. As the Holi arrived next year, with a clear knowledge of the "contexts of its occurrence" and without the "draft of marijuana," Marriott could perceive in the Holi a momentary world of inverse order - an order in which "each riotous act implied some opposite, positive rule or fact of everyday social organization in the village." Each villager had to play his role in this order, including the bird of passage, the anthropologist. In this apparent pandemonium of inverse orders, "the observing anthropologist, inquiring and reflecting on the forces that move men in their orbits, finds himself pressed to act the witless bumpkin..... dancing in the streets, flutting like Lord Krishna with garland of old shoes around his neck."[66]

One final point about participant observation: no one can become a participant observer unless she is fully conscious of her own scientific aims. In one's own society, everyone is a participant observer of a sort. Yet her's is not participant observation in the sense in which we have been discussing it above. Again, when an alien researcher presents herself to a community as a participant observer, she is different from other aliens who might be participants as well as observers in the same community. That is to say, the participating scientist is different from the missionary, the trader or the foreign administrator. These latter are "amateur residents." While it is true, as Malinoswki admits, that sometimes works by them surpass "in plasticity and in vividness most of the purely scientific accounts," their tendency to "transform, or influence or make use" of their relationship with the natives virtually precludes the possibility of "a real, unbiased, and impartial observation."[67] Thus, whether one studies an alien society or her own, as a participant observer, she must have observation as one of her conscious purposes.

Advantages and Disadvantages of Participant Observation

Participant observation as a method of research, as here outlined, has certain great advantages as well as a few disadvantages. The great advantage of this method is the one on which its logic chiefly rests: namely, it helps its practitioners to understand the meaning of actions or events. Mckim Marriott's paper, to which reference has just been made in the previous section, provides a very good illustration of this point.

Marriott, arriving at KrishanGarhi immediately before the Holi, had an opportunity of directly observing, through participation, what it was all about. The riotous pandemonium of the Holi on the one hand, and the villagers' insistence, on the other, that all this was the festival of *Love*, left him in a quandary-- for he was unable to stretch his "mind so far as to include both "love" and these (riotous) performances in one conception," and had him set out for an adequate explanatory understanding of the villagers' perception of unity in these two sharply contradictory phenomena. Since the *Puranic* and mythological roots of the festival were not all too clear or convincing, Marriott went back to the methodological maxim of Radcliffe-Brown that "the meaning of ritual element is to be found by observing what it shares with all the contexts of its occurrence." Through a full year's direct observation of all the ritual performances in the village, Marriott could discern the "underlying connections between the moral constitution of villages like KishanGarhi and the general social form of the Holi festival." The riotous pandemonium of the Holy characterized by momentary structural reversal of social relationships was no longer mere meaningless aberration as it appeared to the observer at first sight. It represented rather a dramatic act of balancing: "world destruction and world renewal, world pollution followed by world purification."

It is needless for us to raise the question whether this is *the* valid interpretation of the festival of Holi. The important thing for us is to note that Marriott has demonstrated here how interpretative understanding can be arrived at through contextualization and participant observation. It is possible that without participant observation the importance of an event like the Holi would never have struck him at all. And even if he was interested in the event, any amount of factual description of the Holi would not have enabled him to get an adequate understanding of it. Contextualization was absolutely essential.

Besides, participant observation, as we have already pointed out, offers an opportunity for secondary socialization. If the scientist is an alien, like Marriott, such secondary socialization is vital. For although it will not reduce the essential difference between the scientist and the "citizens" (i.e., the people or the community under study), nor is it expected to eliminate completely the alien scientist's consciousness of her own culture and achieve an ultimate assimilation between herself and the natives, secondary socialization will help her to build bridges and get a vantage point for understanding the meaning attached to actions by the actors themselves in an entirely different cultural milieu.

Such secondary socialization, or more properly "resocialization," is also essential, as T.N. Madan has shown,[68] in the case of a scientist who is studying her own community. For, it may be assumed that the native scientist must have gone through a process of "distantiation" (to use Louise Dumont's expression) as a result of her University training and acquisition of theoretical knowledge, and probably also by her physical separation from her own community for a considerable period of time. This distantiation and the resulting "desocialization" of the native scientist from her own society can be countered through participant observation and the opportunity for resocialization that it affords.

Secondly, participant observation offers a unique opportunity for knowing not merely how a society actually works but also for capturing the more delicate distinction between how a society actually works and how it says it works. This refers to the distinction between what one says he does and what he actually does. In anthropological literature, it has been expressed as the difference between the *emic* phenomena and the *etic* phenomena. While the emic (from phon*emic*) phenomena incorporate the native's judgement or his point of view about his own behaviour or action, the etic (from phon*etic*) phenomena are "those that are identifiable and studied independently of the natives cultural judgements."[69] Interestingly, therefore, the method (of participant observation) which appears to be the most helpful in permitting one to understand the subjective meaning attached to action by the actors themselves-- that is, in other words, the actor's "point of view," is also an efficient method for understanding action or behaviour independent of such subjective meanings or "points of view." Thus, as John Beattie argues, while through occasional visits and set interviews the inquirer can find "what people think happens or should happen (or perhaps only what they wish her to think happens)," she cannot find what actually happens. "To learn this, people's daily activities must be observed over a long period......"[70]

Srinivas provides a good example of this distinction and of how it could be perceived through participant observation. On his first visit to Rampura, when he was still undecided regarding his choice of that village for study, he was told by the eldest son of the village head man that Rampura was quite unlike neighbouring villages in that it was free from factional politics. To Srinivas, who was looking for a rather typical village, this remark came as a negative feature of the village and he came to doubt the typicality of Rampura as an Indian village. But left with no better choice, and also due to certain aesthetic considerations, he finally chose Rampura as his village for study. Soon after his arrival, however, he discovered that Rampura was no exception in so far as village factionalism is concerned. Two incidents, which we need not recount here, took place within the first few days of his stay in the village in which he found "an implicit repudiation of the claim repeatedly made by the Establishment that Rampura, unlike neighbouring villages, was unified and free from factions."[71]

This, then, was the case of a clear hiatus between what one says and what one does (individually or collectively) and it could easily be detected through participant observation. During his stay in the village Srinivas could see that there indeed was some basis for the villagers' belief about the absence of factionalism in Rampura. For unlike neighbouring villages where factionalism ran deep, it was rather muted there. But it was there all the same, and looking diachronically, Srinivas could demonstrate that even in the recent past, factionalism was quite rampant in Rampura.[72]

Both the emic view and the etic view of our social life are real as well as important and participant observation appears to be a very effective method for capturing both of these dimensions.

Thirdly, participant observation is not merely a very productive method for gathering information but also it is an effective way of knowing what information to seek and what questions to ask. We have, in the very beginning of this chapter, referred to Frederick Frey's advice that configurative and case study approaches may be the best ones to be employed when one is dealing with a completely new area of investigation.

This is a very sound piece of advice. When one confronts a new area, not a very rare occurrence in current social science research, one just does not know what to look for. Only through direct and patient observation one attains the capacity, in such cases, to distinguish the relevant from the irrelevant. William F. Whyte's experience is very instructive on this point. Whyte, in his street corner study, was exploring a rather untrodden area in social research. Once, having asked a wrong question unknowingly, he placed himself in a very uncomfortable situation vis-a-vis his respondents. He was subsequently advised by his chief informant to wait patiently and let people accept him. For once that happens, said his informant," you will learn the answers in the long run without even having to ask the questions." Whyte learned his lesson and, as he said later,

> "... this was true. As I sat and listened, I learnt the answers to questions that I would not even have had the sense to ask if I had been getting my information solely on an interview basis."[73]

While he did not abandon asking questions, Whyte simply "learned to judge the sensitiveness of the question" and his relationship with the people concerned.

In social and humanistic studies this is very important. All issues are not the same. Nor are the people that one encounters. Unless one develops this "sensitiveness," one may get very little by way of asking questions "from without." Sometimes, one may have to pay a price. Srinivas, for instance, says that in order to preserve the " the mutual trust, affection and respect," he gave up " premature display of curiosity about sensitive areas of personal and social life," and he admits that he probably "erred on the side of caution."[74] Yet, we believe it is a price well paid by a scientist belonging to the social and humanistic disciplines.

While such are the strong points of participant observation, it has certain drawbacks as well. The most important drawback of this method arises out of the possibility that the personal bias of the observer may enter unobtrusively into one's observations and inferences and may thus reduce their scientific value. Radcliffe-Brown talked of this as "the personal equation" of the investigator influencing the results, and recognized this as a valid objection.[75] He suggested three remedies for the elimination of such personal equation. First, he recommended "the development of a technique or methodology of interpretation" which could use crucial facts or events to demonstrate the validity of a particular interpretation.

Secondly, he suggested that through multiplication of studies of the same sort and by bringing a larger number of investigators in the field and also by encouraging collaborative efforts among scholars, the effects of personal equation could be reduced. Finally, he discouraged "bare-foot empiricism" and suggested that sociological theories should be developed adequately so that the actual field worker may use such theories as guide for empirical research.

Fortunately, developments have taken place along the lines suggested by Radcliffe-Brown. Collaborative works are much more common these days and at the same time, current social science research shows a much greater theoretical concern than before. Also, detailed statement regarding the field situation and thorough accounts of the procedures for data collection are now usually considered as part of one's research report. A social scientist can hardly disagree these days with Srinivas when he says,

"The assumptions he (the anthropologist) makes about social relationships, his initial mistakes and the gradual diminishing of mutual bewilderment are essential steps in the anthropological knowledge. To leave out all this may make for economy of presentation but it also means the removal of a dimension of reality. How can one be sure that this does not subtract from the reader's understanding of the community if not distort it?"[76]

Besides, as a result of development in communications and easy availability of research support the observations of a researcher these days can easily be cross-checked by another researcher through replication. This surely helps reduce the effects of "personal equation"-- unconscious or deliberate, and contributes to the growth of scientific knowledge about human collectivities through participant observation.

Secondly, while the practice of participant observation may, particularly in the initial stages, generate a spirit of adventure in the scientist, in the long run it places her under severe strain. Living in an alien society or under unfamiliar conditions is not easy. It requires various sorts of adjustments, both physical and psychological. Sometimes these may become so unbearable that the scientist develops a longing for relief. Evans-Pritchard gave expression to this feeling when, apologizing for the pun, he admitted that "after a few weeks of associating solely with Nuer one displays... The most evident symptoms of 'Neurosis.'"[77]

While reading Malinowski's *Diary* one gets a similar picture. As Professor Firth wrote of the *Diary*:

> "The feeling of confinement, the obsessional longing to be back even if for the briefest while in one's own cultural surroundings, the dejection and doubts about the validity of what one is doing, the desire to escape into a fantasy world of novels or daydreams, the moral compulsion to drag oneself back to the task of field observation... have rarely been better expressed than in this diary."[78]

There is yet another problem of participant observation which arises out of the already noted fact that the observer is almost inevitably assigned a role by the community under study. As there are certain unstated expectations around every role, so also is the case with this role and it is almost impossible for the scientist to violate any of the expectations that are attached to her assigned role without damaging her relationship with the community. This often imposes limits even on the scientist's physical movements (and by implication, also on her capacity to collect relevant information) and may create a sense of confinement in her. Srinivas, for instance, had to dismiss the idea of visiting the toddy shop in the village "as it would have been hopelessly inconsistent with the role assigned to me in the village. Even my progressive young friends would not have understood my visiting it."[79]

Similarly, Andre Beteille also found a role assigned to him in the village of Sripuram in Tanjore which he was studying and realized that the villagers "would consider it most unnatural if I decided suddenly to act in ways that were quite contrary to what was expected."[80]

This assigned role playing often creates discomfort and it hardly permits the observer to relax. But these are some of the tribulations of field work and any prospective field worker must get her well prepared for these.

Finally, one more search tribulations must be mentioned as a note of caution. In most cases, a social scientist deals with a stratified society, and in such societies, being too close with certain people or groups may mean for the scientist considerable information blockage. Beteille has particularly focused on this point. Beteille's decision to live in the area within the village where the Brahmins dwell made it impossible for him to be close with the Harijans, for in that case he "would almost certainly become suspect in the eyes of both Brahmans and Harijans."[81]

Similarly, Srinivas by residing in the house provided by the village headman and by developing a close relationship with him deprived himself of the company of those whom the headman disliked. But he "accepted such limitations and tried to work within them."[82]

We discuss this point not because we have any readymade solution for it, for such limitations may just be inescapable in a stratified society. Indeed, as Beteille remarks, in course of "adjusting oneself to stratified community one learns the nature of stratification itself."[83] The important thing for the scientist in this case would be to know, as early during her stay as possible, whether she was mixing with the right people for purposes of her research.

One final point:in a discussion on participant observation it is customary to refer to the problem caused by the act of observation itself, known as the observer effect or the 'Hawthorne effect'. Since human beings constitute the subject of study in the social sciences, either in their individual or collective manifestations, it is almost natural that the act of observation will have an effect on them unless they are particularly naive or the act of observation is kept a secret.

That the simple fact of observation can act as a confounding factor (by affecting and thereby changing the behaviour in question) came to light in connection with the Hawthorne studies on the effect of incentive systems on worker productivity in the General Electric plants outside Chicago conducted between 1927 and 1932 by a team of social scientists.[84] It was discovered that increase in productivity may not as much be due to things such as better lighting or changes in supervision style etc., as to the fact of the workers' recognition that they were being observed by sympathetic social scientists. The discovery was significant, for it pointed out that the interaction between the scientist and the respondents is a two way process and thus, as Barnes says, it drove the first significant nail "in the coffin of the natural science paradigm as used in social science."[85] In a more restricted sense (adequate for our present purposes), however, it raised the question of the validity of what one observes: whether the behaviour in question has not changed due to the fact of observation itself.

This observer effect or the 'Hawthorne effect', however, is particularly confounding in the case of experimental studies.[86] But it is not necessarily so in participant observation. Indeed, as Verba points out, participant observation may be used as a check on observer effect.[87] Verba suggests that participant observation, if concealed can control observer effect, for then, the subjects would remain unaware of the fact that they were being observed and hence, observation could not have any influence on their behaviour. It may, however, be argued that participant observation need not be concealed to avoid observer effect. Whatever observer effect maybe there in the beginning (of the process of participant observation), under the impact of patient and prolonged observation it will surely dissipate.[88]

The social scientist as a participant observer can count on such dissipation for the simple reason that even if the scientist merely assumes an observer role (without even bothering for "living-in" or 'assimilation'), frequent contacts between herself and her respondents will gradually remove the artificially assumed part in the respondents behaviour. It is because of this that a participant scientist can hope to grasp both the etic view and the emic view of human behaviour.

Endnotes

1. Verba, "The Uses of Survey Research," in *Comparative Survey Analysis* by Stein Rokkan, Sidney Verba, Jean Viet and ElinaAlmasy (The Hague : Mouton, 1969)70; Sidney Verba, The Cross- National Program In Political And Social Change: A History and some Comments," in *Cross-National Comparative Survey Research: Theory and Practice*, eds. Alexander Szalai and Riccardo Petrella in collaboration with Stein Rokkan and Erwin K. Scheuch (International Social Science Council Standing Committee on Comparative Research (Oxford : Pergamon Press, 1977), 188-192.

2. Ibid. p.98.

3. Fredrick Frey, "Cross-Cultural Research in Political Science," in *The Methodology of Comparative Research*, eds. Robert T. Holt and John E. Turner (New York: The Free Press, 1970), 258.

4. Frey, Ibid. p.234. By "Multi-Stage Sampling" Frey means that aggregate data concerning the larger units around the individual should be used "before one finally arrives at the individual respondent." In other words, the individual should be placed at the narrower end of the funnel, as it were, and be looked at from the larger end of the funnel.

5. Ibid. p.258.

6. Adam Przeworski and Henry Tune, *The Logic of Comparative Social Inquiry* (New York: Wiley-Interscience, 1970), 5-8; Neil J. Smelser, *Comparative Methods in the Social Sciences* (New Jersey : Prentice Hall, 1976), 202-05. The issue is also of critical significance from Marxist perspectives. We omit such a discussion here as it would require a separate and elaborate treatment. For a brief reference to the issue and for further readings see, Tom Bottomore, *Marxist Sociology* (London : Mcmillan 1975).

7. Following Talcott Parsons, we will use the terms "Verstehen," "Subjective understanding" and "Understanding" interchangeably. Max Weber, *The Theory of Social and Economic Organization*, ed. with an introduction by Talcott Parsons (New York: Oxford University Press, 1947), 87-88.

8. Weber, *The Theory*, 103-4. See also Weber's discussion on " "Objectivity" in Social Science and Social Policy," Max Weber, *The Methodology of the Social Sciences*, eds. E. A. Shils and H. A. Finch (New York: Free Press, 1949), 49-112.

9. Ibid. 94-95.

10. Ibid. 96-99; for a brief but lucid discussion of the point in W. G. Runciman, *Social Science and Political Theory* (Cambridge: Cambridge University Press, 1971), Chap. 1. Runciman makes the interesting observation that "the proper function of a social science is not prediction but diagnosis," 17.

11. Theodore Abel's attack on the idea of *Verstehen* in Abel, "The Operation called *Verstehen*," *The American Journal of Sociology* 54, no. 3 (November 1948): 211-18.

12. Winch questions the logical validity of supplementing *Verstehen* by statistical probability : "...I want to insist that if a proferred interpretation is wrong, statistics, though they may suggest that that is so, are not the decisive and ultimate court of appeal for the validity of sociological interpretations in the way Weber suggested. What then is needed is a better interpretation...The compatibility of an interpretation with the statistics does not prove its validity." Peter Winch, *The Idea of a Social Science* (London:Routledge&Kegan Paul, 1956), p. 113. For a critical and stimulating discussion on the subject see also, Karl R. Popper, *Objective Knowledge* (Oxford: Oxford University Press, 1972), 183-90.

13. See Brian Fay, *Social Theory and Political Practice* (London: Allen and Unwin Ltd., 1975). Fay critically discusses both positivistic and interpretative models and presents, instead, the model of a "Critical Social Science" which asserts that "in order to have subject matter at all the social scientist must attempt to understand the intentions and desires of the actors he is observing, as well as the rules and constitutive meanings of their social order." pp. 94 ff.

14. Abel, "The Operation."

15. Weber, *The Theory*, 90.

16. Ibid. 91.

17. Smelser, *Comparative Methods*, 59.

18. Talcott Parsons, *The Structure of Social Action*, 2 vols. (New York: Free press, 1968),2:635-36.

19. See also Winch's discussion of "meaningful behaviour" in Winch, pp. 45-51. Winch is clearly of the opinion that actions have sense not only when they are linked to 'reason' or 'motive' of the actor, but also when they are symbolic : that is, when the act in question "has a relation to a social context."

20. Murray Wax, "On Misunderstanding *Verstehen*: A Reply to Abel," *Verstehen: Subjective Understanding in the Social Sciences,* ed. by Mercello Truzzi (Massachusetts: Addison-Wesley, 1974), 70-82.

21. Radcliffe-Brown, "The Methods of Ethnology and Social Anthropology," in A.R. Radcliffe-Brown, *Method in Social Anthropology*, ed. M.N. Srinivas (Chicago: University of Chicago Press,1958), 25.

22. Radcliffe-Brown, "The Present Position of Anthropological Studies," in Radcliffe-Brown, *Method in Social Anthropology* , 67 (italics mine).

23. E.E. Evans-Pritchard, *Social Anthropology* (London: Routledge and KeganPaul, 1951),85.

24. Ibid. 80 (italics mine)

25. Robert Redfield, *The Little Community* (Chicago: University of Chicago Press,1956), 168.

26. Ibid. 158.

27. B. Malinowski, *Argonauts of the Western Pacific* (London: Routledge and Kegan Paul, 1922), Foreword, xvi.

28. Ibid. "Preface," by Sir James G.Frazer, ix.

29. R. Firth, *Elements of Social Organisation* (Boston: Beacon Press, 1963), 22-23 (italics mine).

30. Ibid,20.

31. Margaret Mead, *Anthropology: A Human Science* (New York: Van Nostrand, 1964), 15-35.

32. Ibid. 33.

33. Firth, Elements, 23-24 (italics mine).

34. Evans-Pritchard, *Social Anthropology*, 79 (italics mine).

35. David Easton, *The Political System* (New York: Alfred A. Knopf, 1953), 111.

36. Ibid. 113.

37. These questions create real difficulties not merely in studying primitive and non-literate peoples which a political scientist seldom does, but also in studying the political processes within small communities and groups which do not have formal institution.

38. E.E. Evans-Pritchard, *The Neur* (New York: Oxford University Press,1969), 181.

39. F.G. Bailey, *Politics and Social Change-- Orissa in 1959* (Berkeley: University of California Press, 1953).

40. Radcliffe-Brown, *Method*, 68-75.

41. Evans-Pritchard, *Social Anthropology*, 76-77 ff.

42. A.I. Epstein (ed.), *The Craft Of Social Anthropology* (London: Tavistock Publications, 1967).

43. M. Freilich (ed.), *Marginal Natives: Anthropologist at Work* (New York: Harper and Row, 1970).

44. Andre Beteille and T. N. Madan (eds.), *Encounter and Experience* (Delhi: Vikas Publishing, 1975).

45. Michael Martin, "Understanding and Participant Observation in Cultural and Social Anthropology," in *Verstehen*, ed. Truzzi, 112-119.

46. M.N. Srinivas, *The Remembered Village* (Delhi: Oxford University Press, 1976), Chap.2.

47. William F. Whyte, *Street Corner Society* (Chicago : University of Chicago Press, 1943).

48. J.A. Barners, *The Ethics of Enquiry in Social Science* (Delhi: Oxford University Press, 1977).

49. Barnes prefers the term 'citizens' to 'subjects' or 'objects' of study as this term stresses that "they are, or ought to be, both autonomous, responsible individuals possessing rights and duties and, at the same time, members of some collectivity ..." Ibid. 7.

50. Whyte, *Street Corner*, 300-01.

51. T.N. Madan, "*On Living Intimately with Strangers,*" in Andre Beteille and T. N. Madan (eds.), *Encounter and Experience*,151.

52. J. A. Barnes, *The Ethics*, 22-26.

53. Martin, "Understanding and Participant Observation," 112-116

54. John Beattie, *Understanding an African Community:Bunyoro* (New York: Holt, Rinehart & Winston, 1965).

55. B. Malinowski, *A Diary in the Strict Sense of the Term* (London:Routledge and Kegan Paul, 1967).

56. Ibid., p. 167.

57. Evans-Pritchard, *The Nuer*, 13-15.

58. Madan, "On living intimately," in Beteille and Madan (eds.), *Encounter and Experience*, 148.

59. Whyte, *Sreet Corner*, 337-41.

60. Ibid. 304.

61. It should be noted, however, that here also our formulation differs some-what from Martin's. According to Martin, "living-in" means that the ob-server lives in the community under study and while living in, he also "adopts some of the customs and practices" of the natives. "Assimilation sense" means, for him, the observer "lives in a community, develops some social know-how" through following some of the customs of the natives and "is assimilated to a certain extent in the community." Thus, adoption is common to both; assimilation sense differs from the living in sense in that the former assumes that the observer is trying to develop some social know-how. We maintain that thus formulated, the two senses can hardly be distinguishable, for some social know-how will be indispensable even for intelligent adoption just as some amount of adoption of native customs etc., will be necessary for acquiring social know-how. Thus, if the two sens-es are to be *conceptually* distinguished at all, "living-in" must mean mere physical presence. Yet, *in practice*, such simple "living-in" would be hardly feasible without some amount of adoption and/or assimilation.

62. John Beattie, *Bunyoro*, 14; cited in Michael Martin, "Understanding and Participant Observation," 117.

63. Whyte, *Street Corner*, 300.

64. Srinivas, *The Remembered Village*, 40-43.

65. McKim Marriott, "The Feast of Love," in Beteille and Madan (eds.), *Encounter and Experience*,83-97.

66. Ibid. 96-97.

67. Malinowski, *Argonauts*, 18.

68. Madan, "On Living Intimately," in Beteille and Madan (eds.), *Encounter and Experience*, 146.

69. It was the linguistic Kenneth Pike who first proposed this distinction. It has been further elaborated in the context of social anthropology by Mar-vin Harris in his *Culture, People and Nature* (New York: Thomas Crow-ell,1971), 59-61.

70. John Beattie, *Other Cultures: Aims, Methods and Achievements in Social Anthropology* (London : Cohn and West, 1964), 80.

71. Srinivas, *The Remembered Village*, 22-23.

72. Ibid. 221-22.

73. Whyte, Street Corner, 303.

74. Srinivas, *The Remembered Village*, 43.

75. Radcliffe-Brown, *Method*, 70-71.

76. Srinivas, *The Remembered Village*, 51-52.

77. Evans-Pritchard, *TheNuer*, 13.

78. Professor Firth's "Introduction" to Malinowski, *Diary*, XV-XVI.

79. Srinivas, *The Remembered Village*, 50.

80. Andre Betellie, "Tribulations of Field Work," in Beteille and Madan(eds.), *Encounter and Experience* , 104.

81. Ibid.

82. Srinivas, *The Remembered Village*, 47 ff.

83. Beteille, "Tribulations," in Beteille and Madan (eds.), *Encounter and Experience*, 103.

84. F. J. Roethlisberger and W.J. Dickson, *Management and the Worker* (Cambridge: Harvard University Press, 1939).

85. Barnes, *The Ethics*, 46.

86. Sydney Verba, *Small Groups and Political Behaviour* (Princeton: Princeton University Press, 1961), 75-86.

87. Ibid. 79.

88. Malinowski, in fact, perceived this phenomenon of diminishing observer effect very clearly during his stay among the Trobriand Islanders. Very significantly, he noted, "... as the natives saw me constantly, they ceased to be interested or alarmed or made self-conscious by my presence. I ceased to be a disturbing element in the tribal life which I was to study, altering it by my very approach, as always happens with a new comer to every savage community." Malinowski, *Argonauts* 7-8.

8

Focus group research

The simplest test of whether focus groups are appropriate for a research project is to ask how actively and easily the participants would discuss the topic of interest.

David L. Morgan

Focus group discussion (FGD), also known as a focus group interview or group depth interview, is a qualitative research method where the researcher seeks to develop in-depth insights into socio-political issues by listening to people and learning from them. Simply put, it refers to an informal discussion among a selected group of individuals on a particular topic, e.g. a few economists exchanging views on the latest budget proposals of the government; some members of the working class discussing their preferences for candidates contesting the forthcoming elections; or a group of adolescent schoolgirls sharing their experiences of sexual harassment. It needs to be noted that FGD can be used as an exclusive research technique for a particular research project or as one among other techniques used by the same project.

FGD involves a collective conversation among a body of individuals. These individuals, however, do not constitute a statistically selected sample representing a wider population. Rather they are purposely chosen for conducting the group discussion focused on the particular topic which is of interest to the researcher. The members of a focus group are assembled based on their relation to some common interest or 'focus', e.g. sharing some particular belief, experience or social position. The researcher, in the capacity of an anchor/facilitator, engages the group members in a more or less freewheeling conversation. This discussion often yields data – such as those pertaining to the individuals' emotions or unconscious motivations – that could not be accessed through questionnaire-based surveys or formal interviews. Indeed, FGD could be likened to a 'social event' that involves conversation and argumentation within agroup situation, and unravels information through interaction of individuals which makes the outcome of such discussions more than a sum of their parts.

Points to remember

- FGD is a qualitative method in which the researcher aims at gaining insights into socio-political issues by listening to collective conversation among a group of people.

- These individuals are not statistically chosen but purposively selected based on their relation to some common interest or 'focus'.

- Conversation and argumentation within the group context often brings out data otherwise inaccessible through surveys or formal interviews.

This chapter begins with the history of FGD as a research tool, followed by an account of its nature and types. Next, it describes the steps in implementing FGD, together with extensive summaries of two examples of carrying out focus group research. A brief note of the debate between the votaries of quantitative methods and practitioners of focus group research has been noted next. Finally, the strengths and weaknesses of FGD have been commented on in the backdrop of its comparison with two allied qualitative data collection methods, interviewing and participant observation.

History[1]

The use of group interviews by Emory Bogardus in his social psychological research undertaken in the course of developing social distance scale in 1926 perhaps contained the seeds of FGD. The technique was more formally utilized in 1941 by sociologists Paul Lazersfeld and Robert Mertonwho sought to study **how media broadcast shaped popular attitudes** towards US participation in World War II. This project required the respondents to **register their views through button-pushing**; however, this exercise could not fully satisfy the researchers because it failed to reveal *why* the respondents subscribed to particular viewpoints. As a result they modified their approach to resort to **group interviews**. Also, a more **unstructured and qualitative format** was devised so that after listening and responding to the radio programmes, the participants could give their reasons for their individual and collective preferences through an open discussion with the researchers. A new research tool was thus fashioned and the details of its deployment were published in the form of an article jointly authored by Merton and Kendall titled 'The Focused Interview' in the *American Journal of Sociology* in 1946.

However, this initiative failed to hold much appeal for social scientists who remained more fascinated by the promise of quantitative techniques such as questionnaire surveys and individual interviews as a means of data collection; and consequently, the 'focused interview' seemed to fade into oblivion. But though marginalized in the academia, the method attained increasing visibility and popularity in the commercial world as **an effective market research technique in the 1960s.** The person responsible for the development and dissemination of the focus group method in the commercial arena was Thomas Greenbaum. However, while Merton and Kendall sought to impart a qualitative flavour to FGDs, its use in market research constituted **a tightly structured exercise** very much befitting the **quantitatively-oriented** positivist tradition. The primary aim of focus group research as part of marketing strategy is to elicit the views and opinions of a cross-section of clients on new products to assess their potential popularity before launching them in the market. Since the object here is to seek specific answers from the consumer participants, the role of the researcher conducting a group session becomes more akin to that of a proactive interviewer rather than moderator/ facilitator. Similarly, group interaction largely becomes an interaction between the moderator and the participants: the participants answered questions posed by the investigator while exchanges among participants were reduced to a minimum.

The 1980s saw a revival of interest in FGD in academic research when many social scientists and other professionals found its **loosely structured qualitative format** attractive and useful. US political scientists sought to gauge popular perceptions of candidates and their opinions on significant electoral issues through FGDs. This technique was also used during the Reagan presidency to measure people's views on the Soviet Union and its citizens. In UK, the New Labour government tried to take stock of the multiple and at times conflicting perspectives held by various segments of the public on critical policy issues such as government spending on defence, health and education. FGD has been extensively utilized in the field of public health, as part of preventive healthcare strategies and campaigns; once HIV turned into an epidemic, FGDs were relied on to expand the knowledge of researchers and activists about the gay community. Finally, given the potential of FGD to be especially effective in the study of the marginalized and peripheral communities, it has been widely taken up by scholars with a transformative agenda such as the Marxists and the feminists.

Thus Focus group research has passed through three historical phases:

- Emerged as a quantitative social research tool in 1940s which shortly attained qualitative features

- Suffered an eclipse in the academia in 1950s but was revived in 1960s as a quantitative tool of market research
- Back into academic research in a qualitative format since 1980s

Nature[2] and Types[3]

As already noted, focus groups are **group discussions involving six to 10 people** who meet in a conference room-like setting which are arranged to examine a specific topic. Thus, instead of each member being asked the same set of questions by an interviewer, FGDs seek to explore a certain theme in sufficient depth and great detailing in the interactive mode. Through FGD it is thus possible to help the participants to bring out their deeper feelings and reflections on the theme under inquiry which respondents in a large scale survey would not have an opportunity to express. **The members of the group** are selected because they **shared a particular attribute** (such as caste, class, gender, ethnicity, age); had **some particular experience** (e.g. a group of cancer survivors); or are related to **some phenomenon of interest** (e.g. wives of army pensioners). These participants may be unknown to each other or, alternatively, part of a pre-existing natural community.

A focus group aims to **understand a particular issue from the perspectives of group members** by teasing out the meanings and interpretations they attach to the issue at hand. The researcher here is primarily interested not in capturing the individual accounts but in the **emergence of meanings through intra- and inter-personal debates and negotiations**. Interaction thus constitutes the life blood of FGD and the group dynamic enables people to better reflect on and clarify their viewpoints which some scholars describe as 'group effect'. This also helps the researcher to access shared lived experiences of the group participants, **which cannot be wholly uncovered through conventional one-to-one interviews**. The respondents are also enthused by each other to muster the courage to come out with their inner feelings. The success of FGD, however, largely depends on the development of **a permissive, non-threatening environment within the group** so that the participants could share their opinions and experiences comfortably and without fear. If they sense that they would be judged, ridiculed or shouted down while freely and frankly airing their views and concerns, the very purpose of the exercise stands defeated.

In other words, focus group interaction must be **similar to natural social interaction** among its members as far as possible, and the **researcher**

who performs the role of a *moderator* rather than interviewer has a key part to play towards ensuring this. The task of the moderator, who comes equipped with a small number of questions, is to monitor a complex interaction, encourage contributions by the participants while managing diversions and disruptions. Rather than imposing himself/herself upon the group, the moderator must be prepared and willing to hand over a large degree of control to the group members so that the discussion could unfold spontaneously and drift in different directions. The moderator's priority instead would be to observe how the participants are reacting to each other and how their opinions are being influenced by the collective conversation. Thus the moderator's role calls for simultaneous involvement and detachment which at times necessitate the induction of a second moderator into the process to effectively carry out the FGD exercise.

Nyumba et al have sought to present a classification of **various types of focus groups** in terms of size/number of group(s), number/role perception of moderators and online/offline organization of group discussion. This typology which is based on the existing literature pertaining to use of FGD as a research tool, and illustrative rather than exhaustive in nature, could be summarized here. First, the classical FGD involves **interaction among a team of participants and moderator(s) acting as one group** and functioning at a particular place and time. Though the usual number of participants in FGD hovers between six and 10, at times the researcher has to be satisfied with **lesser number of participants**, and hold a 'Mini FGD', especially when the pool of participants is naturally limited (e.g. a body of experts) and their availability also restricted. At times, thirdly, **two groups are used**, one actively engaging in discussion and interaction and the other observing it, usually from behind a glass partition, without being visible to the members of the first group. Based on their observations and the notes taken in its course, the participants of the second group reach their own conclusions which would likely appear sufficiently different from those they would otherwise have drawn.

Another set of innovations relate to the **group moderators: their number, role and identity**, which throws up three further possibilities. In the first case, two moderators who share a well-understood division of labour and yet work in tandem ensure that group interaction advances smoothly and all aspects of the theme are comprehensively addressed. In a second instance, two moderators deliberately take contrarian positions on the concerned topic during the discussion which, it is assumed, would contribute towards more in-depth disclosure of information by the participants. For a change, thirdly, the researcher may encourage one of the participants to lead the discussion as a temporary moderator on the expectation that this experiment might tweak the group dynamics and stimulate more varied and honest responses from the group members.

Finally, the giant strides made of late in the field of information and communications technology (ICT) have enabled even researchers using qualitative methods to take advantage of these **technological advances** and brought into being **online or virtual focus groups**. They do not necessarily represent a different category of focus group but have emerged out of the adaptation of traditional FGDs to the internet revolution, and are conducted with the help of conference calling, chat rooms and other online options. The pragmatic advantages offered by electronically conducted focus group activity include reduction in the cost and time of organizing group discussions, reaching out to geographically dispersed individuals, availability of the complete record of the discussion rendering transcription somewhat redundant, and the anonymity ensured by the research setting that boosted participants' confidence. In pandemic situations generated by Covid-19, or other sorts of disaster may compel researchers to resort to virtual focus groups as a way out. This may be particularly helpful for research projects which want to unravel the impact of the disaster itself by permitting real time investigation. On the downside, however, access to internet (or the lack of it) becomes a key determinant of the composition of the group; technological issues such as connectivity failures might interfere with the smooth progress of the discussion; and the online format by its very nature largely limits gathering of non-verbal data derived from observation of the body language of the participants.

To summarize the nature and types of FGD:

- FGD aims at in-depth exploration of a research theme in an interactive mode.

- The researcher seeks to study how meanings emerge in the context of collective interaction.

- The 'group effect' encourages participants to share their lived experiences as well as innermost thoughts and feelings.

- The researcher assumes the role of a moderator, leaves the discussion to be carried on mostly by the participants while ensuring that each of them can comfortably express their views.

- Focus groups have been classified by composition of the group, number of moderators and online/offline organization.

Description of the technique[4]

Focus group research has four steps or components: **drawing up the research design, conducting group interaction, analyzing the data collected in the process and reporting the findings of the research.** The point of departure is **identification of the aims of research and outlining of its objectives** which usually consist of gathering data for hypothesis testing. However, FGD could also be used for preliminary exploration of an issue, generation of hypothesis, pretesting or supplementing results arrived at through other, quantitative, methodological exercises. Secondly, **a list of questions** has to be developed as a rough guideline for conducting the session which the researcher has to discreetly check off from time to time while overseeing group interaction. Since a session is not supposed to last more than an hour and a half, the researcher could at best use five to six questions which need to be drafted in a way as to effectively cover the various dimensions of the concerned topic.

This is followed by **identification of the participants,** a crucial step given that the success of FGD largely depends on group dynamics and synergy-building among the participants. While the composition of the group would be determined by the aim of the research, it is important to ensure the willingness of the participants to engage in discussion. For some, this object is expected to be better fulfilled if the group members were alike in terms of social characteristics, i.e. age range, gender, ethnic origins, and class background which make it akin to a 'naturally-occurring' group. However, those who disagree with this homogeneity principle argue that groups consisting of strangers could overcome the constraints of pre-existing relationships/ patterns of dominance, and come up with honest and relaxed responses.

As to the **method of recruiting participants,** several options are available ranging between door-to-door canvassing to telephone calls. Further, a consensus has evolved among researchers on two points: (a) participants may be recruited through purposive sampling to ensure that those selected would actually be able to furnish the relevant information; and (b) the respondents may be offered some incentives, including monetary payments, in return for the time and energy invested by them. Using local contacts for roping in participants remains an easy way out though critics maintain that it would make the researcher unnecessarily dependent on the local contact at the cost of his/her control and direction over the recruitment process. Moreover, it would entail 'convenience sampling' which would turn accessibility of the participants the prime criterion for recruitment and might invite 'volunteer bias'.

The **number of participants** gives rise to another thorny issue in this connection. Though researchers seem to agree that the group size should be limited to six to 10 members, some studies have been carried out with as few as four and as many as 15 participants. Since it is difficult to guarantee that all participants who have been contacted would actually turn up for the session, it is advisable to recruit 10 to 15 per cent over and above the targeted group size. In any case, conducting group discussion with more than 12 members becomes difficult to manage and the group tends to get fragmented into several separate and independent discussion clusters. On the other hand, if the group is limited to a few participants, and the discussion time is restricted in order not to tax the patience of the participants, one session might not be sufficient to explore in-depth all aspects of a research theme which has prompted some scholars to hold three to four sessions for meeting their research objectives.

Next, the researcher has to look for a convenient **venue** for holding the discussion, keeping in view participants' comfort, ease of access and levels of distraction among others. The session should be held in **normal and familiar setting**, informal as far as possible in order to stimulate group conversation, and convenient for various kinds of activities the group members might be required to undertake in its course. The venue should be commodious where the participants sit in a circle or around a seminar table so as to have a clear view of each other as well as the moderators with name tags provided to each participant for easy identification. The session gets going as the researcher welcomes the participants, explains the goals of the meeting, undertakes a brief review of its agenda, invites the members to introduce themselves, and spells out the ground rules for conducting the session (e.g. everyone is expected to speak but should wait for one's turn). The participants are required to fill up forms to furnish some basic background information and also to sign the consent document indicating they have understood the purpose of the meeting and chosen to take part in it of their own accord.

This brings us to the second – **data collection** – phase which calls for effectual team work between a moderator and his/her assistant (or two moderators as the case may be). The **moderator's role** is central to taking the discussion forward by creating a congenial and comfortable environment for the group members and managing inter-personal relationships without being overbearing. The principal objective of the moderator should be to ensure that every member could take his or her turn to speak which in practice often becomes a difficult and delicate task as would be evident from the following advisory from Halperin and Heath:

All members should participate as much as possible. If one or two people are dominating the meeting, then call on others. Tell the individuals you want to hear from others. Don't look at individuals, when you ask a question. Raise your hand as if to say stop when the individual tries to talk, and look at someone else. You might say something like 'Let's have someone else go first'. If the participant continues to dominate the session, you might suggest using a roundtable approach, including going in one direction around the table, giving each person a minute to answer the question. If the domination persists, note it to the group and ask for ideas about how the participation can be increased.

Don't be abrupt with the dominating participant, as it may discourage participation from others. And if you feel your efforts to broaden the discussion has led to a withdrawal of participation by the dominating individual, try to re-establish the rapport. If nothing else works, take a break, and privately discuss your concerns with the individual or ask the individual to leave. . .

Indeed, the moderator's job includes maintaining the focus as well as the easy-paced flow of the discussion, and to ensure that the information generated in the process remains meaningful and relevant in terms of the questions framed which calls for reflecting on the discussion that followed each question from time to time.

The task of the **second moderator/ assistant** is to take discussion notes complete with who said what and how, supplemented by observation of non-verbal interactions and the impact of the group ambience on the thought process of the participants. Non-verbal data covered the participants' body language conveying their moods and feelings before, during and after the session which furnished 'thicker' descriptions and interpretations over and above verbal data contents. Nuyamba et al refer to four sources of non-verbal communication data based on participants' behaviour reflected by body displacements and postures (kinesics); use of interpersonal space to communicate attitudes (proxemics); temporal speech markers such as gaps, silences, and hesitations (chronemics); and variations in volume, pitch and quality of voice (paralinguistic).

The **duration of the meeting**, as already suggested should be between one and two hours to avoid respondent fatigue, although in practice it would depend on the complexity of the topic under investigation, number of questions and the size and composition of the group. **Recording** the session through audio/ audio-video recorder, of course with the participants' consent, is extremely important, using high quality yet unobtrusive equipment. However, **transcription** of recorded data may involve several challenges resulting from free flow of the conversation, varying volumes of voices and periodic interruptions which make notes taking and participant observation equally important modes of data collection.

To turn to the **analysis** part, the dominant practice so far has been to indulge in **interpretive analysis**: the researcher gets immersed in the material and develops a thematically ordered account supported by appropriate quotes from the transcripts. This approach, however, is beset with several problems: (a) whether or how far these illustrative quotations represent the broader themes remains questionable; (b) statements quoted in isolation from their immediate context poses another kind of issue; (c) presentation of extracts from group discussion is also not considered adequate for systematic analysis of data. These issues could be addressed, it has been suggested, through mixed content analysis which seeks to integrate interpretive sensitivity with systematic coding.

After the analysis is accomplished, finally the **findings have to be collated into a report** which should be drawn up keeping in view the nature and needs of the target audience. The report, presented either in a narrative or point-wise format, must spell out the objectives of the research project, the background of the participants, the basic questions put before them and the findings duly supported by key quotes derived from the discussion together with the interpretations offered. Before dissemination, the findings should be shared with group participants, a practice known as member checking or participant validation, which would authenticate the findings and buttress the reliability of the report.

Briefly speaking, FGD involves four important steps:

- Formulating a research design involves making a set of decisions as to defining the group size, identification and recruitment of participants, questions to be asked, number and duration of meetings, and selection of an appropriate venue for holding the discussion.

- Conduct of the meeting calls for defining the role of the facilitator, and if there are more than one facilitator, the division of labour among them.

- Analysis is essentially interpretive in nature, though its limitations may be sought to be addressed through adoption of a mixed method strategy.

- Findings to be shared through a report compatible with the nature and needs of the target audience.

Examples

In this section, implementation of focus group method will be illustrated with brief summaries two research articles which aimed at exploring the behaviour of **political elites** and **average citizens** respectively using FGDs. **Rhodes and Tiernan**[5] sought to assess the contribution of focus group research to the study of political elites, which they described as **elite ethnography** and found **useful in accessing the goings on in the innermost recesses of government**. Their point of reference was two closed roundtable FGDs conducted in 2009 with a cohort of 11 former Chiefs of Staff (CoS) to the Prime Minister of Australia who had served during the premiership of Malcolm Fraser to Kevin Rudd. Though CoS to the Australian prime minister played a key role in executive networks, the body of knowledge about the nature of this office remained very limited which constituted the basic impetus for this study. And while it was difficult to *observe* these elite actors at work thanks to access restrictions and secrecy considerations, focus groups conducted with incumbents who were no longer in office offered a second best alternative to ethnographic research. However, **the researchers did not use FGD as a standalone tool** of exploring elite behaviour but chose to **supplement it with documentary resources and informal conversations** as well.

The **battery of questions** developed by the researchers to be addressed in each session included the following:

- How did the job of CoS develop/evolve?

- How did different individuals approach the task of working with the Prime Minister?

- What were the key duties and responsibilities that they were required to perform?

- What were the key challenges confronting the CoS at different stages of the governing cycle? What kind of lessons they wanted passed on to their successors?

In this particular case, the **group participants almost chose themselves** given the nature and objectives of the research, but **contacting them and persuading them to attend** the group interaction proved a long haul. The researchers thought it would be wise to approach these political heavyweights through people they knew and trusted; and for this purpose they relied on their contact networks, including those cultivated during an earlier and similar study conducted by them in the United States. It is only after the initial contacts were thus established that the researchers entered into direct communication with these individuals and dispatched to them a background paper which outlined the aims of the project. However, the hectic schedules of these senior political functionaries impacted the FGD in two ways: **two separate roundtables had to be organized**; and the number of participants – seven in one group and four in the other – did not quite match. Each of the two group meetings, held in Canberra and Sydney respectively, lasted for about four hours with refreshment served in between. Keeping in mind the sociopolitical status of the respondents, the researchers decided against videotaping the proceedings and relied rather on recording and transcriptions though still photographs of the groups and individuals were taken for use in the research report.

The **procedures for conducting FGD** were also modified in keeping with the central objective, i.e. studying governing elites. A list of research questions were circulated to the high profile group members about a week in advance with a request to each respondent to begin discussion with a specific question. This departure from the established FGD norm was required since these elite respondents were used to set their own agendas which reduced the moderators' task only to making sure that the entire range of topics was covered and the conversations did not veer away too much from the discussion schedule. Further, since the members – a group of like-minded colleagues – had agreed to share their experiences openly and in good faith, **they were assured that they did not need to worry about the consequences of any indiscreet remark they might have made during the exercise.** After all, the researchers' purpose was not to feast on their disagreements but to identify the common ground and draw relevant lessons for which quotations would be cited and attributed only with their express consent. Still given the respondents' eminent standing, the researchers almost inevitably had to face issues while managing the group dynamics – for example, one member refused to share discussion table with one former colleague, and another questioned the veracity of the background paper developed by the researchers – which at times gave the moderators a feel of losing control over the group.

The **voluminous output of the discussion** yielded remarkable insights into the functioning of the government. These ranged between the broad connotation of 'the political' that underpinned the understanding of the prime minister's support needs and the importance of protecting his/her health by carefully monitoring the 'safety of food' especially during foreign trips. The researchers were convinced that group discussion alone 'takes you down illuminating byways that would never occur in individual interviews' because 'the researchers don't know what they don't know, so cannot ask relevant questions'. The data churned out by the group engagements ran into 230 pages which prompted the researchers to go through it separately following an agreed coding protocol, compare the transcripts with audio recordings and make corrections wherever necessary. The **interpretive analysis of the data** rested on the assumption that the study of governmental institutions, functions and roles needed to be supplemented by an inquiry into the actions and practices of the incumbent actors which in turn were rooted in the meanings and significance they spin for themselves in terms of their beliefs and preferences. In other words, **the research report**, according to the researchers, was to be based on "a '**thick description**' in which the researcher writes his or her construction of the subjects' construction of what the subject is up to". Thus, through a two-step analysis, first, by scanning the beliefs and practices that impacted the webs of meaning constructed by individual participants; and then matching the patterns of action and corresponding beliefs, they sought to uncover the world of the shared beliefs and practices of the CoS.

Our second example consists of a study of **politicization**, or rather 'de-politicization', of **ordinary citizens** which **Sophie Duchesne and her team**[6] in 2006 sought to assess with reference to their **attitude towards European integration** carried out by. (**De**)-**politicization or apathy towards politics on the part of the masses** is supposed to constitute a threat to legitimate power in a democratic setup, and as such it has long been a major concern for western democracies. But the researchers did not appear to share this pessimism regarding popular apathy towards because they believed that lay citizens do become involved in political affairs. Indeed, when they 'talk politics', **they attach new meanings to political questions and categories** in the light of their everyday experiences. However, their way of engaging with politics is rarely captured through survey research because they are found to avoid discussing politics in the public space. For the same reason they only reluctantly respond to individual interviews: they recoil from opening up before the 'distant' and 'knowledgeable' interviewer who in turn often end up in studying 'de-politicization'. On the other hand, **FGDs appear to be the most appropriate instrument** of ascertaining what kind of competences lay citizens exhibit when confronted with political issues and questions. After all, FGD empowers the interviewees by its open and loosely structured format of interaction, and enables the participants instead to take the questions as a stimulus. They rephrase the questions, and follow them up as per their own preferences, while supporting each other in speaking their minds. After establishing the rationale for relying on focus group research to address the topic the author elaborated on three aspects of their work: **recruitment of participants, logic of sampling and style of moderating the proceedings.**

Usually, researchers who study popular opinion tend to choose those respondents who are interested in politics and usually found to volunteer for participating in such exercises. Ordinary folks, on the other hand, who almost by definition stayed at a remove from the political arena are less likely to respond to these calls. However, the author argued that recruiting only the members of the 'interested' public was likely to defeat the very purpose of the project which proposed to study the political orientations and competences of the 'average citizen', often perceived to be a victim of de-politicization. Hence the focus group members had to be enrolled from lay citizens who reflected the socio-political diversity of the population at large in terms of class, gender, generation and ethnic traits. They were offered rewards for agreeing to take part in the discussion, and traced proactively by the research team rather than waiting for them to 'volunteer'.

A second question that cropped up was whether the participants would be known to each other or pure strangers for a pre-acquainted group is admittedly easier to put together. However, in case of a pre-acquainted group, the author pointed out, it would be likely that the participants are already familiar with the political positions of each other. This would deny the researcher the opportunity to observe if and how far the group members identified with each other's political views,and the grounds of such agreements and disagreements. Hence the researchers went for assembling unacquainted groups though she acknowledged that individuals who are naturally averse to discuss politics in the public realm might further retract in the presence of people they met for the first time.

A final dilemma faced by the research team related to whether the advertisement for the recruitment should contain references to the discussion theme, i.e. the issue of (de)politicization. Disclosing the theme in advance was likely to affect the discussion in two ways: either many potential respondents thanks to their natural aversion to discuss politics in public would refrain from volunteering; or they would be encouraged to do advance 'home work' which would rob the exercise of the desired spontaneity. Thus the researchers ultimately chose to keep the research theme and aim undisclosed in the advertisement astheyconsidered it to be 'scientifically necessary'.

In the matter of **sample selection**, the researchers opted for the principle of combining social homogeneity and political heterogeneity. In other words, they sampled the participant groups according to their national (France, UK and French-speaking Belgium) and social (working class, employees and executives) characteristics. In **conducting the sessions**, the researchers resorted to 'non-directive interview': the moderator was not supposed to ask questions beyond the preliminary ones but rather help the respondents to frame their own questions regarding the central theme; and listen, repeat, or rephrase whatever they had to say.

The **project findings** confirmed the well-documented conclusions regarding widespread popular distrust and disaffection towards politics and politicians. But, the study concluded that this alienation had nothing to do with apathy towards politics or lack of political competence on the part of the participants. Moreover, the group discussions brought out that the working class members displayed greater inclination to rise above their differences to arrive at a consensual viewpoint compared to the executives. However, it was also found that while the executive members identified with a more cosmopolitan viewpoint in the course of the discussion, for the working class members the experience of being governed by or remaining subject to the concerned rules and policies took precedence.

Table 8.1: Lessons learnt from the examples

Example 1	Example 2
Focus on political elites	Focus on lay citizens
Rationale of adopting FGD explained	Rationale of adopting FGD explained
Nature of participants influenced recruitment process: elite participants were automatic choice	Nature of participants influenced recruitment process: enlisting ordinary citizens not necessarily politically inclined and not acquainted with each other was emphasized
Modification of style of conducting FGD to accommodate elite participants	No modification of style reported
Ethical issue: elite respondents were clearly assured that whatever information they shared would not be published without their explicit consent	Ethical issue: keeping in view the average citizen's reluctance to discuss politics in public, the advertisement for recruiting participants kept silent on the discussion theme - somewhat questionable from ethical standpoint - rationalized with reference to demands of scientific research.

FGD as a standalone method? A debate with Robert Merton[7]

Robert Merton, who along with Paul Lazarsfeld shared the paternity of FGD in the 1940s, wrote an article titled 'The focussed interview and focus groups: continuities and discontinuities' in 1988 which appreciated the role of focus groups in producing rich and valid data through a comprehensive engagement with the subjects on a given topic. At the same time, it **accorded focus group method a secondary status vis-à-vis surveys and experiments.** It argued that use of this method should be restricted to the exploratory stages of research – as a supplement to the quantitative methods and as a vehicle of generating hypotheses, designing questionnaires or interpreting survey or experimental results. This argument seemed to rest on **two assumptions**: surveys based on rigorously chosen samples are more reliable and useful for making broad generalizations regarding populations; however, focus groups are selected on purposive sampling which limits its reliability and the scope for drawing causal inferences.

Merton's position has sparked off a debate and attracted **two kinds of responses** which included a strong position and a weak position. The proponents of the **weak position** agree with Merton's core contention and acknowledge the limitations of focus group research from the standpoint of representation and reliability. However, they point out that these are practical problems and rectifiable: thus increased funding could secure a wider representational base of focus group samples. Similarly, the problem of reliability and generalization could be addressed through resort to triangulation. Thus, the researcher is advised to collect data through different techniques, including focus groups, each of which would be given roughly equal weight without letting the quantitative methods take automatic precedence over FGDs.

The **stronger response** – that FGDs can be used as a stand-alone method conducted in its own right – is rooted in critical questioning of the positivist paradigm of research and the 'new qualitative turn' in social sciences experienced over the last couple of decades. These scholars not only express their reservations about the hierarchy of methods implicit in Merton's observations on focus group research but take the critique much further as they questioned the very rationale of causal inferences in social research and assessment of research findings in terms of representativeness. Indeed, they also offer a critique of the survey method which they argue involves reification of the individual and atomization of their responses without taking the social context of communication into account. In their view, social science research cannot be reduced merely to the study of the individual; moreover, the responses of individuals and the meaning they carry for him/her is very much context-dependent, and therefore could be better captured in the interactive milieu of focus group discussions.

In sum:

- The positivists raise doubts about the inferences drawn from FGD research.

- A defiant response to this critique consists of questioning the positivist assumptions and methods of data collection.
- A more accommodative position suggests that focus group method be used conjointly with other qualitative and quantitative techniques.

Assessment[8]

Two principal conventional means of collecting qualitative data are individual **interview** which takes place between individuals where one respondent is engaged by the interviewer in a more or less structured setting; and **participant observation** that occurs in groups involving many participants who interact in a relatively unstructured 'natural' environment. **FGD** is a fairly recent addition to this list which, **as group interview, is positioned in between** these two methods. Though the issue has occasionally come up during our above discussion, it seems worthwhile to wind up by assessing the advantages and disadvantages of focus group in comparative terms with participant observation and individual interview.

Morgan's statement that both the strengths and weaknesses of focus groups could be traced to their two defining features, i.e. the centrality of the researcher's concerns and the format of group interaction, serves as a useful starting point this discussion. **FGD enables the researcher to observe a whole gamut of interaction** pivoting around a particular topic in a limited span of time which indeed is at the root of its reputation as a method quick and easy to execute. This has a clear edge over participant observation because it generates reports on a wide range of situations – which are not necessarily directly observable – and addressed to the researcher's core area of interest. However, **FGD, a variant of the interview method, provides opportunity to observe verbal behaviour alone**, and, through it, the researcher can collect only those data which the participants report themselves. If the research problem demands study of social actions per se rather than second hand accounts of the same (even if presented by the actors themselves), this could only be facilitated by the natural setting of participant observation. In fact, participant observation allows the researcher to study an array of interaction with the participants in their natural surroundings all of which could not be re-created within the simulated ambience of the focus group and provides access to uncontaminated statements of the participants' views and experiences.

The degree of **naturalness of focus group interaction could be impacted by the role of the moderator** who in order to keep the discussion close to the research topic intervened proactively and repeatedly and thereby hindered the flow of the interaction. The **group context could** also leave its imprint on the discussion content and **adulterate the data generated in the process in two ways**: it could encourage a conformist mind-set among the participants who might desist from parting with information they would have shared in private; or cause polarization within the group and thereby prompting some participants to express more extreme views than they would have voiced in private. The group's influence on the data may also relate to the participants' degree of interest in and involvement with the research problem: if the level of involvement is low, it would generate inadequate quantum of data; if it is too high, the moderator might find it difficult to keep the discussion to manageable proportions. **Still a major shortcoming of participant observation** is the problem of locating and finding access to sites which offered the opportunity to gather a substantial set of observations relevant to the researcher's interest. As Morgan aptly put it: 'By conducting focus groups, we admittedly had to sacrifice the immediacy and emotion of a naturally occurring episode such as the lunch conversation, but this was not really a loss because we could not "sacrifice" what we never had access to in the first place'.

On the other hand, **focus groups have relative advantage over face-to-face interview** in amassing **concentrated volumes of data on precisely the topic of interest more quickly and efficiently** because engaging in focus group research virtually amounts to holding several interviews simultaneously. **FGD**, moreover, allows the researcher to **observe interaction and exchanges among participants** which brings out the similarities and differences of their views right away while for individual interviews, such inferences could only be deduced from subsequent analyses of separate statements of multiple informants. However, the **closer communication between the interviewer and the interviewee** gives the former far greater control over the interview process and enables him/her to use more subtle clues to elicit information compared to what is necessary in steering group discussions. Further, **interviews** not only **allow ample time to the respondents to share their ideas**; in a one-on-one setting they also put the onus on the interviewees to clarify their viewpoints without much prodding from their interlocutors. **Focus group moderators, by contrast, are supposed to cede control** of the proceedings largely to the group members which might encourage them to digress from the agenda of discussion though this might be useful in exploratory research where the researcher may not initially be sure about the questions that need to be asked.

Interviews are also credited with fostering **in-depth understanding** of a person's opinions and experiences, though the assumption behind this proposition, i.e. the interviewee has a lot to share with the interviewer, may not always turn out to be correct. On the other hand, if interviews reveal how individuals feel, **focus groups encourage the participants to explore their feelings and attitudes in some depth**, while the researcher takes account of the personal contexts that group members used to frame their accounts, and seeks to understand why particular views were held by individuals and groups. Further, the cool and cozy ambience of **focus groups** which induce members to open up on their own **creates the right ambience for discussing delicate and sensitive issues** especially where participants support each other in self-disclosure. This creates possibilities for the researcher to examine the proverbial gap between what people say and what they do, the hiatus between their beliefs and action. Finally, **focus groups** are said to 'give a voice' to **socially marginalized communities** such as ethnic minorities, poor men and women, or people who often suffer social exclusion/ stigmatization like HIV/AIDS patients. Individuals belonging to these categories who often find it difficult to articulate their thoughts and face-to-face interaction too intimidating or unnerving, would consider focus group environment safe and supportive for sharing their ideas and beliefs.

Table 8.2: Ethnography, Interview and FGD – summing up

Ethnography	Interview	FGD
• Natural setting	• One-to-one scenario	• Presence of a moderator and a pre-selected topic makes focus groups more structured than participant observation
		• Participant-centric nature of group interaction in a focus group makes it less controlled compared to interviews
• Respondents furnish information in a voluntary and spontaneous manner	• Researcher exercises considerable control over informant	• A compromise between these two more popular qualitative techniques, and its flexibility perhaps remains its greatest source of strength

Endnotes

1. Pranee Liamputtong, 'Focus Group Methodology: Introduction and History', in Pranee Liamputtong (ed.) *Focus Group Methodology: Principle and Practice*, (London: Sage 2011), 9-11.

2. Jennifer Cyr, 'The Pitfalls and Promise of Focus Groups as a Date Collection Method', *Sociological Methods and Research*, (Volume 45 Number 2 2016), 233-36; Liamputtong, 3-7.

3. Tobias O. Nyumba et al, 'The use of focus group discussion methodology: Insights from two decades of application in conservation', *Methods in Ecology and Evolution*, (Volume 9 Number 9 January 2018), 24.

4. Ibid 22-24; Peter Lunt and Sonia Livingstone, 'Rethinking the focus group in media and communications research', *Journal of Communication*, (Volume 46 Number 2 1996) http://eprints.lse.ac.uk/409/ 6-7; Sandra Halperin and Oliver Heath, *Political Research: Methods and Practical Skills*, (Oxford: Oxford University Press 2012), 277-78.

5. R.A.W. Rhodes and Anne Tiernan, Focus Groups and Prime Ministers' Chiefs of Staff, *Journal of Organizational Ethnography*, (Volume 4 Number 2, 2015) https://www.semanticscholar.org/paper/FOCUS-GROUPS-AND-PRIME-MINISTERS%27-CHIEFS-OF-STAFF-Rhodes-Tiernan/30c0cebaf2eb1d6bef4e0e822a0a6d593f2c2628)

6. Sophie Duchesne, Using Focus Groups to Study the Process of (de)Politicization, in *A New Era of Focus Group Research*, (Palgrave Macmillan 2017), halshs-01674453.   https://halshs.archives-ouvertes.fr/halshs-01674453/document

7. Lunt and Livingstone, 12-13.

8. David L.Morgan *Focus Groups as Qualitative Research*, (Thousand Oaks and London: Sage 1997), 8-17; Liamputtong, 8-9

PART II

9

Measurement: the Cornerstone of Research

In social science research we often encounter large amount of information or data. These data by themselves signify nothing unless we organize, evaluate and summarise those. This calls for statistical manipulation of empirical data in a legitimate way or in accordance with certain rules. This takes us to the all-important issue of measurement. The empirical data collected by the researchers, rather than being haphazard collection of empirical facts, are aimed at to measure systematically the various aspects of the reality they face. The researchers are interested in assessing the similarities, differences and nature of variation taking place in the different aspects of the physical and social world. Precisely, they focus their attention on the measurement of the variable aspects or attributes of the reality.

Here it seems important to define the term 'measurement.' In the words of Campbell and Jeffreys[1], 'Measurement consists in the assignment of numerals to things or properties.' Now, the things or properties in question possess different dimensions. So, to measure those we need to follow certain rules. Perhaps, this has led Campbell and Jeffrey to come up immediately with the caution that, '…not every assignment of numerals is measurement'[2]. Hence, the properties, dimensions and attributes of Height, Weight, Speed, Political Affiliation, Gender, and Economic Status etc. are all different which necessitates different approaches of measurement. The same measuring principle applied to measure the variable 'Height', for instance, cannot be applied to measure 'Religious Affiliation'. We may assign numerals or other symbols to measure these but the assignment needs to follow the rules which are in tune with the differential nature of the attributes composing the variables. This introduces us to the domain of levels or scales of measurement.

Levels or Scales of Measurement

Depending on the rules determining the assignment of symbols, particularly, numerals, there may be four kinds of levels or scales of measurement. These are: (1) The Nominal Scale; (2) The Ordinal Scale; (3) The Interval scale; and (4) The Ratio Scale.[3]

The Nominal Scale

In nominal scale or level of measurement the numerals are assigned in most 'unrestricted' manner[4]. Here the numbers are devoid of any mathematical implications. These are used to label or name the categories only. Hence, other symbols, like letters or words could also be used. Some variables which can be measured at the nominal level are: gender, political party affiliation, caste affiliations, sectors of cities or wards of municipalities, zip codes of areas, colours of eye, skin etc. Usually numerals are assigned in the nominal level of measurement in two ways. For illustration, (a) assignment of Roll Numbers to students of a particular class in a school, and (b) assignment of numbers to designate each section under the class, like Section – 1, 2 or 3 etc. The first is used to identify the individual students, while the second is used to identify particular section of a class, the students of which are assigned a common numeral. In the first type of nominal scale only the number of cases or the students who are assigned the Roll Numbers is important In the second type where groups of students are clubbed under sections, we can determine, for example, which section is most numerous by inspecting the respective student strengths of the different sections. At the nominal level of measurement, only simple count of frequencies suffices as an operation. Here the numerals do not carry with them the usual mathematical connotations. For example we cannot get the student strength of Section-2 by multiplying the same for Section-1 by 2 or by adding it twice. For this, often it is argued that the nominal measurement cannot be regarded as measurement at all. Accepting the substance of the argument, it can also be claimed that the nominal measurement is not fully devoid of any rules. The rule which determines the empirical operations at the nominal level pertains to the issue of 'equality', which states, 'Do not assign the same numeral to different classes or different numerals to the same class'[5]. This entails that the attributes measured at the nominal level are characterised by their 'exhaustiveness and mutual exclusiveness'[6]. Thus, to classify the Indians along their religious affiliation we need to make it sure that all the religions of India are taken into consideration and no individual can be placed in different classes of religious affiliations. Therefore, when we pick up any Indian, it is sure that s/he bears similarities with the group to which s/he belongs and dissimilarities with all the other groups or classes of religion. It entails that; any two Indians would either be similar or dissimilar in their respective religious affiliations. Beyond this issue of 'equality', the nominal level of measurement cannot provide any other information.

The Ordinal Scale

The ordinal measure can be applied to data which are rank ordered. This is a more sophisticated measure compared to the nominal one. Alike nominal measure, ordinal measures also classifies the scores into exhaustive and mutually exclusive categories. In addition to these, by ranking the scores in terms of 'high or low' or 'more or less' it can actually help in more nuanced inter category comparison. Moving beyond the classification of the cases, here the researchers are more interested in ranking the cases in terms of the degree of the attributes or characteristics of the variable to be measured. Thus, the ordinal measure, for example, is helpful for not only locating the similarities or differences between two persons in terms of intelligence, but also it can indicate which person is more or less intelligent than the other. A classic example of ordinal level of measurement is the caste system in India. We know that hierarchy or ranking of the various castes in terms of the notion of purity and impurity is a ubiquitous feature of the caste system[7]. Here, the upper castes are considered to be more pure than the relatively lower ones. Some other familiar examples are measures of socio-economic status, class status, conservatism, liberalism, attitudes and opinions etc. In order to analyze ordinal level variables we should employ those empirical operations which assume the relative rank order of the data in question. Since the categories in the ordinal level of measurement do not tell us anything about their actual difference so the measures which assume the equal size of the interval among the various categories cannot be employed here.

The Interval Scale

The variables which are measured at the interval level are 'quantitative' in the 'ordinary sense' of the word'[8]. At this level the cases are assigned numbers with almost all of their mathematical implications. Naturally, all the statistical operations, other than the ones which assume the knowledge of a 'true zero point' can be applied to measure the cases. At this level, we can not only classify and rank the categories, but also we know that there are equal intervals among them, which can be measured as well. Since we know the actual distance between the numbers in the number system, so we come to know, for example, the difference between one minute, two minute, and three minute and so on. The zero point in an interval scale is defined conventionally not mathematically. It does not imply the absence of the attribute being measured by the variable. Thus, zero minute or hour does not imply the absence of time. For this arbitrariness of the origin or zero point the scale is not at all affected when the origin is shifted by the addition or subtraction of a constant from it. For example the English calendar starts with January 1, while the Bengali calendar starts with 14th or 15th April, although both of these measure the year with 12 months or 365 days.

Classic examples of the interval scale are the two scales of temperature: the Centigrade and the Fahrenheit. Both these scales measure equal interval of temperature, but their zero points are conventionally agreed upon and do not imply the absence of heat. Hence, we can say that the difference between the two points 20 degree and 30 degree Fahrenheit is equal to the difference between 30 degree and 40 degree Fahrenheit, but it cannot be said that 40 degree Fahrenheit is twice the temperature of 20 degree Fahrenheit. The same can be said about the standardized intelligence test, which nowadays has become a useful tool in social science research. Here we can have measures of equal intervals as the difference between the IQ scores of 100 and 110 is just the same as the difference between 110 and 120. Since, in this scale the person whose IQ score is zero does not mean that s/he is without intelligence, we cannot say that the person with an IQ score of 160 is doubly intelligent than the one with an IQ score of 80.

The Ratio Scale

In ratio scale the attributes of the variables to be measured possess the most crucial 'true zero point', alongside possessing all the structural characteristics of the nominal, ordinal and interval measures. To Stevens, in a ratio scale, '...there exist operations for determining all four relations: equality, rank-order, equality of intervals, and equality of ratios.'[9] Thus, all types of statistical operations can be applied to measure the variable at the ratio level. Thorndike believes that the existence of the true or absolute zero point is one of the important elements of a valid scale, where the 'zero' signifies, '...barely not any of the thing in question...'[10]. Thus, if anyone says that s/he has zero rupees in her/his money purse, it means that s/he really has no money in her/his purse. The absolute zero point, according to Thorndike[11] also allows us to use the 'times judgement', so that, for example, we can say that the length of a particular period of time is twice or half, or one-third or one-fourth times of another period. Here we can also measure the equality of ratios as for example, the ratio of eight and four hours is the same as the ratio of 16 and eight hours. The familiar examples of ratio level measures in social science research are: age, income, years spent in schools, age at marriage, number of family members, population size, number of births and deaths, number of migrants, etc.

Here it is to be noted that all the four scales are cumulative in nature as far as the statistical and mathematical operations required to apply them are concerned. Thus, the ordinal scale, which determines the greater or lesser amount of the attributes of a variable by arranging the cases in rank order also incorporates into itself the operations required to determine equality or difference among the categories of the variable at the nominal level. Similarly, the interval scale in addition to measuring the equality of intervals also takes into consideration the operations required to measure the relative ranks of the attributes and equality of the categories of the variable at the ordinal and nominal levels respectively. A ratio scale measures equality of ratios but it is constructed by incorporating the structural properties of the interval, ordinal and nominal scales into it. Thus, as we move on from nominal to the ordinal, interval and ratio scale the scope of applicable statistical and mathematical operations goes on increasing. Precisely for this, the scales of measurement are also designated as levels of measurement.

Endnotes

1. N.R. Campbell and H. Jeffreys, "Symposium: Measurement and its Importance for Philosophy," *Aristotelian Society* 17, no. 1(1938): 122.
2. ibid.122
3. S.S.Stevens, "On the Theory of Scales of Measurement," *Science* 103, no. 2684 (1946).
4. ibid.
5. ibid., 679.
6. Earl Babbie, *The Practice of Social Research* (Belmont, CA: Wadsworth Cengage Learning, 2010), 143.
7. Louis Dumont, *Homo Hierarchicus* (New Delhi: Oxford University Press, 1980).
8. S.S.Stevens, "On the Theory of Scales of Measurement," *Science* 103, no. 2684 (1946): 679
9. ibid. 679
10. Edward L. Thorndike, "The Measurement of Educational Products," *The School Review* 20, no. 5 (1912): 219
11. ibid. 297

10

Organizing the Data: Frequency Distribution

The researchers in actual research situations collect and analyse information or data to find out reliable and valid answers to their research questions. The data by themselves do not reveal anything unless they are organized following certain principles. If the data are not appropriately organized then we cannot use statistics to measure them or to come to any valid conclusion about their trends and properties. The first step to organize data is to arrange it in a frequency distribution. Here it is important to know what is meant by frequency. To Cramer and Howitt, frequency is 'The number of times a particular event or outcome occurs.'[1] Hence the frequency of Brahmins in a sample, for example, is just the total number of Brahmins in the sample. Since there may be people of other castes in the sample as well, so it is better to have a summary description of all the castes in it. This description is presented in the form of a table known as frequency distribution. In Healey's words, 'Frequency distributions are tables that report the number of cases in each category of a variable'[2]. We can use statistical measures effectively and meaningfully only after we organize the raw data in a frequency distribution. So, frequency distribution is the rudimentary or first step for any statistical application to be applied to measure the underlying trends of a dataset.

To make things clear we can refer to a survey on people's orientation to politics. There are various ways through which people's orientation to politics have been measured in this survey. For the purpose of example we are restricting ourselves to only 30 sampled respondents and three variables viz. sex, level of interest in politics and their age. Consider the following data:

Table: 10.1. *Data of a Survey on People's Orientation to Politics**

Sex	Level of Interest in Politics	Age (in Years)
Female	Not at all Interested	28
Female	Not at all Interested	21
Female	Not very Interested	26
Female	Not at all Interested	52
Male	Not at all Interested	21
Male	Very Interested	50
Male	Not very Interested	27
Male	Not at all Interested	53
Female	Not at all Interested	25
Male	Not at all Interested	28
Male	Not at all Interested	25

Male	Not at all Interested	52
Female	Not at all Interested	20
Male	Somewhat Interested	24
Female	Not at all Interested	60
Female	Somewhat Interested	22
Female	Not at all Interested	67
Female	Not at all Interested	60
Female	Very Interested	20
Male	Very Interested	65
Female	Not at all Interested	39
Female	Very Interested	20
Female	Not very Interested	28
Female	Not very Interested	22
Female	Not very Interested	80
Female	Not very Interested	23
Female	Not very Interested	24
Female	Not at all Interested	75
Male	Somewhat Interested	70
Male	Somewhat Interested	30

Fictitious data

In Table: 10.1 we come across a very low number of cases. To understand the trend of this small sample consisting of only 30 individuals, employment of statistical methods may not seem necessary. Still it is not very easy, for example, to determine any pattern of political orientation out of it without some application of statistical methods. If this is the case for only 30 individuals then one can imagine what could be the situation for say 100, 200 or more cases. Here lies the importance of organizing and summarizing the data to enable us to apply statistical methods meaningfully to gain reliable knowledge about people's orientation to politics.

Since there are different levels of measurement to measure the attributes of different types of variables so there are different forms of frequency distribution as well.

Frequency Distribution of Nominal Data or Variables Measured at the Nominal Level

Since we know that nominal measure only arranges the data in different categories so constructing frequency distribution out of this data is not at all complicated. Researchers only need to count the total number of cases in each of the categories of the variable and report the information in a tabular form. In Table: 10.1 sex is a nominal level variable which has only two categories: male and female. Thus by simple counting of the frequencies of the males and the females in the sample of 30 respondents we can arrive at the following frequency distribution:

Table: 10.2. Distribution of Sex of the Respondents

Sex	Frequency	Frequency (Percentage)
Male	11	36.67
Female	19	63.33
Total	**N= 30**	**100.00**

The table describes the frequency distribution of the variable Sex of the respondents. Here some points are to be noted. The table has a label or number viz. Table: 10.2 and title viz. Distribution of Sex of the Respondents. From the title readers will get an initial knowledge about the nature of the data presented by the table. The table quite clearly mentions the variable in question (here sex of the respondents) and its two categories (male and female) and mentions the number of respondents belonging to these two categories under the column frequency (11 and 19 respectively). Then there is a row mentioning the total number of cases or total frequency or the total number of males and females designated by N (N = 30). In some instances frequency distributions also contain another column describing the percentage frequencies of the different categories of the variable. Here, the column frequency (percentage) presents this. This is obtained by dividing the frequency of each category by total frequency (N) and then multiplying it by 100. These are the essential components of any frequency distribution. Rather than the unorganized data in Table: 10.1, here we can get a summary picture of the data. Just by looking at the table we can know that, it is a table describing the sex of 30 respondents under study, where the number of male is 11 and the number of female is 19.

Frequency Distribution of Ordinal Data or Variables Measured at the Ordinal Level

The construction of frequency distribution of ordinal data follows the same procedure of that of the nominal one. In Table: 10.1, we can see that the variable 'level of interest in politics' is measured at the ordinal level. The categories of this variable has been ranked from 'not at all interested', through 'not very interested' and 'somewhat interested' to 'very interested' in politics. We have the frequency distribution of level of interest in politics in Table: 10.3.

Table: 10.3. Respondents' Level of Interest in Politics

Sex	Frequency	Frequency (Percentage)
Not at all interested	15	50.00
Not very interested	7	23.33
Somewhat interested	4	13.33
Very interested	4	13.33
Total	**30**	**100.00**

From a quick glance at the table we can know that the majority or half of the respondents included in the sample are not at all interested in politics. Sometimes the researchers, in order to have a sharp and more discriminating insight into the respondents' level of interest in politics, can collapse the categories 'Not at all interested' and 'Not very interested' into a single category 'Not interested' and 'Somewhat interested' and 'Very interested' into another category 'Interested'. Doing this the following frequency distribution can be constructed:

Table: 10.4. Respondents' Level of Interest in Politics (Rearranged)

Sex	Frequency	Frequency (Percentage)
Not interested	22	73.33
Interested	8	26.66
Total	**30**	**100.00**

It is evident from the table that 73.33% (almost $\frac{3}{4}$th)of the sampled respondents are not interested in politics against 26.66% (about $\frac{1}{4}$th) who are interested. Such collapsing may result in the loss of detailed information or nature of graded orientation of the people to politics but, nonetheless, it provides a gross and more focused picture of their orientation to politics.

Frequency Distribution of Interval/Ratio Data or Variables Measured at the Interval/Ratio Level

In contrast to nominal and ordinal data the construction of frequency distribution of interval/ratio data is more complicated. This is simply because nominal and ordinal level variable represent a limited number of categories. For example we can mention about sex which at present assumes the categories of male, female, lesbian, gay, bisexual, transgender and queer. Similarly, we can speak about religion which is also represented by a limited number of categories. But, interval/ratio data, in contrast, being numerical in nature can assume any value. Thus, a simple frequency distribution of interval/ratio data for its large number of numerical scores becomes long enough to make it difficult to comprehend. For the purpose of example, in Table: 10.5 we draw a simple frequency distribution of age of the 30 respondents from the data presented in Table: 10.1 before.

Table: 10.5. Simple Frequency Distribution of Age of the respondents

Age of the Respondents	Frequency
20	2
21	2
22	2
23	1
24	2
25	2
26	1
27	1
28	2
30	1
39	1
42	1
45	1
50	1
52	2
53	1
60	2
65	1
67	1
70	1
75	1
80	1
Total	**30**

Here there are 22 different ages of 30 sampled respondents. Undoubtedly, the constructed frequency distribution offers very little advantage to the readers in comprehending the age distribution of the respondents. From the frequency distribution it is also not easy to get the nature of the age distribution of the respondents. We cannot say at a glance whether the respondents represent a young or old population. If this is the case of only 30 respondents, one can imagine what would be the situation if there were more respondents as is usually the case in actual research contexts.

This difficulty calls for a grouped frequency distribution to represent the data with greater amount of clarity and focus. This is achieved by collapsing the scores into a number of smaller groups or categories[3]. To form a group of scores, each of these categories needs to contain more than one score values. These smaller groups or categories are known as **class intervals**. The size of any class interval is determined by the number of score values contained by it. Hence, the size of a class interval 5-9 is five since it contains the scores 5,6,7,8 and 9. Here it is to be noted that the class intervals of any grouped frequency distribution should be exclusive and exhaustive. Any score of the raw data can be placed in one and only one class interval. To illustrate, in Table 10.6 we present a grouped frequency distribution of age constructed by rearranging the ages of 30 respondents of Table: 10.1

Table: 10.6. *Grouped Frequency Distribution of Age of the Respondents*

Class Interval (CI)	Frequency (f)	Percent (%)
20-29	15	50.00
30-39	2	6.67
40-49	2	6.67
50-59	4	13.33
60-69	4	13.33
70-79	2	6.67
80-89	1	3.33
Total	**30**	**100.0**

Here the first column describes the class intervals or age groups of the 30 respondents. The next column after the one on age groups describes the frequencies. From this column we can know the number of cases belonging to each smaller category or class interval. It is evident from the column that the sampled respondents in question constitute a young population since a majority of them compose the age group of 20-29 years. This is clear from the next column which describes the frequencies of all the class intervals in percentages. This is also known as percentage distribution. That the sampled respondents constitute a young population is obvious since the majority or 50% of them belong to the youth category composing the lowest age interval viz. 20-29 years. The column on percentage frequency also enables the researchers to have inter-distribution comparison. We can easily compare the age distributions of different samples through this.

Class Limits

From Table: 10.6 it can be seen that each class interval designates a range from a low score to a high score viz. 20-29, 30-39 and so on. This low and high scores forming each class interval is known as class limits. The lower score from which the class begins is known as lower class limit and the higher one is the upper class limit. Thus, for the class 20-29 years of age, 20 is the lower class limit and 29 is the upper class limit. This way we can have these two limits for each subsequent class intervals in the grouped frequency distribution. From these two limits of each class interval we can calculate the size or width of the class interval. As is mentioned before, the size of the class interval is the actual scores contained by it, so we can find it out by subtracting the lower class limit from the upper class limit. Thus,

$$i = U - L \text{ where,}$$
$$i = \text{size of class interval,}$$
$$U = \text{the upper class limit, and}$$
$$L = \text{the lower class limit.}$$

Hence, the size of the first class interval = 29 − 20 = 10. This way we can calculate the size of all class intervals of the frequency distribution.

Midpoint

Since the class intervals are marked by two points or limits so often it becomes problematic to apply statistical measures or graphically represent the data. To resolve this, a representative score of each interval is required. This is achieved by calculating the midpoint of each class interval. The midpoint of any class, also known as class mark, is exactly the half way between its lower and upper class limits. The midpoint can be obtained by summing up the lower and upper class limit of each class interval and dividing it by two. Hence, for the class 20-29 years the midpoint will be $\frac{20+29}{2}$ = 24.5. Following this way the midpoints of all the subsequent class intervals can be calculated.

Class Boundary or Real Class Limit

Often there are gaps between the class intervals of a frequency distribution. This is due to the non-overlapping nature of the class intervals. In many frequency distributions we can see that the class intervals are not overlapping, meaning, there is a gap between the upper limit of any class interval and the lower limit of the next class interval. This is also the case for the grouped frequency distribution in Table: 10.6 presented here for the purpose of illustration. There are gaps between the class intervals 20-29, 30-39, 40-49 etc. Note the gap between 29 (the upper limit of the first class interval) and 30 (the lower limit of the second class interval). The same gap exists in all the subsequent class intervals. Due to this non-overlapping nature we cannot, for example, tabulate scores the values of which are, for instance, 29.2 or 39.6 etc. This creates problem for organizing interval/ratio level data as the variables which are measured at these levels often are continuous in nature, which theoretically can assume any value. For example we can mention the variables like, age, time, income, height, weight etc. If we cannot tabulate all the values in different class intervals then this is a violation of the rule of exhaustiveness of the frequency distribution. Moreover, for some other purposes like graphical representation of data and application of summary statistical measures, particularly those related to calculation of partition values like median, quartiles etc. overlapping class interval is a theoretical requirement. To resolve this problem the class boundaries or real/actual class limits are calculated. By eliminating the gaps between the class intervals, class boundaries indicate the actual points up to which a particular class is extended. Obviously, it results into changing the lower and upper class limits of any class interval into lower and upper class boundaries respectively.

There are certain steps to convert the class limits into class boundaries. These are:

1. Find out the gap or distance between the class intervals or the gap between the upper limit of any class interval and the lower limit of the next one. This distance can be termed as d. In Table: 6 we can see that $d = 1$

2. Calculate the halfway mark of the distance by dividing it or 'd' by two to get $\frac{d}{2}$

3. Subtract $\frac{d}{2}$ from all the lower class limit of all class intervals to get the lower class boundaries and add $\frac{d}{2}$ to the upper limits to get the upper class boundaries.

Therefore, rearranging Table: 10.6 following the steps mentioned above, we can have Table: 10.7.

Table: 10.7. Grouped Frequency Distribution of Age of the Respondents showing Class Boundaries

Class Boundary (CB)	Frequency (f)	Percent (%)
19.5 -29.5	15	50.00
29.5 – 39.5	2	6.67
39.5 – 49.5	2	6.67
49.5 – 59.5	4	13.33
59.5 – 69.5	4	13.33
69.5 – 79.5	2	6.67
79.5 – 89.5	1	3.33
Total	30	100.0

Here the class intervals are converted into class boundaries. The upper limit of the first class interval here, as describes Table: 10.6, is 29 and the lower limit of the next class interval is 30. So, the difference between these two limits or d = 1. Half of d, or, $\frac{d}{2}$ = 0.5. Now subtracting 0.5 from the lower limit of the first class interval 20, we get the lower class boundary to be 19.5, and adding 0.5 with the upper class limit, that is, 29, we get the upper class boundary of the class interval to be 29.5. This way we find out the class boundaries of the subsequent class intervals.

Procedure or Guidelines for Constructing Class Intervals

At first we need to take utmost care to ensure that the class intervals are non-overlapping or mutually exclusive. They also need to be exhaustive. This can be achieved by ensuring one and only one place for a score in the frequency distribution.

Then we need to decide about the number of class intervals or categories or small groups to represent the interval/ratio level scores in the data. Here, the crucial contradiction pertains to the fact of having a large number of categories or a relatively limited number of categories. If we have a large number of categories then the cases or scores falling within each category would be very low. This may lead to blurring the group distinctions. On the other hand, if we go for a relatively small number of class intervals, then the scores within each category would be large enough to wipe away the benefit of classification of the data. This may erase the desired precision of measurement. So, we need to strike a critical balance between these two positions. Conventionally, it is advisable to restrict the number of categories or class intervals within 5 to 20. But, since it is a guideline or advice, so, depending on their research objectives and the dataset at hand in actual research conditions, the researchers are free to arrive at any feasible decision regarding it.

After deciding about the number of class intervals to be constructed it is time to form the class intervals. Here the guideline is to form the intervals in such a manner so that the size or width of the class interval turns out to be a whole number rather than decimals[4]. This is for enhancing the ease of calculations involving the size or width of the class intervals. For this we need to calculate the range of scores in the dataset, that is, the difference between the highest and the lowest score in it. Then this range should be divided by the number of class interval we want to have. If the result of this is a decimal number then it should be rounded up to the next convenient whole number. This is the size or width of the class. It is conventional to begin the class intervals with the lowest score in the dataset as the lower limit of the first class interval and then go on adding the calculated size or width of the class with it to have the lower limits of all the classes. At the end if we see that the highest score of the data set is not yet covered then we can add one extra lower class limit to incorporate this. Then we need to find out the upper limit of every class keeping into mind that the classes cannot overlap. It is advisable, as argues Levin et. al.[5], to have the lower class limits as some multiples of the size of the class interval. For example, in Table: 10.6 the lower limits viz. 20, 30, 40 and so on are the multiples of the size or width of the classes, that is, 10.

As an example, let us look at Table: 10.6. From the raw data on age of the respondents presented in Table: 10.1, we get 80 years and 20 years as the maximum and minimum age of the respondents respectively. So here the range is $80 - 20 = 60$ years. Initially, we have taken the decision to have six class intervals. So the size or class width becomes $\frac{60}{6} = 10$ years. Thus, starting with the lower score 20 we have the lower limits as 20, 30, 40, 50, 60 and 70. Keeping 10 as the size of the classes we get the upper limits as 29, 39, 49, 59, 69 and 79. Thus we get six non-overlapping class intervals viz. 20-29, 30-39, 40-49, 50-59, 60-69 and 70-79. Since these six classes could not cover the highest score 80, so here we have added one more class 80-89 to incorporate it.

Cumulative Frequency and Cumulative Percentage

The frequency distribution of interval/ratio data describes number of cases belonging to each class interval. It, however, cannot tell us how many cases are lower than a particular score. This requires the frequencies to be presented in a cumulative fashion. It presents the position of a particular class with respect to the total frequency distribution or the overall scores in it. Hence, cumulative frequencies are also useful to obtain positional or partition values. Depending upon this need two more columns can be added to any frequency distribution, namely cumulative frequency and cumulative percentage. From these columns it can be known at a glance how many cases or what percentage of scores are there below a certain score. In Table 10.8, for example, we have added these two columns to the frequency distribution presented in Table: 10.6.

Table: 10.8. Cumulative Frequency Distribution of Age of the respondents

Class Interval (CI)	Frequency (f)	Percent (%)	Cumulative Frequency (cf)	Cumulative Percentage
20-29	15	50.00	15	50.00%
30-39	2	6.67	17	56.67%
40-49	2	6.67	19	63.34%
50-59	4	13.33	23	76.67%
60-69	4	13.33	27	90.00%
70-79	2	6.67	29	96.67%
80-89	1	3.33	30	100.00%
Total	**30**	**100.0**		

In the table we can see that there are 15 respondents within the class interval 20-29 years. This implies that the age of all these 15 respondents are either greater than or equal to 20 years or less than or equal to 29 years. So we can say that altogether 15 respondents are there below or up to the age of 29 years. So the cumulative frequency of this class is 15 because there is no respondent in the dataset whose age is below 20 years. Similarly, in the next interval we can see that there are 2 respondents whose ages are below or equal to 39 years. Now, this is also the fact that the 15 respondents of the preceding class whose ages are below or equal to 29 years are also below the age of 39 years. So cumulatively, there are 15 + 2 = 17 respondents whose ages are below or up to 39 years. Accumulating this way finally we can say that all the 30 respondents are below the age of 89 years. Hence, the cumulative frequency of the highest class interval will always be equal to N, because the upper limit of the highest class interval implies that all the scores must be lower or equal to it. In a similar fashion we can arrive at the cumulative percentage column by accumulating the percentages of respective class intervals. Here we have only concerned us with the scores which are the class limits of the class intervals. But we can use cumulative frequency distribution to ascertain the position or location of any score in the frequency distribution. Since the class intervals are non-overlapping, so to ascertain the position of the score which might theoretically lie at the gap between two class intervals we need to convert the class limits into class boundaries to incorporate all the scores included within the range of the class intervals. For example, we may be interested to know from Table: 10.6, the position of any age within the age range of 20 to 80 years, the lowest and the highest age of the respondents respectively. Hence, from the frequency distribution of Table: 10.6 we can arrive at the cumulative frequency distribution presented in Table: 10.9.

Table: 10.9. *Cumulative Frequency Distribution of Age of the Respondents showing Class Boundaries*

Class Boundary (CB)	Frequency (f)	Cumulative Frequency (cf)
19.5 -29.5	15	15
29.5 – 39.5	2	17
39.5 – 49.5	2	19
49.5 – 59.5	4	23
59.5 – 69.5	4	27
69.5 – 79.5	2	29
79.5 – 89.5	1	30
Total	**30**	

Since here we have overlapping class boundaries, as the upper boundary of any class is coinciding with the lower boundary of the succeeding class, so we can rewrite it by mentioning the pointed class boundaries. Thus, we can have the rearranged cumulative frequency distribution in Table: 10:10

Table: 10.10. *Cumulative Frequency Distribution of Age of the Respondents showing Pointed Class Boundaries*

Class Boundary (CB)	Cumulative Frequency (cf)
19.5	0
29.5	15
39.5	17
49.5	19
59.5	23
69.5	27
79.5	29
89.5	30

45 (arrow pointing between 39.5 and 49.5)   X (box beside 17 and 19)

Now, we have an impression about the position of individual scores in the distribution. This is constructed by just eliminating the coinciding class boundaries. Here the lowest class boundary 19.5 is having cumulative frequency 0 because no respondent is there below the age of 19.5 years. The cumulative frequency of the highest upper boundary viz. 89.5 years is 30 implying that all the respondents are below this age. From this table by applying the method of simple interpolation we can ascertain the position of any score or the cases lying below it.

Application of the Method of Simple Interpolation

Suppose we want to know the number of respondents whose ages are below 45 years. Simple interpolation requires locating this age in the series of class boundaries. Clearly, as marked in Table: 10.10, 45 years is located within the class boundaries 39.5 years and 49.5 years. Since we can see from the cumulative frequency column that there are 17 respondents below the age 39.5 years and 19 respondents below the age 49.5 years so the number of respondents whose ages are below 45 years must be located within these two cumulative frequencies. Let us assume this to be x, as is marked in Table: 10.10. Now to ascertain the number of respondents below 45 years of age we use the formula of simple interpolation, which may be written as:

$$\frac{Partial\ Difference\ in\ Class\ Boundary\ (PD_{CB})}{Total\ Difference\ in\ Class\ Boundary\ (TD_{CB})}$$

$$= \frac{Partial\ Difference\ in\ Cumulative\ Frequency\ (PD_{CF})}{Total\ Difference\ in\ Cumulative\ Frequency\ (TD_{CF})}$$

Here, Partial difference in class boundary (PD_{CB}) refers to the difference between the particular point located within two class boundaries and the class boundary preceding it.

Total difference in class boundary (TD_{CB}) refers to the difference between the class boundaries within which the particular point is located.

Partial difference in cumulative frequency (PD_{CF}) refers to the difference between the particular cumulative frequency (associated with the particular point in the class boundary) located within two cumulative frequencies and the cumulative frequency preceding it.

Total difference in cumulative frequency (TD_{CF}) refers to the difference between the cumulative frequencies within which the particular point is located.

So in our case,

PD_{CB} = 45 – 39.5 = 5.5,

TD_{CB} = 49.5 – 39.5 = 10,

PD_{CF} = x – 17, [Here x is assumed to be the cumulative frequency of 45]

TD_{CF} = 19– 17 = 2

Putting this values in the formula mentioned above we get,

$$\frac{5.5}{10} = \frac{x-17}{2}$$

Or, x = 18.1

Or, x = 18 (appx.)

So, 18 respondents are there whose ages are below 45 years. This way we can find the respondents below any age which lies within the age range of the frequency distribution. Here it is to be noted that, as we know the number of cases below a certain score so we can easily know the number of cases above it by subtracting the cases below it from the total frequency. So, in the example cited above, if there are 18 respondents below the age of 45 years then there are (30 – 18) = 12 respondents who are above the age of 45 years.

Endnotes

1. Duncan Cramer and Dennis Laurence Howitt. *The Sage Dictionary of Statistics* (New Delhi: Sage Publications, 2004), 67.
2. Joseph F Healey, *Statistics: A Tool for Social Research. Ninth Edition* (Belmont: Wadsworth, 2012), 31.
3. Jack A. Levin and James Alan Fox and David R. Forde. *Elementary Statistics in Social Research. Twelfth edition.* (New York: Pearson, 2014).
4. ibid.
5. ibid

11

Measures of Central Tendency

In quantitative research the best way to summarise data is through the application of the various measures of central tendency. Measures of central tendency, or statistical averages (or simply, average, in popular notions) indicate the central point of the distribution of data towards which items tend to show a tendency to coalesce or cluster. The value of a measure of central tendency is of immense importance to the researchers in two ways. First, it is representative of all the scores in a group of scores, thus, helping the researchers to arrive at a summary description of various features or parameters of the group. Second, the value of the measure of central tendency allows the researchers to have intergroup comparison on various desired and pertinent parameters of the groups concerned. There are three measures of central tendency which are commonly used by the researchers. These are: (1) The Mode; (2) The Median; and (3) The Arithmetic Mean, simply known as Mean. Here we shall have a brief consideration of these three one by one.

(1) The Mode

As a measure of central tendency mode refers to that score which occurs most frequently in a series. It is the 'most frequent, most typical, or most common value in a distribution'[1]. For example, in the series 15, 17, 13, 14, 13, 12, 14, 18, 14 and 11, since 14 occurs most frequently, so, here 14 is the mode or modal value of the distribution. Table: 11.1 present another example, which shows the numerical strength of different religious communities in India in 2011. It clearly reveals that the Hindus constitute the mode of the distribution, the single largest religious community in India.

Table: 11.1. *Population (%) by Religious Community in India, 2011*

Religion	Population (%)
Hindu	80.5
Muslim	13.4
Christian	2.3
Sikh	1.9
Buddhist	0.8
Jain	0.4
Others (including Religion not stated)	0.7

Source: Census of India, 2011

Limitations of Mode as a Measure of Central tendency

As a measure of central tendency, mode has some limitations. First, there may be some distributions or series of scores having equal values. In such cases there is no mode at all. Second, some distributions or series might have a number of modal values, which can make this measure dubious, if not meaningless (as is the case in Table: 11.2 below). Third and most important, since mode indicates the most frequent value, so in spite of being most common it may not be the typical value representing the centre of the distribution or any series of data (as is the case in Table: 11.3 below).

Table: 11.2. Marks Obtained by Students in Statistics (fictitious data)

Marks obtained in Statistics (%)	Frequency
85	6
75	6
60	1
55	6
50	2
45	6
40	2
35	6
Total	35

There are five modes in this distribution.

Table: 11.3. Number of personal e-mail ids of the students in a class (fictitious data)

No. of personal e-mail ids	Frequency
5	5
4	4
3	3
2	1
1	1
0	6
Total	20

Here the value of mode is 0, since the majority or six students have no personal e-mail id. This is the most frequent value but cannot represent the distribution.

(2)   The Median

Sir Francis Galton defines the Median as, '…the value which is exceeded by one-half of an infinitely large group, and which the other half falls short of'[2]. To Yule, it is the '…middle most or central value of the variable when the values are ranged in order of magnitude.'[3] Hence, the median is that score which lies at the middle of a series of scores so that half of the scores

(50%) have the values lower and half of the scores (50%) have values higher than it. By identifying the location of the middle most value of a set of scores that, '…cuts the distribution into two equal parts'[4], the median serves as a useful measure of central tendency. Obviously, to achieve the score values higher and lower than the median the scores are to be arranged in a rank order, either ascending or descending.

Median of a Simple Series or Ungrouped Data

To calculate the value of the median first we need to arrange the data in rank order. Then the position of the median can be located by counting the $\frac{N+1}{2}th$ value in the order. Here we are faced with two different conditions: first, when the number of cases in the series is odd, and second, when it is even. Let us take two examples to illustrate the calculation of median value from these two series.

Condition I: When the series contains **odd** number of cases.

Consider the series: 17, 13, 12, 18, 16, 14, and 15

Here there are seven numbers. After arranging the numbers in ascending order the series looks like: 12, 13, 14, 15, 16, 17, 18. Since there are seven numbers, so the position of median will be $\frac{7+1}{2}th$ or 4th in the series. Hence, the value of the median will be 15.

Condition II: When the series contains **even** number of cases.

Consider the series: 17, 13, 12, 18, 16, 14, 15, and 11

Here we have added one more number to the series. So the number of cases in it now stands at eight. After arranging the numbers in ascending order the series now looks like: 11, 12, 13, 14, 15, 16, 17, 18. Since there are eight numbers, so the position of median will be $\frac{8+1}{2}th$ or 4.5^{th} in the series. Hence, the value of the median will lie at the middle of the fourth and fifth score, that is, at the middle of 14 and 15. Thus here the median will be $\frac{14+15}{2}$ = *14.5*.

Median of a Simple Frequency Distribution

In a simple frequency distribution score values or categories and their respective frequencies are presented in separate columns. Let us consider

Table: 11.4, which describe the vote share (in percent) of various economic classes in the 2014 Lok Sabha Election in West Bengal.

Table: 11.4. *Economic Class and Vote Share (in percent) of AITC in the 2014 Lok Sabha Election in West Bengal*

Economic Class	Vote Share (%)	Cumulative Frequency
Poor	16	16
Lower	55	71
Middle	25	96
Rich	4	100
Total	100	

Source: CSDS Lokniti National Election Study 2014

In order to find out the median preference of the electorates belonging to different classes towards AITC, we first need to locate the position of the median. Since here the total vote share is 100 (in percent), so the position of the median would be $\frac{100}{2}$ = 50 or 50th position. To locate the class containing the 50th position we have constructed the cumulative frequency column in Table: 11.4. Now starting with the lowest score value (16) of the class we have to reach the smallest one, the cumulative frequency of which is at least 50. Clearly, it is the Lower Class. So, considered from the angle of class, the AITC finds its median support in the lower class.

Median of a Grouped Frequency Distribution

Suppose in a manufacturing unit the supervisor wants to know the median number of days the workers were absent in a particular year. S/he has arranged the data of the workers' absenteeism in the following frequency distribution:

Table: 11.5 *Number of days the workers were absent in a particular year*

No. of days absent	No. of workers (f)
1-5	5
6-10	9
11-15	12

No. of days absent	No. of workers (f)
16-20	8
21-25	6
Total	N or Σf = 40

Source: Fictitious data

In order to find out the median we must locate the middle case of the distribution. Here since the number of workers absent is 40 so the middle position must be $(\frac{N}{2})$ or $\frac{40}{2}$ or the 20th position. Thus, the value of the median will be the score of absenteeism associated with this position. This will require us to locate the interval that contains the middle, or in this case, the 20th position. To find out the interval we first need to calculate the cumulative frequencies. The following table shows this:

Calculation of Median

No. of days absent	Class boundary	No. of workers (f)	Cumulative Frequency (CF)
1-5	0.5 – 5.5	5	5
6-10	5.5 – 10.5	9	14
11-15	10.5 – 15.5	12	26
16-20	15.5 – 20.5	8	34
21-25	20.5 – 25.5	6	40
Total		N or Σf = 40	

The cumulative frequency column clearly shows that the 20th position lies in the interval 11-15. So, this class can be identified as the median class. But exactly what value in this interval is associated with the middle position? We can find it by the following formula:

$$Mdn = l_1 + (\frac{\frac{N}{2} - F}{f_m}) \times i$$

Where,

Mdn = Median,

l_1 = Lower boundary of the median class,

N = Total frequency,

F = Cumulative frequency preceding the median class,

f_m = Frequency of the median class, and

i = Interval width of the median class.

Now, applying the formula in the present case we get,

$$Mdn = 10.5 + (\frac{\frac{40}{2} - 14}{12}) \times 5 = 10.5 + (\frac{20 - 14}{12}) \times 5 = 10.5 + (\frac{6}{12}) \times 5$$

$$= 10.5 + \frac{30}{12} = 13$$

Thus, the value of the median tells us that half of the absent workers were absent for less than 13 days while half of them were more than 13 days.

Doing it Step by Step

Step 1: Calculate the cumulative frequency from the frequency distribution

Step 2: Locate the median position by calculating $\frac{N}{2}$

Step 3: Find the median class in the class interval

Step 4: Calculate the value of the median by the appropriate formula.

Other Positional Measures: Quartiles, Deciles and Percentiles

As a statistical measure the Median serves two purposes: first it measures the central tendency of a set of scores; second, it identifies the middle most position of the scores, above which there are 50% or one half of the scores and below which there are another 50% or other half of the scores. But often the researchers are also interested in measuring other positional values. They might be interested to know the points which divide the distribution into quarters. These are known as Quartiles since they divide the distribution into four quarters, each containing 25% of the cases. Clearly, to divide a distribution into four equal parts three such points are required. The first point which locates the position of the first 25% of the scores is known as the 'lower' or the First Quartile (denoted by Q_1); the second which identifies the position of the 50% (25% + 25%) of the scores is known as the Second Quartile (denoted by Q_2); and the third which locates the position of the 75% (25% +25% +25%) of the scores is known as the 'upper'[5] or the Third Quartile (denoted by Q_3). It is to be noted here that since the second quartile identifies the 50% position, so for any set of scores the value of the second quartile is equal to that of the median.

Calculation of Quartiles from Simple Series or Ungrouped Data

To calculate the quartiles of a simple series first we need to find out the median or the second quartile. As median divides the scores into two equal parts, so the value of the first quartile would be the middle position of the first half of the scores below the median and that of the third quartile would be the middle position of the other half of the scores above the median.

Once again consider the series: 17, 13, 12, 18, 16, 14, 15, and 11

To find out the median we need to arrange the series in rank order. Arranging in ascending order the series can be rewritten as: 11, 12, 13, 14, and 15,16,17,18. Here there are eight numbers. So the value of the median will lie between the 4th and the 5th position, that is, between 14 and 15. So it is 14.5. Thus, the value of the second quartile (Q_2) is also 14.5.

Now the half of the series below the median is: 11,12,13,14. Applying the same procedure, the value of the middle position of the series is 12.5. So the value of the first quartile (Q_1) is 12.5. Here the half of the series above the median is: 15,16,17,18, the middle position of which is 16.5. So, the value of the third quartile (Q_3) is 16.5.

Quartiles of a Grouped Frequency Distribution

To find out the value of the quartiles from a grouped frequency distribution let us use the same data about the absenteeism of the workers on a manufacturing unit as presented in Table: 11.5 before.

Number of days the workers were absent in a particular year

No. of days absent	No. of workers (f)
1-5	5
6-10	9
11-15	12
16-20	8
21-25	6
Total	N or $\Sigma f = 40$

In order to find out the first quartile (Q_1) we must locate the case located at the 25% position of the distribution. Since the number of workers absent here is 40, so it will be $(\frac{N}{4})$ or $\frac{40}{4}$ or the 10th position. Thus the value of the Q_1 will be the score of absenteeism associated with this position. In order to identify the class interval containing the score at the 10th position, we calculate the cumulative frequencies. We find it in the following:

Calculation of Quartiles

No. of days absent	Class boundary	No. of workers (f)	Cumulative Frequency (CF)
1-5	0.5 – 5.5	5	5
6-10	5.5 – 10.5	9	14
11-15	10.5 – 15.5	12	26
16-20	15.5 – 20.5	8	34
21-25	20.5 – 25.5	6	40
Total		N or $\Sigma f = 40$	

The cumulative frequency column clearly shows that the 10th position lies in the interval 6-10. So, this is the first quartile class. To find out the exact score in this class interval corresponding to the 10th position, we slightly modify the formula used to calculate the median. Hence:

$$Q_1 = l_1 + \left(\frac{\frac{N}{4} - F}{f_{Q_1}}\right) \times i$$

Where,

Q_1 = First Quartile,

l_1 = Lower boundary of the Q_1 Class,

N = Total frequency,

F = Cumulative frequency preceding the Q_1 class,

f_{Q_1} = Frequency of the Q_1 class, and

i = Interval width of the Q_1 class.

Thus, applying the formula we get,

$$Q_1 = 5.5 + \left(\frac{\frac{40}{4} - 5}{9}\right) \times 5 = 5.5 + \left(\frac{10 - 5}{9}\right) \times 5 = 5.5 + \left(\frac{5}{9}\right) \times 5$$

$$= 5.5 + \frac{25}{9} = 8.27$$

The value of the Q_1 tells us that one quarter or 25% of the absent workers were absent for less than 8.27 days or approximately 8 days while three quarter or 75% of them were absent for more than 8 days.

In order to find out the third quartile (Q_3) we need to locate the case located at the 75% position of the distribution. Clearly, it will be $(\frac{3N}{4})$ or $\frac{3X40}{4}$ or the 30th position. Now following the same method adopted in the case of Q_1 we can calculate the value of Q_3 by adjusting the formula of Q_1 a bit. Thus, the formula of Q_3 is:

$$Q_3 = l_1 + (\frac{\frac{3N}{4} - F}{f_{Q_3}}) \times i$$

Putting the appropriate values, we get 18 as the value of Q_3. It can be interpreted that 75% of the workers of the manufacturing unit were absent for less than 18 days while the rest 25% of them were absent for more than 18 days.

Apart from the quartiles there are other positional values like the deciles and percentiles. Decile divides the distribution in ten parts, while percentile divides it into 100 parts. Obviously, 9th decile and 99 percentile points divide the distribution into ten and 100 parts respectively. The nine deciles are represented as D_1, D_2, D_3, ...D_9. Galton termed D_1 and D_9 to be the lower and upper deciles respectively[6]. Lower decile is that position below which falls one-tenth of the scores and the upper decile is exceeded by one-tenth of the scores of any distribution. Similar is the case with percentiles. The percentiles are represented as P_1, P_2, P_3, ...P_{99}. Here P_1 and P_{99} stand for the lower and upper percentile respectively. Needless to mention that, one-hundredth part or one percent of the scores falls short of the lower percentile, while 99% of the scores are located above it. Conversely, below the upper percentile there are 99% of the sores and it is exceeded by one percent of the scores. Being positional values, the calculations of decile and percentile closely follow those of median and quartiles.

From the foregoing discussion of the positional values like the quartiles, deciles and percentiles, it appears that there is a close relation among them. Considered carefully, it can be seen that the first quartile (below which there are one-fourth of the scores) finds its equivalence in the 2.5th decile and the 25th percentile. Similarly, the second quartile or the median is equal to the fifth decile and 50th percentile. Since all these identify the locations or positions of the values in a distribution, so in spite of the differences in their respective approaches, they all point to the same values occupying any particular position in the distribution. Levin et.al[7] describe this relationship among the partition values through the following figure:

Figure: 11.1. *Relationship among the Percentile, Decile and Quartile*

Percentile	Decile	Quartile
95		
90 =	9th	
85		
80 =	8th	
75 =		3rd
70 =	7th	
65		
60 =	6th	
55		
50 =	5th	2nd
45		
40 =	4th	
35		
30 =	3rd	
25 =		1st
20 =	2nd	
15		
10 =	1st	
5		

The Arithmetic Mean (A.M.)

Arithmetic Mean or, simply, average, is the most widely used measure of central tendency. It is obtained by summing up all the scores or measures in a series divided by the number of such scores. If the scores of a series are represented by x, then the Arithmetic Mean is denoted by $\bar{x}$, (read as 'x bar'). For example, if a hill trekker covers 8 km, 10 km, 12, km, 6 km and 4 km in five successive days, the average distance covered by her/him daily is $\frac{8+10+12+6+4}{5}$ km. or, 8 km.

Thus, the formula of Arithmetic Mean can be written as,

$$\bar{x} = \frac{\Sigma x}{N}$$

where, $\bar{x}$= Mean,

Σ(Greek capital letter 'Sigma') = Sum[1]

x = Raw scores in the series,

N = Number of scores in the series.

This is the case of A.M. when the scores compose a simple series. But for the sake of more precise statistical analysis of large volume of data often the scores are arranged in a frequency distribution. To measure the value of the average from such frequency distributions a slight variation in the method of calculation is necessary. In Table: 11.6 below an attempt is made to illustrate this:

Arithmetic Mean of a Grouped Frequency Distribution

Table: 11.6. Age-Group-wise Child Victims of Kidnapping and Abduction in West Bengal during 2016

Age Group (in years)	No. of Cases Reported (f)	Mid point (x)	fx
0-6	60	3	180
6-12	247	9	2223
12-16	1468	14	20552
16-18	1886	17	32062
Total	N or Σf = 3661		Σfx = 55017

Source: 'Crime in India 2016', National Crime Record Bureau (NCRB), Ministry of Home Affairs, Govt. of India

The table reveals the calculation of A.M. or average age of child victims of kidnapping and abduction in West Bengal in the year 2016. A total of 3661 victims have been arranged in a frequency distribution in the above table. Here, we first calculate the midpoints (x_i) of each class or age group. In order to find the midpoint the lower and upper class limits of each class is added and divided by two. Then we multiply or 'weight' the midpoint (x) of each age group by the frequency (f) of that particular group. To get the value of the A.M. or $\bar{x}$, all the values of fx are added and divided by total frequency (N). Thus, the formula of Arithmetic Mean ($\bar{x}$) of a grouped frequency distribution can be written as:

$$\text{Arithmetic Mean } (\bar{x}) = \frac{\Sigma fx}{N}$$

---

[1]Throughout the text the Greek capital letter 'Σ' is used as summation sign.

Applying this formula the average or arithmetic mean of the age of the child victims of kidnapping and abduction in West Bengal during 2016 $= \frac{55017}{3661} =$ *15.03* years or 15 years (appx.)

Doing it Step by Step

Step 1: Calculate the midpoints (x) of each class interval.

Add the lower and upper limits of each class and divide it by two to get the value of x.

Step 2: Multiply the midpoints of each class interval (x) with the respective frequencies (f) of the classes in order to get the values of fx

Step 3. Add or sum up all the values of fx to get the value of Σfx.

Step 4. Get the value of the average or arithmetic mean or $\bar{x}$ by dividing Σfx with the total frequency $(\Sigma f$ or $N)$.

Calculation of Arithmetic Mean (A.M.) by Short Method

Although following the above method, we can calculate the A.M. of a grouped frequency distribution, but it can also be calculated by applying a relatively easy or short method. Known as Step Deviation Method, this is particularly helpful in finding out the mean of a frequency distribution where the numbers measuring the variables are large enough. This is done by calculating the deviations of the midpoints of the various classes of the frequency distribution (x_i) from an arbitrary constant (c) and then dividing it by another constant (d). Usually, 'c' represents a number which lies somewhere at the middle of the distribution of the midpoints (x). For this, often 'c' is also called the arbitrary mean of the distribution. Mathematically, it involves a change in origin because subtraction of a constant 'c' from all the midpoints (x_i) of the class intervals amounts to a shift in its zero point (or origin). The other constant 'd' involves a change in the scale or unit in which the variable is measured. It is commonplace that through multiplication or division we can change the units of measurement, as is done in the cases of conversion from rupees to paisa, dollar to rupee, feet to inch, kilometre to meter etc. Usually, the common difference of the midpoints or the length of the class interval is taken as 'd'.

As the first step, subtracting 'c' from the midpoints (x_i) and dividing these by 'd' we get the deviations as:

$$y_i = \frac{x_i - c}{d}$$

Then in the second step, we need to calculate the mean of y or $\bar{y}$

Finally, we find the required value of $\bar{x}$ by the following expression:

$$\bar{x} = c + d\bar{y}$$

From this expression it appears that the Arithmetic Mean (A.M.) is dependent on or influenced by the change of both origin and scale.

Let us consider the following example:

Table: 11.7. *Distribution of Marks Obtained by 50 Students of a High School in Annual Examination*

Total Marks	Number of Students (f_i)	Midpoint (x_i)	$y_i = \frac{x_i - 455}{10}$	$f_i y_i$
430-440	9	435	-2	-18
440-450	12	445	-1	-12
450-460	16	455	0	0
460-470	8	465	1	8
470-480	5	475	2	10
	N or $\Sigma f_i = 50$			$\Sigma f_i y_i = -12$

Source: Fictitious data

Here, let $c = 455$ and $d = 10$, so, $y_i = \frac{x_i - c}{d} = \frac{x_i - 455}{10}$

We know that, $\bar{y} = \frac{\Sigma f_i y_i}{N}$, so, putting the values from the table we get,

$$\bar{y} = \frac{-12}{50} = -0.24$$

Then, putting the values in the expression $\bar{x} = c + d\bar{y}$, we get,

$\bar{x} = 455 + 10 \, (-0.24)$

Or, $\bar{x} = 452.6$, or 453 (approximately).

Hence, the Arithmetic Mean of the marks Obtained by 50 Students of the high school in annual Examination is approximately 453.

Relation between the Mean, Median and Mode

An 'approximate relation' exists between the Mean, Median and Mode[8]. The following equation expresses the relationship between these three measures of central tendency:

$$Mean - Mode = 3\ (Mean - Median)$$

Hence, if we know or calculate the values of any two of the measures of central tendency, the other one can be known by employing this equation. For example, if for a series of observation the value of Mean is 12 and that of the Median is 11, then putting the values in the relationship equation mentioned above, we get the value of the mode = 9.

Combined Mean

Often the researchers find two or more groups with different sizes and different average values on any particular dimension relevant to the groups. To get an overall picture the researchers then are required to find out the combined mean taking all the groups into consideration. Put simply, the combined mean can be considered as the mean of all the group means. Suppose, a polling booth is composed of 900 electorates among which 400 are Brahmins, 300 are Kayasthas and 200 are Namasudras. If the average ages of the Brahmin, Kayastha and Namasudra electorates are 55, 50 and 40 years respectively, then one might be interested to know the average age of the electorates of that polling booth in general. In order to find it out, let us represent the picture in a tabular form:

Calculation of Combined Mean

Table: 11.8. Caste of the electorates in a polling booth (fictitious data)

Caste of the electorates	Average Age ($\bar{x}$)	Number (N)	N$\bar{x}$
Brahmin	$\bar{x}_1 = 55$	$N_1 = 400$	$N_1\ \bar{x}_1 = 22000$
Kayastha	$\bar{x}_2 = 50$	$N_2 = 300$	$N_2\ \bar{x}_2 = 15000$
Namasudra	$\bar{x}_3 = 40$	$N_3 = 200$	$N_3\ \bar{x}_3 = 8000$

To get the value of combined mean here at the very first stage each group mean needs to be weighted by its size. This is done by multiplying the respective mean ages of the three castes by their respective number of electorates (as is shown in the column N$\bar{x}$ above). Then all the weighted mean ages are summed up and finally divided by the total number of electorates of the polling booth in question.

So, the combined mean age here $= \dfrac{22000+15000+8000}{900} = 50$ years.

Therefore, the formula of combined mean for three groups can be written as:

$$\bar{x}_c = \frac{N_1\bar{x_1}+N_2\bar{x_2}+N_3\bar{x_3}}{N}$$

If there had been two groups instead of three the formula would be written as

$$\bar{x}_c = \frac{N_1\bar{x_1}+N_2\bar{x_2}}{N}$$

Hence, to obtain the combined mean of two or more groups the formula can be generalized as:

$$\bar{x}_c = \frac{\Sigma N_i \bar{x}_i}{N_c}$$

where,

$\bar{x}_c =$ Combined Mean,

$N_i =$ Number of observations or size of a particular group,

$\bar{x}_i =$ Mean of a particular group,

$N_c =$ Combined or total number of cases taking all groups together.

Choosing an Appropriate Measure of Central Tendency

The foregoing discussion presents a brief description of the three measures of central tendency. But in actual research situation the researcher is often confused in selecting the appropriate measure which can best describe the underlying nature and tendencies of the information collected. Levin et al. list three following factors which might help the researcher in arriving at a decision regarding the appropriate measure of central tendency to be employed[9]. These are:

1. Level of measurement of the variable
2. Shape of the distribution of the data
3. Objective of the research

1.   Level of measurement of the variable

The level of measurement of the variable has considerable influence on the appropriate measure of central tendency to be employed to analyse the data. Since Mode requires only frequency count so it can be applied to any level of measurement viz. nominal, ordinal and interval/ratio. But as Mode is measured only by the highest frequency and has nothing to do with the any logical interconnection of the data set, so it is best suited for nominal level data. It is true that it can also be used to ordinal and interval/ratio level data but that will only result in a crude analysis because ordinal and interval/ratio level data contain other information which the Mode is unable to reveal.

As the Median is calculated by arranging the cases in rank order, so it is best suited for ordinal level data. As the nominal level data cannot be ordered in any kind of ranking, so Median cannot be used to analyse this type of data. Median can be employed to analyse interval/ratio level data, but since it requires only an ordering of data and nothing to do with the nature of interval existing among the cases, so applied to interval level data the Median loses some of its analytical power. Because the intervals existing among the cases do not influence the Median, so to analyse the central tendency of a skewed distribution, the Median is the best method.

The use of Mean is exclusively restricted to interval/ratio level data because as a measure of central tendency, it assumes equal intervals of the data, which the data at either nominal or ordinal level cannot guarantee. Logically, it hardly makes any sense to calculate the mean of religious affiliation of the Indians (as describes Table: 11.1) or their caste, gender, linguistic and similar identities. As the mean is based upon the assumption of equal intervals among the cases so it cannot be employed to analyse skewed data also.

The guiding principles to select an appropriate measure of central tendency have been summarized by Healey[10]. We represent it in the shape of Table: 11.9.

Table: 11.9. The Relationship between Level of Measurement and Measures of Central Tendency

Measure of Central Tendency	Level of Measurement		
	Nominal	Ordinal	Intervl/Ratio
Mode	YES*	Yes**	Yes
Median	NO	YES	YES
Mean	No	Yes (?)***	Yes

Capitalized boldfaced 'YES' indicates the most appropriate measure of central tendency
** *'Yes' indicates that the measure is permitted to employ*
***Yes (?) *indicates that the measure is sometimes employed but that violates the principle or measurement logic of levels of measurement*

2.   Shape of the distribution of the data

Shape or form of the distribution representing the data is another important consideration to the researchers in selecting an appropriate measure of central tendency to analyse data. When the data is symmetrical in nature, all the measures of central tendency viz. the mean, the median and the mode coincide in a single point. So, in this case the researchers can employ any one of these depending upon their research objectives. But, the data with which the researchers engage themselves may not always be symmetrical in nature. Often the distribution of the data contains extreme or unusual values to make it skewed. In such cases the researchers cannot use the mean. This is because as the mean, by definition, is based on the consideration of all values, so, the presence of extreme values in a skewed distribution will distort the value of the mean. Here the appropriate measure would be the median because it is based on just the middle most score of a distribution not on all the observations. Thus the presence of extreme values or skewness of the distribution can hardly have any impact on the value of the median. The following example can explain this:

Suppose, we have a series of seven scores which are, 2, 4, 3, 28, 6, 5, 1. Now the mean of the distribution is 7 but the value of the median is 4. It is clear that this difference between the respective values of the mean and median is due to the presence of the extreme score 28 which has been considered while calculating the value of the mean and not considered in the calculation of median. From a close look at the series, hence, we can rely on the value of the median more than that of the mean as a valid measure of central tendency of the data. The presence of extreme values also restricts the use of mode here, since as a measure of central tendency, mode indicates the most frequent score or the highest score in the series. If we consider the above series, the value of mode is 28, which in spite of being a typical value does not seem to represent the series of scores.

3.   Objective of the research

The choice of the appropriate measure of central tendency also depends upon the objective or purpose of the research. If the researcher wants to have a quick and brief reflection of the nature of the data the mode is the best way, since it is a '...preliminary indicator of central tendncy'[11]. But, to have a more precise and in-depth reflection of the underlying trend of the data the researcher must employ either the mean or the median.

The median, as the foregoing discussion makes it clear, can be employed to analyze skewed data. In addition to this, since the median indicates the middle most rank of the scores, it can be used for inter-half comparison to reveal the more subtle aspects of the data. A median value by indicating the middle position of the distribution of a sample of respondents, arranged, for instance, in accordance to their political values viz. liberal or conservative, can actually throw some light on the preponderance of the respective political values in the sample.

The mean, as we have already discussed, can be a useful measure of central tendency of a data set, which is either symmetrical or at least 'roughly symmetrical'[12] in nature. Moreover, the mean possesses all the desirable properties of a suitable average as earmarked by Yule which are:

1. '...an average should be *rigidly defined* and not left to the mere estimation of an observer

2. An average should be *based on all the observations* made. If not, it is not really a characteristic of the whole distribution.

3. ...the average should *possess some simple and obvious properties* to render its general nature readily comprehendible...

4. ...an average should be *calculated with reasonable ease and rapidity.*

5. The average should be as *little affected...by... fluctuations of sampling.*

6. The measure chosen shall lend itself readily to algebraic treatment'[13] (italics added).

Considered against the background of all these properties mentioned by Yule[15], the Arithmetic Mean or simply, the mean appears to be the most appropriate measure of central tendency.

EXERCISES

1. What do the measures of central tendency indicate?
2. What are the important measures of central tendency?
3. What is meant by Mode?

4.   Find the mode of the series, 4, 5, 6, 7, 6, 8, 5, 6, 9, 6   [Ans. 6]
5.   The following table describes the votes secured (in %) by different political parties/coalition in the Assembly Election of West Bengal in 2016:

Party voted	Congress	Left Front	AIT C	BJP	Others
Votes secured (in %)	12.1	26.4	44.7	10.2	6.6

Find the value of the mode.   [Ans. AITC]
6.   How does Galton define Median?
7.   Following are the marks obtained in Statistics by six students of a class: 25, 27, 33, 22, 35, 23. Find the median marks.   [Ans. 26]
8.   The ages (in years) of the contesting candidates of different political parties in an Assembly Constituency are: 36, 45, 28, 33, 57, 48 and 52. Find the median age.   [Ans. 45years]
9.   The following frequency distribution describes the number of COVID 19 cases in India out of 100 by age groups (in years) up to mid July 2020. Find the median age of the cases.

Age Groups	0-14	15-29	30-44	45-59	60-74	75-95
Cases	1	3	8	35	40	13

                                        [Ans. 61 years (appx.)]
10.   The following distribution presents the social categories of the students in a particular undergraduate class of a college Find out the median social category of the students:

Social categories of students	Scheduled Tribe (ST)	Scheduled Cast (SC)	Other Backward Class (OBC)	General	Total
Number of students	4	5	20	21	50

                                        [Ans. OBC]

11.   The following data depict age groups (in years) of a sample of 100 electorates in West Bengal in the Assembly Election of 2016. Find out the median age of the electorates.

Age Groups	0-25	26-35	36-45	46-55	56-85
	15	25	22	19	19

                                        [Ans. 40 years (appx.)]
12.   Suppose, the number of votes polled in five booths of a constituency during the first hour of an election day, are: 56, 74, 54, 45 and 32. Find the Arithmetic Mean (A.M.) of the votes polled in the first hour.

                                        [Ans. 52 (appx.)]

13.   Find the Arithmetic Mean of the data presented in Question No. 7.

[Ans. 27.5]

14.   Marks of the students in Statistics of a class are given below:

Marks	10-20	20-30	30-40	40-50	50-60	60-70
Number of Students (f)	8	10	9	7	4	2

Find the Arithmetic Mean marks obtained by the students in Statistics.

[Ans. 34 (appx.)]

15.   In the following frequency distribution we get the statement of amount of fixed deposits of 20 customers of a bank. Apply the short method to find out the Arithmetic Mean amount of fixed deposits of the customers.

Amount of fixed deposits (Rs.) (x)	20000	25000	30000	35000	40000	45000
Number of Customers (f)	2	5	6	4	2	1

[Ans. Rs. 30500]

16.   If for a distribution the value of the Mean = 10 and the Median = 8; what will be the value of the Mode of the distribution?   [Ans. 4]

17.   In Question No. 9 the value of the Median = 61. By calculation we get the Arithmetic Mean = 60. Use these two values to find out the value of the Mode.   [Ans. 63]

18.   In the following we have a distribution of the Students belonging to three Semesters in an undergraduate course of a college along with their respective average ages:

Semester	Average Age ($\bar{x}$) (in years)	Number of students (N)
1st Semester	$\bar{x_1} = 18$	$N_1 = 45$
2nd Semester	$\bar{x_2} = 19$	$N_2 = 30$
3rd Semester	$\bar{x_3} = 21$	$N_3 = 25$

Find the average age of the students of the undergraduate course as a whole.

19.   In a cyber café of a city in a week the mean time spent by 30 boys and 20 girls for Internet browsing = 5.8 hours. If the average time spent by the boys in that week = 5 hours, what is the average time spent by the girls to browse the Internet in that week?   [Ans. 7 hours]

20.   Why Mode can be used to find out the central tendency of data measured at any level of measurement?

21.   Although Mode can be applied to data measured at any level, but it is best suited to data measured at the _____ level.   [Ans. Nominal]

22.   Why the Median is appropriate to find out the central tendency of ordinal level data?

23.   Consider the following series of data: 5, 7, 9, 8, 4, 45, 6. Which of the three measures of Central tendency viz. Mean, Median and Mode, would you apply here to find out the central tendency of it and why?

24.   Why the Mean cannot be used to measure the central tendency of skewed data?

25.   What, according to Yule, are the desirable properties of a suitable average?

26.   Which of the three measures of Central tendency viz. Mean, Median and Mode, closely follows the desirable properties of a suitable average as mentioned by Yule?

Endnotes

1.   Jack A. Levin and James Alan Fox and David R. Forde, Elementary *Statistics in Social Research. Twelfth edition* (New York: Pearson, 2014), 82.

2.   Francis Galton, "Report of the Anthropometric Committee." *Report of the Fifty-first Meeting of the British Association for the Advancement of Science* (London: John Murray 1882), 245.

3.   George Udny Yule, *An Introduction to the Theory of Statistics* (London: Charles Griffin and Company Limited, 1919), 116.

4.   Jeffery T. Walker and Sean Maddan, *Understanding Statistics for the Social Sciences, Criminal Justice, and Criminology* (Burlington, MA : Jones & Bartlett Learning, 2013), 24.

5.   Galton, "Report of the Anthropometric Committee,"

6.   ibid.

7.   Levin, Fox and Forde, *Elementary Statistics in Social Research. Twelfth edition*, 49.

8.   Yule, *An Introduction to the Theory of Statistics,* 121.

9.   Levin, Fox and Forde, *Elementary Statistics in Social Research. Twelfth edition.*

10.   Joseph F Healey, *Statistics: A Tool for Social Research. Ninth Edition* (Belmont: Wadsworth, 2012), 77.

11.   Levin, Fox and Forde, *Elementary Statistics in Social Research. Twelfth edition*, 95.

12.   ibid. 95.

12

Measures of Dispersion

In the last chapter we have learned central tendency, a particular way to describe a set of scores of a variable. The measure of central tendency indicates the central point of the distribution towards which all the scores in a distribution exhibit a tendency to cluster. If this is an important way to describe a distribution of scores, the other way round is also true. That means, if the scores show a tendency to cluster towards the centre, this tendency is not the same for each and every score in the distribution. Some scores may be close to the centre while others may be relatively away from it. This spread of the scores around the centre is also an important characteristic of the distribution of scores. Measures of dispersion specifically calculate this spread, deviation or variety and diversity of the set of scores in a distribution. Celebrated statistician Karl Pearson in his seminal work 'The Grammar of Science', published in 1900 defines deviation as, '…the amount by which any individual differs in a given character…usually from the mean'[1]. Simply put, it indicates the degree of heterogeneity of a distribution.

An example might help this to understand. Suppose two manufacturing units, A and B, have 100 employees each. The average daily wage of unit A is Rs.275, while that of unit B is Rs.270. So there is little difference in the average daily wage earned by the employees in these two units. But a close scrutiny of the daily wage of the individual employees reveals that in unit A the wage ranges from Rs. 130 to Rs. 400 while in unit B it is from Rs.150 to Rs. 380. Clearly, in unit A the wages are more variable or scattered compared to unit B. Thus, although the average daily wage was almost same in both the units the relatively more spread of it in unit A might be an indication of the greater level of wage inequality existing in it. So, it is not enough to know the central tendency of a set of scores, for a better and complete understanding of the nature of scores of a variable we also need to know its spread or dispersion. From the standpoint of research methodology, measure of dispersion, by pointing out the heterogeneity of a set of scores or measuring the deviations of the scores from a theoretically representative score (often suggested by the measures of central tendency), helps to assess the errors of measurement.

Dispersion can be measured by four measures, which are:

1. Range

2. Mean Deviation (M.D.)

3. Quartile Deviation (Q.D.)

4. Standard Deviation (S.D.)

We will discuss these four measures one by one.

1. Range

Range is the simplest possible way to measure the spread or dispersion of a set of scores in a distribution. It is defined as the difference between the highest (or the greatest) and the lowest (or the least) values of the observed scores in the distribution (Yule[2], Healy[3]). Hence,

Range or R = *Highest score − Lowest score*

Thus, if the highest daily wage in the manufacturing unit A is Rs.400 and the lowest is Rs.130, then the value of Range is Rs.270.

The advantage of range as a measure of dispersion is, it is very easy to calculate. But the same is also the basic disadvantage of it, since it takes into account only two values, the highest and the lowest. So, the entire distribution does not come to its purview. This is why Yule considers it to be the worst of all possible measures which seriously measures dispersion[4] and Levin et.al. claim it to be a crude, rough and preliminary measure of dispersion[5].

2.   Mean Deviation (M.D.)

The Mean Deviation of a set of scores, in Yule's words, is, '…the arithmetic mean of their deviations from some average, taken without regard to their sign.'[6] The deviations can be measured from either the mean or the median of the distribution of scores. If measured from mean then the measure is known as Mean Deviation about mean and if from median then it is known as Mean Deviation about median.

The calculation of Mean Deviation is not very complicated. Here, first, we need to calculate the mean or median of the series of scores. Then, the deviation of each score from the mean or median is calculated. Finally we need to calculate the arithmetic mean of the deviations by ignoring the signs of the deviations.

Hence,

Mean Deviation about Mean = $\frac{\Sigma(x_i-\bar{x})}{n}$ (for ungrouped data) and

Mean Deviation about Median= $\frac{\Sigma(x_i-Median)}{n}$ (for ungrouped data)

For a grouped frequency distribution

Mean Deviation about Mean = $\frac{\Sigma f_i(x_i-\bar{x})}{N}$ and

Mean Deviation about Median = $\frac{\Sigma f_i(x_i-Median)}{N}$

To find out the Mean Deviation about Mean or Median from a simple series of ungrouped data, consider, for example, the following series:

Table: 12.1. *Mean Deviation about Mean and Median of a Simple Series*

Scores	Deviation from mean ($\bar{x}$)	Deviation from median
9	1	2
7	-1	0
5	-3	-2
6	-2	-1
13	5	6

Here the value of mean ($\bar{x}$) = 8, and that of the median = 7

Since, to calculate mean deviation we need to sum the deviations (ignoring the signs), so the sums of the deviations of the scores from their mean and median are 12 and 11 respectively (signs ignored).

So, mean deviation about mean $= \frac{12}{5} = 2.4$ and

Mean deviation about median $= \frac{11}{5} = 2.2$

Mean Deviation (M.D.) about Mean of a Grouped Frequency Distribution

For this purpose, let us refer to the data presented in Table: 16 in the chapter on Central Tendency

Age-Group-wise Child Victims of Kidnapping and Abduction in West Bengal during 2016

Age Group (in years)	No. of Cases Reported (f)	Mid point (x)	Deviation from Mean $(x_i - \bar{x})$	$f_i(x_i - \bar{x})$
0-6	60	3	-12.03	-721.8
6-12	247	9	-6.03	-1489.41
12-16	1468	14	-1.03	-1512.04
16-18	1886	17	1.97	3715.42
Total	N or $\Sigma f = 3661$			$\Sigma f_i(x_i - \bar{x}) = 7438.67$ (ignoring the sign)

Data Source: National Crime Record Bureau (NCRB), 2016

Here, the value of Mean $(\bar{x})$, as we calculated it before stands at 15.03 years.

By the definition of Mean Deviation about mean, we can write:

M.D. $= \frac{\Sigma f_i(x_i - \bar{x})}{N}$

or, M.D. $= \frac{7438.67}{3661} = 2.03$

To find out the value of the mean deviation about median, we just need to replace the mean or x̄ with the value of median in the above mentioned formula.

Doing it Step by Step

Step 1: Calculate the value of the mean or median from the distribution.

Step 2: Calculate the deviations of each score or midpoints of the class intervals from the mean or median to get the values of $(x_i - \bar{x})$ or, $(x_i - Median)$.

Step 3: Multiply the deviations with the respective frequencies of the class and get the values of $f_i(x_i - \bar{x})$ or, $f_i(x_i - Median)$.

Step 4: Sum up all these without paying regard to their signs to get the values of $\Sigma f_i(x_i - \bar{x})$ or, $\Sigma f_i(x_i - Median)$

Step 5: Divide $\Sigma f_i(x_i - \bar{x})$ or, $\Sigma f_i(x_i - Median)$ with total frequency (N), to get the value of the Mean Deviation about mean or median.

3.   Quartile Deviation (Q.D.)

As a measure of dispersion the Quartile Deviation (Q.D.) is defined as the 'semi- interquartile range.'

In the chapter on the measures of central tendency, we have discussed about Quartiles as one of the positional measures of a set of scores. Precisely, we have learnt that there are three quartiles viz. Q_1 (the first or the lower quartile), Q_2 (the second quartile or the median) and Q_3 (the third or the upper quartile). As a measure, Q_1 or the lower quartile indicates the score below which there are 25 percent of the scores and above which lies 75 percent of the scores of a distribution. Q_2 or the second quartile divides the distribution in two equal parts showing the median or the point below and above which 50 percent of the scores are respectively located. Finally, Q_3 or the upper quartile is a point in the distribution below which 75 percent of the scores are located while 25 percent of the scores are above it. The interquartile range implies the difference of scores indicated by the upper and lower quartile values, symbolically which can be expressed as $Q_3 - Q_1$. It measures the distance of the third quartile from the first. The quartile deviation, defined as the semi-interquartile range, therefore, is half of this difference between the upper and lower quartiles. Thus,

Quartile Deviation (Q.D.) $= \frac{Q_3 - Q_1}{2}$

Quartile Deviation of Simple Series or Ungrouped Data

In the chapter on central tendency, we have calculated 12.5 and 16.5 to be the values of Q_1 and Q_3 of the series 17, 13, 12, 18, 16, 14, 15, 11 respectively. Thus, the value of Q.D. of the series will be $\frac{16.5 - 12.5}{2} = 2$

Quartile Deviation (Q.D.) of a Grouped Frequency Distribution

The calculation of Q.D. of a grouped frequency distribution is also simple. To find out the Q.D. of a frequency distribution we need to calculate the values of Q_1 and Q_3 as is done in the chapter on central tendency. Let us take an example:

Table: 12.2. *Age Distribution of a Sample of 150 Children in Two Villages of Mamudpur Gram Panchayat, North 24 Parganas, West Bengal*

Age Group (in years)	No. of Children (f)	Class Boundary	Cumulative Frequency (CF)
1-3	4	0.5 - 3.5	4
4-6	24	3.5 - 6.5	28
7-9	31	6.5 - 9.5	59
10-12	50	9.5 - 12.5	109
13-15	41	12.5 - 15.5	150

Source: Survey data of a Study on Child Rights in Two Villages of North 24 Parganas, West Bengal

Following the method applied in the chapter on central tendency, here we calculate the value of Q_1 through the formula:

$Q_1 = l_1 + (\frac{\frac{N}{4}-F}{f_{Q_1}}) \times i$ (all the notations have their usual meanings)

or, $Q_1 = 6.5 + (\frac{\frac{150}{4}-28}{31}) \times 3 = 6.5 + \frac{9.5}{31} \times 3 = 7.42$

Similarly,

$Q_3 = l_1 + (\frac{\frac{3N}{4}-F}{f_{Q_3}}) \times i$ (all the notations have their usual meanings)

or, $Q_3 = 12.5 + (\frac{\frac{3 \times 150}{4}-109}{41}) \times 3 = 12.5 + \frac{3.5}{41} \times 3 = 12.76$

Applying the abovementioned formula of Q.D. we get,

$Q.D. = \frac{Q_3 - Q_1}{2}$

$= \frac{12.76 - 7.42}{2}$

$= 2.67$

Doing it Step by Step

Step 1: Find the values of the First and Third Quartiles (Q_1 and Q_3 respectively) from a frequency distribution.

Step 2: Calculate the interquartile range or $Q_3 - Q_1$

Step 3: Divide $Q_3 - Q_1$ by 2 to get the value of semi-interquartile range or Q.D.

4. Standard Deviation (S.D.)

The Standard Deviation (S.D.), as a measure of dispersion is defined as the, 'Root mean square deviation from the mean.'[7] Thus, it is the 'square root of the arithmetic mean of the squares of all deviations, deviations being measured from the arithmetic mean of the observations.'[8] The term was introduced by Pearson[9] although it had been in use in alternative names like 'Mean error'[10], 'Mean Square of Error'[11] for about a century before him.

Pearson used the Greek letter 'σ' (sigma) as the symbol to denote the Standard Deviation[12].

Now, if a series of observations $x_1, x_2, x_3 \ldots \ldots x_n$ has the arithmetic mean $\bar{x}$, then, the deviations of the observations from it can be expressed as: $(x_i - \bar{x})$ and, the squares of all deviations be: $(x_i - \bar{x})^2$

Following Yule's definition, the arithmetic mean of the squares of all deviations would be: $\frac{\Sigma(x_i - \bar{x})^2}{n}$.

Therefore, the Standard Deviation (S.D.), or σ can be expressed as: $\sqrt{\frac{\Sigma(x_i - \bar{x})^2}{n}}$

This is the formula of Standard Deviation of a simple series of ungrouped data. Deducing from this we can get the **working formula of S.D.** which is:

$$\text{S.D. or } \sigma = \sqrt{\frac{\Sigma x_i^2}{n} - \left(\frac{\Sigma x_i}{n}\right)^2}$$

For a set of observations classified in a grouped frequency distribution, Pearson (1900) outlined the rule to obtain the S.D. In his words:

> 'Multiply the frequency with which each individual type occurs by the square of its deviation from the mean; add all these products together and divide by the total number of individuals. This is the square of the standard deviation.'[13]

'The square of the standard deviation', Pearson mentioned is known as the Variance. So, to have the standard deviation we just need to find out the square root of it.

Accordingly, for a set of observations $x_1, x_2, x_3 \ldots \ldots x_n$ having the frequencies $f_1, f_2, f_3 \ldots f_n$ and the arithmetic mean $\bar{x}$,

the S.D. or $\sigma = \sqrt{\frac{\Sigma f_i(x_i - \bar{x})^2}{N}}$.

Deducing from this we can get the **working formula of S.D. of a grouped frequency distribution** which is:

S.D. or $\sigma = \sqrt{\frac{\Sigma f_i x_i^2}{N} - \left(\frac{\Sigma f_i x_i}{N}\right)^2}$

Standard Deviation (S.D.) of a simple series

Let us consider the series of observations: 11, 12, 14, 10, and 13

x_i	x_i^2
11	121
12	144
14	196
10	100
13	169
$\Sigma x_i = 60$	$\Sigma x_i^2 = 730$

As we know for an ungrouped data

S.D. or $\sigma = \sqrt{\frac{\Sigma x_i^2}{n} - \left(\frac{\Sigma x_i}{n}\right)^2}$, so by putting the values we get,

$\sigma = \sqrt{\frac{730}{5} - \left(\frac{60}{5}\right)^2}$

$= \sqrt{146 - (12)^2}$

$= \sqrt{2}$

$= 1.41$

As, the value of S.D. = 1.41, so the

Variance = (S.D.)^2 = (1.41)^2 = 2

Standard Deviation (S.D.) of a grouped frequency distribution

To illustrate the calculation of the Standard Deviation from a grouped frequency distribution let us refer to Table: 12.2, which presents the age Distribution of a sample of 150 children in two Villages of Mamudpur Gram Panchayat, North 24 Parganas, West Bengal

Age Group (in years)	No. of Children (f_i)	Midpoint (x_i)	$f_i x_i$	x_i^2	$f_i x_i^2$
1-3	4	2	8	4	16
4-6	24	5	120	25	600
7-9	31	8	248	64	1984
10-12	50	11	550	121	6050
13-15	41	14	574	196	8036
	$N = 150$		$\Sigma f_i x_i = 1500$		$\Sigma f_i x_i^2 = 16686$

As we know that the S.D. or σ of a grouped frequency distribution is:

$$\text{S.D. or } \sigma = \sqrt{\frac{\Sigma f_i x_i^2}{N} - \left(\frac{\Sigma f_i x_i}{N}\right)^2}$$

Putting the values in the equation, we get:

$$\sigma = \sqrt{\frac{16686}{150} - \left(\frac{1500}{150}\right)^2}$$

$$= \sqrt{111.24 - 100}$$

$$= \sqrt{11.24}$$

$$= 3.35$$

Therefore, the value of the Standard Deviation of the ages of the children = 3.35 years, and the value of the Variance $(\sigma^2) = (3.35)^2 = 11.24$ years^2

Doing it Step by Step

Step 1: Find the values of the midpoints (x$_i$) of the class intervals

Step 2: Multiply the midpoints of each class interval with the respective frequencies of the classes to get the values of $f_i\, x_i$

Step 3: Square the midpoints to get the values of x_i^2

Step 4: Multiply each x_i^2 with their respective frequencies (f_i) to get $f_i x_i^2$

Step 5: Sum the $f_i\, x_i$ and $f_i x_i^2$ column to obtain the values of $\Sigma f_i x_i$ and $\Sigma f_i x_i^2$

Step 6: Put the appropriate values in the formula to get the value of the S.D.

Calculation of Standard Deviation (S.D.) by Short Method

The computation of Standard Deviation can be made simpler by adopting the short method. This follows the same procedure of step deviation we have applied to compute the Arithmetic Mean. As the first step, we need to calculate the deviations of the midpoints (x_i) of the class intervals from an arbitrary constant 'c'. Here, 'c', as we have mentioned earlier, is a constant the value of which lies somewhere at the middle of the distribution of the midpoints. This involves, as we know, a shift in the origin or the zero point of the measurement. Then we need to divide such deviations by 'd'. This is yet another constant which usually assumes the value of the common difference of the midpoints or the length of the class interval. We also know that, this division of the deviations by the constant d (it can be multiplied also) results in a shift in the scale or unit of measurement. Thus, subtracting 'c' from the midpoints (x_i) and dividing these by 'd' we get the deviations as:

$$y_i = \frac{x_i - c}{d}$$

Following the same method to obtain Standard Deviation of the scores represented as x_i (denoted as σ_x), we can have the Standard Deviation of the scores represented by y_i (denoted by σ_y). Therefore, if,

$$\sigma x = \sqrt{\frac{\Sigma f_i x_i^2}{N} - \left(\frac{\Sigma f_i x_i}{N}\right)^2}, \text{ then}$$

$$\sigma_y = \sqrt{\frac{\Sigma f_i y_i^2}{N} - \left(\frac{\Sigma f_i y_i}{N}\right)^2}$$

After obtaining the value of σ_y following this method, we can get the value of σ_x through the following expression:

$$\sigma_x = d\sigma_y$$

Thus, we can see that the Standard Deviation (S.D.) is independent of the change of origin but depends on or influenced by the change in unit or scale of measurement.

For the purpose of illustration let us once again refer to Table: 12.2.

Age Group (in years)	No. of Children (f_i)	Mid-Point (x_i)	$y_i = \frac{x_i-8}{3}$	$f_i y_i$	y_i^2	$f_i y_i^2$
1-3	4	2	-2	-8	4	16
4-6	24	5	-1	-24	1	24
7-9	31	8	0	0	0	0
10-12	50	11	1	50	1	50
13-15	41	14	2	82	4	164
	N = 150			$\Sigma f_i y_i = 100$		$\Sigma f_i y_i^2 = 254$

Here, let $c = 8$ and $d = 3$, so, $y_i = \frac{x_i-c}{d} = \frac{x_i-8}{3}$

As we know that:

$$\sigma_y = \sqrt{\frac{\Sigma f_i y_i^2}{N} - \left(\frac{\Sigma f_i y_i}{N}\right)^2}$$

or, $\sigma_y = \sqrt{\frac{254}{150} - \left(\frac{100}{150}\right)^2}$ [putting the calculated values]

$$= \sqrt{1.7 - 0.45}$$

$$= \sqrt{1.7 - 0.45}$$

$$= \sqrt{1.25}$$

$$= 1.118$$

Therefore,

$\sigma_x = 3 \times 1.118$ (since we know that $\sigma_x = d\sigma_y$)

$= 3.35$ (appx.)

Thus, the Standard Deviation of the ages of the children obtained by applying the short method = 3.35 years. Here it is to be noted that the long as well as the short method yield almost the same value of the Standard Deviation.

Composite Standard Deviation

As it has been done in the case of Arithmetic Mean in the previous chapter, a similar situation might emerge where a series of observations is composed of two component series having number of observations N_1 and N_2 respectively, so that the number of observations in the combined series stands at N ($N = N_1 + N_2$). The means of the two component series being $\overline{x_1}$ and $\overline{x_2}$ so that the combined mean ($\overline{x_c}$) as we have found in the previous chapter is:

$$\overline{x_c} = \frac{N_1 \overline{x_1} + N_2 \overline{x_2}}{N}.$$

If the standard deviations of the two series are respectively σ_1 and σ_2, then the standard deviation of the combined series (σ_c) can be found by the following expression:

Standard Deviation of the combined series $(\sigma_c) = \sqrt{\dfrac{N_1\sigma_1{}^2 + N_2\sigma_2{}^2 + N_1 d_1{}^2 + N_2 d_2{}^2}{N}}$

Where,

σ_c = Combined mean of the two series of observations.

σ_1 = Standard Deviation of the first component series

σ_2 = Standard Deviation of the second component series

$d_1 = \bar{x}_1 - \bar{x}_c$ (difference of the mean of the first series and the combined mean)

$d_2 = \bar{x}_2 - \bar{x}_c$ (difference of the mean of the second series and the combined mean)

N_1 = Number of observations in the first series

N_2 = Number of observations in the second series

$N = N_1 + N_2$ (Total number of observations combining the two series)

To illustrate, let us consider the following table which describes the mean ages of 30 boys and 20 girls reading in Class IX in a school along with the respective standard deviations of their ages.

Table: 12.3. *Mean and Standard Deviations of Ages of the Boys and Girls of Class IX in a School**

Students	Average Age (x) in years	Number (N)	Standard Deviation (σ)
Boys	$\bar{x}_1 = 16$	$N_1 = 30$	$\sigma_1 = 3$
Girls	$\bar{x}_2 = 14$	$N_2 = 20$	$\sigma_2 = 4$

*Fictitious data

From this information if we want to calculate the value of the combined standard deviation (σ_c), first we need to find the value of the Combined Mean $(\bar{x}_c)$.

As we know for two component groups,

$$\bar{x}_c = \frac{N_1\bar{x_1}+N_2\bar{x_2}}{N}$$

or, $\bar{x}_c = \frac{30\times16+20\times14}{30+20}$ (putting the given values)

or, $\bar{x}_c = 15.2$

Therefore, the mean age of the combined group of students = 15.2 years

Since the value of $\bar{x}_c$ = 15.2, so, here

$d_1 = \bar{x_1} - \bar{x}_c = 16 - 15.2 = 0.8$ (since $\bar{x_1} = 16$)

and

$d_2 = \bar{x_2} - \bar{x}_c = 14 - 15.2 = -1.2$ (since $\bar{x_2} = 14$)

As we also know that, for two component groups, the combined standard deviation or

$$\sigma_c = \sqrt{\frac{N_1\sigma_1{}^2+N_2\sigma_2{}^2+ N_1d_1{}^2+ N_2d_2{}^2}{N \text{ or } (N_1+ N_2)}}$$

So,

$\sigma_c = \sqrt{\frac{30\times3^2+20\times4^2+ 30\times0.8^2+ 20\,(-1.2)^2}{30+20}}$ (putting all the appropriate values in places)

or, $\sigma_c = \sqrt{\frac{270 +320+ 19.2+ 28.8}{50}}$

or, $\sigma_c = \sqrt{\frac{638}{50}}$

or, $\sigma_c = \sqrt{12.76}$

or, $\sigma_c = 3.57$

Therefore, the combined Standard Deviation of the composite group of boy and girl students of Class IX of that school is 3.57 years.

This way we can calculate the combined standard deviation of a series which is composed of any number of component series. Therefore, to calculate the combined standard deviation of a series being composed of more than two component series we need to generalise the formula in the form of the following expression:

$$\sigma_c = \sqrt{\frac{\Sigma N_i \sigma_i^2 + \Sigma N_i d_i^2}{N}}$$

where,

σ_c = Combined Standard Deviation,

N_i = Number of observations or size of a particular group,

σ_i = Standard Deviation of a particular group,

d_i = Difference of the mean of a particular group and the Combined Mean,

N = Total number of observations combining all the groups

Therefore, for three component series or groups of observations the formula of combined standard deviation, for example, would be:

$$\sigma_c = \sqrt{\frac{N_1 \sigma_1^2 + N_2 \sigma_2^2 + N_3 \sigma_3^2 + N_1 d_1^2 + N_2 d_2^2 + N_3 d_3^2}{N \ or \ (N_1 + N_2 + N_3)}}$$

In this manner the combined standard deviation of any number of groups can be calculated.

Selecting the best measure of dispersion

From the foregoing discussion of the four measures of dispersion, the researchers might get confused about the best measure to apply in their particular research analysis. It is to be noted that all the measures have some disadvantages as well as advantages. But to Pearson (1900) from a theoretical as well as practical point of view the Standard deviation, '…may be considered the best. It is not hard to find, and it occurs and recurs in all sorts of investigations'[14]. In fact, among all the measures of dispersion, the Standard Deviation (S.D.), just like the Arithmetic Mean (A.M.), possesses a majority of the properties of a desirable measure of dispersion. To quote Yule:

> 'It is rigidly defined; it is based on all the observations made; it is calculated with reasonable ease; it lends itself readily to algebraical treatment;...it is... the measure least affected by fluctuations of sampling.'[15]

Thus, as a measure of dispersion the Standard Deviation (S.D.) appears to be the most stable and efficient method. This explains why it has greater applicability in analysing the research data. Moreover, for the relative ease of its calculation the standard deviation is quite a handy tool to measure the spread or dispersion of a series of observation.

Relative Measures of Dispersion

Often there are situations when the researchers want to compare the variability of two or more characteristics of the series of observations in question, which are measured in different units. For example a researcher might be interested to know the variability of monthly wages (measured in the unit Rupees) of the employee of a certain industry and the variability in their period of schooling (measured in the unit years). Precisely, the question is to study in which of the characteristics: monthly wages (measured in rupees) or period of schooling (measured in years), there is greater or lesser variability or spread? Since these are measured in different units, so, mere comparison of the standard deviations of these two characteristics will yield meaningless results. This is because, as we know, standard deviation as a measure of the spread of data depends on the unit or scale of measurement. The number expressing the value of standard deviation will change depending on the change in the unit of measurement. The relative measures of dispersion are of particular importance to achieve such comparability in the variability of two or more characteristics expressed in different units of measurement.

The relative measure of dispersion is the '...ratio of the measure of absolute dispersion (e.g. standard deviation, mean deviation, or quartile deviation) to the average (mean or median) from which the deviations were measured'[16] multiplied by 100. These are expressed as coefficients; hence unit free mere numbers, which allows the comparison of variability of the characteristics measured. There can be various measures of relative dispersion, viz.

1. Coefficient of Mean Deviation (deviations are measured from either mean or median)
2. Coefficient of Quartile Deviation; and
3. Coefficient of Variation.

Coefficient of Mean Deviation (deviations are measured from either mean or median)

Coefficient of Mean Deviation is the ratio of the Mean Deviation (M.D.) to either the mean or the median depending on the average (mean or median as the case may be) from which the deviations are taken and multiplied by 100. Therefore, it can be expressed as:

$$Coefficient\ of\ Mean\ Deviation\ (about\ mean) = \frac{Mean\ Deviation\ (M.D.)about\ Mean}{Mean} \times 100$$

$$Coefficient\ of\ Mean\ Deviation\ (about\ median) = \frac{Mean\ Deviation\ (M.D.)about\ Median}{Median} \times 100$$

Coefficient of Quartile Deviation

Coefficient of Quartile Deviation (Q.D.)is the ratio of the Quartile Deviation (Q.D.) to the median multiplied by 100. Therefore, it can be expressed as:

$$Coefficient\ of\ Quartile\ Deviation = \frac{Quartile\ Deviation\ (Q.D.)}{Median} \times 100$$

Coefficient of Variation (C.V.)

Pearson introduced this measure and defined it as the, '…ratio of standard deviation to mean'[17] multiplied by 100. Thus, it can be expressed as:

$$Coefficient\ of\ Variation = \frac{Standard\ Deviation\ (S.D.)}{Mean} \times 100$$

Since the coefficient of variation or C.V. is based on standard deviation and mean, the most efficient measures of dispersion and central tendency respectively, so coefficient of variation is the best suited to have a measure of relative variability. Hence, to have a general understanding of the relative measure of dispersion it is necessary to understand the coefficient of variation thoroughly. Let us take an example.

The following table presents the values of mean and standard deviation of heights and weights of the secondary level students in a school of a certain city. Among these two characteristics, viz. height and weight, which one is more variable?

Measures	Height (in cm.)	Weight (in kg)
Mean	155	46.5
Standard Deviation	8.5	5.3

From the above mentioned formula:

The coefficient of variation (CV) of height of the students $= \frac{8.5}{155} \times 100 = 0.05 \times 100 = 5\%$

The coefficient of variation (CV) of weight of the students $= \frac{5.3}{46.5} \times 100 = 0.11 \times 100 = 11\%$

By comparing the CVs of height and weight it is found that the weight of the students has greater variability (as the standard deviation of weight is 11% of the average weight) than that of their height (the standard deviation of height is 5% of the average height). So it can be concluded that the weights of the students are more dispersed or scattered from the mean than their height.

Skewness

Skewness refers to the degree of asymmetry of a distribution of scores. A symmetrical distribution is one where the values of the different measures of central tendency viz. the mean, median and the mode are equal. Often this is not the case. To Pearson, when the value of the mean is either greater or lesser than the mode, the distribution can be termed 'skew'[18]. So, when the values of mean, median and mode differ then we have a skewed distribution.

To compare a series of distributions pertaining to different characters of the observations with different levels of asymmetry, some numerical measures of their respective degrees of asymmetry or skewness is necessary. To facilitate comparison the numerical measures should yield some mere numbers independent of the unit of their measurement. For example, the skewness of a distribution of the ages of persons residing in a locality should be independent of the unit of measurement of age like, years, months or days. To Pearson it can be conveniently measured by, '...the ratio of the distance between mode and mean to the standard deviation.'[19] In the following we present it in the form of equation:

Pearson's measure of Skewness

$$\text{Skewness} = \frac{\text{Mean} - \text{Mode}}{\text{Standard Deviation}}$$

What follows from the equation is when the values of mean and mode is equal, then skewness = 0. This is the case of a symmetrical distribution. The distribution would have a positive skewness when the value of mean is greater than the mode and a negative skewness when the value of mean is less than the mode.

Since the mode as a measure of central tendency has several limitations, so Pearson also had suggested a transformation of the above mentioned equation. This is done by replacing the numerator of the equation by 3 (Mean-Median) following the relationship formula of the mean, median and mode as mentioned in the chapter on the Measures of Central Tendency. Hence,

$$\text{Skewness} = \frac{3(\text{Mean} - \text{Median})}{\text{Standard Deviation}}$$

From this expression it is evident that if the value of the mean is equal to the value of median then the value of skewness will be zero. Similar to that of the mode, here also if the value of the mean exceeds that of the median we have a positively skewed distribution and when the median is greater than the mean we have a negatively skewed distribution. Skewness and its different directions can also be comprehended through the following diagrams:

Figure: 12.1 *Skewness and its Direction in Three Distributions*

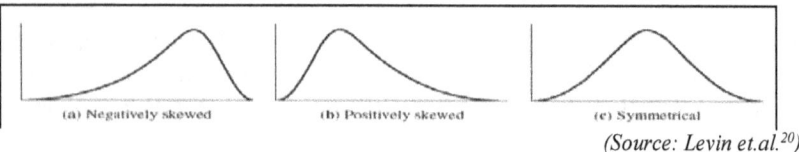

(a) Negatively skewed   (b) Positively skewed   (c) Symmetrical

(Source: Levin et.al.[20])

These measures are known as Pearson's first and second measure of skewness. It is to be noted that both these are dependent on mean and standard deviation, which often find problems in dealing with data with greater degree of asymmetry as well as extreme values in the series of observations. Perhaps, on a consideration of these Bowley had come up with an alternative measure of skewness based on quartiles[21]. This is also known as Yule's coefficient of skewness. Since, Bowley's measure is based on the quartiles of any distribution of scores, so it is largely unaffected by the presence of extreme values. This is also known as quartile measure of skewness.

Bowley's Measure of Skewness

$$Skewness = \frac{(Q_3 - Q_2) - (Q_2 - Q_1)}{(Q_3 - Q_1)} = \frac{Q_3 - 2Q_2 + Q_1}{Q_3 - Q_1}$$

Here it should be noticed that for a symmetrical distribution the difference between Q_3 and Q_2 will be equal to that of between Q_2 and Q_1, so the coefficient of skewness will be zero. The presence of skewness will be there whenever these differences are not equal. If the difference between $(Q_3 - Q_2)$ is greater than $(Q_2 - Q_1)$, then skewness will be positive and will be negative when the difference between $(Q_3 - Q_2)$ is less than $(Q_2 - Q_1)$.

EXERCISE

1. What is meant by dispersion or deviation?
2. What is the importance of the measure of dispersion from the standpoint of research methodology?
3. What are the different measures of dispersion?
4. What is meant by range?
5. Find the range of the series, 18, 24, 15, 17, 27, 13, 25, 12
   [Ans. 15]
6. The Gross State Domestic Product (GSDP) per capita of six states viz. Gujarat, Goa, Karnataka, Tamil Nadu, West Bengal, Maharashtra during 1993-94 to 1998-99 (as mentioned by the Planning Commission of India) was 6.2, 4.5, 6.4, 5.8, 5.0 and 5.4 respectively. Find the range of the GSDP per capita of these states.   [Ans. 1.9]
7. What is meant by Mean Deviation?
8. Find out the Mean Deviation about Mean and Median of the following series: 11, 9, 6, 7, 10   [Ans. 1.68; 2]

9. The following table describes the number of road accidents and the number of days the accidents happened in a month in a certain city. Calculate the Mean deviation about Mean of the data:

Number of Road Accidents	30-40	40-50	50-60	60-70	70-80
Number of Days	8	9	6	4	3

[Ans. 10.5]

10. Calculate the value of Mean Deviation about Median from the data of Question no. 9
11. Define Quartile Deviation (Q.D.).
12. Calculate the value of Quartile Deviation from the data of Question no. 5   [Ans. 5]
13. Calculate the value of Quartile Deviation from the following data:

Height (inches)	60-64	65-69	70-74	75-79	80-84	85-89
Frequency	8	28	118	66	16	8

[Ans. 3.3 inches]

14. What is meant by Standard Deviation?
15. Calculate the Standard Deviation of the series: 22, 24, 28, 20, 26

[Ans. 2.82]

16. What is meant by Variance of a set of scores?
17. Find the variance of the set of scores given in Question no. 15.

[Ans. 7.95]

18. 50 students were asked to write the total number of hours per day they spent on browsing the Internet. With this information find the standard deviation of hours spent per day by the students for Internet browsing.

Time Spent (hrs.) (x)	4	5	6	8	2	7	3
F	3	5	10	12	9	6	5

[Ans. 2.19]

19. The marks obtained by the students in an Internal Assessment are given below.

Marks Obtained (x)	6	9	12	10	7
f	7	8	6	5	4

Find the standard deviation of their marks. [Ans. 2.14]

20. Marks of the students in Statistics of a class are given below:

Marks	10-20	20-30	30-40	40-50	50-60	60-70
Number of Students (f)	8	10	9	7	4	2

Find the standard deviation by applying the short method of calculation.
[Ans. 14.35]

21. In sample A (N = 100), the mean = 70, and standard deviation = 20, in sample B (N = 80), the mean = 50 and standard deviation = 10. Find the value of the standard deviation of the combined group of 180 cases.
[Ans. 19.12]

22. Consider the following data:

Students	Average time (in hour) spent for watching Television per day (x)	Number (N)	Standard Deviation (σ)
Urban	$\overline{x_1} = 4$	$N_1 = 50$	$\sigma_1 = 5$
Rural	$\overline{x_2} = 8$	$N_2 = 20$	$\sigma_2 = 2$
Semi Urban	$\overline{x_3} = 5$	$N_3 = 30$	$\sigma_3 = 3$

Find the combined standard deviation of the time spent for watching Television by the three groups taken together. [Ans. 4.28 hours]

23. Why does Yule consider Standard Deviation (S.D.) to be the most stable and efficient method of dispersion?

24. What is meant by the relative measure of dispersion?

25. What is the importance of the relative measure of variability?

26. From the data presented in Question no. 9, calculate the values of coefficient of mean deviation about mean and median.
[Ans. 21% and 22.39%]

27. Calculate the value of coefficient of quartile deviation from the data given in Question no. 13. [Ans. 4.5%]

28. How coefficient of variation is measured?

29. If the value of standard deviation = 10 and the mean = 30, what will be the value of the coefficient variation? [Ans. 33.33%]

30. Find the value of coefficient variation from the data given in Question no. 20.   [Ans. 42.52%]

31. The following table presents the values of mean and variance of monthly income (in Rs.) of the employees of two software farms A and B. In which of these two farms the monthly income of the employees is more stable?

Measures	Farm A	Farm B
Mean	25 (in thousand)	28 (in thousand)
Variance	121	196

[Ans. Coefficient of variations of farm A and B = 40% and 50% respectively. Farm A is more stable.]

32. What does Karl Pearson mean by Skewness?

33. If the value of Mean = 20, Mode = 10 and S.D. = 2, then find the value of Pearson's first measure of Skewness.   [Ans. 5]

34. If for a distribution of scores the value of the Mean = 25, Median = 30 and the S.D. = 5, what will be the value of Pearson's second measure of skewness?   [Ans. −3]

35. Find the value of Skewness of the data given in Question no. 20.
                                                                [Ans. 0.32]

36. Find the value of Bowley's measure of Skewness from the data in Question no. 13.   [Ans. 0.19]

37. Considering Pearson's first and second measure of skewness, point out the conditions when the distribution will be symmetrical (skewness = 0), positively skewed and negatively skewed.

Endnotes

1. Karl Pearson, *The Grammar of Science. Second Edition* (London: Adam and Charles Black, 1900), 385.

2. George Udny Yule, *An Introduction to the Theory of Statistics* (London: Charles Griffin and Company Limited, 1919).

3. Joseph F Healey, *Statistics: A Tool for Social Research. Ninth Edition* (Belmont: Wadsworth, 2012).

4. Yule, *An Introduction to the Theory of Statistics.*

5. Jack A. Levin and James Alan Fox and David R. Forde, *Elementary Statistics in Social Research*. *Twelfth edition* (New York: Pearson, 2014).

6. Yule, *An Introduction to the Theory of Statistics*, 144.

7. ibid. 134.

8. ibid.

9. Karl Pearson, "III. Contributions to the mathematical theory of evolution." *Philosophical Transactions of the Royal Society of London. (A.)* 185 (1894)

10. Carl Friedrich Gauss, *Theory of the Combination of Observations Least Subject to Errors: Part One, Part Two, Supplement (Classics in Applied Mathematics, Series Number 11)*, trans. G.W. Stewart (Philadelphia: SIAM, 1823), 8.

11. George Biddell Airy, *On the Algebraical and Numerical Theory of Errors of Observations and the Combination of Observations* (London: Macmillan and Co., 1875), 47.

12. Karl Pearson, *The Grammar of Science. Second Edition*.

13. ibid., 387.

14. ibid., 387.

15. Yule, *An Introduction to the Theory of Statistics*, 143-44.

16. ibid.149.

17. Karl Pearson, "VII. Mathematical contributions to the theory of evolution.—III. Regression, heredity, and panmixia.." *Philosophical Transactions of the Royal Society of London. Series A, Containing Papers of a Mathematical or Physical Character* 187 (1896), 277.

18. Karl Pearson, *The Grammar of Science. Second Edition*.

19. ibid. 408.

20. Levin, Fox and Forde, *Elementary Statistics in Social Research. Twelfth edition*, 68.

21. Arthur Lyon Bowley, *Elements of Statistics* (London: P.S. King and Son, 1901).

13

Correlation and Regression

Correlation

So far we have only concerned ourselves with the description of data in the various properties or dimensions represented by it like, age of the individuals, their monthly or annual income, age at marriage, educational achievement measured in terms of number of schooling years, family size etc. Although the measures through which we have attempted to describe such traits of the series of observations are quite reliable, but often we are interested to know the interaction or relation between the different traits of the data in question. For example, we might be interested to know whether family size is related to the educational attainment of the individuals or whether their monthly or annual income in any way is related to their educational attainment. It might also be of considerable importance to know whether educational attainment is more/less intimately associated with family size than the monthly income of the individuals. We can know these by the method of correlation.

From the standpoint of research methodology the measure of association or correlation is of paramount importance. In the research process the basic aim of the researcher is to analyse or explain the facts in the light of the existing theories or to develop new theoretical schemes if the existing ones are unable to provide appropriate analytical insights into the facts studied. Since theories can be defined as systematic explanations about how and why the events in the universe occur, so the basic task of theory is to establish logical connections or associations between the apparently haphazard facts. It is commonplace that facts appear to us through their properties and attributes which are variable in nature. In the physical world these may imply properties of matter like mass, weight, height, volume, density etc., while in the social world we get hold of the facts through their various aspects as expressed by, for example, people's caste, class, race, ethnicity, gender, religion etc. Theory asserts the logical connections between these variables in the shape of causal framework like variable x causes y or the variable y is a function or effect of the variable x. For example, the secularization thesis states that with the increasing unfolding of the process of modernization in different societies the level of secularization is also increasing. Quite simply, here modernization has been shown to be the cause of secularization. In a methodological sense, modernization here is the independent variable and secularization is the dependent variable. Measures of association or correlation, by studying, measuring and quantifying the degree of association between the independent (or the cause) and the dependent variable (or the effect), thus, helps in causal analysis: the fundamental aim of scientific research.

The statistical technique to measure the relationship quantitatively is known as the coefficient of correlation denoted by the symbol 'r'. Put simply, the coefficient of correlation (r) measures the degree or strength of association between two or more variables. Moreover, correlation coefficient also helps in assessing the nature of the relationship between two or more variables. For example, we might be interested to know whether with increasing or decreasing family income family size also increases or decreases. If with increasing family income the family size increases then the correlation between them is positive and it is negative when the reverse is true. Hence, it is evident that coefficient of correlation measures two aspects: the degree or strength of association and the nature or direction of association. In order to develop a basic understanding of correlation coefficient, in this chapter we will restrict ourselves to bivariate correlation or the discussion and measurement of association between two variables.

Strength of Association

It is not enough to know that there is an association between two variables. Often it is more important to know the degree or strength of this association. For example, we may know that educational attainment is associated with monthly income of the individuals. This is because generally the more educated a person is more is her/his monthly income. But, empirically there are counter evidences to this since there are relatively less educated individuals earning more than the relatively more educated persons. We know that with increasing age at marriage of the females their fertility tends to decline. But here also reverse instances are there. So, not only the existence of association is enough, it is more important to know the degree or strength of such association. As a preliminary measure we can visualise this association between two variables, for example, x and y, through a scatter diagram or scatter gram or scatterplot.

Scatter Diagram

A scatter diagram, in the words of Cramer and Howitt is, 'A graph or diagram which plots the position of cases in terms of their values on two quantitative variables and which shows the way the two variables are related to one another....'[1] In a scatter diagram, it is a convention to locate the scores of the variable 'x' along the horizontal axis and those of the variable 'y' along the vertical axis. The Figures 13.1 and 13.2 describe the scatter diagrams. Figure: 13.1 depicts the relation between years of schooling of males and their monthly income measured in Rupees and Figure: 13.2 presents the same for the females. Here, the variable 'years of schooling' implies the amount of time spent for educational pursuits. It is to be noticed that each point in the scatter diagrams represents values of two variables: one in the horizontal axis (years of schooling) and the other in the vertical axis (monthly income). Thus, among the males, as represented in Figure: 13.1, the person with 15 years of schooling is found to earn Rs. 20,000 per month.

Figure: 13.1 *Scatter Diagram of Years of Schooling and Monthly Income (in Rs.) of Males**

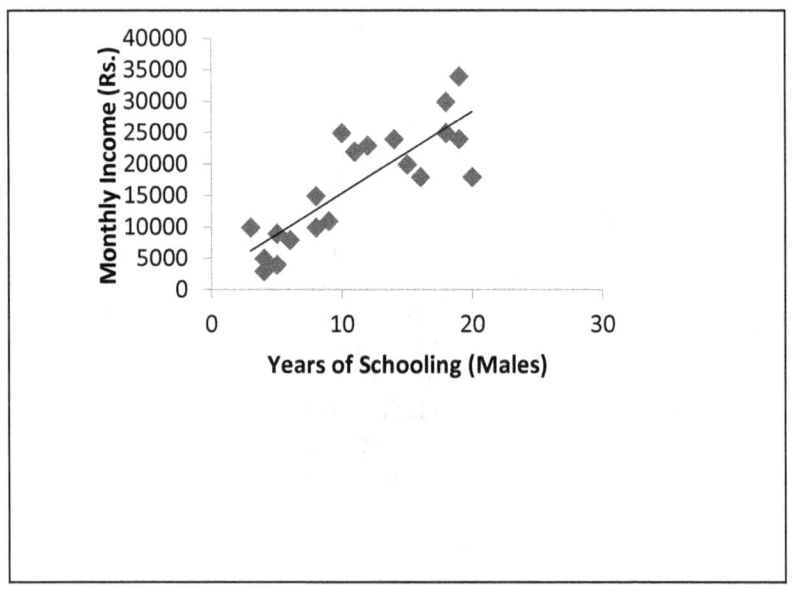

*Fictitious Data

Figure: 13.2 Scatter Diagram of Years of Schooling and Monthly Income (in Rs.) of Females

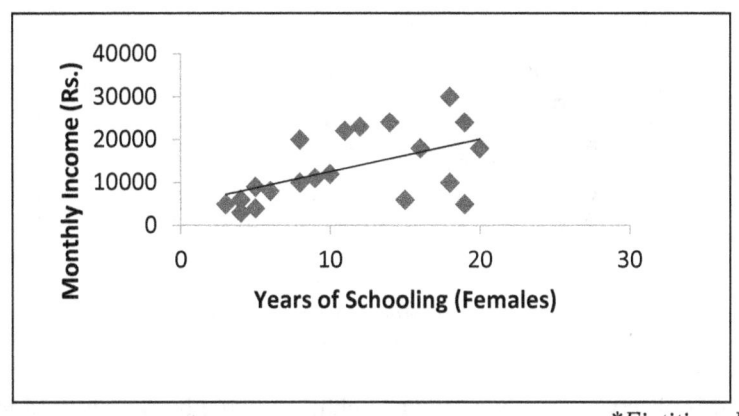

Fictitious Data

From the figures it is revealed that the scattered points in the plots tend to form a trend line which passes through the centre of these points. This trend line, although not a necessary component of the scatter diagram, has been shown here to have an overall perception of the strength of association existing between the two variables. It is observed that closer the scattered points are around the trend line the stronger is the correlation. Hence, for the males in Figure: 13.1, there exists a stronger correlation between years of schooling and monthly income compared to the females as depicted in Figure: 13.2.

Direction of Association

The coefficient of correlation also measures the direction of the association between two variables. In Figures: 13.1 and 13.2 it can be observed that, whatever might be the strength of the association, for both males and females the monthly income of the persons increases with the increase in their years of schooling. So there exists a positive correlation between these two variables. There are several instances where the association follows a reverse direction, that is, the values of one variable (x) tend to decline with the simultaneous increase in the values of the other variable (y). This is the case of a negative correlation. The scatter diagram presented in Figure: 13.3, which describes the age at first marriage of women and the number of children borne by them, is an example of this.

Figure: *13.3 Scatter Diagram of Age at First Marriage of Women and Number of Children borne by them**

*Fictitious Data

Here it is observed that the number of children borne by women tend to go down with the increase in their age at first marriage. Thus, it is evident from the diagram that there exists a negative correlation between age at first marriage of women and the number of children borne by them. There may be several other examples of this, as for instances, with increasing modernization the level of religiosity declines, people with greater amount of liberal values tend to vote less for the conservative parties, with increasing degree of urbanization the rigidity of the caste system tends to decline and so on.

So far we have only discussed associations between two variables where the increase/decrease of the values of one variable is associated with the simultaneous increase/decrease in the values of another variable. This is called linear association or linear correlation. However, there may be instances where the increase in the values of any one of the variables is initially associated with an increase in another variable but only up to a threshold point. Whenever the threshold is reached, further increase in the values of the variable may result in decreasing values of the other variable. Similar may be the case with decrease in the values of one variable resulting into simultaneous decrease in the values of the other variable up to a point after which the values of the latter start to increase with any farther decrease in values of the former. This is the case of curvilinear correlation. In the present chapter we will limit ourselves to the discussion of linear correlation only.

Correlation Coefficient between x and y (r_{xy})

The correlation coefficient as a single measure assesses the strength and direction of the association between two variables. As far as strength is concerned, the correlation coefficient can range from perfect to no correlation in either direction viz. positive or negative. The perfect correlation between two variables is found when change in the values of one variable is related to an equal change in the values of the other variable. Since strength of the correlation is independent of the direction of it, so it may be perfectly positive or perfectly negative depending upon the nature of the data in question. Perfect correlation is denoted by 1.00 in either direction. So, if we find that the value of the correlation coefficient between age and political radicalism to be −1.00, then we can say that there exists a perfect negative correlation between the variables implying that with an increase in the age of the people by a certain unit there would be an equal decrease in the degrees of their political radicalism and the vice-versa. Similar may be the cases of perfect positive correlation expressed as +1.00 or simply, 1.00. The variables may be uncorrelated if the strength of association measured by the coefficient of correlation between them is equal to zero. This implies a situation where change in any one of the variable is noted to have no impact on the values of the other variable. For instance, if the percentage of votes polled by any party across the different age groups of the electorates remains unchanged then there is no relation between the votes polled by that party and the age of the electorates. In other words, the correlation coefficient between these two variables is equal to zero.

Thus, the value of the correlation coefficient varies from perfectly negative to perfectly positive or from −1 to + 1. The following figure describes it:

Figure: 13.4. *The Strength and Direction of Correlation*

⇓	⇓	⇓	⇓	⇓	⇓	⇓	⇓	⇓
−1.00	−0.60	−0.30	−0.10	0	+0.10	+0.30	+0.60	+1.00
Perfect	Strong	Moderate	Weak	No	Weak	Moderate	Strong	Perfect
Negative				Correlation				Positive
Correlation								Correlation

Hence, the correlation coefficient varies from the 'perfect negative correlation' (−1.00) to 'strong negative correlation' (−0.60) to 'moderate negative correlation' (−0.30) to 'weak negative correlation' (−0.10) to 'no correlation' (0). Starting with 'no correlation' it varies in a similar fashion to the positive side as well. Since the strength of correlation is independent of its direction, so we can say that a correlation of −0.60 is equal to +0.60 in strength, as both imply strong correlation.

Pearson's Correlation Coefficient

In the year 1895 Karl Pearson first came up with a formula to measure the strength and direction of association between two variables. Since then it is being used as the most efficient technique to determine the association between two variables measured at the interval and ratio level. According to Pearson[2], if (x_1, y_1), (x_2, y_2)........(x_n, y_n) is a series of n pair of observations, where the mean of $x_1, x_2, ...x_n = \bar{x}$ and standard deviation $= \sigma_x$ and the mean of $y_1, y_2....y_n = \bar{y}$ and standard deviation $= \sigma_y$,

Then, the correlation coefficient between x and y represented as r_{xy} is as following:

$$r_{xy} = \frac{Covariance_{(x\,with\,y)}}{\sigma_x \sigma_y}$$

Here Covariance $_{(x\ with\ y)}$ or simply, Covariance $_{xy}$, like correlation, 'is a measure of linear association between variables.'[3] It refers to the shared variance of x and y and expressed as:

$$Covariance_{xy} = \frac{\Sigma(x_i - \bar{x})(y_i - \bar{y})}{n}$$

Putting the value of covariance $_{xy}$ in the expression of correlation coefficient (r_{xy}) above, we get,

$$r_{xy} = \frac{\Sigma(x_i - \bar{x})(y_i - \bar{y})}{n\sigma_x \sigma_y}$$

Deducing the expression we arrive at the:

Working formula of Pearson's Correlation Coefficient:

$$r_{xy} = \frac{n\Sigma xy - \Sigma x \Sigma y}{\sqrt{\{n\Sigma x^2 - (\Sigma x)^2\}\{n\Sigma y^2 - (\Sigma y)^2\}}}$$

Pearson's correlation coefficient (r_{xy}) is a dimensionless or unit free pure number. As mentioned earlier, its value lies between −1 and +1.

To illustrate the working formula of Pearson's correlation coefficient let us consider Table: 13.1, which describes the age at marriage of seven mothers (x) and the age at marriage of their seven daughters (y) measured in years.

To employ the formula we need to compute, xy, x^2, y^2 which is also done in the table.

Table: 13.1. *Age at Marriage (in Years) of Seven Mothers and their Seven Daughters**

Age at Marriage of Mothers (x)	Age at Marriage of Daughters (y)	xy	x^2	y^2
16	23	368	256	529
19	25	475	361	625
20	27	540	400	729
22	28	616	484	784
17	24	408	289	576
23	21	483	529	441
21	22	462	441	484
Σx = 138	*Σy = 170*	*Σxy = 3352*	*Σx² = 2760*	*Σy² = 4168*

*Fictitious data

As we know, the Pearson's Correlation Coefficient,

$$r_{xy} = \frac{n\Sigma xy - \Sigma x \Sigma y}{\sqrt{\{n\Sigma x^2 - (\Sigma x)^2\}\{n\Sigma y^2 - (\Sigma y)^2\}}}$$

Putting the values in the expression we get,

$$r_{xy} = \frac{7 \times 3352 - 138 \times 170}{\sqrt{\{7 \times 2760 - (138)^2\}\{7 \times 4168 - (170)^2\}}}$$

$$= \frac{7 \times 3352 - 138 \times 170}{\sqrt{\{(19320 - 19044)(29176 - 28900)\}}}$$

$$= \frac{7 \times 3352 - 138 \times 170}{\sqrt{276 \times 276}}$$

$$= \frac{23464 - 23460}{\sqrt{276 \times 276}}$$

$$= \frac{4}{276}$$

$$= 0.01$$

Hence, there is a weak positive correlation between age at marriage of the mothers and age at marriage of their daughters.

Doing it Step by Step

Step 1: Calculate the values of Σx, Σy, Σxy, Σx^2, Σy^2

Step 2: Put the values in Pearson's formula of correlation coefficient

$$r_{xy} = \frac{n\Sigma xy - \Sigma x \Sigma y}{\sqrt{\{n\Sigma x^2 - (\Sigma x)^2\}\{n\Sigma y^2 - (\Sigma y)^2\}}}$$

Calculation of Pearson's Correlation Coefficient by Short Method

Like the Arithmetic Mean and Standard Deviation, the Pearson's Correlation Coefficient can also be calculated with relative ease by employing the Step Deviation method. This can be done by calculating the deviations of the values in 'x' series from an arbitrary constant (c) and then dividing it by another constant (d). Similarly, we calculate the deviations of the values in 'y' series from an arbitrary constant (p) and then dividing it by another constant (q). Here the constants c, d and p, q implying, as usual, changes in origin and scale in the two series of observations.

Thus, the deviations in the 'x' series can be expressed as:

$$u_i = \frac{x_i - c}{d}$$

And the deviations in the 'y' series can be expressed as:

$$v_i = \frac{y_i - p}{q}$$

Through the changes in the origin and scale, the 'n' pair of observations represented as (x_1, y_1), (x_2, y_2)........(x_n, y_n) gets transformed into (u_1, v_1),

$(u_2, v_2)........(u_n, v_n)$. The coefficient of correlation of the transformed series is represented by the symbol r_{uv}.

The correlation coefficient of the original series represented by (x_1, y_1), $(x_2, y_2)........(x_n, y_n)$ can be found by the following expression:

$$r_{xy} = r_{uv}$$

This implies that the correlation coefficient is independent of the change of origin and scale.

To illustrate the method, let us consider the following data:

Six students of a particular class in a college were questioned regarding (x) their attitudes toward the abolition of Triple Talaq and (y) their attitudes toward the Reservation of seats for women in the Parliament (greater the values of x and y more favourable is the attitude). Table: 13.2 presents the data in tabular form. Here we need to compute the Pearson's correlation coefficient between the two attitudes of the students.

Table: 13.2. *Attitude of the Students towards Abolition of Triple Talaq and Reservation of Seats for Women in the Parliament*

Student	X	Y	$u = \dfrac{x-14}{2}$	$v = \dfrac{y-15}{3}$	uv	u^2	v^2
A	8	12	-3	-1	3	9	1
B	18	21	2	2	4	4	4
C	14	15	0	0	0	0	0
D	12	15	-1	0	0	1	0
E	10	9	-2	-2	4	4	4
F	20	12	3	-1	-3	9	1
			$\Sigma u = -1$	$\Sigma v = -2$	$\Sigma uv = 8$	$\Sigma u^2 = 27$	$\Sigma v^2 = 10$

As we know that the Pearson Correlation Coefficient for the variables u and v

$$r_{uv} = \frac{n\Sigma uv - \Sigma u \Sigma v}{\sqrt{\{n\Sigma u^2 - (\Sigma u)^2\}\{n\Sigma v^2 - (\Sigma v)^2\}}}$$

Putting the values in the expression we get,

$$r_{uv} = \frac{6 \times 8 - (-1) \times (-2)}{\sqrt{\{6 \times 27 - (-1)^2\}\{6 \times 10 - (-2)^2\}}}$$

$$= \frac{48 - 2}{\sqrt{\{162 - 1\}\{60 - 4\}}}$$

$$= \frac{46}{\sqrt{161 \times 56}}$$

$$= \frac{46}{94.95}$$

$$= 0.48$$

Since we know that:

$$r_{xy} = r_{uv} \text{ , so}$$

$$r_{xy} = 0.48, \quad [\text{as the value of } r_{uv} = 0.48]$$

Therefore, through the application of the short method (also known as step deviation method), we get a moderate to strong positive correlation between the students' attitudes toward abolition of Triple Talaq and their attitudes toward reservation of seats for women in the Parliament. It is evident that the calculation is much easier in this method.

Regression

The correlation coefficient tells us the degree or strength of association between two variables. Methodologically, as has been discussed before, correlation can be conceptualised as the degree of association between the independent and the dependent variable, which is of considerable edge to arrive at a causal analysis. So, by the correlation coefficient we can know the manner in which the independent variable is related to the dependent one. But, the correlation coefficient cannot say how much a dependent variable will change as a result of a certain change in the values of an independent variable. A positive correlation coefficient, for example, between level of modernization and degree of secularization can be indicative of the fact that modernization is a cause of secularization, but we cannot assess, from this correlation, the extent of increase/decrease in the degree of secularization in a society resulting from a certain increase/decrease in the level of its modernization. This is precisely the task of regression. Based on the value of the independent variable, in regression analysis we try to regress the value of the independent variable. By measuring or quantifying the extent of concomitant variation in a dependent variable due to variation in the associated independent variable, regression helps in prediction: yet another cornerstone of scientific research. From a known value of the predictor (the independent variable) it can predict the most likely value of the outcome variable (the dependent variable). Obviously, such prediction is made on the basis of correlation coefficient between the two variables in question.

The Regression Equation

In the bivariate framework of analysis, regression helps in predicting the value of the dependent variable (generally denoted by y) on the basis of the independent variable (generally denoted by x) through a mathematical equation. This equation is expressed as:

$$y = a + bx$$

This is the equation of a straight line. The trend lines, which we have seen in the scatter diagrams represented in the Figures: 13.1, 13.2 and 13.3 in this chapter, are basically the regression lines we are now discussing. It expresses that the dependent variable y is the sum of two components.

To understand the mathematical implication of this through an example, let us consider the scatter diagram in Figure 13.1, which describes the association between years of schooling (x) and monthly income (in Rs.) of the males (y). The equation indicates that the income earned by a particular male is a sum of two components: (1) A baseline amount earned by all the males. It refers to the monthly income earned by a male without any year of schooling ('a' in the equation); (2) the amount earned by a male for each year spent for schooling ('b' in the equation).

Graphically, 'a' is designated to be the 'y intercept', a constant value for a bivariate distribution. It indicates the value of y when $x = 0$. Hence, it is the point where the regression line crosses the y axis. In our case, it is the monthly income earned by anyone without any time spent for schooling. This entails that monthly income earned by anyone is not exclusively determined by years of schooling. There may be several other factors responsible for it. The term 'b' denotes the slope of the regression line. It is also known as the regression coefficient. This represents the concomitant change in 'y' or the monthly income of the males due to an increase of each unit of 'x', or year of schooling in our example. For its geometrical root in the straight line, bivariate regression is also known as linear regression.

From the regression equation, theoretically or mathematically we can predict the monthly income of any male if we know the years spent by him for educational pursuits. But, practically, there are several socio-economic and cultural factors, which impose limits on it. Thus, usually, we cannot expect anyone, for example, to spend 50 years for educational attainment.

There are two types of regression lines. These are:

1. Regression Equation of y on x; and
2. Regression Equation of x on y.

Regression Equation of *y* on *x*

It is used when we are to predict or estimate the value of the dependent variable '*y*' for any given value of the independent variable '*x*'. This is expressed by the equation $y = a + bx$. Through mathematical deduction it can be expressed as following:

$$y - \bar{y} = b_{yx}(x - \bar{x})$$

Here, $\bar{x}$ and $\bar{y}$ represent the means of the variable x and y. The factor b_{yx} is known as the regression coefficient of y on x. It is also the slope of the regression line represented by the equation.

Mathematically, it can be shown that:

$$b_{yx} = \frac{y - \bar{y}}{x - \bar{x}}$$

$$or, b_{yx} = \frac{Cov_{xy}}{\sigma_x^2} \left[since, Cov_{xy} = \frac{\Sigma(x_i - \bar{x})(y_i - \bar{y})}{n}\right]$$

$$or, b_{yx} = r_{xy} \times \frac{\sigma_y}{\sigma_x} \left[Since\ r_{xy} = \frac{Cov_{xy}}{\sigma_x \times \sigma_y}\right]$$

Where,

b_{yx} = The regression coefficient of y on x,

r_{xy} = The correlation coefficient of x and y,

σ_y = The Standard Deviation of y, and

σ_x = The Standard Deviation of x

Regression Equation of *x* on *y*

It is used when '*y*' becomes the independent variable, for any given value of which we want to predict or estimate the value of the dependent variable '*x*'.

This can be expressed by the equation $y = p + qx$. Following mathematical deduction it can be expressed as following:

$$x - \bar{x} = b_{xy}(y - \bar{y})$$

Here, $\bar{x}$ and $\bar{y}$ represent the means of the variable x and y. The term b_{xy} is known as the regression coefficient of x on y. The slope of the regression line represented by this equation is $\frac{1}{b_{xy}}$.

Mathematically, it can be shown that:

$$b_{xy} = \frac{x - \bar{x}}{y - \bar{y}}$$

or, $b_{xy} = \frac{Cov_{xy}}{\sigma_y^2}$ [Since, $Cov_{xy} = \frac{\Sigma(x_i - \bar{x})(y_i - \bar{y})}{n}$]

or, $b_{xy} = r_{xy} \times \frac{\sigma_x}{\sigma_y}$ [Since $r_{xy} = \frac{Cov_{xy}}{\sigma_x \times \sigma_y}$]

Where,

b_{xy} = The regression coefficient of x on y,

r_{xy} = The correlation coefficient of x and y,

σ_x = The Standard Deviation of x, and

σ_y = The Standard Deviation of y.

Since regression, or the prediction of the values of a dependent variable from the given values of the independent variable, is centred upon the correlation coefficient, so its calculation is also similar to that of the correlation coefficient. The equations, mentioned above, also point out this.

To illustrate, let us refer back to Table: 13.1, which presents the data of the age at marriage of seven mothers and their seven daughters.

Age at Marriage (in Years) of Seven Mothers and their Seven Daughters

Age at Marriage of Mothers (x)	Age at Marriage of Daughters (y)	xy	x^2	y^2
16	23	368	256	529
19	25	475	361	625
20	27	540	400	729
22	28	616	484	784
17	24	408	289	576
23	21	483	529	441
21	22	462	441	484
$\Sigma x = 138$	$\Sigma y = 170$	$\Sigma xy = 3352$	$\Sigma x^2 = 2760$	$\Sigma y^2 = 4168$

From this data, suppose we are to predict the age at marriage of a daughter (y) whose mother's age at marriage is 18 years and the age at marriage of the mother (x) whose daughter's age at marriage (y) is 30 years.

Such predictions, as is mentioned before, require regression analysis. For this we need to calculate the two regression equations first.

Calculation of Regression equation of y on x

We know that the regression equation of y on x is

$$y - \bar{y} = b_{yx}(x - \bar{x})$$

Where,

$\bar{x}$ and $\bar{y}$ represent the respective means of the variable x and y and b_{yx} is known as the regression coefficient of y on x.

It is known that, $b_{yx} = r_{xy} \times \dfrac{\sigma_y}{\sigma_x}$

Here,

r_{xy} = The correlation coefficient of x and y,

σ_y = The Standard Deviation of y, and

σ_x = The Standard Deviation of x

Thus, the regression equation of y on x can be rewritten as:

$$y - \bar{y} = r_{xy} \times \frac{\sigma_y}{\sigma_x}(x - \bar{x})$$

It has been calculated earlier that the correlation coefficient (r_{xy}) between the age at marriage of mothers and age at marriage of their daughters = 0.01. So, we need to calculate the values of $\bar{x}, \bar{y}, \sigma_y$ and σ_x from the table.

We know that:

$$\bar{x} = \frac{\Sigma x_i}{n}$$

Putting the values as calculated in the table we get,

$$\bar{x} = \frac{138}{7}$$

or, $\bar{x} = 19.71$ years

Similarly,

$$\bar{y} = \frac{170}{7}$$

or, $\bar{y} = 24.29$ years

Now for the Standard Deviations(σ_y and σ_x), we know that,

$$\sigma_y = \sqrt{\frac{\Sigma y_i^2}{n} - \left(\frac{\Sigma y_i}{n}\right)^2}$$

or,

$$\sigma_y = \sqrt{\frac{4168}{7} - \left(\frac{170}{7}\right)^2}$$

$$= \sqrt{595.43 - 590}$$

$$= 2.33 \text{ years}$$

Similarly,

$$\sigma_x = \sqrt{\frac{\Sigma x_i^2}{n} - \left(\frac{\Sigma x_i}{n}\right)^2}$$

Putting the values from the table, we get:

$$\sigma_x = \sqrt{\frac{2760}{7} - \left(\frac{138}{7}\right)^2}$$

or, $\sigma_x = 2.41$ years

Since the regression coefficient of y on x or,

$$b_{yx} = r_{xy} \times \frac{\sigma_y}{\sigma_x}$$

So, putting the values of r_{xy}, σ_y and σ_x we get,

$$b_{yx} = 0.01 \times \frac{2.33}{2.41}$$

$$= 0.01 \text{ (appx.)}$$

Now, putting the values in the regression equation of y on x, we get:

Regression equation of y on x

$$y - \bar{y} = b_{yx}(x - \bar{x})$$

or, $y - 24.29 = 0.01 (x- 19.71)$

or, $y - 0.01x = 24.09$

Calculation of Regression equation of x on y.

We know that that the regression equation of x on y is

$$x - \bar{x} = b_{xy}(y - \bar{y})$$

Since we know that:

The regression coefficient of x on y or,

$$b_{xy} = r_{xy} \times \frac{\sigma_x}{\sigma_y}$$

So, by putting the calculated values of r_{xy}, σ_x and σ_y we get,

$$b_{xy} = 0.01 \times \frac{2.41}{2.33}$$

$$= 0.01 \text{ (appx.)}$$

Now, putting the values in the regression equation of x on y, we get:

Regression equation of x on y

$$x - \bar{x} = b_{xy}(y - \bar{y})$$

or, $x - 19.71 = 0.01(y - 24.29)$

or, $x - 0.01y = 19.47$

Now in order to predict the age at marriage of the daughter (y) whose mother's age at marriage (x) is 18 years, we need to employ the regression equation of y on x.

We have found out that the regression equation of y on x for the data is:

$y - 0.01x = 24.09$

Hence, putting the given value of x, we get:

$y - 0.01 \times 18 = 24.09$

or, $y = 24.09 + 0.18$

or, $y = 24.27$ or 24 years (appx.)

Therefore, the age at marriage of the daughter will be approximately 24 years whose mother's age at marriage is 18 years.

Again, to predict the age at marriage of the mother (x) whose daughter's age at marriage (y) is 30 years, we need to employ the regression equation of x on y.

We have also found out that the regression equation of x on y for the data is:

$x - 0.01y = 19.47$

Hence, putting the given value of y, we get:

$x - 0.01 \times 30 = 19.47$

or, $x = 19.47 + 0.3$

or, $x = 19.77$ or 20 years (appx.)

Hence, the age at marriage of the mother will be approximately 20 years whose daughter's age at marriage is 30 years.

Doing it Step by Step

Step 1: Calculate the values of Σx, Σy, Σxy, Σx^2 and Σy^2 from the distribution of scores of the variables x and y.

Step 2: Calculate the values of $\bar{x}$, $\bar{y}$, σ_x, σ_y, and r_{xy} by employing these values in their appropriate formulas.

Step 3: Calculate the values of b_{xy} and b_{yx} applying their appropriate formulas.

Step 4: Find out the two regression equations by employing all these values.

Step 5: Make predictions of either x or y, as the cases might be, by employing the appropriate formulas viz. regression equation of x on y or y on x, for the purpose.

Properties of Linear Regression

i.   Two regression lines always intersect at their mean or average values ($\bar{x}$ and $\bar{y}$) . This is because, the point where these two lines intersect happens to be the representative values of both the distributions represented by x and y. Since, we know that the mean of any distribution best represents it, so, here the two lines intersect at the point comprised of their mean values. In other words, if we solve the two regression equations we get the values of $\bar{x}$ and $\bar{y}$.

ii. The product of the two regression coefficients is equal to the square of the correlation coefficient. Therefore,

Product of the two regression coefficients $= b_{xy} \times b_{yx}$

$$= [r_{xy} \times \frac{\sigma_x}{\sigma_y}] \times [r_{xy} \times \frac{\sigma_y}{\sigma_x}]$$

$$= r_{xy}{}^2$$

iii. The two regression coefficients b_{yx}, b_{xy} and the correlation coefficient 'r_{xy}' all have the same sign. This is because the regression coefficients (b_{xy} and b_{yx}) are rooted in the correlation coefficient (r_{xy}) and the standard deviations of x and y (σ_x and σ_y). Since, for socio-economic, political and cultural data the standard deviations cannot be negative, so, if the correlation coefficient is positive then both the regression coefficients will be positive and if it is negative then both the regression coefficients will also be negative.

iv. If the correlation coefficient (r_{xy}) = 0, then values of both the regression coefficients will be 0. This implies that in this condition the two regression equations turns out to be $x = \bar{x}$ and $y = \bar{y}$. Hence, if the correlation coefficient = '0' the two variables are uncorrelated or independent, so there is no scope for prediction. Graphically, the two regression lines represented by the equations $x = \bar{x}$ and $y = \bar{y}$ will be perpendicular, having a 90^0 angle.

v. If the correlation coefficient (r_{xy}) = ±1, then the slopes of the two regression lines viz. b_{yx} and $\frac{1}{b_{xy}}$ will be equal. In such a situation the two regression lines will merge or coincide. The angle, in this case, between the two regression lines will be 0^0. Thus, from the properties iv and v we can say that with the numerical increase in the value of the correlation coefficient from 0 to ± 1, the angle between them decreases from 90^0 to 0^0

We can understand some of these properties through an example.

Let, $3x - 7y = 10$ be the regression equation of x on y and $14y - 5x = 20$ be the regression equation of y on x. Following the properties of linear regression, we can find out the values of $\bar{x}$, $\bar{y}$ and r_{xy} from these two equations. If, for example, it is known that $\sigma_x = 3.3$, then we can also find out the value of σ_y.

As we know that the regression equations always intersect at the point $(\bar{x}, \bar{y})$, so we can get the average or representative values of x and y by solving the two equations. Hence, by multiplying the equation of x on y by 5 and that of y on x by 3 and then adding the two equations we get $y = 15.7$. Now putting this value of y in any one of the equations we get $x = 39.97$. Thus the value of $\bar{x} = 39.97$ and $\bar{y} = 15.7$

Here, the regression equation of x on y is $3x - 7y = 10$.

It can be written as, $x = \left(\frac{7}{3}\right)y - \left(-\frac{10}{3}\right)$

The equation is rewritten in this form because the equation of straight line is classically represented as:

$$y = a + bx$$

From this equation we get that $x = \left(\frac{1}{b}\right)y - \frac{a}{b}$ [This implies that the coefficient of y or $\left(\frac{1}{b}\right)$ is basically the regression coefficient of x on y or b_{xy}]

So, in the above example, the regression coefficient of x on y or $b_{xy} = \left(\frac{7}{3}\right) = 2.33$

Similarly, the regression equation of y on x is $14y - 5x = 20$,

This can be written as, $y = \left(\frac{5}{14}\right)x + \frac{20}{14}$

So, the regression coefficient of y on x or $b_{yx} = \left(\frac{5}{14}\right) = 0.36$

As we know that, $r^2 = b_{xy} \times b_{yx}$

So, putting the values of b_{xy} and b_{yx} we get,

$r^2 = b_{xy} \times b_{yx}$

$\quad = 2.33 \times 0.36$

$\quad = 0.84$

or, $r = \sqrt{0.84}$

$\quad = \pm 0.92$

Since both the regression coefficients are positive, so here the value of correlation coefficient will also be positive.

Hence, $r_{xy} = 0.92$

Now, here we also know that $\sigma_x = 3.3$. Thus, we can find out the value of σ_y in the following way:

We know that,

$b_{xy} = 2.33$

or, $r_{xy} \times \dfrac{\sigma_x}{\sigma_y} = 2.33$ [Since it is known that, $b_{xy} = r_{xy} \times \dfrac{\sigma_x}{\sigma_y}$]

Therefore, $0.92 \times \dfrac{3.3}{\sigma_y} = 2.33$ [putting the values of r_{xy} and σ_x]

Hence, $\sigma_y = 1.3$

Similarly, we can also find out the unknown value of σ_x when we know the value of σ_y

Thus, here we see that, if we know the values of the two regression coefficients (b_{xy} and b_{yx}) we can find out the value of r_{xy}. Along with these if we know the value of either σ_x or σ_y, we can also find out the value of the other.

EXERCISE

1. What is meant by Correlation?
2. What is a Scatter Diagram?
3. What is meant by perfect correlation?
4. A study found that the correlation between conservative values possessed by the people and their height to be zero. Interpret the result.
5. What is meant by covariance?
6. Find out the Pearson Correlation Coefficient (r_{xy}) from the following information:

   $\Sigma x = 18$, $\Sigma y = 14$, $\Sigma xy = 61$, $\Sigma x^2 = 86$, $\Sigma y^2 = 66$ and $n = 4$

   [Ans. −0.22]
7. A statistics instructor at an Indian university is interested to know the relationship between the number of optional homework problems students do during the semester (x) and their final course grade (y). She randomly selects 10 students for study and asks them to keep track of the number of these problems completed during the course of the semester. At the end of the course each student's total is recorded along with their final grade. The data are presented in the following table. Compute the linear correlation coefficient (r_{xy}) for this data set:

Student Sl. No.	Number of Homework Problems (x)	Final Course Grade (y)
1	11	22
2	18	28

3	22	26
4	25	26
5	28	27
6	36	32
7	37	33
8	38	38
9	44	33
10	51	35

[Ans. 0.87]

8. The following table represents the age in years (x) and degree of caste prejudice (y) of 10 persons in a locality. Find the Pearson's correlation coefficient (r_{xy}) between age and conservative values by applying the short method.

| Age in years (x) | 20 | 35 | 25 | 45 | 55 | 65 | 25 | 60 | 30 | 40 |
| Degree of caste prejudice (y)* | 2 | 4 | 5 | 6 | 5 | 7 | 3 | 6 | 5 | 4 |

*Higher scores in the degree of caste prejudice indicate greater caste prejudice.   [Ans. 0.8]

9. i. Find the regression equations of (a) x on y and (b) y on x from the following data: $\bar{x} = 508.4$, $\bar{y} = 26.7$, $\sigma_x = 36.8$, $\sigma_y = 4.6$, $r_{xy} = 0.52$

[Ans. (a): x − 4.16y = 397.33, (b): y − 0.065x = − 6.35]

ii. If for any set of data $b_{yx} = 1$ and $b_{xy} = 0.25$, what will be the value of r_{xy}?   [Ans. 0.5]

10. From the data in Question No. 8, find the regression equation of y on x and regression equation of x on y. From these find
    i.   Degree of caste prejudice of the person whose age is 50 and
    ii. Age of the person whose degree of caste prejudice is 8

[Ans. Regression equation of y on x: y − 0.08x = 1.5,
Regression equation of x on y: x − 8.45y = 0.285;
(i) 6 (appx.), (ii) 68 years (appx.)]

11. If the regression equation of x on y is 2x − 3y = 5 and y on x is 15y − 6x = 3,

(i) What will be the values of $\bar{x}$ and $\bar{y}$?   [Ans. 7 and 3]

(ii) What will be the value of r_{xy}?   [Ans. 0.77]

(iii) If the value of $\sigma_y = 2.1$, then what will be the value of σ_x? [Ans. 4.1]

Endnotes

1. Duncan Cramer and Dennis Laurence Howitt, *The Sage Dictionary of Statistics* (New Delhi: Sage Publications, 2004), 146.

2. Karl Pearson, "VII. Mathematical contributions to the theory of evolution.—III. Regression, heredity, and panmixia," *Philosophical Transactions of the Royal Society of London. Series A, Containing Papers of a Mathematical or Physical Character* 187, (1896), 265.

3. Rodgers Joseph Lee and W. Alan Nicewander, "Thirteen Ways to Look at the Correlation Coefficient," *The American Statistician* 42, no.1(1988), 62.

14

Nonparametric Measures of Correlation

In the last chapter on Correlation and Regression we have learnt Pearson's correlation coefficient which measures the strength of association between two interval or ratio level variables. But, in actual research situations we are often confronted with data which are not measured at the interval or ratio level. This is especially true of the different social categories and identities which are expressed through variables couched at the nominal or ordinal level of measurement. Obviously Pearson's Product Moment Correlation Coefficient (r_{xy}) cannot be applied to find out the strength of the association between these variables. The interval and ratio level data as required by the Pearson's measure of correlation coefficient implies that the variable in question should be continuous in nature like age, height, weight, size of family, votes secured by political party, hours spent for television viewing etc. It is also based on a fundamental assumption that at least one of the variables should represent a normal, or unskewed, distribution[1]. This is known as distributional assumption and the statistical methods which share this, primarily the mean and standard deviation, are called parametric methods[2].The methods which are free from such distributional assumptions are known as non-parametric methods. To measure the correlations between nominal and ordinal level variables hence, we need to employ the non-parametric methods of correlation. In this chapter we will focus on some of the well known non-parametric methods of correlation such as, Spearman's Rank Correlation Coefficient, Phi coefficient, Contingency coefficient, and Cramér's V

Spearman's Rank Correlation Coefficient

In order to measure the strength of association of ordinal data, which are ordered or ranked along any given attribute of the variable, Spearman's rank correlation coefficient is employed. We may be interested, for example, in measuring the association between adherence to liberal political values (ranked from maximum support to minimum support) and attitude towards women's liberation (ranked from most favourable to least favourable) in society. To have a better understanding of the Spearman's Rank Correlation Coefficient, let us consider the following table as an example, which describes the caste ranking of the electorates and their support to the Left parties (ranked) in the 2014 Parliamentary election in West Bengal.

Table: 14.1. *Distribution of Ranks of Support to Left Parties in 2014 Parliamentary Election in West Bengal and Caste/Community of the Electorates*

Respondent	Caste Status (Ranked) (x)	Support to Left Parties (Ranked) (y)	d*** (difference of the ranks)	d^2
Brahmin	1*	7	-6	36
Kayastha	2	9	-7	49
Vaishya	3	3	0	0
Other Upper Caste	4	2	2	4
OBC	5	5	0	0
Rajbanshi	6	6	0	0
Namasudras	7	4	3	9
Other Dalit	8	8	0	0
Adivasi	9	1**	8	64
				$\Sigma d^2 = 162$

Data Source: Ranked from CSDS National Election Study 2014 data

* *Rank of the Castes according to Popular Perception of Social Status. 1 denotes highest rank.*

** *1 Signifies Highest Support to Left Parties*

*** *Calculated by subtracting the rank of y from that of x*

Here support to left parties has been calculated from the percentage of votes secured by them in a sample of 875 electorates in West Bengal in 2014. It is true that this could be measured in an interval scale but the other variable caste/community status is ordered and typically expressed through ranks. This ordinality requires the application of a method appropriate to calculate the degree of association of ordinal data. Thus, here the Spearman's Rank Correaltion Coefficient needs to be employed.

The data in the table show that the Brahmins occupy the highest rank in the caste ranking or hierarchy, but they rank 7th in their support to the Left parties. The Kayasthas, the 2nd ranked caste, secure the lowest rank (9th) as far as their support to the left parties is concerned. This way we can explain the cases of other caste/communities as well.

In a 1904 article Spearman first talked about the correlation calculated by 'rank difference.'[3] Like Pearson's Correlation coefficient, Spearman's correlation coefficient also varies from -1 to $+1$. Therefore, it can be considered to be same as Pearson's correlation coefficient but applied to on ordinal level data. Spearman's Rank Correlation Coefficient is denoted by the Greek letter ρ (Rho) although sometimes it is also denoted by the expression r_s. It can be calculated through the following formula:

$$\rho \text{ or } r_s = 1 - \frac{6\Sigma d^2}{N(N^2-1)}$$

where,

ρ or r_s = Spearman's rank correlation coefficient

d = difference in rank between the variables x and y

N = Number of ranked scores pairs.

Putting the values obtained in the table above in the formula we get:

$$r_s = 1 - \frac{6\times162}{9(9^2-1)} \text{ [as } \Sigma d^2 = 162, \text{ and } N = 9]$$

$$= 1 - \frac{972}{9\times80} \quad = 1 - \frac{972}{720} \quad = 1-1.35 \quad = -0.35$$

Hence, there is a moderate to strong negative correlation ($r_s = -0.35$) between caste/community rank of the electorates and their support to the left parties. So, it is evident that the upper the caste/community rank of the electorates is, lower is their support to the left parties.

Tied Ranks

In actual research situations we often have respondents some of whom have similar or equal scores in the variables measured. We may find, for example, few castes are occupying equal rank in popular perception, there may be students of a class who have attained equal marks in an examination to yield equal ranks, there may be some countries, states within a country or districts within a state having equal infant mortality rate etc. Let us consider Table: 14.2 as an illustration:

Table: 14.2. *Distribution of Economic Class and Support to Democratic Politics*▲

Respondent	Economic Class (x)	Rank of Economic Class	Support to Democratic Politics (y)	Rank of Support to Democratic Politics	d (difference of the ranks)	d²
A	Very Poor	7	15	7	0	0
B	Middle Class	4	20 ↘	5	−1	1
C	Poor	6	20 → tied	5	1	1
D	Lower Middle Class	5	20 ↗	5	0	0
E	Upper Middle Class	3	22	3	0	0
F	Upper Class	2	25 ↘ tied	1.5	0.5	0.25
G	Rich	1*	25** ↗	1.5	−0.5	0.25
						Σd² = 2.5

▲Fictitious data

* Highest economic class

** Highest support to democratic politics

In Table: 14.2 we have a distribution of economic class of seven respondents ranked from Rich to very poor and their respective support to democratic politics (measured in a scale of 30) ranked from high to low support, where higher score in the scale represents higher support. Here we can see that respondents G and F have scored the highest in the scale of support to democratic politics (25), so in ranking their position is tied for the 1st and 2nd position. Similarly, the positions of the respondents B, C and D are also tied for the 4th, 5th and 6th rank in the same scale.

In order to assign exact ranks to the tied positions we need to 'add the tied ranks and divide by the number of ties'[4]. So, the rationale is to assign average rank by adding the tied position and dividing it by the number of cases involved in the tie. Thus, as shows Table: 14.2, the 25 score of support to democratic politics, occupying the 1st and 2nd position should be assigned an average rank of:

$$\frac{1+2}{2} = 1.5$$

In the same way we can find the average rank of the score 20 occupying the 4th, 5th and 6th position as:

$$\frac{4+5+6}{3} = 5$$

Here also, to find out the value of the Spearman's Correlation Coefficient (r_s), we need to calculate the rank differences (d) between economic class of the respondents and their support to democratic politics. To find out Spearman's rank correlation coefficient, we then apply the same formula as before:

$$r_s = 1 - \frac{6\Sigma d^2}{N(N^2 - 1)}$$

Putting the values as calculated in Table 14.2, we get:

$$r_s = 1 - \frac{6 \times 2.5}{7(7^2 - 1)} \text{ [as } \Sigma d^2 = 2.5, \text{ and N} = 7]$$

$$= 1 - \frac{15}{7 \times 48}$$

$$= 1 - \frac{15}{336}$$

$$= 1 - 0.04$$

$$= 0.96$$

Hence, there is a very strong positive correlation ($r_s = 0.96$) between economic class of the respondents and their support to democratic politics. So, it is evident that upper the class of the respondent, higher is their support to democratic politics.

Doing it Step by Step

Step 1: Rank respondents' scores along the two variables x and y

Step 2: Calculate the difference of the ranks (d)

Step 3: Calculate square of the each difference (d^2) and sum it up to get Σd^2

Step 4: Put the values in the formula to get the value of Spearman's Rank Correlation Coefficient (ρ or r_s)

Phi Correlation Coefficient (φ)

In social science research often a large range of data measured at the nominal level is encountered. This is more often the case in comparative research involving a number of categorical variables like, gender, nationality, race and ethnic groups, religious affiliations, marital status etc. Comparison of these variables often makes it necessary to have an idea about the nature and degree of association among them. Since the nominal level variables, like the ordinal ones discussed above, do not make any assumption about the normality of the distribution of scores in the data, so to assess the correlation of these variables non-parametric methods should be employed. As, nominal and ordinal level data are often represented in the form of cross tabulation, so here the non-parametric methods of correlation attempts to find out the correlation between two variables which are spread across the rows and columns of the cross tabulated data. Among the several techniques, the phi coefficient of correlation, denoted by the Greek letter 'φ' (phi), is an important non-parametric technique to assess the association between nominal variables. It is most suitable for the variables which are cross tabulated in a dichotomised manner (having only two possible values) and, hence, can be represented through a 2 × 2 contingency table.

The formula to calculate the phi coefficient of correlation is: $\varphi = \sqrt{\dfrac{\chi^2}{N}}$

Where:

φ = phi Correlation Coefficient

χ^2 = Calculated value of Chi square

N = total number of cases

Chi square (χ^2)

Here, we have a new term 'chi-square'. Let us have a very brief look at this. It is often symbolised by the Greek letter 'χ' (chi), squaring which we get the expression chi-square. It is also known as Pearson's chi-square as he introduced it into statistical analysis. It is primarily used as a measure of goodness of fit of a frequency distribution involving one variable or as a measure to assess the independence of two variables. It does so by, comparing'…the observed frequencies with the frequencies expected … of one variable or all the combinations of categories of two variables.'[5]

In a cross tabulation, as has been discussed in Chapter 4 of this book, the cells represent the categories of the two variables. Hence, the number of categories of the variables will be equal to the number of cells. If a variable, for example, has four categories then it will have four cells. The value of Chi-square is based on the comparison of the observed frequency of a cell with the expected frequency of that cell. This is done by calculating the differences between the observed and the expected frequencies. Since, these differences are squared, so the value of chi-square cannot be negative. The following expression is used to calculate the value of the chi square:

$$\chi^2 = \sum \frac{(f_o - f_e)^2}{f_e}$$

Where,

χ^2 = Chi-square

f_o = observed frequency

f_e = expected frequency

In a bivariate framework, chi-square, thus, assesses the independence of two nominal and ordinal variables. Although such measure of independence is theoretically rooted in the logic of correlation, but chi-square as a measure cannot give any value of correlation or degree of association between the variables. Measures, which are typically designed to assess the strength of correlation between two categorical variables, often use the chi-square to come up with a value of the correlation coefficients between these variables. The phi-coefficient, as can be seen from its formula mentioned above, is one of these.

Let us consider the following cross tabulation constructed by Feierabend and Feierabend[6] and presented in Chapter 4 of this book as an example to show the calculation of the phi-coefficient.

Table: 14.3. Level of Systemic Frustration and Degree of Political Stability

Degree of Political Stability	Index of Systemic Frustration		Total
	High systemic frustration	Low systemic frustration	
Unstable	34	6	40
Stable	2	20	22
Total	36	26	62

The table describes the observed degree of political stability in 62 countries and the prevailing level of systemic frustration in those countries. It reveals that out of 40 politically unstable countries 34 and 6 have high and low systemic frustration levels respectively, while in 22 politically stable countries two and 20 countries exhibit high and low systemic frustration levels respectively. From these observed frequencies of the two variables viz. political stability and level of social frustration, we need to calculate the correlation coefficient between them.

Here, first we need to calculate the expected frequencies out of the observed frequencies presented in Table: 14.3. To find out the expected frequency for any cell, we multiply the column and row marginal totals of that cell and divide the product by N.

Hence, expected frequency of a cell

$$(f_e) = \frac{marginal\ total\ of\ row \times marginal\ total\ of\ column}{N}$$

Thus, the expected cell frequency (f_e) of the observed cell frequency (f_o) 34 $= \frac{40 \times 36}{62} = 23$ (appx.)

Hence, we can get the table of expected frequencies as following:

f_e Table

23	17
13	9

Then, at the next step we find out the table of $\frac{(f_o-f_e)^2}{f_e}$. This is done by calculating the difference of the observed and expected frequencies of each cell, squaring it and then dividing it by the expected frequency of that cell. Hence, we get:

$\frac{(f_o-f_e)^2}{f_e}$ Table

5.26	7.12
9.31	13.44

Therefore, from the table it can be found that:

$$\chi^2 (\text{chi square}) = \sum \frac{(f_o-f_e)^2}{f_e} = 5.26+7.12+9.31+13.44 = 35.13$$

Finally, we calculate the value of the phi correlation coefficient by the formula:

$$\varphi = \sqrt{\frac{\chi^2}{N}}$$

$$= \sqrt{\frac{35.13}{62}}$$

$$= \sqrt{0.57}$$

$$= 0.75$$

Hence, we find that there is a strong correlation between political stability and systemic frustration among the countries studied. The phi correlation coefficient, thus, confirms the main finding of the study, which according to Feierabend and Feierabend[7] is, '…the higher the level of systemic frustration…the greater the political instability.'

Contingency Correlation Coefficient (C)

In actual research context we often have nominal data which are arranged in more than two categories. Here we need to calculate the correlation between two variables which have been measured in more than two categories. The table representing the data, therefore, is comprised of more than 2 × 2 cells. Here to find out the correlation coefficient we need to have a simple extension of the calculation of chi square value and find out a different coefficient of correlation known as Contingency Correlation Coefficient. (C). The formula through which the Contingency Correlation Coefficient can be calculated is:

$$\text{Contingency Correlation Coefficient (C)} = \sqrt{\frac{\chi^2}{N + \chi^2}}$$

To illustrate, we can consider Table: 14.4, which describes the choice of optional subjects (Political Science, Sociology and History) of 50 students having Bengali, Oriya and Telugu mother tongues, in an undergraduate class of a college. Here, we need to find out the correlation coefficient between choice of optional subjects and mother tongues of the students.

Clearly, the data in Table: 14.4 are comprised of more than 2 × 2 categories. So, here we need to employ the Contingency Correlation Coefficient to get the strength of association between the variables viz. choice of optional subjects and mother tongue of the students.

Table: 14.4. *Mother Tongue of Students and Choice of Optional Subjects**

Mother Tongue	Subjects Opted			Total
	Political Science	Sociology	History	
Bengali	8	5	6	19
Oriya	5	6	6	17
Telugu	4	6	4	14
Total	17	17	16	50

*Source: Fictitious data

Here also, we first need to calculate the value of the chi square. As we have done before, we need to calculate the expected frequencies (f_e) from the table of the observed frequencies (f_o). Following the same method we obtain the table of expected frequencies in the following:

f_e **Table**

6.46	6.46	6.08
5.78	5.78	5.44
4.76	4.76	4.48

At the next step we find out the table of $\frac{(f_o - f_e)^2}{f_e}$. This is done by squaring the difference of the observed and expected frequencies of each cell, and dividing it by the expected frequency of that cell. Hence, we get:

$\frac{(f_o - f_e)^2}{f_e}$ **Table**

0.37	0.33	0.001
0.11	0.01	0.06
0.12	0.32	0.05

Therefore, from the table it can be found that:

$\chi^2 \text{(chi square)} = \sum \frac{(f_o - f_e)^2}{f_e} = 1.37$

Finally, we calculate the value of the Contingency correlation coefficient by the formula:

$$C = \sqrt{\frac{\chi^2}{N + \chi^2}}$$

$$= \sqrt{\frac{1.37}{50 + 1.37}}$$

$$= \sqrt{\frac{1.37}{51.37}}$$

$$= \sqrt{\frac{1.37}{51.37}}$$

$$= 0.16$$

Thus, we obtain a weak to moderate correlation between mother tongue of the students and their choice of optional subjects.

Cramer's V

The Contingency coefficient is a highly popular method to find out the correlation coefficient between two nominal variables. But, it has some disadvantages as well. First, the value of the contingency coefficient (C) is influenced by the number of columns and rows in a contingency table. For this it does not always range between the values 0 to 1. Although it will never exceed 1 numerically, but its maximum value rarely reach 1. Second, contingency coefficient is not a plausible method to employ in the case of contingency tables where the number of rows and columns are unequal. That means instead of 3 × 3, 4 × 4 when the table is 3 × 2 or 4 × 3 etc. To avoid these limitations of the contingency correlation coefficient, Cramer[8] has come up with an alternative correlation coefficient known as Cramer's V. Like contingency coefficient, Cramer's V can be employed to calculate the correlation between nominal level variables but with the added advantage that it can be employed to any contingency table larger than 2 × 2 size. The formula through which the Cramer's V can be calculated is:

$$V = \sqrt{\frac{\chi^2}{N(k-1)}}$$

Where:

V = Cramer's V

N = Number of cases

k = number of columns or rows whichever is smaller (if the number of rows and columns are equal then any one number can be used).

To illustrate Cramer's V let us refer to the 3 × 3 cross tabulated data in Table: 14.4, representing the choice of optional subjects and mother tongue of 50 undergraduate students in a college.

We know that:

Cramer's V or $V = \sqrt{\dfrac{\chi^2}{N(k-1)}}$

Plugging the values calculated before in the expression we get,

$V = \sqrt{\dfrac{1.37}{50(3-1)}}$ [since here are 3 columns and 3 rows, so, here $k = 3$]

$= \sqrt{\dfrac{1.37}{100}}$

$= \sqrt{0.0137}$

$= 0.12$

Thus, we obtain an almost weak correlation between the choice of optional subjects and mother tongue of the undergraduate students in the college through the application of the method of Cramer's V.

EXERCISE

1. What is meant by distributional assumption?

2. What is the basic difference between parametric and non-parametric methods?

3. To assess the correlation between two variables at least one of which is measured at the ordinal level, which method should be used?
   [Ans. Spearman's Rank Correlation Coefficient]

4. The following table describes ranks of seven students of Class X in a school and their relative proficiency in English language rankled from 1 to 7, where 1 denotes the highest proficiency and 7 denotes the least proficiency. Calculate Spearman's Rank Correlation Coefficient (r_s) between class ranks and degree of proficiency in English language of the students:

| Class rank of the students (x) | 1 | 2 | 3 | 4 | 5 | 6 | 7 |
| Rank of proficiency in English language (y) | 4 | 2 | 1 | 6 | 3 | 7 | 5 |

[Ans. 0.54]

5. The following table describes the time spent (in minutes) by eight persons in viewing news programme in Television per day and their perception about elections in West Bengal to be naturally violent, ranked in a scale of 1 to 8, where 1 denotes the highest perception about electoral violence to be natural and 8 denotes the lowest.

| Time spent to watch news in Television per day (in minutes) (x) | 30 | 55 | 45 | 25 | 70 | 110 | 80 | 40 |
| Rank of perception about election to be naturally violent (y) | 6 | 5 | 8 | 4 | 3 | 2 | 1 | 7 |

Find the Spearman's Rank Correlation Coefficient from the data.

(Hint: Arrange the variable x in ranks so that 1 denotes the highest time spent to watch news in television and 8 the lowest).   [Ans. 0.64]

6. The following data represent the time spent by 10 children for video games in a week and the rank obtained by them in an aggression measurement test conducted just after the week.

| Time spent for video games (in hrs) | 25 | 30 | 11 | 10 | 32 | 25 | 25 | 12 | 8 | 11 |
| Rank * obtained in the aggression measurement test | 8 | 7 | 3 | 4 | 10 | 9 | 5 | 2 | 1 | 3 |

*1 denotes lowest aggression, 10 denotes highest aggression

Find the correlation coefficient between time spent for video games by the children and their rank in the aggression in the measurement test.

[Hint: Arrange the time spent for video games in rank order from 1 to 10 denoting low to high, and then calculate Spearman's rank correlation coefficient]   [Ans. 0.84]

7. To find out the correlation between two variables measured at the nominal level, which method should be employed?

[Ans. Phi Correlation Coefficient (φ)]

8. To assess the correlation between two nominal variables which are measured in a dichotomised manner, which method of correlation should be used?   [Ans. Phi Correlation Coefficient (φ)]

9. The following table describes the believers and non-believers of astrology among 40 literate and 60 illiterate respondents of a study.

Status of Literacy	Belief in Astrology		Total
	Belief	Non Belief	
Literate	15	25	40
Illiterate	40	20	60
Total	55	45	100

Find out the correlation coefficient between status of literacy and belief in astrology.   [Ans. $\varphi = 0.29$]

10. The following table depicts the gender wise status of COVID – 19 infections in a sample of 100 respondents. Find the correlation coefficient between gender and COVID – 19 infections in the sample.

Gender	Status of COVID – 19 Infections		Total
	Infected	Not Infected	
Male	37	23	60
Female	15	25	40
Total	52	48	100

[Ans. =0.24]

11. Which method can be employed to find out the correlation of nominal data not cross tabulated in a dichotomised manner?
                                          [Ans. Contingency Correlation]

12. When Cramer's V as a method of finding the correlation coefficient can be employed?

13. The following table describe the Locality and Electoral Preference of the Electorates in West Bengal Assembly Election, 2011 as reports the CSDS Lokniti West Bengal Assembly Election Study, 2011.

Locality	Electoral Preference in 2011 Assembly Election in West Bengal (%)		Total
	Left	Non-left	
Rural	35	47	82
Urban	6	12	18
Total	41	59	100

Find the correlation coefficient between electoral preference of the electorates and their locality.   [Ans. $\varphi = 0.05$]

14. In the CSDS Lokniti Postpoll study of the West Bengal Assembly Election 2016, the following data describing the gender wise percentage distribution of electoral preferences of 3472 respondents were obtained. Find out the correlation between gender and electoral preferences from the data.

Gender	Party Voted for					Total
	Congress	Left Front	Trinamool Congress	BJP	Others	
Male	6	13	21	5	3	48
Female	5	12	23	5	3	48
Others	1	1	1	0	1	4
Total	12	26	45	10	7	100

[Ans. Contingency Correlation Coefficient C = 0.23]

15. Calculate Cramer's V from the data presented in Question Number 12 and 13.

16. The following table describes the marital status of 60 women and their attitude towards single motherhood. Find out the correlation coefficient between marital status of the women and their attitude towards single motherhood.

Marital Status	Attitude toward single Motherhood		Total
	Favourable	Unfavourable	
Unmarried	14	6	20
Married	10	15	25
Divorcee	9	6	15
	33	27	60

[Ans. Contingency Correlation Coefficient C = 0.26]

Endnotes

1. Philip Sedgwick, "Spearman's Rank Correlation Coefficient," *BMJ: British Medical Journal* 349, (2014).

2. Douglas G Altman and J Martin Bland, "Statistics Notes: Parametric v Non-parametric Methods for Data Analysis," *BMJ: British Medical Journal* 339, no. 7713 (2009).

3. Charles Spearman, "The Proof and Measurement of Association between Two Things," *The American Journal of Psychology* 15, no. 1 (1904), 86-87.

4. Jack A. Levin and James Alan Fox and David R. Forde, *Elementary Statistics in Social Research. Twelfth edition* (New York: Pearson, 2014), 447.

5. Duncan Cramer and Dennis Laurence Howitt, *The Sage Dictionary of Statistics* (New Delhi: Sage Publications, 2004), 22.

6. Ivo K. Feierabend and Rosalind L. Feierabend, "Aggressive Behaviors Within Politics, 1948-1962: A cross National Study," *The Journal of Conflict Resolution* 10, no. 3 (1966), 259.

7. Feierabend, and Feierabend, "Aggressive Behaviors," 258.

8. Harald Cramér, *Mathematical Methods of Statistics* (Bombay: Asia Publishing House, 1962).

List of Important Formulas

Measures of Central Tendency

Median of a Grouped Frequency Distribution, $\text{Mdn} = l_l + \left(\dfrac{\frac{N}{2} - F}{f_m} \right) \times i$

First Quartile, $Q_l = l_l + \left(\dfrac{\frac{N}{4} - F}{f_{Q_1}} \right) \times i$

Second Quartile or Median or, $Q_2 = l_l + \left(\dfrac{\frac{N}{2} - F}{f_{Q_2}} \right) \times i$

Third Quartile, $Q_3 = l_l + \left(i \dfrac{\frac{3N}{4} - F}{f_{Q_3}} \right) \times i$

Simple Arithmetic Mean, $\bar{x} = \dfrac{\Sigma x}{N}$

Arithmetic Mean ($\bar{x}$) of a grouped frequency distribution, $(\bar{x}) = \dfrac{\Sigma f x}{N}$

Combined Mean, $\bar{x}_c = \dfrac{\Sigma N_i \bar{x}_i}{N_c}$

Interrelationship formula of Mean, Median and Mode

Mean – Mode = 3 (Mean-Median)

Measure of Dispersion

Mean Deviation (M.D.) about Mean (Simple Series), $M.D. = \dfrac{\Sigma(x_i - \bar{x})}{n}$

Mean Deviation (M.D.) about Median (Simple Series), $M.D. = \dfrac{\Sigma(x_i - Median)}{n}$

Mean Deviation (M.D.) about Mean of a Grouped Frequency Distribution

$M.D. = \dfrac{\Sigma f_i(x_i - \bar{x})}{N}$

Mean Deviation (M.D.) about Median of a Grouped Frequency Distribution

$M.D. = \dfrac{\Sigma f_i(x_i - Median)}{N}$

Quartile Deviation, $Q.D. = \frac{Q_3 - Q_1}{2}$

Standard Deviation (S.D.), or σ (Simple Series) $= \sqrt{\frac{\Sigma(x_i - \bar{x})^2}{n}}$.

The working formula of S.D., or σ (simple series) $= \sqrt{\frac{\Sigma x_i^2}{n} - \left(\frac{\Sigma x_i}{n}\right)^2}$

Standard Deviation (S.D.), or σ of Grouped Frequency Distribution
$= \sqrt{\frac{\Sigma f_i(x_i - \bar{x})^2}{N}}$.

Working formula of S.D. of a grouped frequency distribution:

$S.D.$ or $\sigma = \sqrt{\frac{\Sigma f_i x_i^2}{N} - \left(\frac{\Sigma f_i x_i}{N}\right)^2}$

Variance $= \sigma^2$

Standard Deviation of the combined series $\sigma_c = \sqrt{\frac{\Sigma N_i \sigma_i^2 + \Sigma N_i d_i^2}{N}}$

Coefficient of Mean Deviation (about mean) $=$

$$\frac{Mean\ Deviation\ (M.D.)about\ Mean}{Mean} \times 100$$

Coefficient of Mean Deviation (about median) $=$

$$\frac{Mean\ Deviation\ (M.D.)about\ Meadian}{Median} \times 100$$

Coefficient of Quartile Deviation $= \frac{Quartile\ Deviation\ (Q.D.)}{Median} \times 100$

Coefficient of Variation $= \frac{Standard\ Deviation\ (S.D.)}{Mean} \times 100$

Pearson's First Measure of Skewness $= \frac{Mean - Mode}{Standard\ Deviation}$

Pearson's Second Measure of Skewness $= \frac{3(Mean - Median)}{Standard\ Deviation}$

Bowley's Measure of Skewness $= \frac{(Q_3 - Q_2) - (Q_2 - Q_1)}{(Q_3 - Q_1)}$ or, $\frac{Q_3 - 2Q_2 + Q_1}{Q_3 - Q_1}$

Correlation and Regression

Covariance $_{xy}$ or $Cov_{xy} = = \frac{\Sigma(x_i - \bar{x})(y_i - \bar{y})}{n}$

Pearson's formula of correlation coefficient,

$$r_{xy} = \frac{Covariance_{xy}}{\sigma_x \sigma_y} = \frac{\Sigma(x_i - \bar{x})(y_i - \bar{y})}{n\sigma_x \sigma_y}$$

Working formula of Pearson's correlation coefficient,

$$r_{xy} = \frac{n\Sigma xy - \Sigma x \Sigma y}{\sqrt{\{n\Sigma x^2 - (\Sigma x)^2\}\{n\Sigma y^2 - (\Sigma y)^2\}}}$$

Regression Equation of y on x: $\quad y - \bar{y} = b_{yx}(x - \bar{x})$

Regression Coefficient of y on x or b_{yx} $= r_{xy} \times \frac{\sigma_y}{\sigma_x}$

Regression Equation of x on y : $\quad x - \bar{x} = b_{xy}(y - \bar{y})$

Regression Coefficient of x on y or b_{xy} $= r_{xy} \times \frac{\sigma_x}{\sigma_y}$

Nonparametric Measures of Correlation

Spearman's Rank Correlation Coefficient: ρ or $r_s = 1 - \frac{6\Sigma d^2}{N(N^2 - 1)}$

phi coefficient of correlation or $\Phi = \sqrt{\frac{\chi^2}{N}}$

chi square: $\chi^2 = \Sigma \frac{(f_o - f_e)^2}{f_e}$

Contingency correlation coefficient: $C = \sqrt{\frac{\chi^2}{N + \chi^2}}$

Cramer's V or $V = \sqrt{\frac{\chi^2}{N(k-1)}}$

Bibliography

Abel, Theodore. "The Operation called *Verstehen.*" *American Journal of Sociology* 54, no.3 (1948): 211-18

Airy, George Biddell. *On the Algebraical and Numerical Theory of Errors of Observations and the Combination of Observations.* London: Macmillan and Co., 1875.

Alker, Hayward R. *Mathematics and Politics.* New York: The Macmillan Co., 1965.

Altman, Douglas G. and J Martin Bland. "Statistics Notes: Parametric v Non-parametric Methods for Data Analysis." *BMJ: British Medical Journal* 339, no. 7713 (2009): 170. Accessed March 7, 2021. http://www.jstor.org/stable/25672138.

Babbie, Earl. *The Practice of Social Research.* Belmont, CA: Wadsworth Cengage Learning, 2010

Bailey, F.G. *Politics and Social Change – Orissa in 1959.* Berkeley: University of California Press, 1963.

Banks, Arthur S. and Greg, Philip M. "Grouping Political Systems: Q-Factor Analysis of A Cross-Polity Survey." In *Macro-Quantitative Analysis: Conflict, Development, and Democratization,* edited by John V. Gillespie and Betty A. Nesvold, 311-20. Beverly Hills: Sage Publications, 1971.

Banks, Arthur S. *Political Handbook of the World.* New York: McGraw-Hill, 1971.

Barnes, J.A. *The Ethics of Inquiry in Social Science.* Delhi: Oxford University Press, 1977.

Basu, Partha Pratim. *Press and Foreign Policy in India.* New Delhi: Lancers, 2003.

Beattie, John. *Other Cultures: Aims, Methods and Achievements in Social Anthropology.* London: Cohn and West, 1964.

Beattie, John. *Understanding an African Community: Bunyoro.* New York: Holt, Rinehart and Winston, 1965.

Bendix, Reinhard. "Concepts and Generalizations in Comparative Sociological Studies." *American Sociological Review* 28, no. 4 (1963): 532-39.

Bendix, Reinhard. *Embattled Reason, Essays on Social Knowledge.* New York: Oxford University Press, 1970.

Berelson, Bernard, ed. *The Behavioural Sciences Today.* New York: Harper, 1968.

Beteille, Andre. "Tribulations of Field Work." In *Encounter and Experience – Personal Accounts of Field Work*, 99-113. Edited by Andre Beteille and T.N. Madan. Delhi: Vikas Publishing House, 1975.

Bhatt, Anil. "Some Social and Human Aspects of Conducting Large-Scale Field Surveys in India."*Political Science Review* (Jaipur) 17 (1978): 30-41.

Blalock, H.M Jr. *Social Statistics.* New York: McGraw-Hill, 1960.

Bottomore, Tom. *Marxist Sociology.* London : Macmillan, 1975.

Bowley, Arthur Lyon. *Elements of Statistics.* London: P.S. King and Son, 1901.

Bridgman, P.W. *The Logic of Moden Physics.* New York: Macmillan, 1927.

Bryman, Alan. *Social Research Methods*, Oxford: Oxford University Press, 2012.

Campbell, Donald T. and Stanley, Juian C. *Experimental and Quasi-experimental Designs for Research.* Chicago: Rand McNally and Co. 1970.

Campbell, Donald T. "Factors Relevant to the Validity of Experiments in Social Settings." In *Stages of Social Research: Contemporary Perspectives,* 116-31. Edited by Dennis P. Forcese and Stephen Richer. New Jersey: Prentice-Hall, 1970.

Campbell, Donald T. and Ross, H.L. "The Connecticut Crackdown on Speeding : Time-Series Data in Quasi-Experimental Analysis." In *The Quantitative Analysis of Social Problems,* 110-125. Edited by Edward R. Tufte. Reading, Massachusetts : Addison-Wesley Publishing Co., 1970.

Campbell, N. R., and H. Jeffreys. "Symposium: Measurement and Its Importance for Philosophy." *Proceedings of the Aristotelian Society, Supplementary Volumes* 17, no. 1 (1938): 121-51.

Caporaso, James A. and Pelowski, Alan L. "Economic and Political integration in Europe: A Time-Series Quasi-Experimental Analysis." *American Political Science Review* 65, no. 2 (1971) : 418-33.

Chatterjee, Jyotiprasad, and Suprio Basu. *Left front and After: Understanding the Dynamics of Poriborton in West Bengal.* Los Angeles: Sage Publications, 2020.

Chatterji, Rakhahari, and Anasuya Basu Ray Choudhury. *Indian Media's Perceptions of China: Analysis of Editorials,* Kolkata; Observer Research Foundation, 2016.

Cohen, Morris R. and Nagel, Enest. *An introduction to Logic and Scientific Method.* New York: Harcourt, Brace and Co. 1937.

Collier, Rex Madison. "The Effect of Propaganda upon attitudes following a crucial examination of the propaganda itself." The *Journal of Social Psychology* 20, no. 1 (1944): 3-71.

Cramer, Duncan, and Dennis Laurence Howitt. *The Sage Dictionary of Statistics.* New Delhi: Sage Publications, 2004.

Cramer, Harald. *Mathematical Methods of Statistics.* Bombay: Asia Publishing House, 1962.

Cyr, Jennifer. "The Pitfalls and Promise of Focus Groups as a Date Collection Method." *Sociological Methods and Research* 45, no. 2 (2016): 231-259.

Dasgupta, Biplab and Morris-Jones, W.H. *Patterns and Trends in Indian Politics.* Bombay: Allied Publishers Private Ltd., 1975.

Devi Prasad, B. "Content Analysis: A Method in Social Science Research." In *Research Methods for Social Work*, edited by Lal Das, D.K and Bhaskaran, V. New Delhi: Rawat, 2008.

Deutsch, Karl W. "Social Mobilization and Political Development." *The American Political Science Review* 55, no. 3 (1961): 493-514.

Dumont, L. *Homo Hierarchicus.* New Delhi: Oxford University Press, 1980.

Durkheim Emile. *The Rules of Sociological Method.* New York: The Free Press, 1964.

Duchesne, Sophie. "Using Focus Groups to Study the Process of (de)Politicization." in *A New Era of Focus Group Research, Palgrave Macmillan,* edited by Rosaline S. Barbour; David L.Morgan 2017, halshs-01674453. https://halshs.archives-ouvertes.fr/halshs-01674453/document

Easton, David. *The political System.* New York: Alfred A. Knopf, 1953.

Easton, David. *A Framework for Political Analysis.* New Jersey : Prentice-Hall, 1965.

Epstein, A.L. *The Craft of Social Anthropology.* London :Tavistock publications, 1967.

Evans-Pritchard, E.E. *Social Anthropology,* London: Routeledge and Kegan Paul, 1951.

Evans-Pritchard, E.E . *The Nuer :A Description of the Modes of livelihood and Political Institutions of a Nilotic People.* New York : Oxford University Press, 1969.

Fay, Brian. *Social Theory and Political Practice.*London : Allen Unwin Ltd., 1975.

Feierabend, Ivo K., and Rosalind L. Feierabend. "Aggressive Behaviors within Polities, 1948-1962: A Cross-National Study." *The Journal of Conflict Resolution* 10, no. 3 (1966): 249-71. Accessed September 5, 2021.

Feierabend, Ivo K., and Rosalind L. Feierabend. "Aggressive Behaviour within Polities, 1948-62 : A Cross-National Study." In *Macro-Quantitative Analysis*, 141-66. Edited by John V. Gillespie and Betty A. Nesvold. Beverly Hills: Sage Publications, 1971.

Firth, Raymond. *Elements of Social Organization*. Boston: Beacon Press, 1963.

Freilich, M. ed. *Marginal Natives: Anthropologists at Work.* New York: Harper and Row, 1970.

Frey, Frederick W. "Cross-Cultural Survey Research in Political Science." In *The Methodology of Comparative Research in Political Science"*, 173-294. Edited by Robert T. Holt and John E. Turner. New York: The Free Press, 1970.

Galton, Francis. "Report of the Anthropometric Committee." *Report of the Fifty-first Meeting of the British Association for the Advancement of Science.* London: John Murray (1882): 245-60.

Gauss, Carl Friedrich. *Theory of the Combination of Observations Least Subject to Errors: Part One, Part Two, Supplement(Classics in Applied Mathematics, Series Number 11).* Translated by G.W. Stewart. Philadelphia: SIAM, 1823.

Gheyls, Niels and Thomas Jacobs. 'Content Analysis: A Short Overview', https://www.researchgate.net/publication/321977528_Content_Analysis_a_short_overviw

Giddens, Anthony. *New Rules of Sociological Method.* London: Hutchinson, 1976.

Gillespie John V. and Nesvold, Betty A. eds. *Macro Quantitative Analysis.* Beverly Hills: Sage Publications, 1970.

Goode, William J. and Hatt, Paul K.*Methods in Social Research*. New York :McGarw-Hill, 1952.

Goode, William J. and Hatt, Paul K . "The Interview : A Data Collection Technique." In *The Conduct of Political Inquiry,* pp. 115-201.Edited by Louise D. Hays and Ronald D. Hedland. New Jersey : Prentice-Hall, 1970.

Gregg, Philip M. and Banks, Arthur S. "Dimensions of Political Systems: Factor Analysis of A Cross-Polity Survey". In Macro-Quantitative Analysis, pp. 289-309. Edited by John V. Gillespie and Betty A. Nesvold. Beverly Hills: Sage Publications, 1971.

Gurr, Ted and Ruttenberg, Charles. "The Conditions of Civil Violence : First Tests of Casual Model." Princeton : Princeton University Centre for Internal Studies, Research Monograph 28, April, 1967.

Halperin Sandra and Oliver Heath, *Political Research: Methods and Practical Skills*, Oxford: OUP, 2012.

Harris, Marvin. *Culture, People and Nature.* New York : Thomas Crowell, 1971.

Healey, Joseph F. *Statistics: A Tool for Social Research. Ninth Edition.* Belmont: Wadsworth, 2012.

Hempel, Carl G. *Fundamental of Concept Formation.* Chicago : University of Chicago Press, 1952.

Hempel, Carl G. *Aspects of Scientific Explanation and other Essays in the Philosophy of Science.* New York : The Free Press, 1965.

Hempel, Carl G. Philosophy of Natural Science. New Jersey : Prentice-Hall, 1966.

Johnson, Jannett Buttolph and Richard A. Joslyn. Political Science Research Methods, New Delhi: Prentice Hall India, 1989

Kelly, A. P. *Social Research Methods*, London: London School of Economics and Political Science, 2016.

Key, V.O. *A primer of Statistics for Political Scientists*. New York: Thomas Y. Crowell, 1954.

Krippendorff, Klaus. Content Analysis: An Introduction to Its Methodology, Thousand Oaks, Sage, 2004.

Kuhn, Thomas. *The Structure of Scientific Revolutions.*Chicago : University of Chicago Press, 1962.

Lazarsfeld, Paul F. and Rosenberg, Morris. Eds. *The Language of Social Research.*New York : The Free Press, 1955.

Lerner, Daniel. *The Passing of Traditional Society : Modernizing the Middle East*. New York : The Free Press, 1955.

Levin, Jack A. and James Alan Fox and David R. Forde. *Elementary Statistics in Social Research. Twelfth edition*. New York: Pearson, 2014.

Liamputtong, Pranee, 'Focus Group Methodology: Introduction and History', in Liamputtong (ed.) *Focus Group Methodology: Principle and Practice*, London: Sage, 2011.

Lijphart, Arend. "On Living Intimately with Strangers." In *Encounter and Experience-Personal Accounts of Fieldwork. Pp. 131-56*. Edited by Andre Beteille and T.N. Madan.Delhi :Vikas Publishing House, 1975.

Lunt, Peter and Sonia Livingstone, 'Rethinking the focus group in media and communications research', *Journal of Communication*, 46:2, 1996 http://eprints.lse.ac.uk/409/

Mallinowski, Bronislaw. *Argonauts of the Western Pacific*. London: Routeledge and Kegan Paul, 1922.

Mallinowski, Bronislaw. *A Diary in the Strict Sense of the Term*. London :Routeledge and Kegan Paul, 1967.

McKim Marriott, "The Feast of Love." In Encounter and Experience: Personal Accounts of Fieldwork, edited by Andre Beteille and T.N.Madan, 83-97. Delhi: Vikas Publishing, 1975

Martin, Michael. "Understanding and Participant Observation in Cultural and Social Anthropology." In *Verstehen : Subjective Understanding in the Social Sciences,* pp.102-33. Edited by Marcello Truzzi.Massachusetts : Addison-Wesley Publishing Co. 1974.

Mckinlay, R.D. and Cohan, A.S. "Performance and Instability in Military and Non-Military Regime Systems."*American Political Science Review* 70 (1976): 850-64.

Mcintyre, Alasdair. "Can There be a Science of Comparative Politics?" Chicago : University of Chicago, 1971 (Mimeographed).

Mead, Margret. *Anthropology : A Human Science.* New York : Van Nostrand, 1964.

Merton, Robert K. *Social Theory and Social Structure.*Glencoe, Illinois : The Free Press, 1949.

Merton, Robert K. "The Mosaic of the Behavioural Sciences." In *The Behavioural Sciences Today,* pp. 247-72. Edited by Bernard Berelson, New York : Harper, 1968.

Middleton, Russell. "Alienation, Race, and Education." *American Sociological Review* 28, no. 6 (1963): 973-77

Mill, John Stuart. *John Stuart Mill's Philosophy of Scientific Method.* Edited by Ernest Nagel. New York :Hafner Publishing Co., 1950.

Mills, C. Wright. *The Sociological Imagination.* London: Oxford University Press, 1959.

Monk-turner Elizabeth et al. 'A Content Analysis of Violence in American War Movies', *Analyses of Social Issues and Public Policy* 4, no. 1 (2004): 1-11 https://devl1980.files.wordpress.com/2011/05/content-analysis-on-movies.pdf

Morgan David L., *Focus Groups as Qualitative Research*, Thousand Oaks and London: Sage, 1997.

Neuendorf, Kimberly, A. *The Content Analysis Guidebook*. Thousand Oaks, Sage, 2002.

Neuman,W. Lawrence. *Social Research Methods: Qualitative and Quantitative Approaches*, Essex: Pearson, 2014.

Nie, Norman H., Bent, Dale H. and Hull, Hadli. *SPSS: Statistical Package for the Social Sciences.* New York : McGraw-Hill, 1970.

Nowak, Stefan. "The Strategy of Cross-National Survey Research for the Development of Social Theory." In Cross-National Comparative Survey Research : Theory and Practice, pp. 3-48. Edited by Alexander Szalai and Riccardo Petrella in Collaboration with Stein Rokkan and Erwin K. Scheuch.International Social Science Council Standing Committee on Comparative Research.Oxford :Pergamon Press, 1977.

Parsons, Talcott. *The Structure of Social Action*, 2 Vols. New York: The Free Press, 1968. Vol. 2 : Weber.

Nyumba, Tobias O. et al, 'The use of focus group discussion methodology: Insights from two decades of application in conservation', *Methods in Ecology and Evolution* 9, no.9 (January 2018): 20-32. https://www.researchgate.net/publication/322405274_The_use_of_focus_group_discussion_methodology_Insights_from_two_decades_of_application_in_conservation

Pearson, Karl. "III. Contributions to the mathematical theory of evolution." *Philosophical Transactions of the Royal Society of London. (A.)*185 (1894): 71- 110. http://doi.org/10.1098/rsta.1894.0003.

Pearson, Karl. "VII. Mathematical contributions to the theory of evolution.—III. Regression, heredity, and panmixia." *Philosophical Transactions of the Royal Society of London. Series A, Containing Papers of a Mathematical or Physical Character*187 (1896): 253–318. http://doi.org/10.1098/rsta.1896.0007

Pearson, Karl. *The Grammar of Science. Second Edition*. London: Adam and Charles Black, 1900.

Popper, Karl R. *Poverty of Historicism.*London :Routeledge and Kegan Paul, [paper] 1961.

Popper, Karl R. *Conjectures and Refutations.* London :Routeledge and Kegan Paul, 1969.

Popper, Karl R. *Objective Knowledge – An Evolutionary Approach.* New York : Oxford University Press, 1972.

Przeworski, Adam and Teune, Henry.*The Logic of Comparative Social Enquiry.* New York : Wiley Interscience, 1970.

Putnam, Robert D. "Toward Explaining Military Intervention in Latin American Politics." *World Politics* 20, no. 1 (1967): 83-110.

Radcliffe-Brown, A.R .*The Andaman Islanders.*Glencoe, Illinois: The Free Press, 1948.

Radcliffe-Brown, A.R. *Method in Social Anthropology.*Edited by M.N. Srinivas.Chicago : University of Chicago Press, 1958.

Redfield, Robert. *The Little Community.* Chicago: University of Chicago Press, 1956.

Retzlaff, Ralph H. "The Use of Aggregate Data in Comparative Political Analysis." *The Journal of Politics* 27, no. 4 (1965): 797-817.

Rhodes, R. and Anne Tiernan. "Focus Groups and Prime Ministers' Chiefs of Staff." *Journal of Organizational Ethnography* 4 (2015): 208-222. https://www.semanticscholar.org/paper/FOCUS-GROUPS-AND-PRIME-MINISTERS%27-CHIEFS-OF-STAFF-Rhodes-Tiernan/30c0c ebaf2eb1d6bef4e0e822a0a6d593f2c2628

Rodgers, Joseph Lee and W. Alan Nicewander. 1988. "Thirteen Ways to Look at the Correlation Coefficient." *The American Statistician* 42, no.1(1988): 59-66.

Roethlisberger, F.J. and Dickson, W.J. *Management and the Worker.* Cambridge: Harvard University Press, 1939.

Rokkan, Stein "Cross National Survey Research: historical, analytical and Substantive Contexts." In *Comparative Survey Analysis*, 5-55. Stein Rokkan, Sidney Verba, Jean Viet and ElinaAlmasy. The Hague : Mouton, 1969.

Rose Susan, Nigel Spinks, Ana Canhoto. *Management Research applying the Principles*, Oxon: Routledge, 2015 (Expanded content to Chapter 6 file:///C:/Users/HP/AppData/Local/Temp/Quantitativecontentanalysis-1.pdf).

Rosenberg, Morris. *The Logic of Survey Analysis*. New York: Basic Books, 1968.

Rudolph, Lloyd I. and Rudolph, Susanne H. "Survey in India : field experience in Madras." *Public Opinion Quarterly* 22 (1958) : 35-44.

Runciman.W.G. *Social Science and Political Theory*. Cambridge: Cambridge University Press, 1971.

Russett, Bruce M. Alker, Hayword R. Deutsch, Karl W. and Lasswell, Harold D. *World Handbook of Political and Social Indicators*. New Haven: Yale University Press, 1964.

Sartori, Giovanni. "Concept Misformation in Comparative Politics." *The American Political Science Review* 64, no. 4 (1970): 1033-053

Scheuch, Erwin K. "Cross-National Comparison using Aggregate Data : Some Substantive and Methodological Problems." In *Comparing Nations : The Use of Quantitative Data in Cross-National Research*, pp. 131-67. Edited by Richard L. Merritt and Stein Rokkan. New Haven : Yale University Press, 1966.

Scheuch, Erwin K. "The Cross-Cultural Use of Sample Surveys : Problems of Comparability." In *Comparative Research Across Cultures and Nations*, pp. 176-209. Edited by Stein Rokkan. The Hague : Mouton, 1968.

Schmitter, Philippe C. *Interest Conflict and Political Change in Brazil*. Stanford: Stanford University Press, 1971.

Sedgwick, Philip. "Spearman's Rank Correlation Coefficient." *BMJ: British*

Medical Journal 349 (2014). Accessed March 9, 2021. https://www.jstor. org/stable/26518805

Smelser, Neil J. *Comparative Methods in the Social Sciences.* New Jersey: Prentice-Hall, 1976.

Spearman, Charles. "The Proof and Measurement of Association between Two Things." *The American Journal of Psychology* 15, no. 1 (1904): 72-101. Accessed November 20, 2020. doi:10.2307/1412159.

Srinivas, M.N. *The Remembered Village.* Delhi : Oxford University Press, 1976.

Stan, Lavinia. 'Content Analysis.' In *Encyclopedia of Case Study Research*, edited by A. J. Mills, G. Durepos and E. Wiebe, 29-31., , Thousand Oaks: Sage, 2010.

Star, Shirley A., and Helen MacGill Hughes. "Report on an Educational Campaign: The Cincinnati Plan for the United Nations." *American Journal of Sociology* 55, no. 4 (1950): 389-400.

Stevens, S. S. "On the Theory of Scales of Measurement." *Science* 103, no. 2684 (1946): 677-80.

Stouffer, Samuel A. "Some Observations on Study Design." *American Journal of Sociology* 55, no. 4 (1950): 355-61

Taylor. Charles L. ed., *Aggregate Data Analysis : Political and Social Indicators in Cross-National Research.* Paris : Mouton, 1968.

Thorndike, Edward L. "The Measurement of Educational Products." *The School Review* 20, no. 5 (1912): 289-99.

Shorter, Edward, and Charles Tilly. "The Shape of Strikes in France, 1830-1960." *Comparative Studies in Society and History* 13, no. 1 (1971): 60-86

Truzzi, Marcello, *Verstehen: Subjective Understanding in the Social Sciences.* Massachusetts : Addison-Wesley Publishing Co., 1974.

Tufte, Edward R. ed. *Quantitative Analysis of Social Problems.* Masachusetts: Addison-Wesley Publishing Co., 1974.

Tufte, Edward R. *Data Analysis for Politics and Policy*. New Jersey: Prentice-Hall, 1974.

Turkey, John W. and Wilk M.B. "Data Analysis and Statistics." In *Quantitative Analysis of Social Problems*, pp. 437-49. Edited by Edward R. Tufte. Masschusetts: Addison-Wesley Publishing Co., 1970.

Verba, Sydney. *Small Groups And The Political Behaviour*. Princeton : Princeton University Press, 1961.

Verba, Sydney."Some Dilemmas In Comparative Research". *World politics* 20 (1967) : 111-27.

Verba, Sydney. "The uses of Survey Research". In *Comparative Survey Analysis*, pp. 56-106.Stein Rokkan, Sydney Verba, Jean Viet and ElinaAlmasy. The Hague : Mouton ,1969.

Verba, Sydny, Ahmad, Basiruddin and Bhatt, Anil. *Caste, Race and Politics: : A Comparative Study of India and the United States*. Beverely Hills: Sage Publications, 1971.

Verba, Sydny and Nie, Norman H. *Participation in America : Political Democracy and Social Equality*. New York: Harper and Row,1972.

Verba, Sydny "The Cross-National Programme in Political and Social Change: a History and some Comments". In *Cross-National Comparative Survey Research-Theory and Practice*, pp. 169-201. Edited by Alexander Szalai and Riccardo Petrella in collaboration with Stein Rokkan and Erwin K. Scheuch. International Social Science Council Standing Committee on Comparative Research Oxford :Pergamon Press, 1977.

Walker, Jeffery.T, and Sean Maddan. *Understanding Statistics for the Social Sciences, Criminal Justice, and Criminology*. Burlington, MA : Jones & Bartlett Learning, 2013.

Wax Murray. "On Misundertanding Verstehen: A Reply to Abel". *Sociology and Social Research 51(1967): 323-33.*

Weber, Max. *The Methodology of the Social Sciences*. Edited by E.A. Shils and H.A. Finch. New York: The Free Press,1949.

Weber, Max. *Theory of Social and Economic Organization.* Edited by Talcott Parsons. New York: The Free Press, 1964.

Weber, Rocert. *Basic Content Analysis*, Thousand Oaks, Calif: Sage, 1990.

Whyte, William F. *Street Corner Society.* Chicago: University of Chicago Press,1943.

Winch, Peter. *The Idea of Social Science.*London:Routeledge and Kegan Paul, 1956.

Wolfe, A.B. "Functional Economics". In *The Trend in Economics.*Edited by R.G.Tugewell. New York: Alfred A. Knopf, 1924.

Yule, George Udny. *An Introduction to the Theory of Statistics.* London: Charles Griffin and Company Limited, 1919.

Zagoria, Donald S. 'The Ecology of Peasant Communism in India'. *American Political Science Review* 65(1971): 144-60.

Index

For Product Safety Concerns and Information please contact our EU
representative GPSR@taylorandfrancis.com
Taylor & Francis Verlag GmbH, Kaufingerstraße 24, 80331 München, Germany